T0265473

The Bluestockings

Also by Susannah Gibson

Animal, Vegetable, Mineral?
The Spirit of Inquiry

THE BLUESTOCKINGS

A HISTORY OF
THE FIRST
WOMEN'S MOVEMENT

SUSANNAH
GIBSON

W. W. NORTON & COMPANY

Independent Publishers Since 1923

For Irene – friend, inspiration and fellow bluestocking

Contents

She rises, conscious of her worth;
And, at her new-found powers elated,
Thinks them not rous'd, but new created.

Hannah More, 'The Bas Bleu', 1783

PROLOGUE

WHEN ELIZABETH MONTAGU first visited Hill Street in 1746, it was barely a street at all. The countryside to the east of Hyde Park was slowly being taken over by the expanding edges of London. As the old rambling farmland was parcelled up into neat plots, and straight roads were laid over meandering tracks, Mayfair began to take shape. This process was repeated across the capital as it swelled from half a million souls at the beginning of the century, to three quarters of a million by the midway point. The rising population expanded outwards from the old City of London, edging towards Westminster and Marylebone, absorbing rural villages such as Bethnal Green and Knightsbridge into its new sprawl. Old London Bridge, still topped by rows of houses precariously overhanging the river, was the only link connecting the City with Southwark. Traffic jams that lasted for hours finally inspired the frustrated Londoners to build a wooden bridge at Putney in the 1720s, and the sturdy stone bridge at Westminster in 1750. Across the new bridges and throughout the city, carriages clattered over cobblestones and metallic horseshoes struck granite – the city existed always in a din. Wandering street vendors trod the footpaths offering fresh milk and fruit, catch of the day, or breads straight from the oven. Tradesmen set up on street corners, offering repairs and renovations – a sharper knife, a shinier shoe, anything made new. Down at the docks, ships arrived from all over the world, carrying rare or precious cargos – sometimes traded, sometimes looted in the name of empire. They brought news from across Europe – word of new fashions, new ideas, new science, new politics. The expanding city felt vibrant, full of energy. London was becoming a place where anything was possible.

Montagu was in her late twenties when she first saw the plot on Hill Street and began to picture her future life there. The house they would build on that small portion of land would become not just a home for herself and her husband, but the start of something unprecedented. The salons that Montagu would host in that new house – a fine six-storey edifice in what would soon become one of London's most fashionable streets – were to be the centrepiece of the first women's liberation movement.

In the Great Room, guests began to assemble. Dusk had fallen many hours ago but candles in silver sconces lit the room almost as bright as noon. The room was resplendent in rococo plasterwork. Its three elegant sash windows overlooked Hill Street, allowing passersby a glimpse into Montagu's lavish life. One visitor compared the salons to Paradise – a place where the lion sits down with the lamb.[1] The guest list was diverse. It felt as though every nation in Europe was represented: Italians and French mingled with Scottish and Swedish. There were politicians, artists, aristocrats. Montagu moved among them. She had always come alive in the evenings; nothing thrilled her like a roomful of lively company set against a blaze of wax lights.

She appraised her guests and seated them accordingly. The most honoured guests would be seated directly opposite Montagu's fireplace. At the salon, one did not win these seats of honour according to conventional social standing; rather, it was the guests who displayed wit, wisdom or learning that were most esteemed. Montagu sat beside the brightest wits while the rest of the company took their places along a semicircle of chairs.[2]

Montagu's greatest joy was having a woman take pride of place. It might be the classicist Elizabeth Carter whom Samuel Johnson described as 'my old friend Mrs Carter [who] could make a pudding, as well as translate Epictetus from the Greek'.[3] Perhaps it would be the writer Hester Mulso Chapone who had once dared to argue with the revered novelist Samuel Richardson about a woman's right to refuse an arranged marriage. The playwright and poet Hannah More was another popular guest at the salons, known for her sense of fun and an exceptionally quick mind. Many guests longed to see Hester Thrale

at Hill Street – this rival *salonnière* was one of the few who could equal
Montagu in wit, erudition and style.

At the heart of the salon was conversation. Here, it was elevated
to an art form. The assembled guests might talk of literature, fine
art, history, foreign affairs, science or philosophy. In a world where
women were generally discouraged from partaking in intellectual pursuits, this was a rare treat for those who longed for something more
cerebral. Hannah More has left us a lively description of the salons in
a poem called 'The Bas Bleu: or, Conversation'. She had despaired at
the way card-playing and dancing quadrilles dominated most social
events (or at least the ones women were permitted to attend) until
the *salonnières* opened up a whole new world. Then things began
to change. A reader can still hear the awe More felt when she tells
how, in the salons, 'Genius prevails, and Conversation/Emerges into
Reformation'. Her verses describe the eclectic nature of the salon. She
captured the essential oddness of a room filled with people whose
paths might never cross in the ordinary course of events:

> Here sober duchesses are seen,
> Chaste wits, and critics void of spleen,
> Physicians, fraught with real science,
> And Whigs and Tories in alliance;
> Poets, fulfilling Christian duties,
> Just lawyers, reasonable beauties;
> Bishops who preach, and peers who pray,
> And countesses who seldom play;
> Learned antiquaries, who, from college,
> Reject the rust, and bring the knowledge;
> And, hear it, age, believe it, youth, -
> Polemics really seeking truth;
> And travellers of that rare tribe
> Who've seen the countries they describe.[4]

Elizabeth Montagu loved to hear so many different voices chatter-
ing away with affable ease on a hundred different subjects. Everywhere
she turned she heard something new. The morning after one such
entertainment, Montagu penned a letter to a friend telling of the joy
she felt at witnessing a philosopher, a fine lady, an officer, a macaroni,

a poet, a priest, a beauty and a guest who had travelled all the way from Tahiti gathered together to practise the art of conversation. 'Witts let off epigrams like minute guns,' she wrote.[5]

The salons were fun, but there was more to them than that. They were the only place where women and men could converse on intellectual topics as equals. For women, the salons were a chance to prove (to themselves and others) that they were capable of so much more than anyone believed possible. For many men, the salons were the first place where they began to wonder if women might, like themselves, actually be rational creatures.

It was all very well for a woman to prove she was a rational creature, but the reality of women's lives in the eighteenth century was often far removed from the glamour of an evening at Hill Street or any of the other great salons. There were many barriers a woman had to overcome before she could participate in this intellectual life. Many women found it near impossible to escape the burden of domesticity placed upon them – running a household and caring for children could easily fill every hour of a woman's day, leaving no time for anything else. Endless pregnancies could ruin a woman's health; the loss of a child or even several children could bury her beneath an avalanche of grief. Fathers or husbands had to be appeased before a woman was granted time for herself. It took a concerted effort for a clever woman to find like-minded friends; it took a single-minded tenacity to carve out time for herself to think and to write. Then there was the question of respectability. Reputation was everything to a middle- or upper-class eighteenth-century woman. By stepping outside the social norms, she might risk accusations of indecency: conversing on scholarly topics with men as though she was their equal certainly seemed indecent to many observers.

Despite this, there were women who managed to claim the time and the space to pursue a life of the mind. It might seem like a small thing, but these women who attended the salons were pushing back against the patriarchy. These women who thought so clearly, who spoke so eloquently, who argued so forcefully set something in motion. Their actions would have ramifications across society. Quietly, they would help to create a new world for women.

I

A WOMAN'S PLACE

'I WISH WITH all my heart Lady Ilchester had brought forth a son instead of a daughter, for they are much more convenient things,' wrote the politician Edward Digby to his uncle Lord Ilchester in 1750. A few years later, Lady Ilchester was pregnant once more and again her husband hoped for a son. It was not to be. Following the birth of the baby, Lord Ilchester wrote sadly to friends to inform them, 'I have nothing but a little Frances Muriel.'[1]

It was not an uncommon reaction to the birth of a female child. Women were held in low regard in the eighteenth century. A baby girl was not seen as an asset to a family in the same way that a boy was. A boy might have a distinguished or lucrative career; he might win honour that would reflect well on the family; at the very least he might pass the family name on to a new generation. A girl was unlikely to do any of those things. Instead, she was another mouth to feed. When she grew older, her father would either have to pay a dowry to have her taken off his hands, or accept the cost of maintaining a spinster. In return, she would provide domestic labour – sewing or washing, cooking or childcare – but, though every household needed these chores done, they were deemed trifling and unimportant.

When young, any decisions that might materially affect a girl's life were taken by her father; after marriage, by her husband. The ancient rules of coverture meant that a married woman did not legally exist as an entity independent of her husband. She could not sign a contract, she could not own property, if she earned money she could not keep it for herself. The legal system treated her as not quite a full person – she could be prosecuted for a crime, but could not sit on a jury. Traditional centres of power or prestige such as parliament, the church and the universities were off limits.

The historian Catharine Macaulay wanted to understand how this inequality had come about. In 1790, she published her theory of how

> some degree of inferiority, in point of corporeal strength, seems always to have existed between the two sexes; and this advantage, in the barbarous ages of mankind, was abused to such a degree, as to destroy all the natural rights of the female species, and reduce them to a state of abject slavery.[2]

Nothing had changed in millennia. Men still used their physical strength as the basis for a system of oppression that permeated almost every human society. In 1786 the milkmaid poetess Ann Yearsley was also thinking about female oppression. She too saw that much of the prejudice faced by women stemmed from the simple fact of men being bigger and stronger: 'Active strength / The boast of animals, is clearly thine', she wrote dismissively before arguing that physical strength was not necessarily the pinnacle of human achievement and pointing out that women could possess intellect and spirit to equal a man's.[3]

Though women could see the roots of the problem, that did little to alleviate their situation. A woman's place in the patriarchal society of eighteenth-century Europe was still very much in the home. If married, her chief duty was to produce children. Though essential to society, the arduous (and often dangerous) task of bearing and rearing children was not particularly valued by those whose job it was to value things – men. As one male commentator wrote: 'I cannot see the Reason why [women] are to be considered on a Level with the Men they bring forth, any more than that the Mould in a Garden is to be equally valued with the Fruits it produces.'[4]

Alongside this narrow view of a woman's role in society, sat the belief that educating girls past a basic level was a waste of everyone's time. Since girls were generally uneducated, they grew into women unable to take any part in public life; therefore, they were best left at home and kept busy in the kitchen or the nursery. It was, of course, a self-fulfilling prophecy.

Centuries of under-education led to a widespread belief that girls were not really capable of being taught much. While boys learned Latin and Greek, rhetoric and logic, mathematics and natural philosophy, girls were told that learning such subjects would frazzle their brains, damage their wombs and destroy their looks. Anything to do with the intellectual realm was considered unsuitable: it was unacceptable for a woman to be clever, to be bookish, to seek out the same kind of education that her brothers would enjoy. While boys learned about *male* subjects – history and politics, empire and the military – girls made endless needlework samplers, dutifully practised their scales, or attempted to impress their dancing masters. But these girls (girls of the upper and middle classes) were not expected to put their sewing, their music or their dancing to any practical use. Their crafts weren't intended to be used to earn a living, for that was another thoroughly unwomanly activity. These skills were merely ornamental, intended to give the girls a polished air, to attract a suitable husband, to fill up the girls' days, to keep them docile. A pretty face, a nice figure and a biddable demeanour counted for more than any educational attainments. As Elizabeth Montagu put it: 'the world does not mind our intrinsic worth so much as the fashion of us, and will not easily forgive our not pleasing . . . in a woman's education little but outward accomplishment is regarded.' Since the education system was controlled by men, Montagu could only conclude that men had a self-serving reason for limiting women's education: 'they know that fools make the best slaves.'[5]

Women were scorned by men for their lack of education and worldly experience. 'Women, then, are only children of a larger growth,' wrote the statesman Lord Chesterfield to his son in 1748, 'they have an entertaining tattle, and sometimes wit; but for solid reasoning, good sense, I never knew in my life one that had it, or who reasoned or acted consequentially for four-and-twenty hours together.'[6]

If uneducated women were the victims of male scorn, surely educated women were held in high regard by men? A 1739 pamphlet titled *Man Superior to Woman; or, a Vindication of Man's Natural Right of Sovereign Authority over the Woman* explained why this was not the case. The anonymous author described the disdain, bordering on disgust, that he felt for those women who sought out education. These were the dreaded 'learned ladies'. The author told how these educated women neglected important things (such as their appearance) in favour of their studies:

> she neither knows how to set her Cap strait, nor can remember to buckle her Shoes; and is so blinded with poring over Books as not

to be capable of discerning the Difference of Shades between a dirty Smock-sleeve and a clean apron . . . It must be owned, that if this Lady is a scholar she is a very sluttish one; and the much she reads is to very little Purpose, since it can make nothing better of her than a *bookish Slattern*. It is happy for her, and much more for our Sex, that she is unmarried.[7]

The learned lady – a stereotype that appears again and again in eighteenth-century culture – was not just untidy in her person, not just a bad housekeeper distracted from her domestic duties, she would make a bad *wife*. And that was the key point for many who disdained female education: a woman's purpose in life was to be defined by her relationship to a man. She only had value if she was useful to a man. Her own happiness, her personal achievements, her contributions to society amounted to nothing if she did not first tend to her husband's needs. Women were seen as innately subordinate.

One conduct manual from the 1760s discouraged women from reading overly taxing books; instead, the author wrote, 'your business chiefly is to read Man, in order to make yourselves agreeable and useful.'[8] Occasionally, a conduct manual might suggest that there were times when it was acceptable for a woman to read a book. A 1771 manual titled *The Nunnery for Coquettes* opined that a small amount of appropriate reading could help a girl remain chaste. That suggestion was followed instantly by this caveat: 'But then beware after this you do not affect the character of a learned lady, which is of all other affectations the most odious in a woman . . . the only end of female reading is to make you agreeable in conversation.'[9] On balance, it was probably better to be thought unchaste than clever. Other manuals advised women not to aspire to anything beyond pleasing their husbands: 'a Woman is the downy pillar on which a Man should repose from the severer and more exalted duties of life.'[10]

Learned ladies were rare. This was not just because schooling for girls was rare (nor because women had to spend so much time acting as reposeful downy pillars), but because the few women who were given a little learning, or who managed to educate themselves, then faced a wall of societal prejudice. Elizabeth Montagu once wrote that 'extraordinary talents may make a Woman admired, but they will never make her happy.' She knew that men of exceptional talent found themselves praised and exalted but talented women had to beg pardon for their uncommon excellence.[11]

Worse still, much of the prejudice came from other women, as Montagu knew. Other learned ladies reported the same. Attacked from all sides, Montagu felt that life sometimes resembled continual warfare.[12] When the novelist Frances Burney first experienced success as an author, her friend Hester Thrale wrote these words of caution:

> you must be more careful than ever of not being thought Bookish, for now you are known for a Wit, & a belle Esprit, you will be watched, &, if you are not upon your Guard, all the misses will rise up against you.[13]

Hannah More also wrote about the opprobrium learned ladies faced from other women. In the epilogue at the end of an all-female play, she spoke of the negative reactions she had experienced from other women when they learned that she wrote for a living:

> 'What! – does she *write*? A slattern, as I live –
> I wish she'd leave her books, and mend her cloaths
> I thank my stars I know not verse from prose.'[14]

Women were so conditioned by the patriarchy to believe themselves incapable of intellectual achievements that they ridiculed any of their sisters who dared step out of line. Just as future centuries would see women rail against university education for their sisters or votes for themselves, some eighteenth-century women could not comprehend why any woman would want to attain a 'manly' education or speak in public. For a working-class man, a good education might be a way to raise his status in the world, but for a woman (of any class) it was more likely to be a pathway to a lifetime of derision.

Everyone in the eighteenth century knew what place a woman occupied. It had been ordained by God that woman was subservient to man. Few gave it much thought. Fewer still contemplated that there might be any other way to arrange society, or any particular merit in doing so. The act of beginning to imagine a different relationship between the sexes demanded enormous vision. Almost nobody took it seriously. But those few who did took it very seriously indeed.

2

THE SALON

IT BEGAN WITH a breakfast. A long table, draped in the finest white linen, heaved with endless cups of gold, silver and delicate porcelain, each filled with exotic treats from faraway lands: coffee, chocolate and exquisite tea. Arranged around the cups were plates bearing the homelier treats of biscuits, cream and freshly buttered toast. But the breakfast table, glinting with hundreds of pounds worth of gold and silver plate, was not the first thing the guests noticed when they were welcomed into Elizabeth Montagu's opulent Chinese Room.

Though she joked that the style was barbarously gaudy, Montagu threw herself into collecting and making pieces in this European pastiche of Asian design. The room abounded with bright colours and intricate craftsmanship. Black and gold japanned furniture was specially commissioned, adorned with landscape scenes and precisely rendered plants and pebbles. A flamboyant looking-glass sat above the chimney-piece, decorated with the bustling figures of musicians and gardeners. In the evenings, pier mirrors placed between the windows reflected back the light from flickering candles in their ornately branched stands. Montagu's two sailor brothers brought her gifts from the Far East – lanterns and vases, screens and porcelain figurines. Hand-painted wallpaper seemed almost to bloom with flowers. 'My house looks like an Indian warehouse,' she exclaimed with some pleasure to her sister Sarah in 1748, shortly after she had begun assembling her *objets d'art*. Two years later, the room still unfinished, she wrote about the changes she had made since Sarah's last visit: '[it] is like the Temple of some Indian god . . . The very curtains are Chinese pictures on gauze . . . with cushions of Japan satin painted.'[1]

The breakfast given in this room was a feast for the senses. The guests were enchanted by the delicious food, the richness of the setting, the stunning *chinoiserie* (which many of them saw in all its glory for the first time here in Hill Street), and the perfection of their hostess. Montagu was now in her thirties; no longer in the first flush of youth but still 'comely, plump and jolly'.[2] She loved clothes as much as she loved interiors, and her gowns were expensively made and festooned with ribbons and bows. But it was not her pretty face or her luxurious silks that held her guests' attention. The poet and playwright Anne-Marie Fiquet du Boccage, visiting from Paris, declared that Montagu deserved to be served at the table of the gods. Boccage, who hosted a salon herself, was a celebrity in French literary circles and had been called the Sappho of Normandy by Voltaire. She could not have been an easy person to impress. But she was in awe of Montagu – in awe of her learning, her wit, her grace and her hospitality. After the breakfast, Montagu presented Boccage with a new edition of Milton – perhaps a clue as to what the ladies discussed in the Chinese Room that morning.[3]

Boccage's account of that breakfast, held in 1750, is the earliest surviving report of one of Montagu's sumptuous gatherings of literary guests. Montagu chose her guests carefully. She deliberately sought out foreign visitors who could bring word of new books and new ideas, and surrounded herself with writers, critics, wits and, above all, brilliant women.

Montagu longed for brilliance. With Boccage's praise ringing in her ears, she began to plan her next literary breakfast, and the one after that. Soon the breakfasts grew much more elaborate. By the winter of the following year, Montagu was hosting parties at which, she recorded, 'the Chinese Room was filled by a succession of people from eleven in the morning till eleven at night.' A few months later she reported to her husband (who had retreated to their country house with a bad cold) that she had had more than a hundred guests the night before and that the house held them with ease. These larger parties were held in the Great Room, next to the Chinese Room. The evening parties suited Montagu better than the breakfasts – she had never been a morning person. Once, in her youth, sent away from the family home to escape an outbreak of smallpox, she complained bitterly of the revered clock that ruled the lives of the farming family she stayed with: 'even me it governs, sends me to bed at ten, and makes me rise, oh barbarous! at eight . . . I only wish they could sleep in their beds in the morning, and wake in a chair in the evening.'[4]

Slowly, Montagu began to combine the serious literary flavour of her breakfasts with the light gaiety of her day-long revelries to create something new in London. Where once she had had fifty guests come and play cards, now she wanted something more substantial. She looked to the centre of the world for inspiration – Paris. Though she had not yet visited the city when she began hosting, its salons were famous. Longingly she listened as friends returning from France told of soirées where exalted men of letters mingled with the greatest thinkers from the worlds of the arts, natural philosophy or politics. With these stories swirling through her mind, Montagu began to shape a salon of her own.

She believed that salons, like oysters, should only be had in months with a letter R in them.[5] This meant that her events were held during the London season when the fashionable crowd were in town for the winter. Though she sometimes found women (and men) of fashion to be dull conversationalists, Montagu liked the sparkle they brought to her evenings – and her salon would be as sparkling as any in Paris. But she was not interested in simply imitating Paris; her salons featured several innovations of her own devising. While many of the French salons were hosted by a woman, the guests were predominantly male; Montagu went one step further and invited large numbers of women to her assemblies. She gave those women licence to speak. For the first time, here was a forum where women's voices had equal billing with men's.

Men-only clubs were very much in vogue in eighteenth-century London. There were clubs for playing whist or chess, clubs for discussing politics, clubs for gambling and even clubs for blaspheming. It has been said that up to twenty thousand men met in clubs in the capital each night.[6] Women were excluded and had no equivalent of their own. For many men, this exclusion of women was key to their enjoyment of a night out. One commentator wrote that

the strange fashion introduced of late years of mixing in company on almost all occasions with Women; will eventually turn out to our destruction, as it must render us effeminate, luxurious, and ignorant; and I am astonished that Government [do not] restrict the liberty of Women and punish in an exemplary way indiscriminate mixtures of Men and Women . . . [and] banish them, as banes to Society, the TABLE and CONVERSATION-ROOM.[7]

But Montagu was firm that mixing the sexes like this could be a positive experience for both men and women. She had to be careful, though, to avoid accusations of impropriety. Her salons were set up in such a way as to exclude any hint of debauchery – so often an undercurrent in the stories she heard from Paris. She made it clear that her salon was not a place for sexual intrigues. Unlike some other hostesses, she never dreamed of issuing invitations that demanded 'no husband to bring his wife, or wife her husband, or young lady her chaperon'.[8] Instead of alcohol, she poured fine teas, concocted orgeats from almonds and orange flower water, or served lemonade – still a rare luxury in those days. The playing of cards (and the losing of fortunes that often went with it) – a popular pastime in this social circle – came to be gently but firmly forbidden, and discussion of politics was always steered back towards the safer ground of literature or art.

The void left by the banning of sex, alcohol and gambling was filled with something that Montagu valued much more highly: wit. The ultimate accolade in her world was to be considered witty. It implied not just a quick brain and a clever turn of phrase, but a deep kind of understanding that drew together different strands of learning. Wit implied not just intellect but sensibility. Now, in the salon, witty conversation was elevated to high art.

'Her conversational powers were of a truly superior order; strong, just, clear, and often eloquent,' wrote the novelist Frances Burney after spending an evening with Montagu.[9] Burney (a generation younger than Montagu) idolised the older woman who always seemed so knowledgeable and self-assured. 'Our sex's Glory', Burney called her as she had prepared for their first meeting, unable to imagine a more perfect embodiment of womanhood.[10] Burney would attend countless salons at Hill Street over the years. As an inveterate people-watcher, she loved to look on as Montagu managed things. Once Montagu had carefully orchestrated the seating arrangements around the fireplace, the evening could unfold before her. It was almost like watching a sport.

The subject at hand would be turned inside out and upside down, seen through a hundred different lenses, compared to this or that, carefully examined for deeper meaning. And all in a way that was somehow as pleasing to one's sense of fun as to one's intellect. Montagu herself was witty, erudite and enormously well-read, and she often led the conversation, spiralling upwards as she followed ideas wherever they took her, amazing her guests with her effortless performances.

For the women who attended the salon it was a lifeline. In her youth, the courtier and diarist Mary Hamilton had revealed to her (male) guardian that she hoped to learn Greek and Latin. He firmly told her that 'a Lady's being learned is commonly looked on as a great fault, even by the learned.'[11] He urged her to keep this terrible desire a secret, for fear that it would damage her marriage prospects. Similar sentiments were repeated in every conduct manual for young ladies: 'if you happen to have any learning, keep it a profound secret, especially from the men, who generally look with a jealous and malignant eye on a woman of great parts, and a cultivated understanding,' was standard advice.[12]

As a girl, Hamilton had taken such advice seriously. Though she wanted an intellectual life, the prospect of being known as a learned lady made her uneasy. Her guardian's words had instilled a deep-seated fear in her. She was afraid of appearing too clever, and afraid for other young women who strived for an education. After meeting a bright young woman at dinner one night, Hamilton confided in her diary:

> Miss Boyle is too well educated. It will prevent her enjoying the innocent pleasure of society, for every other female will not only envy her but be afraid of her, and the men in general are so jealous of our being as wise as themselves, they will shun her.[13]

At Hill Street, the women did not envy, and the men did not shun.

Yet Hamilton's words show how deeply embedded the dread of the 'learned lady' had become. Even the learned ladies themselves were conditioned to believe the stereotypes. Her diary entry continued:

> An affected 'Femme savante' is, in my opinion, a most disagreeable animal. The reason of this is that they always pretend to more

knowledge than they possess, that they are ignorant of what they ought to know, are pert, affected, useless members of society. Mrs Carter, Miss Hannah More, Mrs Chapone, and two or three others I could name, I would except out of the list of what I call 'Femmes savantes', for their talents and amiable precepts have been a great service to society.[14]

The three she excused from the dreaded epithet – Elizabeth Carter, Hannah More and Hester Mulso Chapone – were all part of Montagu's inner circle. To be close to Elizabeth Montagu was to become something new: a socially acceptable intelligent woman. Whatever magic Montagu weaved within the walls of her salon, the old spell was broken and the learned lady – so despised elsewhere – suddenly became a desirable person to know, an agreeable visitor to one's house, even an aspirational figure. But Montagu's reach only extended so far, and it was only those women who were close to her or who were active participants in her salon or a handful of other salons who managed to escape opprobrium. Elsewhere, clever women remained figures of fun or suspicion. Montagu had created something extraordinary.

For decades, Montagu's salon thrived. Almost thirty years after her first literary breakfasts, a visitor to London (who had known the famous salon of Madame du Deffand in Paris) described how

the 'Gens de Lettres,' or 'Blue Stockings,' as they were commonly denominated, formed a very numerous, powerful, compact phalanx, in the midst of London . . . Mrs. Montague [sic] was then the madame du Deffand of the English capital; and her house constituted the central point of union, for all those persons who already were known, or who emulated to become known, by their talents and productions.[15]

The word 'Bluestocking' had begun as a joke. In 1757, Montagu used it to poke fun at the botanist Benjamin Stillingfleet. He was a good friend of hers, a learned man who had thrown himself into the new Linnæan botanical system. Coming in from fieldwork to the parlour, he would neglect to change from his rough worsted blue stockings – coloured with cheap woad dye – to the expensive white silk ones usually worn to formal events.[16] The word caught on, and came to imply a kind of informality, a way of valuing intellectual endeavours above fashions. James Boswell once lamented when Stillingfleet was absent from a gathering that 'we can do nothing without the blue stockings.'[17] Somehow the word, at first specifically associated with Stillingfleet, evolved to mean the circles Stillingfleet moved in, and especially Montagu's circle. From the 1750s to the 1770s, the word was applied equally to women and men; later, it was reserved for the women who surrounded Montagu; and, later still, for any clever woman. Until almost 1800, the word was neutral; after that, it became pejorative.

Shortly after Frances Burney was first welcomed into the Bluestocking Circle, she heard that Hester Mulso Chapone had praised her work. 'There's for you!' exclaimed Burney, pleased to have won heartfelt praise from a writer she admired, 'who would not be a blue-stockinger at this rate?'[18]

In the fireside glow of Hill Street, each guest replete after Montagu's lavish hospitality, each guest taking their proper place in the circle, it was clear to them that this salon was more than just a place for an evening's entertainment. Montagu's salon could be the beginning of a career, the route to fame, the most satisfying part of a day. Some of those guests even saw it as a sort of informal university for women. At a time when the two English universities were reserved solely for men, Montagu's salon offered women a way to learn about new literature, about the classics, about writing, and to do so communally – like a genteel and overdressed seminar group. She 'makes her Drawing Room the Lyceum of the day', enthused one learned male guest.[19] If the Hill Street house was the Lyceum, then Montagu must have been its Aristotle.

The idea of a female Aristotle would have been laughable in Montagu's time. Even with every advantage that she had had from youth, no one would have expected a mere girl to rise to such heights. Elizabeth Montagu had been born Elizabeth Robinson in York in 1718. Her mother Elizabeth and father Matthew had twelve children, of whom nine survived to adulthood. The family, fairly comfortably off (thanks to an inheritance on mother Elizabeth's side) and educated, was an unusual environment in which to grow up.

Matthew, who had studied at Cambridge, adored the fashionable coffee-houses of London. There, he would mix freely with the metropolitan literati, exchanging views on the latest books or the political intrigues of the day. He would show off his most recent paintings, or throw himself into animated discussions on science or religion. Mother Elizabeth was an educated woman and also fond of witty conversation. Later, after her children had grown up and most had left home, she got herself a pet squirrel so that she would always have someone to listen to her talk.[20]

The Robinson family was part of the gentry but they could not afford to keep a house in London, so they moved between family properties in Yorkshire, Cambridge and Kent. To spirited, outgoing Matthew, who craved company and excitement, this rural life seemed irredeemably dull. He daydreamed of London. No doubt a trip to the capital would have raised his spirits but, unable to leave their home at Monk's Horton, Kent, he tried a different cure: 'my Pappa has ordered me to put a double quantity of saffron in his tea,' wrote young Elizabeth to a friend.[21] But the saffron, a common folk remedy for low spirits, did little to alleviate his boredom and so he encouraged his children to entertain him. He trained them in the arts of conversation and disputation; he made sure they could read the newest books in several languages. He attempted to recreate the atmosphere of a coffee-house in his own parlour.

The household was a lively place as the children competed for their father's attention, trying to outdo each other in wit and erudition. Their mother Elizabeth became known as The Speaker, as she attempted to keep the peace between her children as though governing a small flock of Whigs and Tories. Not so much for their own benefit as for Matthew's, Elizabeth and her younger sister Sarah were educated to a much higher standard than was common for girls of the time.

Each evening in Monk's Horton, the family would gather around the fireplace to hear Shakespeare or the classics read aloud – something that would shape Elizabeth profoundly. The Robinson children also spent much time at the house of their maternal grandmother in Cambridge. Grandmother Sarah had married the well-known scholar Conyers Middleton and through Middleton, a kindly old man with a great deal of tenderness for his step-grandchildren, the world of the university was opened up to them. The Robinson children, keeping quiet as mice, would sit in the corner of his study while he entertained the fellows and professors of the university. Knowing what was to come, they listened to every word that those black-gowned old gentlemen spoke. When the fellows had gone, Middleton would quiz the children, turning it into a game, making them repeat what they had heard, encouraging them always to pay close attention to the spoken word, and teaching them how to follow complex arguments seemingly far beyond their years. In that sombre Cambridge study, the children began to learn that conversation could be an art form.

Back in rural Kent, the Robinson family gave themselves up to less cerebral entertainments. They travelled all over the county to see plays, to watch horse-racing, or to enjoy tavern suppers with young gentlemen. Fun, pretty Elizabeth, with her animated blue eyes, high arched eyebrows, and dark hair contrasting against her pale skin, was a popular guest. She received constant invitations, and with excitement. She and her sister and brothers once travelled eight miles over bad roads on a cold winter's evening to hear a fiddler play; they danced all night, not coming home until two o'clock in the morning. The letters of her girlhood are scattered with dances and late nights, 'I am so fond of dancing,' she wrote, 'that I cannot help fancying I was at some time bit by a tarantula, and never got cured of it.'* It seems to have been a family trait, for even her father Matthew would cast aside his country gloom at a ball, and dance as nimbly as a man half his age.[22]

Kentish balls were often held at the full moon to allow the guests to travel more easily. In the sparsely populated countryside, it was common to invite all the neighbourhood to a ball, regardless of social status. Elizabeth and her siblings delighted in the silliness of it all. She described how one hostess invited 'all the parsons, apprentices, tradesmen, apothecaries, and farmers, milliners, mantua-makers, haberdashers of small wares, and chambermaids. It is the oddest mixture you can imagine – here sails a reverent parson, there skips an airy apprentice, here jumps a farmer.'[23] These parties, where unexpected combinations of guests mingled freely, captured the teenage Elizabeth's imagination.

---

* There is an old folk belief that the cure for a spider bite is to dance.

Then, in her early teens, Elizabeth began a close friendship with Margaret Cavendish Harley. The two girls met through Elizabeth's family in Cambridge – Margaret's family home being just a few miles away at Wimpole Hall. Margaret, the daughter of an earl, was a few years older, but Elizabeth's quick mind, her wit and her endless joyful energy charmed Margaret, and from the very beginning the two girls behaved as equals and revelled in a playful friendship. When they were apart, letters flew from one to the other, sharing snippets from their daily lives, updates on their families, painstakingly copied-out verses, or their musings on art and literature. Elizabeth's visits to Wimpole made her old Kentish entertainments seem suddenly insipid and provincial as Margaret introduced her to a realm of glamour and wealth, grand houses, fabulous parties and a glittering social life. Margaret nicknamed her lively new friend 'Fidget' – a name that stuck for many years. 'There are long tables in the room that have more feet than [a] caterpillar . . . Why so many legs are needful to stand *still*, I cannot imagine when I can fidget on two,' Elizabeth exclaimed as she dashed headlong into her new social world.[24]

Margaret married in 1734 and became the Duchess of Portland. Her life changed as she took on the responsibilities of her new role. Elizabeth's life changed too as she became a kind of unofficial companion to her dear friend. The Duchess split her time between her magnificent London residence in Whitehall and the beautiful country estate of Bulstrode in Buckinghamshire. Bulstrode captured Elizabeth's heart from her very first visit there, becoming almost a second home to her. It was not just the beauty and opulence of the place that moved Elizabeth, she was struck by a quiet female charm that pervaded everything there. The Duchess, a bright woman, was fond of literature and natural history. The Duke was often away on business, or entertaining himself with other friends, so the Duchess could do as she pleased. Her father had always surrounded himself with wits and had spent a fortune collecting books and manuscripts, paintings and objects of curiosity. Now the Duchess was mistress of her own house and she too chose to furnish it with a fine library and all manner of natural history objects but, more importantly than that, she chose to fill it with a coterie of smart, engaging women. Her circle included the celebrated Mary Delany – still famed today for her intricate botanical art; the Irishwoman Anne Donnellan, a friend of Jonathan Swift; Catherine Dashwood, later a lady-in-waiting to Queen Charlotte; and fashionable Mary Catherine Knollys (Lady Wallingford). Elizabeth – Fidget as she was always called at Bulstrode – slipped seamlessly into this world, and Pen (as Delany was nicknamed from her first husband's name of Pendarves), Don, Dash and Wall became her most treasured friends. It was a respectable group of women, engaged in appropriately female pursuits. If they were intellectual, they were intellectual *in private*, thus making them seem less threatening to society at large.

At Bulstrode, the women would read and write together, they would sew and spin and knit together, they would take long walks through the grounds gathering plants for the Duchess's herbal, or feed the birds in the menagerie, they would converse for hours about the arts and sciences, politics or society. When Elizabeth had first arrived, supper was served at nine o'clock in the evening, but that was pushed back to ten o'clock as the women found they needed more time for their writing – a favourite activity of Elizabeth's. Hunched around candles in the Duchess's dressing room, the women would write late into the night.[25]

When they tore themselves away from Bulstrode and bundled into the carriage for the twenty-mile drive to Whitehall, another new world unfolded. The Duchess introduced teenage Elizabeth to the joys of the London season. Like her father before her, Elizabeth found the capital thrilling: the gay company, the worldly gentlemen and sophisticated women, the easy luxury of it all gladdened her heart. In London, she could hear the words of Shakespeare drop from the lips of the greatest actors, while she watched from a plush velvet-lined box, surrounded by the *bon ton*, as the fashionable elite were called. She could attend balls, promenade in the new squares and parks, accept invitations to tea parties and card parties. She could see how the aristocracy lived, and begin to imagine herself immersed in such a life.

Elizabeth had been formally introduced into society some years before, but her parents had never been able to afford a full London season for her, packed as it was with extravagant balls and outings, each requiring just the right dress, a coach, extra servants.

The Duchess knew about the Robinson family finances, and she knew how much Elizabeth wanted a life in London. Then a solution presented itself: the Duchess was pregnant with her third child and she needed a companion to be with her through the months before her confinement. The Duchess realised that an act of charity would have offended the Robinsons; instead, she asked Elizabeth to help *her*. Elizabeth had made herself indispensable to the Duchess – a wise move, and one which shows Elizabeth's understanding of the games that had to be played if she were to advance in the world.

The Duchess had already borne two daughters: Elizabeth in 1735 and Henrietta in 1737. Now she wanted a friend to be with her for the final dull, heavy months before her third baby arrived, and to stay with her during her lying-in after the birth. This was common practice in the eighteenth century: a new mother would rest for a period of about a month after the birth while female relatives and friends tended to her. For a woman of the Duchess's status, lying-in was as much a social activity as a medical one; it was expected that all her aristocratic friends would call on her in that month to congratulate her and see the infant.

Here was a chance for Elizabeth to shine. But shining was expensive. She wrote to her father and explained the situation to him: she would be meeting all the *bon ton* of London, but she had nothing suitable to wear. 'I must be in full dress,' she explained to him, 'I shall never so much want a handsome suit as upon this occasion of first appearing with my Lady Duchess.'[26] Elizabeth loved fine clothes and jewels – she was well aware that vanity was one of her weaknesses. She knew that she could not compete with the Duchess's friends but she still wanted to look her best. Matthew, who was not much given to spending money on his children, sent her £20 – a considerable sum for him. He was a sharp man and he saw this as a good opportunity for Elizabeth to catch the eye of a wealthy nobleman. He had not budgeted for large dowries for his two daughters; instead, he was hoping that Elizabeth's looks and charming manner would attract a man, so that minimal financial input from himself would be required. The sum of £20, though a lot, was nothing compared to what a proper dowry would cost him.

Together, Elizabeth and the Duchess began to visit cloth merchants, examining bolts of silks, beautifully patterned with new designs from the East. They eventually found one that suited Elizabeth's purposes. There was a small fault in the silk due to an error made by the loom, but Elizabeth knew she could hide the damaged parts within the cut of the dress. She bought the silk at a discount, and well within her father's tight budget.[27] Canny Elizabeth would always be good with money. To go with the silk for her new mantua gown, Elizabeth also bought a new hoop which, she proudly told her mother, was 'of the first magnitude'. In an age when dress hoops regularly caused women to become entangled in doorways, a hoop of the first magnitude must have been quite something.

Elizabeth and the Duchess passed the winter pleasantly together in London, and, in the spring of 1738, a boy was born. William Henry, a tiny mewling creature, would go on to become the third Duke of Portland, would twice be Prime Minister, and would be the great-great-great-grandfather of Queen Elizabeth II.

When the month was up, Elizabeth's family summoned their daughter back to Kent. 'You must get your Papa to stay [in London] next year: it is really insufferable going out of town at the most pleasant time of the year,' admonished the Duchess as she tauntingly filled Elizabeth in on all the excitements she had enjoyed since her friend's departure – operas, parks, assemblies and Vauxhall pleasure gardens. Elizabeth, meanwhile, was thoroughly bored.[28]

But the two would be together again before too long. In London once more, the pair would dance at lavish balls, have their portraits painted (Elizabeth incongruously dressed as Anne Boleyn), frolic at Vauxhall, or even try out new-fangled medical fads such as cold plunge baths, the terrified Duchess watching as Elizabeth disappeared beneath the water. But the thing that touched Elizabeth most profoundly was their visits to the theatre. 'I have been to the play *As you Like it*,' she wrote to her sister Sarah after seeing the famous actor James Quin perform at Drury Lane, 'I have never heard anything spoke with such command of voice and action as the "seven stages of man" . . . it was really prodigious, the alteration of the voice, he spoke the slippered pantaloon just like my Uncle Clark.'[29] She had heard the words of Shakespeare read aloud at Monk's Horton, but this night marked the beginning of a new relationship between Elizabeth and the Bard – it would be one of the most satisfying relationships of her life.

There were other relationships to consider too. Elizabeth may not have met a suitable husband during the Duchess's lying-in, but her family still had high hopes of her making a good match. She was ambivalent about the prospect of marriage. Elizabeth enjoyed a modicum of independence and was afraid of losing it if she married a controlling husband. It was not socially acceptable for a woman to voice such thoughts aloud. Instead, Elizabeth joked that perhaps she was not suited to marriage. To a (male) cousin, she wrote that

> I should make a very silly wife, and an extremely foolish Mother, and so have as far resolved as is consistent with deference to reason and advice, never to trouble any man, or spoil any children. I already love too many people in this world to enjoy a perfect tranquility, and I don't care to have any more strings to pull my heart; it is very tender, and a small matter hurts it.[30]

Those last words would prove to be painfully prophetic.

The idea of a beautiful, healthy young woman of good family choosing not to marry was absurd and her somewhat alarmed cousin could not help but nag at her, asking 'when you set sail, *i.e.* when you are to be manned, and who is to be your Captain'. She patiently explained that she was in no rush:

> I am not going to set sail yet; the ocean of fortune is rough, the bark of fortune light, the prosperous gale uncertain, but the Pilot must be smooth, steady and content, patient in storms, moderate and careful in sunshine, and easy in the turns of the wind, and changes of the times. Guess if these things be easily found? . . . So I wait on the shore, scarce looking towards this land of promise, so few I find with whom I would risk the voyage.

Moreover, she was extremely open about what financial incentives might induce her to consent to a proposal: 'gold is the chief ingredient in the composition of worldly happiness. Living in a cottage on love is certainly the worst diet and the worst habitation one can find out.'[31] Elizabeth was no dreamy romantic.

She was aware that a woman's whole life was shaped by her husband. He would decide where the family should live and what kind of life they would have, he would control the family's finances, be his wife's legal guardian and decide where to send any sons for their education. A lucky woman might enjoy many day-to-day freedoms but higher level decision-making was almost always considered a role for the man of the house.

Elizabeth's vivacious spirit might have made people think she was passionate in affairs of the heart but it was not so. Elizabeth knew how society worked, she understood the lowly place occupied by women; and she was willing to play the game. 'Love has a good right over the marriages of men, but not of women,' she wrote once to her mother, 'for men raise their wives to their ranks, women stoop to their husbands, if they choose below themselves.'[32] She could not overturn the patriarchy – indeed such a thought never crossed her mind – but she could improve her lot in life by marrying well. Having spent several years in the intimate company of the Duchess of Portland, Elizabeth craved her fine lifestyle; but perhaps more than that, she craved the ability to surround herself with clever and interesting women, to build a good library, to have time to write – things that could be achieved more easily if she had money and an understanding husband.

Early in 1742 her father took her north to look over one of the family properties. Matthew Robinson tempted Elizabeth on the journey with a promise of a trip to the York races. Whether or not the visit to the racetrack ever occurred is unrecorded but on the trip she met Edward Montagu. Edward had an estate not far from some Robinson lands at Rokeby; perhaps it was there that they met. Elizabeth's letters, usually so voluble on all manner of topics, barely mention this new acquaintance. One brother teasingly wrote that he had heard about his sister 'converting a Mr. M- to dancing'. While Anne Donnellan, replying to a letter of Elizabeth's (now lost), advised that

> if you meet with a person who you think would be proper to make
> you happy in the married state, and they show a desire to please you,
> and a solidity in their liking, give it the proper encouragement that the
> decency of our sex will allow of, for it is the settlement in the world

24

that we should aim at, and the only way we females have of making ourselves of use to Society and raising ourselves in this world.[33]

Donnellan, herself an extremely useful member of society and a great supporter of the arts and of women, never married.

With Donnellan's advice in mind, Elizabeth began to consider this new man's qualities. Edward was the grandson of an earl. He was a nice, sensible, quiet and extremely wealthy man. Much of his family money came from coal mines in the North of England. He was just what Elizabeth had been looking for. She was in her early twenties and he in his fifties, but Elizabeth hadn't been searching for a romantic hero and had no need of a whirlwind love affair. She did not mind that Edward, soon to be elected a fellow of the prestigious Royal Society, would rather devote himself to mathematics in his study than accompany her to fashionable assemblies. With appropriate modesty and decency, Elizabeth began to show an interest in Edward, and soon the couple had come to an understanding. She was so modest that news of this new relationship spread slowly. Her sister Sarah, to whom Elizabeth had always been close, and who was one of her most frequent correspondents, was left to rely on rumours to find out about the engagement. Sarah was a little hurt to be kept from her sister's confidence: she wrote, 'I hear that you are going to be married . . . you are very private in it to us.'[34] Once word was out, approval rained down upon the pair. Elizabeth's step-grandfather Conyers Middleton knew that it would be a happy match because, as he wrote to her: '[Edward] values you, not so much for the charms of your person, as the beauties of your mind.'[35]

Their wedding was announced in the *Gentleman's Magazine* of August 1742. The announcement did not name Elizabeth, an omission which neatly summed up the position of women in marriage: 'August 5th. Edward Montagu, Esqr., Member for Huntingdon, to the eldest daughter of Matthew Robinson, of Horton in Kent, Esqr.' The wedding took place in London on a bright summer's day; it was a simple ceremony with just a few family members present. The bride wore her best dress and carried a modest bouquet. 'My mind was in no mirthful mood,' she wrote the next day to the Duchess, confessing that though she hoped for happiness, she was beset by 'a thousand anxious thoughts'.[36] She had no way of knowing what kind of husband Edward would be, or what her life as a married woman might bring.

Elizabeth Robinson was now Elizabeth Montagu. Her anxieties soon passed as Edward proved himself to be everything she had wished for in a husband. The family was delighted to see their eldest daughter so well married, and happy too.

Now Elizabeth Montagu had everything she needed: her privileged childhood had given her a rare education for a girl, allowing her to cultivate her fine mind; her years with the Duchess had taught her the social graces she needed to live in high society; and her devoted, wealthy husband gave her the freedom and the funds to begin to imagine a new world for herself, and for other women. More important than any of these, Montagu was possessed of a deep and abiding belief that women were capable of great intellectual feats. She wanted to give herself and her sisters a chance to shine. She understood, however, that she would have to go about it carefully. She knew the pitfalls faced by clever women; she knew that everything they did would have to rest on a foundation of the most unimpeachable respectability; and she knew that male egos would need soothing. She wrote once that women who wanted power had to 'command while seeming to submit, and win their way by yielding to the tyde'.[37] It was a fine balancing act; nevertheless, Montagu was certain she could pull it off. Everything was in place. But it would take a tragedy to drive Montagu to create her salon.

3

THE STREATHAMITES

E LIZABETH MONTAGU APPEARED always the consummate hostess. On first meeting her, the poet Hannah More gushed that Montagu was 'not only the finest genius, but the finest lady I ever saw'. Hester Thrale declared that she was 'brilliant in diamonds, solid in judgement, critical in talk'. Thrale was perfectly poised to appraise Montagu and her salons, for she herself hosted a literary assembly to rival that of Hill Street. North of the River Thames, Montagu reigned over her chic Mayfair salon with stately aplomb; a few miles due south, Thrale presided over a different kind of literary mêlée in the rural idyll of Streatham.

The land on which Streatham Park was built was said to have been bought in exchange for a ten-year supply of ale from the famous Thrale brewery. To escort them on the six-mile journey from London down to Streatham the Thrales's guests could hire armed guards to ward off the highwaymen who roamed the roads in the bandit country that surrounded the capital. But the dangerous journey was worth it once the delights of Streatham Park were revealed. In the hundred acres of the park were woodlands and meadows, a ha-ha, a large lake complete with its own island and drawbridge, formal gardens, kitchen gardens and greenhouses that could supply everything from cabbages to pineapples, an ice-house for added luxury, orchards, stables, a dairy, an extensive collection of rare poultry, a quaint summer-house and a two-mile circular gravel walk. The house itself was a three-storey brick mansion, covered in stucco and painted a gleaming white. Henry Thrale was a man possessed by a mania for building and he frequently re-invented the house, adding new wings, a pedimented front and a magnificent library.[1]

But the beauty of the place was not the reason that everyone longed for an invitation to Streatham. Hester Thrale, mistress of the house, was known for her wit which flashed brilliantly, for her spirit, her intellect, her sweet good humour, her merriment and her common sense. The diminutive Welshwoman was charming to look at with her chestnut hair, a clear complexion ('the Red very bright, & the White eminently good and clean', as she once described it) and large, light grey eyes.[2] More than that, she was known to be extremely well-read, as comfortable with the classics as with modern literature. She liberally scattered her many diaries and notebooks with original poetry, often copying the best verses out for friends or sending them anonymously to journals for publication. As a hostess, she was famed for her easy generosity, designing elaborate menus for her guests who would swoon over dinners they described as 'most splendid and magnificent – two courses of 21 Dishes each, besides Removes;[*] and after that a dessert of a piece with the Dinner – Pines and Fruits of all sorts, Ices, Creams &c., &c. without end – everything in [gold] plate, of which such a profusion'.[3] At Streatham, these feasts were held not in a dining room, but in the library at a table that could expand to seat more than thirty guests. There, surrounded by her books, Thrale would bask in the witty conversation that flowed so effortlessly around her.

Besides Thrale, there was another star at Streatham. It was not her husband Henry, but that giant of eighteenth-century letters – Samuel Johnson – who added lustre to the many soirées she hosted. His *Dictionary of the English Language* was an astonishing book that had propelled him to fame when it appeared in 1755. This meticulous work of scholarship had taken Johnson only a decade to complete, working with just a few assistants. In contrast, the French equivalent had taken forty years and dozens of scholars. Johnson's dictionary, which in someone else's hands might have been a staid affair, managed to be functional yet elegant. He included hundreds of examples from a wealth of books to illustrate his definitions, and the finished work overflowed with his erudition. In the years that he was working on his dictionary, Johnson also managed to find time to write

---

* A 'remove' was an extra dish which replaced one that had been emptied.

multiple essays, plays and poems. He was a charitable and pious man, but could be blunt to the point of rudeness at times. He was unusually tall, bore the marks of scrofula, had many tics and often grunted involuntarily. This unusual physical appearance led many to underestimate him at first glance, but as soon as he began to speak, his eloquence, wit and learning shone through.

Thrale and Johnson had first met on a gloomy Thursday in January 1765. She had heard so much about the lexicographer that she longed to know him. She was spending the winter in Southwark, at the townhouse next to the brewery. Baby Queeney, her first child, was four months old and Thrale, dutifully nursing this adored infant herself (rather than employing a wet nurse as many of her contemporaries would have done), was tied to the nursery. She was bored and tried to entice visitors to see her, but few would come. The new bridge would not be built from Blackfriars for another few years, making the area hard to reach from the West End and, besides, Southwark was an unfashionable area, filthy and poor, filled with foul smells from the tanneries and noise from the manufactories. The riverbank echoed with the coarse shouts of the lightermen as they ferried passengers and cargo along the Thames. The notorious Clink prison was the area's most notable building. Street names such as 'Dirty Lane' did little to inspire confidence. The Thrale brewery was itself nestled at the end of Deadman's Place – a name derived from the old pesthouses built there during the plague. The brewery was spread over several acres; its malt-houses, storehouses, brewhouse with its gleaming copper vats, the coopers' workshops, and stables for a hundred horses added much to the noises and odours of Southwark. Another brewer once told Hester that other women had rejected Henry's marriage proposals because they would not countenance living for any part of the year in 'the Borough'. Hester would not learn about these other women, and the discomforts of the brewery, until she was already wed. 'God help me,' she wrote in her diary when she did.[4]

Samuel Johnson was not a man to be put off by the unpleasant odours of this lively corner of London. Knowing that Johnson kept an eclectic circle of friends, Thrale tempted him to Southwark with the promise of an introduction to 'the poetical shoemaker' James

Woodhouse. This Staffordshire man had trained as a cordwainer before discovering that he had a talent for verse. He had come to London hoping to raise his profile and further his career. Excited to receive Thrale's invitation, Woodhouse arrived at Deadman's Place promptly at four o'clock that Thursday afternoon, just as Johnson appeared. The dinner was a great success, with Thrale and Johnson taking to each other immediately. Woodhouse seems to have been less of a hit with Thrale: 'the next Thursday was appointed for the same company to meet – exclusive of the Shoemaker,' she wrote dismissively (Woodhouse would later find a patron in Elizabeth Montagu). This was the beginning of an intense friendship between Thrale and Johnson. In the summer, when the brewery was quiet and the Thrales had decamped from the banks of the murky Thames to the open space of Streatham, they invited Johnson to visit. His trip to Streatham was a success – such a success that he decided to move in with the Thrales. He would spend the next decade and a half living much of the year with them.

The Thrales frequently had guests stay for weeks or months and seemed barely to bat an eyelid at Johnson taking up habitation with them. They had no problem seeing their house as a sort of residential salon. Unlike the Hill Street salon (which came to life only as Montagu directed, her evenings carefully planned in advance), at Streatham, any moment, any meal, any chance encounter in the library could become an event.

After a few years, the Thrales built a special room for Johnson, directly above the library. Johnson's room looked out over the gardens and park from bow windows. It was a far cry from the house he kept in London, overlooked on all sides and crammed always with his friends and charity cases. When he was not in his bright and airy room at Streatham, he could often be found in the wooden summer-house where he would read and write for hours. The summer-house was also where Johnson and little Queeney Thrale would celebrate their birthdays – fifty-five years and a day apart – together. Ink pot and papers would give way to elaborate dishes, the usual contemplative silence was broken by fiddle music and the servants spilling into the garden to enjoy this high day.[5] Years later, Frances Burney would sit in that same 'sweet cool summer House' to read

Johnson's play *Irene* – which 'though not a good *play*, is a beautiful poem', she concluded.[6]

Johnson made himself at home at Streatham and the Thrales looked upon him with mingled awe and affection. Growing used to his eccentricities, they took to keeping spare wigs for Johnson, knowing that his practice of holding a candle between his weak eyes and the pages of a book often led to his hair going up in smoke. His idea of building a chemistry laboratory next to the pump in the kitchen garden seemed a good one and Thrale and the children spent much of the summer of 1771 happily distilling essences and experimenting with colouring liquors. But Henry Thrale, not normally a cautious man, put an end to all furnace-based experiments when he found Johnson, closely surrounded by children and servants, bending over a particularly fierce flame – his poor eyesight had left him unable to see just how close they all were to that dangerous blaze.[7] Dismantling the brick furnace, Henry advised Johnson to take up something safe, such as natural history, but it never caught his imagination in quite the same way.

When not endangering her children and servants, Johnson was a sort of muse to Thrale, encouraging her to write. Knowing that she was a bright woman, clever and sensitive, and seeing that she had no real creative outlet of her own, he advised her to set her thoughts down on paper. He had been encouraging her to write since their earliest days of friendship. But from the time of her marriage in 1763, Thrale had rarely had a break from pregnancy, nursing and the care of small (and often sickly) children. It was 1776 before she managed to carve out time to write. On 15 September that year, just a few days before the annual joint festivities for Johnson and Queeney's birthdays, she sat down in front of a brand new notebook. On the cover, a red label was stamped in gold with a single word: 'Thraliana'. The blank pages, bound in undressed calf-skin, called out to her.[8] The notebooks, six in all, had been a present from Henry – partly a gift for their upcoming thirteenth wedding anniversary, and partly a silent and shame-faced thank you to her for tending to his hideously swollen testicles after he had contracted another bout of venereal disease.[9]

'It is many Years since Doctor Samuel Johnson advised me to get a little Book,' she began, 'and write in it all the little Anecdotes which might come to my Knowledge, all the Observations I might make or hear; all the Verses never likely to be published, and in fine ev'ry thing which struck me at the Time.' The *Thraliana* (the name derived from the -ana genre popular in France) was part personal diary, part literary musings, part biography of Johnson. It was an extraordinary record of Thrale's days and her circle at Streatham. She veered from comments on society and politics, to incredibly intimate details of her daily life. At certain times, she seemed to think of publishing it; at others, of burning it. Though it gave her solace to write in it, she felt guilty about every minute it took her away from her domestic duties, thinking that it was not really the best use of a woman's time. After a despairing entry of 1781, touching on the Dutch war, recent hurricanes in the Caribbean, the aftermath of the Gordon Riots and Henry's ill health, she chided herself: '& I! writing in the Thraliana! I do not do it often tho', & am always ashamed when I do.'[10]

Thrale felt that the notebooks were taking up too much of her time, yet her friends felt that she didn't write enough, and especially that she did not write enough about Johnson. Every sentence he uttered was so perfectly formed, so witty and erudite, that his admirers longed to have a record of all he said. Thrale felt uneasy about writing down each of Johnson's words. She had seen James Boswell do it and disapproved, calling it 'ill-bred' and 'inclining to treachery'.[11] Even if Thrale had approved of the practice, she would have the problem of carving out writing time at the expense of family time. Ever since she had first known Johnson, she had been a mother,

> and little do these wise Men know or feel, that the Crying of a
> young Child, or the Perverseness of an elder, or the Danger however
> trifling of any one – will soon drive out of a female Parent's head a
> Conversation concerning Wit, Science or Sentiment . . . If one is to
> listen all Even[ing] and write all Morning what one has heard; where
> will be the Time for tutoring, caressing, or what is still more useful,
> for having one's Children about one.[12]

Johnson encouraged Thrale to write, but he also made it more difficult for her to do so by adding greatly to her domestic burden. She never resented having him as a house guest, but she did resent him demanding that she nurse him through an eye infection while her mother was dying of breast cancer and her little girl Lucy (Johnson's god-daughter) was gravely ill. But despite his demands for attention, Thrale loved Johnson dearly. Contradicting the well-known maxim that no man is a hero to his valet, Thrale affirmed that 'Johnson is more a Hero to me than to any one - & I have been more to him for Intimacy, than ever was any Man's Valet de Chambre.'[13] Thrale admired him not just because of his great intellect, but because of his kindness – it was he who brought little sugar animals for the children when they were drooping in their beds with chickenpox, and it was he who loved the tiny Susanna – born two months prematurely – when no one else would dare to let themselves become attached to her.[14]

Johnson, in his turn, gruffly appreciated Thrale's care for him. He could see too how many admirable attributes she had, and valued them: 'you have as much *sense*, & more *Wit* than any woman I know!' he declared at dinner one night, embarrassing her with his praise as he compared her favourably to Elizabeth Montagu.[15] But he could never quite separate these attributes from Thrale's being a woman. An ode Thrale wrote on a robin redbreast which used to sing at her window each morning in exchange for a few crumbs was, he thought, 'very pretty . . . a good one . . . for a *Lady*'. Occasionally he would break out with more heartfelt praise, as when he made an impromptu toast to her one evening, 'Mercy on Me!' she declared afterwards, 'what noble what generous Praise! – I sate & cryed almost at the hearing of it - & yet to be so loved by such a Man! – who can wonder that my head is turned with Vanity?'[16]

An invitation to Streatham meant admission to a rarefied world, as Frances Burney knew. Burney (called Fanny by her family and friends) had been a slow child: unable to read until she was eight years old, her family worried that she was perhaps a little backward. But then, quite suddenly, listening to one of her sisters recite Pope, her letters came to her. By the time she was ten, she had written her first novel. Much to her family's horror she began to write incessantly; she wrote elegies and odes, plays, songs, stories, farces, tragedies and epic poems. By the time she was fifteen, knowing that such fits of writing were unbecoming in a girl and afraid of upsetting her family, she had burnt all of this work. One of the pieces that went up in smoke was that first novel, *The History of Caroline Evelyn*. Though the words were lost, the story stayed with Burney and some years later she began to work on its sequel, assembling scraps and fragments of prose in her spare moments.[17]

The Burney family had moved in 1774 to a house built for Isaac Newton in St Martin's Street, near Leicester Fields (now Leicester Square). The house was well situated in the heart of the West End of London, close to the opera houses, theatres and coffee-houses. Frances Burney's father Charles Burney, the famous harpsichordist, was well connected in the world of the arts and he gave weekly concerts in the house, throwing open its doors to actors and painters, writers and fellow musicians each Sunday evening. The family was proud to show off their new house, especially the attic, which had once been Newton's observatory – the London skies still clear enough for star-gazing. The house bustled always. Though she loved the liveliness of the visitors (and of her throng of brothers and sisters, step-siblings, and a growing set of half-brothers and sisters too), Burney struggled to find a secluded spot to write. Quiet moments were rare. Her stepmother disapproved of her unladylike hobby, and Burney tried to placate her by finishing all her needlework for the day before taking up a pen:

> I make a kind of rule, never to indulge myself in my two most favourite pursuits, reading and writing, in the morning – no, like a very good girl I give that up wholly . . . to needle work, by which means my reading and writing in the afternoon is a pleasure I cannot be blamed for by my mother, as it does not take up the time I ought to spend otherwise.[18]

Her father frequently co-opted her to act as his amanuensis for his own books on the history and theory of music, which left her little time to herself.

Burney shared a room on the second floor with her sister Susan and there she would hide and write. She worked in secret, confiding only in her sisters, one brother and a cousin. Slowly, the collection of scraps began to grow into a new book: *Evelina*. It was 1777 before Burney, aged twenty-five, finished the book. So great was her desire for secrecy that she disguised the handwriting in the manuscript (which appeared frequently in the manuscripts of her father's books). Her brother Charles, then an undergraduate at Cambridge, was delegated to carry the manuscript to a potential publisher. His sisters wrapped him up in an oversize greatcoat and muffled him up with scarf and hat 'to give him a somewhat antique as well as vulgar disguise' before sending him out on a dark evening. A Fleet Street bookseller accepted the manuscript from this strange emissary, and paid twenty guineas to the anonymous writer.[19]

In January 1778, *Evelina* was published. In the spring, it began to attract attention. By April, the reviewers were calling it 'one of the most sprightly, entertaining and agreeable productions of this kind'. The painter Joshua Reynolds (a neighbour of the Burneys) liked it so much he was 'quite *absent* all the Day' that he began reading it. He barely heard a word that was said to him and refused to put it down at mealtimes. The statesman Edmund Burke sat up all night to finish it. By summer, Hester Thrale was reading it. She was recommended the book by a friend during her lying-in after the birth of her daughter Henrietta Sophia (always called Harriett). She found the novel enchanting: 'a very *pretty* Book & a very *clever* Book and a very *comical* Book', she called it. She was struck by the power of the writing, the deftly drawn characters, and the perfectly observed satire of the society she knew so well. She heartily recommended the book to her eldest girl's music tutor – Charles Burney – declaring that she longed to know who the anonymous author was.[20]

Charles Burney had only found out his daughter's secret himself that summer, let slip by Frances's younger sister Susan. Though he had learned that she had written a book, it was some time before he could find out which book. When he finally ferreted out the secret and got hold of a copy, he was struck dumb by the dedication – to him:

> O, Author of my being! – far more dear
> To me than light, than nourishment, or rest,
> Hygeia's blessings, Rapture's burning tear,
> Or the life-blood that mantles in my breast!

The dedication brought tears to Charles's eyes. Burney cried too when her sister Charlotte reported this to her, tears of relief that her father was not angry at her deception, and tears of pride when she heard that he admired her work.

Charles was unable to control his laughter when Thrale had spoken of finding out the author of *Evelina*: 'I want to know him of all things.' Still laughing, he revealed the author's identity to her – no great man, but simply 'our Fanny'. Charles was as surprised as anyone that his daughter had written such a book, admitting to a friend that 'she has had very little Education but what she has given *herself*, - less than any of the others!'[21] Thrale had already heard about the girl as she had chatted to Charles about his family. She had even met her once. It was a meeting that had made a great impression on Burney, and none at all on Thrale.

Thrale was thrilled to be let in on the secret, and to hear of such an accomplished young woman. As soon as she found out Burney's identity, Thrale prevailed upon Charles to bring her to Streatham, keen to have such a bright new talent join her circle. Burney longed to visit Streatham too, having heard so much about the luminaries that resided there. She was flattered and happy at the prospect, yet she was anxious too, 'in a kind of *twitter*', she said, at the prospect of her first 'public' appearance as an author.[22]

The date for Burney's first visit to Streatham was set for August 1778 – 'the most *Consequential* Day I have spent since my birth', she called it when she wrote about it in her journal afterwards.[23] She travelled to Streatham from the home of a family friend named Samuel Crisp (always affectionately called 'Daddy Crisp' by Burney, while he addressed her as 'Fannikin'). Crisp's house in Chessington, Surrey had become a retreat for Burney when she needed space to write; she had written part of *Evelina* there. Leaving this quiet refuge for the glamour of Streatham made Burney nervous. She fidgeted constantly on the dusty ten-mile journey over the sun-baked summer roads. As her chaise rolled up the driveway to Streatham Park, Burney had her first glimpse of the fine white house set neatly in its acres of parkland. Hester Thrale, who was out in the grounds taking a stroll when she heard the rumbling chaise, came to meet her. Taking both Burney's hands in hers, she welcomed her to Streatham, heralding the beginning of a new life for the young writer.

The Streathamites, as Burney called them, centred their day upon the library. This well-stocked room, scattered with comfortable chairs, lit by large windows looking out over the estate, was a haven for these literati. There they could read or converse for hours, recommending volumes to each other or plucking a book off the shelf to win an argument. Above the rows of wooden bookshelves, hung thirteen portraits commissioned by the Thrales. These 'Streatham Worthies' (a nod to the British Worthies of Stowe Gardens) were painted by Joshua Reynolds in the 1770s and 1780s. A double portrait of Hester and Queeney Thrale was displayed above the mantelpiece: Hester resplendent in a white silk gown, the rosy cheeks she was so proud of much in evidence, gazed serenely into the middle distance. The other portraits showed some of the key members of Thrale's circle: Henry Thrale himself, not much of a wit, but a jovial host whose brewery funded the whole Streatham enterprise; the writer Oliver Goldsmith; the Italian critic and translator (and one-time tutor of Queeney) Giuseppe Baretti; statesman and philosopher Edmund Burke; a self-portrait of Reynolds, cupping his hand to his ear to show his deafness; Samuel Johnson, whom Reynolds had wished to paint squinting to show his poor eyesight, until Johnson firmly quashed that idea; Charles Burney (though this portrait had not been completed at the time of Frances Burney's first visit); the actor David Garrick; and several other notable figures from the world of the arts. To go with each portrait, Thrale composed a character-sketch in verse of the sitter. About herself, perhaps finding her gaze *too* tranquil, she wrote:

> In Features so placid, so smooth, so serene,
> What Trace of the Wit – or the Welch-woman's seen?
> Of the Temper sarcastic, the flattering Tongue,
> The Sentiment right – with th' Occasion still wrong.
> What Trace of the tender, the rough, the refin'd,
> The Soul in which all Contrarieties join'd?[24]

That first day in Streatham, Frances Burney spent several hours in the library, conversing with her hosts and other guests, reading alone (not something considered at all stand-offish at Streatham), and fending off questions about her authorship of *Evelina* from an impudent young man, who was quite unaware of her embarrassment at being thrust into the limelight. She dropped into the music room to hear Queeney play. She took her place at the table for dinner, served in the early afternoon, next to Thrale. On her other side was an empty seat. Already almost overwhelmed by the events of this most consequential day, her nerves were strained even further when Samuel Johnson entered the library and sat down beside her. She had heard from Thrale how much Johnson had enjoyed reading *Evelina*, saying that it excelled even the novels of his friend Samuel Richardson. 'We talk of it forever,' Thrale had told the Burneys, leaving Frances feeling rather dazed with joy. '*Dr. Johnson's* approbation! – Good God, it almost *Crazed* me with agreeable surprise! – it gave me such a flight of spirits, that I Danced a Jigg.' She had met him in passing before, but had never attracted his notice. Now she sat demurely at the dinner table trying to keep her emotions in check. Upon his entrance, she was inspired with a sense of reverence. At first she was struck by the contrast between his reputedly brilliant mind and his odd appearance, but, within minutes, she had lost herself in listening to him. She was mesmerised by the conversation that rolled around the table that first day: lines of verse in English, French and Latin; a dissection of one of David Garrick's epilogues; a bawdy story about a woman who drank pints of ale; a comic turn by Thrale on the fatiguing life of a wit. After dinner, Burney and Thrale – the only two ladies present – withdrew. 'Delightful,' Burney called their first proper time together, 'she was all good humour, spirits, sense & *agreeability*.'[25]

Afterwards, Burney gushed in her letters and diary that Thrale was 'so entertaining, so gay, so enlivening, when she is in spirits, and so intelligent and instructive when she is otherwise, that I almost wish to record all she says'. Thrale was less instantly enamoured of Burney, remarking that 'her Conversation would be more pleasing if She thought less of herself,' and that '[Burney] is a graceful looking Girl, but 'tis the Grace of an Actress not a Woman of Fashion.' Thrale did not consider that Burney's nerves might have stilted her conversation in front of the heroes she had so long dreamed of meeting. Burney's almost debilitating shyness frequently caused her to rush from the room when someone questioned her too closely about *Evelina* or her new-found status as an author. She considered herself a 'poor mere *Worm* in Literature', and even at Streatham was embarrassed to be seen reading 'lest I should pass for being *studious*, or *affected*, & therefore, instead of making a *Display* of Books, I always try to *hide* them.' But Thrale must have seen something to admire in Burney for she invited her to Streatham again a few weeks later. This time, Burney's nerves were a little calmer, her manner more composed and Thrale began to warm to her. Burney stayed for several days and Thrale put her in a bedchamber adjacent to her own dressing room. Thrale liked to leave the communicating doors open so that the pair could converse easily whenever they liked. By the end of Burney's second visit, the two women had become friends.[26]

When Burney returned to Streatham for that second, longer, visit, Johnson was delighted to see her again. He nicknamed her 'Little Burney' and began to take a fatherly interest in her. Together Johnson and Burney indulged in literary chats over breakfast and enjoyed gaily sociable teas. Johnson tried to feed Burney up, insisting that she have extra cake at tea time, and that rashers of bacon be cooked for her supper: 'a *Rasher*, – a *Rasher*, I believe, would please her,' he announced to Thrale, insisting that a table be laid for a perplexed Burney, not hungry in the least. He kept her up conversing for hours after she tried to slip off to bed, but made up for it with his comical good humour, composing extempore dialogues to entertain the party. When Burney began to get over her shyness about *Evelina*, Johnson began to talk to her of it. From memory, he quoted lines from his favourite characters, saying that even Henry Fielding had not written such good characters. 'Madam,' he assured her, 'there is *no* Character better drawn *any* where – in *any* Book, or by *any* Author.'[27]

The days at Streatham passed easily: breakfasts together in the library, then mornings alone, with most of the inhabitants giving these hours to writing. The guests came together again in the library from noon to read or converse. They encouraged each other to undertake new things, as when Thrale earnestly implored Burney to try her hand at writing a comedy for the stage. The party would then dress for their afternoon dinner, the centrepiece of the day, where everyone could show off their wit (their 'flash' as they called it at Streatham) as the meal unfolded at a leisurely pace. Then there would be walks in the grounds – visiting the lake or the summer-house, the orchard or walled gardens; seeing the pineapples ripen in the hothouses or Thrale's elaborate assortment of poultry; or just meandering along the miles of gravel paths with one of the many Streatham dogs following along. Neighbours were visited, or correspondence completed. Tea and confabs in the library followed, and as the darkness closed in and the candles were lit, the party would assemble again for conversations that ran deep into the night.

A huge volume of written work was produced at Streatham over the years. There were informal works such as the *Thraliana*, but also poems and plays, novels and histories that would be published to much acclaim. Johnson wrote there, Frances and Charles Burney both wrote there. Most guests seemed to find stimulation in Thrale's company but, just as importantly, she was able to provide the luxuries of time, space and peace for her guests, if not always for herself.

Streatham was also a place of learning. In her second summer there, Burney joined in Queeney's Latin lessons – with Johnson as Latin master. Women were rarely given the chance to study classical languages, so this was a special opportunity for them. Hester Thrale had studied Latin as a child and revelled in her knowledge of the language. Henry Thrale, surprisingly enlightened on questions of female education, said that it was 'better to each of them than a Thousand Pounds added to their Fortune'. Burney was not so sure. Just a few months earlier, on being asked by a clergyman whether she knew Latin, she replied with an offended 'No, indeed! not at all!' She assumed that a scurrilous rumour had got about that she must have known Latin in order to be accepted as a Streathamite. A few months later, when Thrale and Johnson persuaded her to join Queeney's lessons, she remained unconvinced that it was a proper thing for a woman. 'I heartily wish I rejoiced more sincerely in this *Classical plan*,' she confessed to her sister Susan, 'but the truth is, I have more fear of the malignity which will follow its being known, than delight in what advantages it may afford.' Two months into the lessons, Burney had still not made peace with the idea of learning Latin and wrote again to Susan of her dread that people would find out how she spent her spare time. Burney was greatly relieved when she found out that her father believed that 'Latin was too Masculine for Misses' and dissuaded her from keeping up the lessons. Thrale suspected that really he feared being overtaken by his daughter in intellectual achievements – a common worry amongst men.[28]

In truth, Burney was happier playing parlour games than attending Latin lessons. The Streathamites were known for a sense of fun, and they could while away whole afternoons playing the fool – assigning a colour or a silk to represent the character of each member of the circle ('Miss Burney a lilac Tabby, & myself a Gold Colour'd Watered Tabby', recorded Thrale afterwards), or trying to imagine each other as flowers, foods or animals. Johnson, bulky and wise, was an elephant; the easily startled Burney was a doe; Thrale herself was a rattlesnake – 'you have its *Attractions*, I think you have its *Venom* too, and all the World knows you have its *Rattle*,' Johnson told her more than once. The eighteenth-century craze for classification ran riot at Streatham. The new Linnæan system for grouping plants had caught the public imagination. Thrale decided to see if she could devise a similar system to classify her friends. Men, she ranked according to their religious feeling, morality, scholarship, general knowledge, person and voice, manner, wit, humour and good humour. According to her scale, Johnson scored the highest mark of 20 for religion, morality and general knowledge, and none whatsoever for person and voice, manner, or good humour. No one else earned any 20s. Joshua Reynolds had passable general knowledge but failed on most other accounts; Charles Burney scored well across the board, failing only on wit; David Garrick was another high scorer, but was let down by his poor scholarship and bad humour. Henry Thrale was awarded no points for wit or humour, but otherwise acquitted himself reasonably well.[29]

Women, she thought, needed a separate system, and so she devised a new set of criteria: worth of heart; conversational powers; person, mien and manner ('it is general Appearance rather than Beauty that is meant'); good humour; useful knowledge; ornamental knowledge ('Singing, Dancing, Painting & suchlike'). Thrale did not include any category pertaining to virtue for the women because 'they must possess *Virtue* . . . or one would not keep em Company, so that is not thought about.' Several prominent learned ladies appeared in her classification: poet Hannah More scored a perfect 20 for worth of heart, but nothing for person, mien and manner; writer Hester Mulso Chapone scored highly on everything except good humour and person, mien and manner; classicist Elizabeth Carter apparently possessed a great deal of ornamental knowledge. But highest ranked of all was Elizabeth Montagu, earning a 20 for her legendary conversational powers, and above 15 points in all other categories.[30]

Thrale and Montagu had first met in February 1775. They were introduced at a dinner hosted by Joshua Reynolds at his house in Leicester Fields. Montagu was sitting for a portrait at the time – she would have visited the house often, reposing in an armchair on a raised dais beneath a single high window as Reynolds appraised her. Sitting for Reynolds could be an alarming experience: he would observe his easel and his subjects side by side before dashing to the canvas and jabbing his brush at it with a kind of manic fury. 'I sometimes thought he would make a mistake and paint on me instead of the picture,' one sitter recalled after the ordeal.[31] But Montagu did not find Reynolds alarming. They had moved in the same circles for many years – he was a frequent guest at her salons and dinner parties, and she often came to his studio to keep friends company while they sat for him, or to visit the gallery that he had built onto the back of the house, where his own paintings hung next to old masters. Reynolds often hosted open days, allowing the public to move through his studios, his upper-class guests mingling with an intriguing world of artists and performers. But on that February night, Reynolds kept the party small. He did not wish to be distracted from the sure-to-be brilliant first meeting of Montagu and Thrale.[32]

Montagu (then in her mid-fifties) immediately saw something she recognised in Thrale (in her mid-thirties). They spoke of literature, they admired each other's fluent conversation and revelled in easy wit. Though many saw them as rivals, really they were each of them happy to meet a like-minded woman. Afterwards, Montagu made it clear that she desired Thrale's friendship. Thrale was delighted. 'She is a very high bred Lady,' wrote Thrale, 'a very conspicuous Character in the World, and her Conversation flows very freely from a very full Mind.' It was praise that could have been applied to either woman.

After that first meeting, they saw each other often. In London, they would meet at Hill Street or other assemblies or they would dine at private parties. They attended Court together. They met at Streatham too, with Montagu describing dinner parties there as 'the best of all feasts, sense, and witt, and good humour' and praising the hostess as 'a Woman of very superior understanding, and very respectable as a Wife, a Mother, a Friend, and a Mistress of a Family'.[33] But Montagu, anxious about travelling on account of the highwaymen, would never stay late at Streatham.[34]

In the autumn of 1778, Montagu received a note from Thrale inviting her to dine at Streatham the next day. Thrale wanted to show off Frances Burney, her new friend. Burney was torn between desperately wanting to meet the woman she called 'our sex's Glory' and embarrassment at the thought of taking up any of the great lady's time. When Thrale told Johnson that Montagu was to dine with them the next day, he began to rock with silent laughter, trying to keep a straight face. He was imagining the first meeting of Montagu and Burney – the reigning Queen of the Blues faced with the newest witling. '*Down* with her, Burney!' he shouted suddenly,

> *down* with her! – spare her not! attack her, fight her, & *down* with her
> at once! – *You* are a *rising* Wit, – *she* is at the *Top*, – & when *I* was
> beginning the World, & was nothing & nobody, the Joy of my Life
> was to fire at all the established Wits![35]

Nothing could have been further from shy little Burney's mind.

Johnson was often dismissive of women, and especially of women who could out-talk him. Once, while in the company of one such female, he was heard to say that 'I am very fond of the company of ladies; I like their beauty, I like their delicacy, I like their vivacity, and I like their silence.'[36] Though he praised Elizabeth Carter, as we have seen, he valued her pudding-making abilities as highly as her skills as a translator. He valued Thrale too, but often just as much for her domestic service to him as for her mind or writing. Despite his esteem for these women, he was able baldly to declare that 'a man is in general better pleased when he has a good dinner upon his table, than when his wife talks Greek.'[37]

This attitude had crumbled in the face of Montagu. Though Johnson might joke about bringing Montagu down, like everyone else at Streatham, he held her in high regard. The two had first met in the late 1750s, introduced by Elizabeth Carter, who was one of Montagu's closest friends. It was some years after their first introduction before he condescended to visit Hill Street but when he finally did, reported a supercilious Montagu, 'he came early and staid late.' Montagu's wit won round this man who had claimed to rejoice in the silence of females. 'I believe he is not hard to please in conversation', she told friends, 'for I hear he expresses himself delighted with the evening he pass'd here, and some of my friends tell me that since Polyphemus was in love there has not been so glorious a conquest as I have made over Mr Johnson.' Johnson found in Montagu an equal in the conversational arts. He admitted that 'Mrs. Montagu is a very extraordinary woman; she has a constant stream of conversation, and it is always impregnated; it has always meaning.'[38]

Over the years, Montagu and Johnson had a tumultuous friendship, sparring first when they penned competing critiques of Shakespeare, and later when Johnson slighted a poet friend of Montagu's. Yet the two were well-matched, and always made up, perhaps knowing that they complemented each other so perfectly, and that they shone so brightly in each other's company. It was he who dubbed Montagu 'the Queen of the Blues'. It was meant perhaps as a barb, for he first said it during one of their spats, but it was a title that stuck, and was used with reverence by many.

When Montagu accepted Thrale's invitation to dinner that September day, Johnson was ordered to be on his best behaviour. Burney must have wondered what had passed on Montagu's previous visit when she overheard her hostess telling Johnson that 'you *did* put her a little out of countenance last Time she came . . . when a lady *changes Colour*, we imagine her feelings are not quite *composed*.' Thrale tartly reminded Johnson that Montagu was the foremost woman of literature in the country and bid him temper his mischief. Johnson agreed that Montagu was worthy of respect: 'She diffuses more knowledge in her Conversation than any Woman I know,' he admitted and then added as an afterthought, 'or, indeed, *almost* any man.'[39]

Elizabeth Montagu, along with her young companion Dorothy Gregory, arrived before one o'clock in the afternoon. Burney, who had heard so much about Montagu, was pleased to note her sensible face and penetrating eye along with a general air of one comfortable with her own greatness (an air that Johnson claimed she had practised for many years before perfecting it). Burney's attempt at quiet observation was interrupted by Thrale's favourite terrier, Presto, bustling to the library door, yapping at the guests and distracting everyone from formal introductions. When Presto had been calmed, the party settled down into polite chit-chat. Burney relaxed into listening in happy anticipation of hearing these two great women converse. But within ten minutes, Montagu had sent little Burney into spasms of anxiety with an innocent enquiry about the popular book *Evelina*. Montagu had sent to her bookseller for a copy but he was all out; she hoped to procure a copy elsewhere soon. 'I began, now, a vehement *Nose-blowing*,' Burney wrote to her sister later, 'for the Benefit of *Handkerchiefing* my Face.' Hiding conspicuously behind her handkerchief, Burney listened with a sense of mounting dread as Thrale began to praise *Evelina*, telling how Joshua Reynolds was now offering £50 for information that would identify the author. Intrigued, Montagu said that she hoped to have the book before her next trip to her country seat at Sandleford in Berkshire so that she could read it in her carriage. Thrale, eager to help, sent Queeney off to find her own copy. Feeling increasingly awkward, Burney went and stood at the furthest window and pretended to contemplate the fowl. Thrale rhapsodised on, comparing the novel to the works of Henry Fielding and saying how much Johnson had liked it. 'Indeed,' agreed Montagu, '*that* I did not expect, for I have been informed it is the work of a Young lady, – & therefore . . . I expected a very pretty Book . . . but *Life & manners* I never dreamt of finding.' And then Thrale could contain herself no longer: she suddenly looked over at her young friend by the window and exclaimed, 'we are *killing* Miss Burney, who wrote the Book herself!'[40] The startled Burney could take no more and ran from the room.

Despite Thrale's entreaties to her to rejoin the party, Burney hid in her room until it was time to eat. Unable to concentrate on reading or writing, she just sat alone, rueing missing out on Montagu's conversation, and wishing that she was not so abashed about being a female author. She was still a bundle of nerves at dinnertime. Montagu spoke to her kindly, avoiding all mention of the book, but Gregory could not help staring at the secret author of *Evelina*, hardly taking her eyes off Burney's face. Johnson joined them for dinner (doing his best not to provoke Montagu), but even his genial presence did little to restore Burney's equilibrium. When eventually, inevitably, someone mentioned *Evelina*, Montagu, still with the greatest deference to Burney's shyness, declared that she was '*proud* that a work *so* commended should be a *woman's*'.[41] Johnson joined in the praise, and Burney finally began to feel something other than panic, especially when she caught the delight on Thrale's face at seeing the reigning king and queen of literature say so much in favour of her shy authoress friend. Finally, Burney unwound enough to enjoy herself. She began to make up for all the amusement she had missed while hiding in her room. But just as Burney was beginning to have some fun, Montagu became aware of the beginning of an autumn twilight and called for her coach, determined to get back to town before the footpads began to roam.

Burney barely heard a word of the famous conversation of Montagu that day, but she would have many chances to hear her again in the future. Burney would particularly relish listening to Montagu and Thrale together. Those two great ladies continued to meet in London and Streatham, and their paths crossed now and again in the more fashionable resort towns. Their impromptu meetings in the drawing rooms of Tunbridge Wells or Bath were as much of an occasion for the other visitors as any of the formal entertainments on offer. The spring of 1780 saw them together at Bath. Thrale described how each night brought a new invitation for both herself and Montagu, for

> People think they must not ask one of us without the other, & there they sit gaping while we talk: I left it to her for the first fortnight & she harangued the Circles herself; till I heard of private Discussions why Mrs. Thrale who was so willing to talk at other Times, was so silent in

Mrs. Montagu's Company – then I began, and now we talk away regularly when there is no Musick.[42]

Burney, also in Bath that season, was delighted to see the two together every evening, conversing late into the night in high spirits. The evenings were not enough, and so they began to meet in the afternoons too: 'Mrs Montagu & my Mrs Thrale both flashed away admirably,' wrote Burney to her sister Susan, evoking the ambience of their afternoon tea parties, and the hushed crowd of listeners who gathered round. After some weeks in Bath, having assessed Montagu from close quarters, Burney felt able to contrast the conversational powers of the two great *salonnières*. In a letter to her father she wrote:

I am very glad at this opportunity of seeing so much of [Montagu], [for] she is always reasonable and sensible, & *sometimes* instructive and entertaining, - & I think of our Mrs. Thrale we may say the reverse, - for *she* is *always* entertaining and instructive, & *sometimes* reasonable & sensible, - & I write this because she is just now looking over me, - not but what I *think* it too.[43]

★

In a constant swirl between London and Streatham, Bath and Sandleford, and even occasionally (when she could not excuse herself from duties at the brewery) Deadman's Place, Thrale and Montagu created a new sphere for women. They could be bookish, they could lose themselves in 'manly' pursuits such as reading the classics, they could raise their voices and be heard just like men. Their fame and success gave others courage to try to emulate them.

More salons began to grow up in London and around the country, each with a different flavour. Montagu's was an unashamedly intellectual salon. Thrale's was light and literary, always with space for humour or a bawdy tale. Thrale herself once described the difference between them: 'Mrs Montagu's Bouquet is all out of the Hothouse – mine out of the Woods and Fields & many a Weed there is in it.'[44]

Montagu in particular gained a reputation as a heavyweight. The prestigious *Monthly Review*, sometimes scathing about female writers, called Montagu a 'literary amazon'.[45] Even her critics, such as the playwright Richard Cumberland, though he satirised her, grudgingly admitted that she had a mesmerising ability to inspire literary feeling wherever she went: 'she can make a mathematician quote Pindar.'[46] Montagu's salon came to be seen as a national asset, with one statesman writing to her that

> George the third does not know how much he is indebted to the chearful and Classic Assemblies of your Chinese Room. You gave that sweetness and refinement to the thoughts of our Statesmen which could alone counteract the acid and gloom of their Dispositions . . . we are all indebted to you.[47]

Two of the other great Bluestocking hostesses were Frances Boscawen and Elizabeth Vesey – friends of Montagu's since her early days in Hill Street. Both set up their salons in Mayfair, within a few minutes' walk of Montagu's house: Boscawen's was in South Audley Street, while Vesey's was in Clarges Street. Boscawen was famed for her elegant correspondence, and for the warm maternal glow she emanated at her salons. Her husband was an admiral in the navy, and talk at her evening assemblies sometimes drifted towards military and political matters. Vesey (nicknamed the Sylph on account of her otherworldly air) specialised in bringing the most disparate elements of society together. Even Montagu was in awe of her hosting skills.

There were other salons too: if one wanted music, one went to the Duchess of Norfolk's or Countess Spencer's; for a light mixture of art, music, masquerade and books one went to the Honourable Miss Monckton's; for polite discourse to Lady Hillsborough's assemblies; and for politics, to the Duchess of Cumberland's Thursday drawing room.

But even in this proliferation of salons, Montagu and Thrale remained the most eminent of this new breed of clever women. They themselves were the focal points of the Bluestocking movement; their homes were among the most desirable social spaces of eighteenth-century England. Everyone from royalty to revolutionaries clamoured for an invitation. Montagu and Thrale filled their houses with the brightest thinkers, the greatest writers and the sharpest wits. They welcomed their glittering friends into some of the most sumptuous interiors in the capital. Onlookers marvelled at their learning and their quick brains; many envied their ready access to money, their beautiful houses, or supportive husbands.

But there were those who viewed these new places for women to socialise with suspicion. 'I hope you have met with an absurd paragraph in the Morning Herald,' Montagu wrote one day with much mirth to Elizabeth Carter, continuing with an account of how the newspaper reported that a brawl had broken out at a Bluestocking salon and that the event had nearly ended with a fatality. According to the reporter, the Bluestockings had now split into two rival factions. Montagu shrugged off these idle rumours.[48] It was not likely that any Bluestocking gathering ever came close to ending with a murder. But to some readers of gossipy newspaper columns, the idea that a group of clever women spending time together could only end badly chimed neatly with the idea that the 'learned lady' was an unnatural figure in society. This imaginary woman could not blend seamlessly in with her peers, could not live a happy blameless life, but must always upset the natural balance of the world.

To an outsider, the Bluestocking salons seemed like a piece of theatre peopled with dramatic figures so far from the ordinary that no one could predict their actions. But from within, the salons were places of acceptance and sorority, places where women could show their true selves without fear of judgement.

4

THE MILKING PARLOUR

THE WINTER OF 1784 was the coldest anyone could remember. The River Severn froze over for miles and miles. They said that you could walk across the Thames from Rotherhithe to Wapping New Stairs on the ice. They said that the post-boys fell frozen from their ponies. The cattle perished where they stood. The ground was hard as rock. Benjamin Franklin thought that the extreme weather had been brought on by the strange fog that had enveloped much of the northern hemisphere since the previous summer. This dense, dry fog – like smoke – sat heavily over the land for months and months. Through it, the noonday sun looked like a clouded-over moon. Daylight looked rusted and tarnished. The sky at sunrise and sunset was the colour of blood. At first, the dust made everything hotter – meat would rot within a day and the land was plagued with flies. Then, as summer dwindled into autumn, the dust seemed no longer to intensify the sun's heat but to block it out. Overnight frosts failed to thaw, light snows refused to melt. The air was cold, and the winds colder still.

Franklin and the men of science speculated that the fog had come from Iceland, where there were reports of massive volcanic eruptions. Witnesses had recorded how the land seemed to howl and cry before it swelled and shattered, ripped open by explosions. Flames leaped up from the bowels of the earth, huge rocks were flung to impossible heights, fountains of ash darkened the skies.[1] For eight months, the eruption continued. Twenty villages were destroyed by unrelenting lava flows. Smoke and cinders poisoned the land, killing livestock and withering crops. The famine that followed killed a quarter of the population of the island.

The wind swept the toxic plumes upwards and outwards, darkening half the world and bringing that preternatural winter. Records from dozens of countries tell the same story. As the men of science tried to explain the portentous events of that year, as they debated the mysteries of volcanoes at meetings of their academies, Ann Yearsley knew only that she had to do something to save her family.

Her four young children were growing thinner daily, she herself was heavily pregnant, her elderly mother was becoming weaker. Deep snow covered the ground, and her cows were steadily munching through the reserves she had put aside to last until the spring. From her home in Clifton, a village slowly being subsumed into the nearby city of Bristol, Yearsley could look down from the heights of St Vincent's Rocks to the river below. She was used to seeing the water flash and wind its way through the narrow gorge, but now it was solid and still. 'Crystal streams in frozen fetters stand,' she would write later, thinking back on that harsh year.[2] But she had little time for poetry that winter.

Yearsley depended on the cows for her livelihood – she was a milkwoman. This respectable occupation had been taught to her by her mother. Milkwomen were a vital part of the rural economy and of urban life: they brought fresh milk daily into the cities and sold it door to door. Milkwomen usually had their own animals and worked for themselves, giving them a higher status than many other rural workers. But that winter, as the land lay covered in snow and the fodder supplies ran short, Yearsley struggled. Agriculture ground to a halt and day labourers were laid off at alarming rates. The churches stepped in to distribute alms. But the Yearsleys – used to being independent – were too proud to ask for help. They lost their house and took refuge in a stable. It was only by chance that a gentleman stumbled across the family there and sent for aid. He provided food and clothes and brought them to the attention of the alms-givers. It was too late for Yearsley's elderly mother: she perished just as winter turned to spring.

With help, the rest of the family survived until the warmer weather came. Yearsley's daughter Jane was born in May 1784 and Yearsley resumed her work. Her route took her up and down the Bristol hills, through the narrow old lanes and on to the wide modern streets being built in the expanding city. On Park Street, one of the newest streets, Yearsley could always count on selling some milk to the girls' school. She could also rely on the school cook selling her the kitchen slops cheaply, as food for the pigs she kept. Gradually, Yearsley and the cook came to know each other a little. They became friendly enough for Yearsley to share details of her life with the cook, friendly enough that Yearsley began to share something else – her poetry.

Yearsley had been taught to read by her mother when she was a child, and taught to write by her older brother. She had learned stories from the classics by looking at prints which hung in a shop window near her house.[3] The family owned a handful of books – Virgil, Shakespeare and Milton – which the little girl would pore over. Her favourite poem was Edward Young's *Night Thoughts*, with its musings on death, loss and human frailty. When she began to write poetry herself, she found that there was often a melancholy note to her verses. She found great comfort in writing.

Yearsley had married in 1774 at the age of twenty-one. Her husband John was listed as a yeoman in the parish register – meaning that he had land of his own. John's family earned enough money that they had to pay the 'poor rates' – a tax levied on those above a certain income to enable the churches to fund poor relief. But at some point after the marriage, John's family lost their land and their income slipped lower and lower. Yearsley bore her first child, Henry, in 1775; then William in 1776; John in 1778; Charles in 1780; and Ann in 1782.* With the arrival of each new child and John's loss of income, the family grew more dependent on the money Yearsley could earn from selling milk. John would take on work as a labourer when he could but the wages were only a few shillings a week. Her mother took in washing, which might add a few shillings more. It was a hard life with little time for poetry, but Yearsley would write at night when her work for the day was done and the children asleep. She said that poetry assuaged the hunger pangs she felt from missed meals, and that it soothed her anxious mind. It is not surprising that her poems often had a certain darkness to them.

Yearsley wrote for herself, not for an audience, but the few people who read her poems praised them. She probably never intended to

---

* Henry died in January 1779, aged four.

share them beyond a small circle but when she showed them to the cook at the girls' school on Park Street, everything changed.

The school was run by the More sisters: Mary, Elizabeth (Betty), Sarah (Sally), Hannah and Martha. The girls had been educated by their father, a schoolmaster himself. But though he was liberal enough to educate his daughters, he refused to teach them any higher mathematics, for fear that he would turn them into 'female pedants'.[4]

The two eldest More girls had set up the school with nineteen-year-old Mary as headmistress, Betty as housekeeper, and the three youngest sisters still among the pupils. As the younger More girls finished school, they joined the teaching staff until all five ran the establishment together. The curriculum included French, reading, writing, arithmetic, needlework and, later, due to popular demand, dancing.[5] The school filled up instantly and had to move to larger premises within just a few years of its foundation. At its new home in Park Street, the school could accommodate around sixty pupils.

Yearsley was not the only poet known to the school cook; she knew that one of the More sisters was a poet too. Hannah More was in her late thirties and already an established literary phenomenon and acknowledged Bluestocking when the cook showed her a copy of Yearsley's verses in the summer of 1784. More was astonished by what she read. She had been told that the author of these verses was 'a poor illiterate woman in the neighbourhood'. More had had low expectations but as she read, she found herself drawn in by the strik-ing imagery and powerful language of Yearsley's work.

Intrigued, More asked for an introduction to the poet. When the two women met, More was impressed by the simplicity of Yearsley's manners, by her lack of pretension or affectation. Yearsley admired More's learning as well as her wit and spirit. As they talked, they found they had similar tastes in poetry and similar opinions on liter-ary criticism. More's letters about the beginning of her relationship with Yearsley reveal that the two women had much in common. They also reveal an unbridgeable gulf between the pair: class. In a letter to Elizabeth Montagu, More marvelled that 'without having ever conversed with any body above her own level, [Yearsley] seems to possess the general principles of sound taste and just thinking.'[6] More's words might sound condescending today but at the time condescension was built in to the system and none of More's correspondents seemed at all troubled by the supercilious approach she took to Yearsley. Yearsley also seemed to accept More's manner – at least, in the beginning.

Yearsley struck More as being that most romantic of eighteenth-century phenomena – a natural genius. More believed that Yearsley's work welled up from 'the true fountain of divine Inspiration'. She saw Yearsley's talent as akin to a gift from God. Being a devout Christian, More believed it was her duty to nurture this gift and to help Yearsley publish her poetry. On a practical level, More believed that she could help Yearsley to earn money for her writing and so save the family from poverty. With these noble aims, More decided to become Yearsley's patron.

It was not More's first experience of patronage – she herself had been mentored when she was in her twenties by the great actor David Garrick. More had first met him in London in 1774, having carefully arranged for their paths to cross. Garrick had been in London for almost forty years by then. He had come to the city with his old schoolteacher and friend Samuel Johnson and had half-heartedly tried a career as a vintner before befriending several actors and deciding to give the theatrical life a go himself. On stage, Garrick was a sensation. He was vital, intense, dynamic and expressive – a world away from the formal, declamatory style that had dominated until then. By the time he met More, Garrick was already long established as the king of the London stage.

'Tuesday was the Day of Days!' More wrote to a neighbour in Bristol after she saw Garrick in *King Lear* at the Theatre Royal in Drury Lane. She had waited a long time to see him perform and she was not disappointed. 'I felt myself annihilated before Him,' she wrote afterwards. She felt that her soul itself was captivated and that she might actually suffocate with grief as she watched him play the aging, broken king. 'In short I am quite ridiculous about him,' she admitted, 'whether I eat, stand still, or walk – Still I can nothing but of Garrick talk.'[7]

It was no coincidence that the neighbour to whom More sent this gushing letter was an acquaintance of Garrick's. Aware of More's theatrical ambitions, the neighbour wrote to Garrick about this 'young Woman of an amazing Genius, & remarkable Humility'. He piqued Garrick's interest by quoting More's exuberant praise for his Lear.

Nor was it a coincidence that More and her sisters had taken lodgings for this trip in Southampton Street, halfway between Drury Lane, where Garrick worked, and the Adelphi, where he lived. In fact Garrick and his glamorous wife Eva (a retired dancer and another favourite with the Bluestockings) had once lived in Southampton Street themselves.

Garrick invited More and her sisters to visit him at home, courteously sending his coach, though it was only a short walk away. At the Adelphi, the sisters marvelled at this modern mansion, ornately decorated with marble pillars, bronze balustrades and painted ceilings. The Garricks welcomed the sisters warmly. Almost immediately, Hannah More and David Garrick began to discuss her work. The two whiled away several hours dissecting her words, her structures, her themes.

This was the beginning of an important phase of More's life. Garrick was taking her seriously as a writer. He took to calling her 'Nine' as he considered her to embody the talents of all nine Muses.[8] The year after their first meeting, Garrick wrote an epilogue for More's play *The Inflexible Captive* and helped to have it staged at Bath. Next, he helped as she prepared her new play *Percy* to be performed at the Theatre Royal in Covent Garden (Garrick had by then retired from Drury Lane).[9] For *Percy*, Garrick wrote the prologue, clearly inspired by his clever young female protégée:

> A *woman* here I come – to take a *woman's* part.
> No little jealousies my mind perplex,
> I come, the *friend* and *champion* of my sex;
> I'll prove, ye fair, that let us have our swing,
> We can, as well as men, do anything.[10]

As well as artistic advice and support, Garrick also provided crucial financial advice. Though no money ever changed hands between Garrick and More, the Garricks made life easier for More by providing her with rooms both in the Adelphi and at their country house at Hampton. At the Adelphi, More had use of the whole house, as well as her own bedchamber and a dressing room in which she could receive guests privately. She joked about the Garricks as excellent housemates, being 'well-behaved sensible people [who] are fond of books, and can read, and have a shelf of books which they will lend me'.[11] In fact the Garricks possessed a rather grand library. At Hampton meanwhile, just a little upriver from Hampton Court Palace, sat the Garricks' villa with its fine lawn running down to the Thames and its solemn temple to Shakespeare. Here, More could write in peace, away from the bustle of London which she found increasingly distracting.

When More's plays began to earn money, Garrick was on hand to guide her through the complicated process of investing it sensibly. For *Percy*, More earned about £600 (a combination of money from publication of the script, and fees from the theatres including 'author's nights' from which More could keep the profits). Garrick invested the money in a 5 per cent security on More's behalf. This writing income (together with an annuity More received from a man to whom she had once been engaged but who was unable ever to commit to a wedding date) allowed her enough independence to step back from her teaching responsibilities at the Park Street school.[12]

Hester Thrale used the story of More's financial success to try to encourage Frances Burney to write a play of her own, chiding that 'Hannah More got near 400 pounds for her foolish play, – & if you did not write a better than *hers*, I dare say you deserve to be *whipped*.'* Thrale was not More's biggest fan. Yet, years later she wrote in the *Thraliana* that 'Hannah More is the cleverest of all us Female Wits at last I think, her Florio is a very excellent Piece of writing in its way: We none of us much love the Author though.'[13] Still, Thrale was always cordial, and the other Bluestockings welcomed More much more warmly.

Very soon, More built up a circle of acquaintances in the capital. She became friendly with the painter Frances Reynolds who then introduced More to her brother Joshua Reynolds. It was at the Reynoldses' home that More was introduced to Samuel Johnson. Just as

---

* Burney did try her hand at writing for the stage but her play *The Witlings* was never performed for fear that it was too satirical and might offend Elizabeth Montagu and others.

she was about to enter the drawing room for this momentous introduction, Reynolds warned her of Johnson's occasional sombre moods.
She need not have worried: when she went into the room, More found
Johnson with a macaw perched upon his hand, smiling broadly. Instead
of greeting her in the conventional manner, he burst into a recitation of a
poem written by More herself. Years later, Johnson would call More 'the
most powerful versificatrix in the English language'.[14]

More's early trips to London were such a success that she continued
to make a pilgrimage to the capital each year for the next three decades.
Each visit was crammed with theatre trips, teas with friends, evenings at
salons and what More termed 'the hurry, bustle, dissipation, and non-
sensical flutter of a town life'. Her letters, and those of her sisters who
often accompanied her, were filled with fine dinners and even finer
conversation: 'Monday we dined, drank tea, and supped, at the amiable
Sir Joshua Reynolds'; there was a brilliant circle of both sexes . . . we
were not suffered to come away till one,' ran one early letter. Though
More loved these soirées, she dreaded the preparations they entailed. In
advance of one grand dinner, More complained to her sisters that she
was compelled to have a hairdresser attend to her:

> Nothing can be conceived so absurd, extravagant, and fantastical, as
> the present mode of dressing the head . . . I have just escaped from
> one of the most fashionable disfigurers; and though I charged him
> to dress me with the greatest simplicity, and to have only a very dis-
> tant eye upon the fashion . . . yet in spite of all these sage didactics, I
> absolutely blush at myself, and turn to the glass with as much caution
> as a vain beauty, just risen from the small pox.

More was baffled too by the large displays of fruit worn on the head
and the abundance of ostrich feathers. There was a (thankfully brief)
vogue for powdering wigs with turmeric to create the effect of blonde
hair but, as evenings wore on, the yellow powder would trickle down
onto the faces and the necks of the wearers, making them appear like
a field of crocuses.[15]

In 1775 More had her first invitation to dine at Elizabeth Mon-
tagu's Hill Street home. The guests included Elizabeth Carter, Samuel
Johnson, the naturalist Daniel Solander, Frances Boscawen, Frances
Reynolds, Joshua Reynolds, and a few others. More was initially

overwhelmed by the grandeur of her dining companions. 'I felt myself a worm,' she wrote to her sisters afterwards – almost the exact same words that Frances Burney used when she was first invited to Streatham. But Montagu's warmth and generous hosting soon made More feel at home. One evening of Montagu's conversation was enough to allow More to conclude that Montagu was 'the finest genius' she had ever met. She described Carter as having 'a great deal of what the gentlemen mean when they say such a one is a "poetical lady",' but, despite this, More liked her very much. Her favourite, however, was Frances Boscawen who was 'at once polite, learned, judicious, and humble'. For More, the climax of that dinner came when she was asked her opinion on a new tragedy playing at Drury Lane. 'I was afraid to speak before them all, as I knew a diversity of opinion prevailed among the company,' she admitted. But speak she did and was most gratified to have Samuel Johnson turn to her and gravely pronounce: 'you are right, madam.'[16]

From then on, More became a great favourite with Johnson, Boscawen and Montagu. At assemblies, Johnson would seek her out and the pair would converse for hours in high spirits, seeing who could 'pepper the highest' and drawing crowds round to listen. Boscawen often invited More to smaller, more intimate gatherings at her house on South Audley Street. More described one to which only herself, Montagu, Carter and Hester Mulso Chapone were admitted: 'we spent the time, not as wits, but as reasonable creatures . . . the conversation was sprightly but serious.' She frequently attended Montagu's salons, spending some of her happiest London days with the Queen of the Blues, who would invite twenty guests for dinner and then let them sort themselves into smaller groups for after-dinner tête-à-têtes, as was described by More:

> I spent my time in going from one to the other of these little societies, as I happened more or less to like the subjects they were discussing. Mrs. Scott, Mrs. Montagu's sister, a very good writer, Mrs. Carter, Mrs. Barbauld, and a man of letters, whose name I have forgotten, made up one of these little parties. When we had canvassed two or three subjects, I stole off and joined in with the next group, which was composed of Mrs. Montagu, Dr. Johnson, the Provost of Dublin, and two other ingenious men.[17]

In 1783 More wrote her poem 'The Bas Bleu: or, Conversation' which shows so well her delight at finding herself among like-minded people who preferred sprightly conversation to fashionable pursuits such as gambling or dancing. She intended to write only a few couplets, but this paean to Bluestocking life grew and grew until it was several hundred lines long.

Word of the poem spread quickly. The Bluestockings were immediately enamoured of it and began to ask for manuscript copies. Frances Burney, who had heard that she was the inspiration for the character of Attention in the poem ('Mute angel, yes! thy looks dispense / the silence of intelligence'), was keen to see a copy. Samuel Johnson called it 'a very great performance'. Elizabeth Carter (singled out as being 'deeply wise [and] never vain') was delighted by it. The famous writer and wit Horace Walpole ('polish'd Walpole shew'd the way, / how wits may be both learn'd and gay') began a correspondence with More after reading it, and praised her for her learning.[18]

More did not mind this informal circulation of the work, but she had no intention of publishing it; indeed, she did not imagine that anyone outside the inner Bluestocking circle would be much interested in her in-jokes and witticisms about the group. She was mistaken. A few weeks after she had penned the verses, a friend asked her permission to make a copy for himself; More granted this permission, on the condition that he not share it beyond their mutual friends. 'Thank you for your licence,' he replied,

> but a fig for your restrictions . . . when you must know that not only
> every reading and writing Miss at Margate has got a copy of them,
> but that copies of them are, by this time, dispersed over every part of
> the kingdom, to all their correspondents.[19]

A few months later, More had to sit up all night copying out the poem for a would-be reader who had insisted on having a copy of his own – King George III.[20]

London life was stimulating and inspiring for Hannah More. There were only two parts of it that she could not abide: cards and opera. Playing cards was not generally popular among the Bluestockings. More and Montagu fastidiously avoided it (and were gently mocked for their puritanical attitudes). Boscawen would sometimes set up a card table in a side room at her salons and More had to admit that this was a useful tactic for weeding out those she considered the duller members of the assembly.[21] On going to the opera, More had only this to say: 'like getting drunk, [it] is a sin that carries its own punishment with it, and that a very severe one.'[22] She never had an ear for music.

Each time More travelled home to the West Country, she brought a little bit of London with her. The ideas she formed about how to live a literary life, how to be a writer, how a clever woman should conduct herself were all coloured by what she had seen in the capital. Her ideas of patronage were also heavily influenced by her experiences there. More had sought Garrick out from the beginning, had praised him extravagantly, and had welcomed his criticism of her works. That first night she saw him performing in *King Lear*, she had written those striking words – 'I felt myself annihilated before Him'. It was an extraordinarily intense response. Even that capital letter 'H' hints towards More seeing Garrick as a kind of god-like figure.

When More was presented with the poetry of Ann Yearsley, she very quickly made up her mind to become its author's patron. It was early in the summer of 1784 that More and Yearsley first met in Bristol. They spent some time together over the next few months, More tactfully winkling stories of Clifton life out of Yearsley. Yearsley was initially wary of this attention, careful not to give out too much information, not even letting More know where she lodged. By the middle of the summer, More felt that she was finally getting to know Yearsley a little. Yearsley, meanwhile, grew to respect More and found herself inspired by this warm, genteel and educated Bluestocking. This new friendship, together with the end of that awful period of deprivation she had experienced just a few months before, lifted Yearsley's mood and wrought a change in her melancholic verses.

One of the poems she wrote that summer was called 'Night. To Stella'. In it, Yearsley grappled with the darkness of the events of the previous winter, and particularly with the death of her mother. Then she wrote in a more hopeful tone as she described how her family was rescued and how her writing was encouraged by More.

'Stella', to whom the poem was addressed, was Yearsley's poetical name for More. After vivid descriptions of her mother's suffering and death, Yearsley paused to pay tribute to More: '. . . I will view thee as the fount of light, / Which pierc'd old Chaos to his depth profound.'[23] Yearsley presents herself as an uncouth, uncivilised, unpolished creature; while More is a shining light, illuminating her mind and banishing the chaos of her past. It was exactly the kind of tribute that More hoped for from her protégée.

More began to write to her Bluestocking friends in London to tell them of the talented milkwoman. It was the first step in becoming Yearsley's patron. But patronage was not something that Yearsley had sought out. Poems such as 'Night. To Stella' and several others written around the same time show that Yearsley found much satisfaction in what she saw as a literary friendship with More and they show that Yearsley was grateful for More's willingness to help her publish her work. But if More expected a similar intensity of relationship between herself and Yearsley as that she had experienced with Garrick, she would be sorely disappointed. Yearsley had no wish to be annihilated by anyone.

Yearsley was aware that More was telling her London friends about her poetry and was initially appreciative of this support. One of the first people to whom More wrote was Elizabeth Montagu: she was impressed by Yearsley's poetry and wanted to know more about her life. More gave her as much detail as she could, and enclosed an extract from 'Night. To Stella'. 'Indeed she is one of nature's miracles,' replied Montagu as soon as she read it, 'what force of imagination! . . . Her native fire has not been damped by a load of learning.'[24] More agreed with this sentiment. She praised Yearsley's 'wild wood-notes' and wrote that she would 'be sorry to see the wild vigour of her rustic muse polished into elegance, or laboured into correctness'.

This obsession with natural genius reflected the fashion of the day, but it did Yearsley a great disservice. Yearsley was more a conduit than a poet in the eyes of some of her readers. More emphasised that Yearsley was someone 'who does not know a single rule of Grammar, and who has never even *seen* a Dictionary'. What More intended as praise often reads as cutting criticism: 'there is sometimes great felicity in the structure of her blank verse,' More wrote to Montagu, before adding dismissively – 'and she often varies the pause with a happiness which looks like skill.'[25] Yearsley did not yet know about these letters; she was told only that the famous Elizabeth Montagu had praised her verses and sent a guinea in tribute.

With this positive response from Montagu, More began sending snippets of Yearsley's work to more of her friends. She sent some to the courtier and diarist Mary Hamilton who happened to be staying with the Duchess of Portland, along with Mary Delany. All three of these women read Yearsley's poems together and declared them remarkable. More sent some of Yearsley's work to Horace Walpole who admitted that he saw genius in the verses but expressed grave reservations about Yearsley pursuing poetry as a career, 'lest it should divert her from the care of her family, and after the novelty is over, leave her worse than she was'.[26] This was a sentiment that recurred in many of the letters More sent and received during these months. Yes, everyone agreed, Yearsley was talented; but should working-class women be encouraged to pursue any interests outside the home or their manual work? Again, the upper- and middle-class Bluestockings agreed – this was a risky proposition. More assured her correspondents that she was taking a suitably paternalistic attitude to Yearsley.

By the autumn, More had formed a concrete idea of gathering together a selection of Yearsley's poems and publishing them as a book. A common mode of publication in the eighteenth century was to enlist subscribers who paid in advance for their copies of the work (and might also contribute extra to provide additional income for the author). More decided that this was the best way to go about putting Yearsley's words into print and once she had Montagu and a few other powerful figures on board, More began to canvass potential subscribers. If the project was a success, it might earn hundreds of pounds for Yearsley, as well as paving the way for future publications. This kind of money could be life-changing for Yearsley and her family; but More was determined that it should not be. Not only did More worry that a change in circumstances might detrimentally affect Yearsley's natural genius, she worried that access to such a large amount of money might affect Yearsley's morals and make her forget her station in life. 'It is not intended to place her in such a state of independence as might seduce her to devote her time to the idleness of Poetry,' More assured the potential subscribers:

> as a wife and mother she has duties to fill, the smallest of which is of more value than the finest verses she can write: but as it pleased God to give her these talents, may they not be made an instrument to mend her situation?[27]

All through the winter, More wrote endless letters and by the spring of 1785, she had enlisted the support of over a thousand subscribers. These included several dukes and duchesses, earls and countesses, a smattering of bishops, several well-known politicians, numerous literary figures and, of course, many Bluestockings. The book was a slim volume published in June 1785 under the title *Poems, on Several Occasions*. Ann Yearsley's name on the title page was followed by the description 'a milkwoman of Bristol'.

More (who had made most of the decisions around publication without much consultation with Yearsley) had decided to highlight More's status as a woman, and particularly as a working-class woman. This was in stark contrast to the anonymity that many of the Bluestockings sought when they published. The Bluestockings did not put their names on their publications, they tried to avoid drawing attention to their sex, and they certainly did not say anything explicit about their social class. By stating Yearsley's occupation, More was marking her out as distinct from other Bluestockings.

Even though Yearsley's name appeared on the title page, few people thought of her as 'Ann Yearsley'; they thought of her as 'Lactilla'. The name had begun as a joke in a letter from Horace Walpole to More. He had been concerned that poetry would distract Yearsley from her real duties, and so he wrote: 'She must remember that she is a Lactilla, not a Pastora, and is to tend cows, not Arcadian sheep.'[28] The name had tickled More and her friends and it had stuck and spread so that most of the subscribers knew it by the time the book appeared.

Montagu was delighted by the book, as were all who read it. The *Critical Review* declared that 'the poems before us are entitled to a superior degree of praise; there are evident traces to be found in them of a strong and fervid imagination.' The *Monthly Review* agreed, writing that 'these Poems present us with a very striking picture of a vigorous and aspiring genius, struggling with its own feelings. We see an ardent mind exerting itself.'[29] The book was one of the most successful poetry debuts of the period.

The book contained something else besides Yearsley's poems. It was a 'Prefatory Letter' written by Hannah More, explaining how Yearsley had suffered the previous winter, how poetry had helped her to overcome her difficulties, and vouching for her upright character. The letter was similar to the thousands More had sent to potential subscribers. In fact, it was addressed to Elizabeth Montagu and it doubled as a dedication. Montagu commended this letter almost as highly as she did Yearsley's poems. The *Critical Review* gave almost equal space to praising More as it did Yearsley. The reviewer mentioned the Prefatory Letter specifically, and pointed out that by buying the book, a reader could derive as much enjoyment from supporting a charitable cause as from the poems themselves. The *Monthly Review* went even further, quoting several pages of the Prefatory Letter and emphasising how indebted Yearsley should feel to More.

The Prefatory Letter placed great weight on Yearsley's working-class background, her lack of education, the occasional errors in her writing – all to emphasise her natural genius. More seemed to suggest that Yearsley's work was brilliant almost in spite of Yearsley herself. More wrote about how she had been excited on first seeing Yearsley's work, but also made clear that early drafts were 'incorrect'. Perhaps she meant that they had some grammatical errors, or that they strayed from conventional metre and rhyme. It is impossible to know how Yearsley's early drafts were written because More later burned them all. More wrote openly about what she considered faults in Yearsley's poems: 'she abounds in false concords, and inaccuracies of various kinds.' And of course there were those back-handed compliments, as when More wrote that she would be sorry to see Yearsley 'polished into elegance, or laboured into correctness'.[30]

More herself was guilty of several inaccuracies in the Prefatory Letter. She inflated the number of Yearsley's children (from four to six) as she told the story of that dismal winter in a stable. Perhaps this was to make the events seem more tragic, or perhaps it was because she was ignorant of the basic facts of Yearsley's life. The letter finished in the same paternalistic tone that had coloured More's earlier letters to potential subscribers. More assured readers that she had only undertaken to support Yearsley because she was convinced that Yearsley would not become puffed up by the glory of being a published author, and that she would continue to know her place in society. More wrote that she sought 'not fame, but bread' for her protégée.

There were several problems with the letter, the most pressing of which was that Yearsley had not seen it before publication. Very probably, Yearsley knew that More intended to write a few introductory words and that Montagu would be singled out as a supporter of the edition. After having been so private and reserved with More when the two first met, Yearsley did not expect to see details of her life and poverty laid out for all to see. Nor can she have expected to see More being so heartlessly dismissive of her writing, or so high-handed about the class difference between them. As far as Yearsley was concerned, More was only a few rungs above her on the social ladder. Yearsley's husband's family had been landowners until recently, and Yearsley's career as a milkwoman placed her in the upper echelons of the working class. Yearsley saw More – the daughter of a schoolteacher who herself had had to teach or write to earn a living – as sitting at the very bottom of the middling classes. More, who adored her high-class London friends, was perhaps keen to be seen as higher up the social ladder than her profession or family background might actually place her.

Yearsley's feelings on reading More's Prefatory Letter for the first time are scarcely recorded. For on the same day that Yearsley received the first copies of her book – what should have been a day of triumph – Yearsley also received something else from More. It was a deed of trust: a lengthy legal document that Yearsley and her husband were ordered to sign immediately and return to More's attorney in London. Mary More, Hannah's eldest sister, read the deed aloud to the Yearsleys and handed over the pen. Yearsley was barely able to make sense of the dense legal language but the More family had been good to her thus far. And so, in haste and confusion, they signed.

It was not until later that Yearsley understood what she had signed. The document set up a trust to be administered jointly by Hannah More and Elizabeth Montagu. All proceeds of the book would be placed in the trust and a tiny salary would be paid out to cover Yearsley's basic living expenses. 'My feelings were all struck at,' Yearsley wrote afterwards when the enormity of what she had done set in, 'I felt as a mother deemed unworthy the tuition or care of her family.' Yearsley realised that she would not be entitled to the interest from the trust fund – More could spend it as she thought proper. Perhaps worst of all to a woman who had worried so much over her children, *they* would have no claim on the money in the event of Yearsley's death.[31]

Yearsley had felt that she had to sign the deed as proof of her gratitude to More. To be seen as ungrateful to such a magnanimous patron would be a stain on Yearsley's character. Yearsley worried too what the public perception of her must be if this deed was thought necessary – did the public imagine her as a wanton spendthrift who would fritter away her funds without a thought about her children's futures? She signed the deed to show that she was no such thing. She very soon regretted it. Yearsley had not even had time to make a copy of the deed before it was whisked off to London. She could only remember a few key clauses. Seeking a little clarity, she asked More if she could have a copy of the deed.

More was away from Bristol when *Poems, on Several Occasions* was first published. In fact she was staying with the Garricks at the Adelphi that week – happily showing off copies of the book she had championed to the man who had once helped her so much. When she returned to Bristol, she met up with Yearsley. This meeting should have been a celebration, but the Prefatory Letter and the deed had soured Yearsley's initial happiness at seeing her words in print. Things became more tense when it became clear that the More family had been keeping tabs on Yearsley, and another of the sisters reported to More that Yearsley owed some money in the town. Yearsley's debt was a small one, just a few pounds. There were £350 in the trust by then. More demanded that Yearsley write out an account of everything she owed and to whom, down to the last shilling and penny. In a disapproving tone, More agreed to pay Yearsley's creditors. Perhaps in shock, Yearsley took this first meeting surprisingly meekly.

She was not so meek when she was invited for supper at Park Street a few days later. The women dined cordially enough, More handed over the few pounds Yearsley needed to pay her bills. Then the tone changed. More said that she had heard Yearsley had other debts – 'we hear it from every quarter,' she said, hinting again that she was spying on Yearsley.[32] Yearsley vehemently denied the existence of these debts. On the subject of the deed, she said that she was concerned that her children did not have access to the trust funds in the case of her death, and that she did not have a copy of the document. In Yearsley's telling of the event, More then burst out, 'Are you *mad*, Mrs. Yearsley? or have you drank a glass too much? . . . I am certain you have drank, or you would not talk to me in this manner.' Shocked at this accusation, Yearsley denied being drunk and reiterated that she was simply concerned for her children.

Betty More intervened at this point saying that she could see Yearsley's point – 'but', she said gently, 'there is a manner of speaking.' Yearsley, already stung by the references to her class in More's Prefatory Letter, felt again that the More sisters saw her as so far below themselves as to be almost another kind of creature. 'As to the manner of speaking', Yearsley replied, the hurt audible in her voice, 'I fear I shall always err in that, as I have not been accustomed to your rules of polished life.'[33]

The women were at an impasse. Yearsley was making what she felt was a reasonable request. More saw this request as a slight on her own character – a sign that Yearsley did not trust her to manage the funds honestly. Yearsley saw the very existence of the deed as a slight on *her* character. Years before, when David Garrick had invested More's money on her behalf, More had been delighted. She trusted him completely. Perhaps More was trying to replicate something of that arrangement here. The major difference between the two situations was that More had been able to access her capital whenever she wished, whereas Yearsley had to make formal applications to More or Montagu to access hers.

In a letter to Elizabeth Montagu written not long after that supper, More gave her own version of events:

> she accused me in the openest and fullest manner of a design to defraud her of the Money, and demanded it . . . When I recovered my Speech I told her the money was in the Bank of England, that Mrs. Montagu had condescended to be joint Trustee; but nothing wou'd appease her fury but having the Money to spend.[34]

Whether More had actually misunderstood what Yearsley wanted (a copy of the deed, and a clause to protect her children's future finances) or whether she deliberately twisted Yearsley into a grotesque caricature of the grasping underclass is unclear. The letter from More to Montagu continued: 'I do not see her [but] I hear she wears very fine gauze Bonnets, long lappets, gold Pins etc. Is such a Woman to be trusted with her poor Children's money?'[35]

That summer, as the existence of the deed hung over Yearsley, and the bad publicity and acrimony ate away at More, each woman became more entrenched in her position. More took to writing to the Bluestockings and to the subscribers explaining why she was so intent on leaving the trust in place. Her letters play up her own benevolence and piety while demonising Yearsley. To Elizabeth Carter, More wrote, 'my conscience tells me I ought not to give up my trust for these poor children, on account of their mother's wickedness.'[36]

Perhaps More's main feeling was embarrassment. She was painfully aware that she was of a much lower class than many of the Bluestockings. She had felt proud to become a patron – not just for the good it could do Yearsley, but for the status it would bestow on More herself. She had been thrilled to have had her letter to Elizabeth Montagu published as the preface to *Poems, on Several Occasions*, so that all could see her association with the great woman. She had vouched for Yearsley's character, thus earning the goodwill of all those aristocrats who subscribed to the volume. Now, in front of all of them, it appeared (to her, at least) that her judgement of Yearsley had been sorely misguided.

To save her own reputation, More tried to distance herself from Yearsley. She shifted the blame for her own mishandling of the situation onto external factors. 'I grieve most for poor fallen human nature,' More wrote to a friend, before going on to suggest that Yearsley was a trial sent by God to test her Christian principles. And then there was Yearsley herself who, of course, made an excellent scapegoat. 'Prosperity is a great trial and she could not stand it,' sighed More in a letter to Carter. Plenty of More's friends accepted this explanation. More had described Yearsley as 'a milker of Cows, and a feeder of Hogs' in an early letter to one of her fellow Bluestockings. Yearsley the individual was erased by such mechanical descriptions. By negating Yearsley as a person, it became easier to see her as a faceless member of a homogenous working class. And everyone knew that the labouring classes could not be expected to deal with fame and success in the same level-headed manner as their betters. To Boscawen, More had once written, 'I hope all these honours will not turn her head, and indispose her for her humble occupations.'[37] More had primed the subscribers for future disappointment with Yearsley, and appointed herself a sage at the same time. With a disappointed shake of her head, More could tut and say that she had always seen that it might end this way.

Elizabeth Montagu was sympathetic to More. She had once had a similarly unfortunate experience when her patronage of James Woodhouse the shoemaker poet (catalyst to the friendship of Hester Thrale and Samuel Johnson) had ended acrimoniously. When More had first mentioned Yearsley's poetry to Montagu, the latter had urged caution. Hinting at her relationship with Woodhouse, Montagu had written to More:

> It has sometimes happened to me, that, by an endeavour to encourage talents and cherish virtue, by driving from [the poor] the terrifying spectre of pale poverty, I have introduced a legion of little demons: vanity, luxury, idleness, and pride, have entered the cottage the moment poverty vanished.

And of course everyone knew the famous story of Stephen Duck, thresher turned poet. Duck's earliest poems had earned him a reputation for natural genius and had attracted the attention of Queen Caroline. In the 1730s, she had awarded him an annuity and a house and had appointed him keeper of one of the royal libraries. Many saw parallels between Yearsley and Duck – some favourable, some less so. Hannah More was well aware of Duck's story, and had considered it carefully before deciding to become Yearsley's patron, writing that 'I am *utterly* against taking her out of her station. *Stephen* was an excellent Bard as a *Thresher*, but as a Court Poet, and Rival of Pope detestable.'[38] It was not just Duck's poetry that had deteriorated after he found fame and courtly success, his mental health suffered too and he later took his own life.

There was another aspect of the row between More and Yearsley that highlighted Yearsley's working-class background: hogwash. After the June dinner at which More had accused Yearsley of being drunk, the two women did not see each other again for several weeks. But throughout this period, Yearsley visited the Park Street school every day to collect the kitchen scraps – the hogwash – from her old friend the cook. This was a longstanding arrangement between Yearsley and the cook, part of an informal economy outside the control of the More sisters. More was enraged that Yearsley still had this dealing with her household. To placate her employers, the cook offered to refund Yearsley the money paid for the hogwash and put an end to the deal. Yearsley, needing all the food she could get for her pigs, refused.

In the midst of all this bad feeling, another meeting was arranged between Yearsley and More for July. They hoped to resolve the dispute in the presence of witnesses. Unfortunately the witnesses did little to dispel the tension. According to Yearsley's version of events, she herself was in low spirits, quiet; More was full of vitriol, calling Yearsley 'a savage', 'a bad woman'.[39] More's account, naturally, differs.

Yearsley by now found her entire connection to More to be insupportable, and asked that the agreement be ended, and her original manuscripts returned to her. This was when More was forced to admit that the manuscripts had been burnt. They had been left at the printer's and thoughtlessly disposed of after being set. Yearsley was horrified to hear this, but could see that More had not done it maliciously and felt for the woman as she blushed and stumbled through her confession. In the end, More was at least able to present Yearsley with a copy of the deed – the one thing she had wanted since the beginning – and the two parted for the final time.

Only one letter between the two women is known to survive. It was written by Yearsley a few months after that last meeting. Yearsley began with words of gratitude before describing how that gratitude had evaporated. Whoever controlled the purse strings, controlled the family, and Yearsley felt that More was trying to take charge of her children. Yearsley wrote that she felt degraded by the trust fund, humiliated by More's attitude to her poverty. Yearsley wrote clearly, explaining exactly what issues she had with the trust, and the financial and emotional ramifications the trust fund had had for her. Though much of the letter was matter of fact, it also had a defiant tone. It finished by mentioning that Yearsley was planning to publish a second book, without More's help, and hinted that this second book might contain favourable or unfavourable sentiments about More, depending on how the question of the trust fund was resolved.[40]

More was most put out by the letter. Rather than responding to Yearsley and addressing her concerns, she wrote immediately to Montagu, including a long extract from Yearsley's letter. Except that it was no such thing – some parts she paraphrased, some she rewrote, some she completely invented. One line she added to her re-telling of Yearsley's letter read: 'as it's necessary for *my* character to be *wrecked* to do justice to *yours* I submit to it; in this it is your turn to be grateful.' It neatly summarised how the women had created a situation in which neither could back down – neither could see a way out without one woman being hailed as a villain and the other a hero.

By now, the story had spilled out into the public arena and news-paper articles began to appear. More wrote to Montagu, 'I hear they have put me in the Papers: I take not the least notice of any of *their* scurrilities.'[41] More's only public comment on the row was a note added to the beginning of the second edition of *Poems, on Several Occasions* which assured readers that all proceeds from the work were placed in a trust for the benefit of the poet. More had overseen the production of this second edition while the row between her and Yearsley blazed, and she would go on to oversee a third edition before finally ending all association with her former protégée.

In October 1785, More and Montagu finally agreed to give up the trust. Rather than just signing the funds over to Yearsley, More kept the trust intact and put it under the control of a Bristol man named Richard Vaughan – the man who had discovered Yearsley and her family starving in the stable the previous year. Vaughan was the only person the two women could agree upon to take on this role. Vaughan allowed Yearsley control of the funds and she finally found financial freedom.

The problem of the trust was resolved, but neither woman could quite let go of the bitterness they felt over it. While More complained about Yearsley in private letters to friends, Yearsley's complaints were rather more public. After More walked away from future involvement with *Poems, on Several Occasions*, Yearsley decided to produce a fourth edition herself. The first three editions had been published by Thomas Cadell – a publisher with strong links to More and other Bluestockings. Now, Yearsley approached the progressive publishers George and John Robinson and found them supportive of her cause. They agreed to include a 'Narrative' written by Yearsley as a preface to the book. This lengthy essay told the story of her involvement with More and the row that had ensued.

'I am said to have proved ungrateful to my patroness,' began Yearsley's Narrative. There followed thirteen pages of the most deliciously juicy gossip any reader could wish for. Yearsley laid out in detail every twist and turn of the saga – the deed, the hogwash, the recriminations.[42] This edition was a great success. Yearsley had lost most of the high-status subscribers who funded the earlier editions, but now she found a new audience: some who appreciated her story-telling skills; and some who saw her as the unlucky underdog in her tussle with More.

Yearsley soon found a new patron in the form of the eccentric Earl of Bristol. Here was a bishop who had once declared himself agnostic; a peer who opposed ancient feudal systems; a British politician who supported Irish liberation. He was anything but conventional and was mocked by many in upper-class English society. 'How suitable the Patron to the Protegee,' wrote More to Montagu when she heard.[43] He was a good patron to Yearsley, bringing in many new subscribers for her later books.

Yearsley found other supporters too. Anna Seward, known as the Swan of Lichfield, was a provincial poet who moved in influential circles. She had ties to the famous Lunar Society, particularly to Erasmus Darwin, and was an old acquaintance of Samuel Johnson's. Later, she would be linked to the Romantic poets. When she had first read Ann Yearsley's *Poems, on Several Occasions*, she had noticed the tone of More's Prefatory Letter, writing that it 'struck me with an air of superciliousness towards the Being she patronized'. She was one of the few middle- or upper-class observers to see More's attitude as problematic. Sitting a little outside the mainstream herself, Seward saw how Yearsley's sex and social position set her apart from other so-called geniuses:

> So, in a similar situation, would surly Samuel Johnson have spurned the hand that, after it had procured him the bounty of others, sought to dictate to him its use; and that resentment, which, in her, is universally execrated, would, coming down to us now as a record of his emerging talents, have been generally excused, and probably, with whatever little reason, admired.[44]

Seward was not at all surprised when Yearsley revolted against More's high-handed treatment.

Romantic poets such as Robert Southey were generally well-disposed towards Yearsley and her poems. The intense emotions and sensuous language in her work appealed to them. The Bristol-based publisher Joseph Cottle who worked with many Romantic poets including Samuel Taylor Coleridge became a great supporter to Yearsley in later years. The *Monthly Review* supported Yearsley too. When she published her next volume of poetry (called *Poems, on Various Subjects*) in 1787, the review touched on the earlier scandal and acknowledged that many thought success had made her vain before coming down firmly on Yearsley's side.[45] The reviewer applauded Yearsley for her self-respect, and for defending herself with calm courage in her 'Narrative'. More importantly, the review highlighted the bold imagery in Yearsley's new verses, the grandeur of them, the loftiness of her mind. The *Critical Review* likewise took Yearsley's side in the dispute and lauded her new work, calling it original and just, strong and animated. Yearsley had proved that even without More to edit her work, she could produce good poetry.

Yearsley continued to be a prolific writer through the 1780s and 1790s, despite recurring bouts of ill health. She branched out from poetry, first trying her hand at plays, later at novel-writing – both with notable success. In poetry, she experimented with new forms – writing an ode about Bristol's new Magdalen Hospital – but she also continued to write the intensely personal and unconventionally structured poems that had first won her an audience. Her 1790 'Stanzas of Woe' was written after an assault on one of her children, following which a shocked Yearsley suffered a miscarriage. More, who usually only spoke of Yearsley with bitterness in these years, heard what had happened and wrote to one of her sisters:

> I think very often with concern of poor Yearsley's situation. I could get a famous medicine which has done wonders, if you can contrive to find out if she would take it; but I suppose the poor creature would be afraid to take anything of my recommending.[46]

Yearsley also turned her mind to politics, penning several poems on the hottest topic of the day – the French Revolution. Her 'Reflections on the Death of Louis XVI' and 'Elegy on Marie Antoinette' placed her firmly on the side of the moderates.

It was not Yearsley's first foray into political poetry. A few years earlier, she had written a work titled *A Poem on the Inhumanity of the Slave Trade* which told the story of a man named Luco who had been betrayed into slavery and who later rebelled against his captivity. The poem ran to more than four hundred lines of heart-wrenching blank verse. Yearsley used her gift for imagery to underscore the brutality of the slave trade. Though many British poets wrote against slavery at this time, Yearsley's poem was unusual in its direct descriptions, in her giving its hero such agency and in her writing approvingly of his attempt to win his freedom by force.

Hannah More published an anti-slavery poem the same year as Yearsley. More's aim in *Slavery: A Poem* was not so much to make her readers *feel* the inhumanity of the trade as rationally to argue against it on intellectual grounds in carefully measured couplets.

Both were worthy efforts. Yearsley's was addressed particularly to the residents of Bristol, many of whom were already well aware of the inhumanity of the slave trade, and some of whom had begun protests against it. More's poem had been commissioned by the nascent Society for Effecting the Abolition of the African Slave Trade and was circulated widely among politicians and men of influence. Though the two women no longer had any connection, these poems were often reviewed in tandem in the press.

Apart from her writing, Yearsley's other great project of these later years was the establishment of a circulating library in 1793. The first circulating libraries had appeared in Britain earlier in the century. For a small fee – a few shillings per quarter – readers could borrow books rather than going to the trouble and expense of buying, binding and storing books themselves. Such libraries were particularly popular with women and came to have a reputation as storehouses for trashy novels. A character in Richard Brinsley Sheridan's 1775 play *The Rivals* referred to the circulating library as 'an evergreen tree of diabolical knowledge'. In reality, the libraries were stocked with a wide range of books. A surviving catalogue for Yearsley's shows plenty of novels; but also works by Shakespeare, Johnson and Pope; travel books; scientific books; and French books by writers such as Rousseau.

Yearsley's library was located in the fashionable crescent colonnade by the Hotwells spa just outside Bristol where two springs flowed from deep underground before bubbling up on the river-bed. Only accessible when the tide was low, and tucked under the hulking St Vincent Rock, the Hotwells never achieved the popularity of other eighteenth-century spas, but they were still a popular enough tourist destination. Pump rooms and assembly rooms were built nearby, and a host of enterprising residents set up shop to cater to the visitors. Like many other librarians of the time, Yearsley stocked more than just books to keep her business afloat: perfumes, essences and medicines could all be bought on the premises.

Yearsley thrived in these years. Hannah More's career as a playwright had stalled after the death of her beloved patron, David Garrick; but Yearsley blossomed once she set out on her own. More never again risked taking on a protégée like Yearsley, but she continued her benevolent work in a different way. She moved to a country cottage (with two cats called Passive Obedience and Non-Resistance) and there she set up a network of charitable schools for poor children in the West Country.[47] She set up 'female clubs' where poor women could pay in a few pennies a week and then receive payments to help with the costs incurred by childbirth or illness. She set up benevolent funds to help workers who lost their jobs, and she campaigned on all kinds of social issues. Though she gave up writing for the theatre, More did continue to write extensively on various topics, including manners and morality. Her most successful works were the *Cheap Repository Tracts* — tales designed to promote Christian values and to counter some of the politically radical books that appeared in England following the French Revolution. More was the primary author of the series, though some were also penned by her sisters and by friends. Published from the 1790s until the 1830s, they easily outsold competing books of the day, including those by Jane Austen.

Briefly, the two very different lives of these women had overlapped. When they had spoken of poetry together, when they had read together, or discussed works of criticism, nothing mattered but their commonalities. But the complexities of the British class system and the question of money would never have allowed their tentative friendship to survive.

If it was difficult for a middle- or upper-class woman to break into the world of literature and to find a public voice for herself, it was almost impossible for a working-class woman. Yearsley had needed More's support to take her first steps to publication, but after that she had succeeded by her own merit and had emerged largely unscathed from her brush with More. She forced people to think differently about working-class women: she was living proof that it was not just the wealthy who could write.

5

THE COMMUNE

.

S ARAH SCOTT WAS the younger sister of Elizabeth Montagu. They were just two years apart in age and looked so alike that when they were girls, many confused one with the other. The two sisters were close: 'the peas', they were called. But as they grew into womanhood, their lives diverged. While Montagu busied herself in London with opulent furnishings and high-society guests, Scott was leading a very different life in the West Country.

Scott had been born Sarah Robinson in Yorkshire in 1720 and had shared in that same unusual upbringing as her sister. As well as all the traditional female pursuits such as needlework, Sarah and Elizabeth were taught to read, to think and to argue. Sarah attended all the Kentish balls with her sister and brothers, but, though she enjoyed them, she was not moved by them in quite the same way as Elizabeth. After Elizabeth befriended Margaret Cavendish Harley (later the Duchess of Portland) and began to spend time away from her family, Sarah was left to a rather more sedate life with her parents and brothers. She spent her hours rambling through verdant countryside, improving her languages, enjoying witty family repartee, reading or knitting by the fireside, and writing copious letters to her sister. Sarah, always quietly practical, never resented their differing lifestyles.

Life trundled along calmly for Sarah until she reached the age of twenty. That was the year that smallpox came to the house. In the eighteenth century the disease was still rampant across the globe. This highly contagious illness began with a fever, burning through the patient's body; next came rushes of nausea and vomiting, headaches and aching muscles; then a rash, getting progressively worse until large fluid-filled pustules erupted on the skin. As many as one in three patients did not survive the disease. Of those that survived, many were left blind, and almost all suffered some disfigurement.

The smallpox pustules concentrated themselves on the face – a particularly cruel fact for young women whose marriage prospects (in effect, their livelihoods) often depended on a pretty face. As soon as Sarah contracted the disease, it was decided that Elizabeth must be kept away from her. Though a part of her must have longed to nurse her ill sister, she was sent to stay on a farm a few miles away until the disease had passed. After more than a month apart, the two sisters were reunited: 'I had the joy of seeing my dear Pea yesterday,' Elizabeth wrote to a friend.[1] But, though Sarah was over the worst of the fever, Elizabeth was still afraid that the disease might be contagious; she kept her distance. She stood two yards away from Sarah in the open air. Sarah, not yet used to her scarred face, held her hat low, covering the scabs, but promising that she would let Elizabeth see her once the redness had reduced.

Sarah did make a full recovery. But her looks were ruined. Elizabeth knew better than to offer false comfort; instead she bluntly advised her sister to give up any hope of charming people with her face and to take up good works instead.[2] After Sarah's recovery, no one ever referred to the sisters as 'the peas' again. Sarah resigned herself to this and, even years later when the scars had faded somewhat, she would gently bat away attempts at flattery from Elizabeth.

Though Sarah seemed to take her misfortune in good part, her horror of the disease never left her. She became determined to ensure inoculation for as many of her household as possible. Inoculation against smallpox had been used in many countries for centuries, but it was only brought to Britain in 1721 by Lady Mary Wortley Montagu who had lived in Constantinople and had seen the practice there.[3] During an outbreak of the disease in England, Wortley Montagu (who had lost a brother to the disease and who had been scarred by it herself) inoculated her children. The practice worked by exposing a healthy person to a small amount of the fluid from a smallpox pustule. Typically, a scratch was made on the arm or hand and the infected material rubbed into it. If all went well, the patient would develop some mild symptoms of the disease, but then would be rewarded with lifelong immunity. (Occasionally, things did not go to plan and the patient could become seriously ill.) News of the practice spread, and the technique received royal approval when the Prince and Princess of Wales had their children inoculated. Though the practice had become more common as the century progressed, the Robinsons had not thought of it for their children. It was too late for Sarah, but the younger Robinson boys were inoculated shortly after her recovery, and thereafter she took a lively interest in promoting inoculation whenever possible.

She was well again, but Sarah felt that her life lacked purpose. The family had few hopes of marriage for her now, not helped by the fact that her father was reluctant to settle a decent dowry on her. Her sister was largely absent by this time, now truly enmeshed in the Bulstrode circle. Later that year, Elizabeth married Edward Montagu, moving her one step further from Sarah.

It was an isolating time for Sarah. But she was saved from her loneliness by a friend called Williamina-Dorothy Cotes. Late in the autumn of 1743, Cotes took Sarah to Bath. Bath at that time was a fashionable spa where the middle and upper classes would go to drink the healing waters and enjoy the benefits of the thermal springs. Cotes (the daughter of a surgeon, and wife of a physician) would have been familiar with Bath and it seemed an ideal place to winter pleasantly. But for Sarah, Bath would become so much more than just a fashionable retreat: it would be the city in which she would live much of her adult life; meet the friends who would so profoundly shape her ideology; and begin her first experiment in creating a community for women.

Sarah's mother and sister had visited Bath previously, so Sarah had heard a little about the city and its strange mish-mash of visitors with their various maladies and eccentricities. Elizabeth had once told her a story of an aristocratic lady at the Cross Bath who had demanded that the level of the water be raised until it reached her chin. The lady, however, was rather tall, and the other bathers were almost drowned before the rising waters forced them to flee. The Cross Bath dated back to medieval times at least and, behind an elegant new stone facade, it stood in the open air on top of a spring which carried hot water up from deep within the earth. The water had fallen ten thousand years earlier as rain on the nearby Mendip hills; it had percolated down through layers of soil and rock, run along the Pennyquick fault line, and gathered in a large underground lake thousands of metres below the surface. There, the Earth's heat brought it to almost 100°C before a tremendous pressure forced it upwards. These hot waters had been used by people since prehistoric times and the area had long been a focal point for healing and religious beliefs. The Romans had built a temple and several baths at the site (though these had not yet been rediscovered when Sarah first visited).

The water was not only hot – above 40°C when it reached the surface, a little cooler by the time it had been pumped into reservoirs and flowed into the baths – it contained dozens of minerals and metals, leached slowly from the rocks, as it meandered its way below ground. For centuries, it had been thought that drinking this strange-tasting water could cure countless medical conditions, but it was not a particularly pleasant experience, as one seventeenth-century female travel writer described: 'it's very hot and tastes like the water that boyles eggs.'[4] Notwithstanding the sulphuric taste, taking the waters became highly fashionable in the eighteenth century, and the sleepy city of Bath exploded into the national consciousness. At the beginning of the century, its population had been about two thousand; by the end, it was close to forty thousand.

As thousands flocked to Bath hoping for cures for everything from heart problems to infertility to leprosy, a modern new city began to grow up. The visitors required not just access to the waters, but places to live, to eat, to socialise. In 1706, work was begun on a new Pump Room. It was initially built in the style of an orangery, but it was enlarged and redesigned regularly throughout the century as more and more people made their pilgrimage to the springs. Each morning in the Pump Room the public could buy carefully measured glasses of the mineral water according to their doctors' orders. An orchestra would play while the patients perambulated about the room, meeting friends and catching up on the latest gossip. Next to the Pump Room sat the King's Bath – the hottest of the town's baths – and from the Pump Room's windows, those drinking the waters could look out and observe the strange spectacle of the bathers. Men and women bathed together, but to preserve their modesty, the women wore dark-coloured petticoats and jackets and covered their hair with bonnets, while the men wore lightweight full-body suits with hats or, occasionally, periwigs. Only their heads emerged above the gently steaming surface of the water.

Shortly after the Pump Room was completed, the Lower Assembly Rooms were built – this was a place where the public could pay to take part in dancing and gambling. A little removed from the warm and odorous spring waters, the rooms stood near the parade gardens by the banks of the River Avon. The new buildings of the city were made of the beautiful buttery-yellow Bath stone which gave the city its luminous quality. From the 1720s onwards (thanks to the vision of the architect John Wood) the new streets and houses, squares and promenades of Bath were all built harmoniously in the Palladian style. While Wood created the city, his contemporary Beau Nash conjured a social scene around himself. Nash became unofficial master of ceremonies for Bath, organising dinners, concerts and balls, introducing new arrivals, and playing matchmaker. He was famous as a dandy, a gambler and a womaniser. He left behind him a trail of debts and broken hearts; one lover was so distraught by their break-up that she spent most of the remainder of her life living in a hollowed-out tree. Cad though he was, Nash created a kind of magic in Bath, effortlessly mingling aristocrats, the gentry and the middle classes.

It was into this melee that Sarah Robinson arrived towards the end of 1743. She and Mrs Cotes took a small set of rooms just north of the Abbey. It was a lively area filled with public houses, shops and coffee-houses, including a ladies-only coffee-house. Sarah was anxious to visit the Assembly Rooms and the Pump Room. She began sewing trimmings to her gowns, ready to fit in with the fashionable crowd. She endured the unpleasantness of having her hair curled with tongs straight from the fire, she powdered over her scars. But her first night in the Assembly Rooms was not a success: 'theirs is not much company & what there is is bad, I met with nobody I knew.' Things did not go much better at one of the city's famous 'music breakfasts' where over a hundred people were crushed into an airless room, leaving Sarah feeling ill, tired and hot. The Pump Room was also over-heated, so much so that the humidity destroyed the ladies' elaborate hairstyles – 'In about forty couples of dancers,' grumbled Sarah, 'I don't believe you could find one curl by nine o'clock at night.'[5] Worse still, Sarah complained to her sister, she had not met any men who had made her *rougir* – blush – as she put it delicately.

But despite these first disappointments, Sarah soon settled in to Bath life – on her own terms. She found that she preferred the quieter pursuits on offer: playing the card game Pope Joan with genteel ladies; drinking tea and eating French rolls; and taking up the sport of shuttlecock (an early form of badminton). There was other fun to be had too: one of Sarah and Mrs Cotes's favourite hobbies was dressing up their maid Jenny Miller and sending her to balls in the hope that a nobleman would fall in love with her. Jenny, probably only a few years younger than her mistresses, was game, and the three would spend hours preening and curling, choosing outfits and jewellery, a hoop and a handkerchief. For Jenny it never came to much but she touchingly described how she was 'so happy in being taken for a Gentlewoman & call'd Miss & the young Lady by all those about her, but so miserable in not being Gentlewoman enough to go into the bottom of the room where there was less crou'd'.[6] Sarah herself gradually warmed to the idea of balls and suppers and would attend if they were not too busy. She visited the Pump Room each morning and downed her allotted portion of the queer-tasting water with great relish. She was recovering, finally, from the effects of the smallpox – both physical and mental. Her spirit was renewed and her body grew in energy and vigour.

She spent the rest of that winter in Bath, keeping an eye out for any potential suitors. She had once confessed that 'I think Men more necessary at a ball than a fiddle, having often thought a Partners voice more musical than the finest Opera, & his eyes more enlivening than the briskest tune which had ever been play'd.' Sarah's letters from these months in Bath are peppered with coquettish references to dancing partners and shuttlecock opponents, men who joined their card parties or called for tea.[7] Sarah didn't know it, but she had already met her future husband before ever arriving at Bath.

George Scott had escorted Sarah and Mrs Cotes for part of their journey to the West Country. Mrs Cotes had begun by insisting on driving their carriage herself. She was an experienced driver but the speed with which she attempted to take the rough country roads was alarming. Sarah was much relieved when George took over the driving and proceeded at a steadier pace. Despite his best efforts, the women arrived in Bath aching all over. Mrs Cotes complained particularly of a bruised 'bumfiddle', then begged Sarah not to mention such an indelicate thing in her letters home. Sarah, finding her sudden prudery hilarious, ignored her.

It is not clear how George Scott came to be on the journey with them; he may have been a family friend of one or the other. At any rate, he took care to look after and rest their horses, to temper Mrs Cotes's speed, and to give peace of mind to the young ladies – after all, highwaymen were still active in the countryside, and it had only been a few years since the notorious Dick Turpin had been hanged. The three travellers dined together along the way, making a lively little party. George was known as an animated and fun raconteur; Frances Burney once described him as 'very sociable and facetious'.[8] George was the son of an ambassador and he was used to moving effortlessly between social groups. He had been born to Scottish parents in Hanover, Germany in 1708, where his father was stationed at the time, and he moved in courtly and political circles throughout his life.

Sarah may have seen George again that winter in Bath. There is a mysterious reference to a handsome man walking her home one cold October evening:

> You would not fear my catching cold with walking home if you had seen how well I was taken care of the last time I practised that thriftiness . . . His face [is] handsome enough to make me forget it cou'd be cold, he met me going out & wou'd not for the world trust me to go home alone so very obsequiously escorted me to the door.[9]

Then George quietly disappeared from Sarah's life for some time.

He reappeared in a flash of drama two years later. It was December 1745 and Sarah was living again in Kent with her parents. England was being invaded. From the north, Scottish troops had crossed the border and had marched as far south as Derby within just a few weeks. This was the Jacobite Rebellion. Charles Stuart – popularly known as the Young Pretender, or Bonnie Prince Charlie – was attempting to retake the British throne on behalf of his father James Stuart, whom many believed to be the rightful heir. As Catholics, the Stuarts had been cut out of the line of British succession, but now they hoped to regain their place in it. The Jacobites' plan relied on support from Catholic France, and they hoped that troops would cross from France, land on the Kent coast and march northwards to meet them.

Living just a few miles from the Kentish ports, the Robinson family began to worry. Any troops landing at nearby Hythe or Romney would pass right by Monk's Horton on the road to London. Matthew Robinson anxiously sent to Canterbury for news. But Sarah relied on a better source: George Scott. He himself was rumoured to be a Jacobite supporter and was certainly well-informed on their movements. George reassured Sarah that she was unlikely to see French soldiers passing by her garden gate and advised her to stay put. But the fear of an invasion drove her to London, to stay with her old friend Mrs Cotes. In the end, George was right: the French never invaded. It seems unlikely that they had ever had any serious intention of doing so. The Scottish troops in the north retreated, the Battle of Culloden in the Scottish Highlands a few months later put an end to hopes for a revival of the Stuart line, and support for the cause slowly dwindled.

But Sarah's reliance on George in her time of crisis had created a bond between them. The whole family was grateful to him for his clear-headed counsel. Soon he came to be intimately entwined in the Robinsons' affairs, passing messages between different family members and advising on all manner of topics. Sarah's relationship with him would grow stronger. Meanwhile her family's circumstances altered radically when her mother died in 1746 following a long illness, throughout which Sarah had attentively nursed her. The house in Kent passed to Sarah's eldest brother Matthew. Her father Matthew, who had only ever taken an interest in his children as a source of entertainment for himself, left Sarah to fend for herself while he moved to London where he began an affair with his housekeeper, Mrs Betty, whom he would later marry. The three youngest Robinson boys – William, John and Charles – were also effectively abandoned in this period; sent away to school, they did not even see their family during the holidays. Without their mother Elizabeth to regulate Matthew's selfish nature, the Robinson children were scattered. None of the family was especially keen to take on the burden of housing a grown daughter or sister, so Sarah was left to wander aimlessly from friend to friend, cobbling together a life with a few months spent here, a few there. She had no income of her own, just whatever pittance her father might throw to her occasionally, erratically.

Like all women of her class, she had no trade and no means of making a living for herself. She was entirely at the mercy of the male members of her family. Even her sister who was now married and living in luxury couldn't offer independent assistance: her assets and money were hers in appearance only – in reality, everything belonged to her husband. Perhaps this was the first time that the starkness of women's lives hit Sarah with full force. A single woman had some legal rights but (in Sarah's class at least) had no real means to earn a living. A married woman might be more financially secure but was considered entirely subordinate to her husband. Women (especially non-working-class women) were only considered economically useful if they were married and providing 'legitimate' heirs to their husbands' wealth. A single woman like Sarah, whose scars severely diminished her prospects of marriage, was of almost no use to this society. She had no home, little support from her family, and a sinking heart. But Sarah was on the verge of an epiphany – she was beginning to understand the pitiless machinations of the world around her.

In the winter of 1747, without any clear plan, Sarah accepted an invitation to visit Bath with Montagu and her husband Edward. The city had drawn her back. It was just a few years since she had wintered there with Mrs Cotes, and she still knew enough people to be able to eke out an existence there. Besides, it was cheaper than London, and the waters might be able to help with the headaches that had begun to plague her. It was in Bath that winter that Sarah met, or perhaps renewed a former acquaintance with, Lady Barbara Montagu (a very distant relation of Edward's). Like Sarah, Lady Barbara – Lady Bab, as she was always known – was a young woman considered essentially useless by her family. She was the daughter of an earl, and should have been a desirable marriage prospect; but a heart condition meant that she was considered too frail to endure a pregnancy, and therefore of limited use to a man.

The friendship that grew between Sarah and Lady Bab was intense, captivating and utterly fulfilling. Some have suggested a romantic element to it, although there is no particular evidence for this, nor much against. Whatever their relationship, the two young women found themselves on the fringes of society together, unwanted. They bonded over their similar beliefs and values, their similar prospects. This new friendship would lead each to seek to understand the world around them in new ways. They dissected notions of family relationships, marriages, companionships, and saw all the ways in which these supposed pillars of society were fundamentally flawed, how they were dictated by the powerful to the weak, how they created cruel dependencies.

It was because of Lady Bab that Sarah determined to settle in Bath. Sarah praised her in the highest terms, moved by her gentleness and goodness. Montagu saw at once how much Lady Bab meant to her sister. The relationship played out almost like a courtship. Indeed, Montagu wrote directly to Lady Bab, teasing her about the intensity of her feelings for Sarah: 'My sister tells me you have been very good to her, the Girl is good enough, I allow you to coquet a little with her but do not fall in love.'[10]

By the summer of 1748, Sarah and Lady Bab had set up house. Lady Bab had a small income from her father and she pooled this with Sarah's resources so that the pair could rent a modest place together in pretty Trim Street. The two shared everything, as Sarah later described: 'I speak of Lady Babs Pension [i.e. income] as if it were my own, & in truth it is as much mine as hers, we having as little distinction of property as any married couple.'[11]

But of course, the two were not married. And when George Scott (now in Bath again) showed an interest in courting Sarah, it would have been foolish for her to dismiss him out of hand. As he made advances towards her, she found that she had a real affection for him. Matthew Robinson looked upon the potential union benignly enough. George Scott could take Sarah off Matthew's hands, and he was suitably well-connected and entertaining to appeal to Matthew's tastes. George was not a wealthy man so Matthew would have to provide a dowry, but it seemed a reasonable price to pay. But Montagu was strongly against the union from the start. There seems to have been a long-standing animosity between her and George, dating back to the days of the Jacobite Rebellion at least. It threatened to drive a wedge between the sisters. Montagu angrily accused Sarah of letting a 'violent love passion' cloud her judgement. Sarah stood her ground. She calmly pointed out that neither she nor George was beholden to anyone else, and that their mutual affection was pure and not deserving of censure.[12]

A large part of convincing her family that it was a good match involved the practical question of money, or lack of it. George had been called to the bar but had never actually practised. He dabbled in music and mathematics and natural philosophy, but none of this provided an income. By 1748 Sarah and George were betrothed, but she would have to wait three years for him to find a suitable job before they could wed. For a man who was used to moving in aristocratic and royal circles (though he was neither himself), no ordinary post would do. In 1750, George finally got lucky: he was appointed as tutor to a pre-pubescent boy – the future King George III. Though Horace Walpole joked that 'The Princess, finding that Prince George, at eleven years old, could not read English . . . introduced a new Preceptor, one Scot', in reality Prince George was a serious and bookish young boy.[13] He could already read and write in several languages, and George Scott's job would be to teach him history, natural philosophy and chemistry.

George Scott had had to petition hard to be appointed to such an important role. Sarah told Montagu that he had been recommended for the job by a great number of people, but it was Sarah who petitioned hardest, writing beseechingly to her cousin Anne whose husband was secretary to the Princess of Wales, the little boy's mother. The post became even more significant in 1751 when the Prince of Wales died suddenly. This meant that the boy became Prince of Wales himself, and heir apparent to the throne.

Finally, George Scott had an income and the couple could marry. It was June 1751 when they wed. Eight years had passed since they had met on the road to Bath, jolted together by the terrible driving of Mrs Cotes. Sarah was thirty now, older than the average bride, and George was forty-two. The ceremony was held at St Michael Bassishaw in the City of London. It was a strange little church designed by Christopher Wren: a muddle of materials plastered over to give a harmonious look, all sitting atop weak foundations – it was not an auspicious place to begin a life together.[14] Sarah's family, and especially Montagu, still doubted whether the marriage was a good idea, but Matthew handed over a modest dowry (or part of it). The new couple rented a tall, narrow townhouse in Leicester Fields in order to be close to the young Prince of Wales in Leicester House.

Just one letter in Sarah Scott's hand survives from the time of the marriage. It was written that summer, the day before the couple were due to take possession of their new house. Scott mused on humdrum activities such as airing the beds and buying new furniture; she chatted idly about her friends and social engagements; the single drama in the letter was a violent cold suffered by her friend Lady Sandwich. Only one line strikes a discord: 'Lady Bab is middlingly well, Mr Scott quite so.'[15] Lady Bab, who was to be part of the newlyweds' household, seemed to get higher billing than George in Sarah's mind.

To a woman such as Lady Bab – whose frail health meant that she would likely never marry – the chance to become part of a family was a welcome one. The system of 'companionship' had been around for centuries as a neat way to solve the problem of what to do with unmarried women. It also saved married women from loneliness, for it was not generally expected that their husbands would spend much time with them. The system allowed a married woman to engage a genteel-but-impoverished woman to live with her. It was a complex relationship – neither simple unfettered friendship, nor a classic servant-and-master arrangement. The two women were frequently equals in social status, and the idea of formal servitude would have been repellent to the companion. Often there was no actual salary involved, but room and board would be provided, and perhaps a little pin money. Lady Bab had a small income of her own and, being the daughter of an earl, was considered of higher social rank than Scott, so she was not a typical companion. And yet the arrangement was sufficiently recognisable to those outside the family that no one gave it a second thought.

So Scott and George and Lady Bab moved into the house in Leicester Fields. And then the letters stop. All is silent. In Scott's correspondence, in Montagu's, in the writings of every member of the Robinson family, there is a gap. A handful of letters from Montagu's friends in which they call George 'a very bad man' have survived.[16]

But that is all. Copious letters must have existed once, before being carefully and deliberately destroyed. Nobody knows why. All that is known is that in the spring after her marriage, after just ten months with George, Sarah Scott's family helped her to leave her marital home.

This was incredibly unusual. There were, of course, plenty of unhappy marriages, and it was generally women who bore the brunt of the misery. Women were expected to put up with a huge amount of terrible behaviour: infidelity (and consequent infection with venereal diseases), violence, alcohol abuse, gambling away the family income, to name but a few. Unless very severe, most of these would not have been considered grounds for separation. Even rarer than separation was divorce. A divorce could only be granted by an act of parliament. A man could apply for such a divorce on the grounds of adultery; a woman had to prove that her husband had committed adultery *and* that she was the victim of life-threatening cruelty. Apart from this inequality, the process was public and expensive. Fewer than three hundred divorces were granted in England in the whole of the eighteenth century. Though Scott and George never saw each other again, they never applied for a divorce.

What happened in the ten months of their marriage was a mystery. Speculation abounded. The presence of Lady Bab was said by some to have been the problem, with the implication that she and Sarah Scott were having an affair, but that was mere conjecture, and George was already aware of their close relationship before the marriage. It was possible that George had committed adultery, but that would hardly have been seen as remarkable. It was also possible that he was guilty of some kind of financial misconduct, or that his radical politics were leading him into trouble. Many years after the separation, a rumour circulated that he had attempted to poison his wife, but that was probably just a Victorian fantasy.

George, fearful that any hint of a scandal might affect his position in the royal household, anxiously explained away the matter to his employer – the Princess of Wales. When word of his explanation reached Scott, she scornfully reported his tale to her family: George had told the Princess that his wife had confessed that madness ran in her family. Worried that she would pass this madness on to any children she bore, Scott decided she should sleep separately from George, and thus began a rift in their marriage.[17] The Princess seemed to believe this version of events and Scott heard that this story was being repeated by the Princess's ladies in waiting. While it was true that Scott's younger brother John had a mental illness, it did not stop her siblings from marrying and having children, so it was unlikely that she would have taken this course.

It was a difficult balancing act for Scott and her family. They had to imply publicly that things were bad enough to merit a separation, while being careful that scandal did not cause George to lose his job, or offend him so much that he cut off financial support for her. Scott's older brother Morris, a solicitor, handled the separation with incredible tact and eventually negotiated a settlement whereby George (who, as Scott's lawful husband, was still responsible for her upkeep) would pay her £100 each year. In exchange, the Robinsons would keep their silence. They did this very successfully: their secret is still unknown. Half of the dowry was returned, not to Scott, but to Matthew who was delighted to have offloaded the burden of upkeep for his spinster daughter *and* kept hold of most of his capital.

Now Scott found herself in an odd position. She wasn't single, she wasn't a widow, and yet she wasn't living as a married woman. Though she had been through a difficult experience, Scott emerged not just intact, but in a better position than she had been before. Not only did she no longer have to beg money from her father, she could go where she liked and do as she pleased without needing permission from a husband. So she returned to Bath with Lady Bab, travelling west once again along the rutted road that she had come to know so well. In Bath, she blossomed.

As before, the two friends set up home together. With Montagu's help, Scott begged a few hundred pounds from the dowry her father had so swiftly reclaimed. She used this to rent a house in John Street, in the centre of Bath. Scott felt light as she began to unpack her belongings, weight lifting from her now that she was away from London, away from the gossip, and away from whatever secret that house in Leicester Fields had held.

Scott's happiness came not just from leaving her past behind, but from embracing her future. The arrangement for the shared house in John Street began from practical considerations – pooling their meagre incomes meant that they could live more comfortably – but it grew into something neither had foreseen. There were hints from the beginning that their household would defy convention. First came Mary Arnold. Arnold was Scott's niece, the daughter of Morris Robinson and Rosamond Arnold. She had been born in 1733 when the Robinson family was living in Yorkshire; Morris, aged about seventeen, had had an intrigue with Rosamond, and Mary was born out of wedlock. This could be a damning fate for a child at the time, but the Robinson family always acknowledged her and ensured she was provided for. As an 'illegitimate' person, Arnold had only limited marriage prospects. Like Scott, who had once been considered unmarriageable because of her scars, and Lady Bab because of her heart condition, Arnold was seen as superfluous to the needs of society, but she found refuge in Bath. Then there were the servants: one was a woman with learning disabilities; another was a deaf woman; later, there was a woman with leprosy. Almost all of the women and girls they employed over the years either had a disability, or were considered unclean or morally unfit for work in regular households. Scott and Lady Bab made their home a sanctuary for unwanted women.

The Bath where Scott and Lady Bab moved now seemed a very different place from the one where Scott had arrived a decade earlier. Though both women were still devoted to taking the Bath waters, they no longer circulated in the fashionable Assembly Rooms or Pump Rooms, and they avoided the balls and concerts. Instead, they found an alternative social sphere for themselves. Their new friends were independent women (sometimes by choice, sometimes by necessity), generally well-read and strong-minded. The best-known member of the group was Sarah Fielding, sister of the novelist Henry. Like Scott and Lady Bab these women did not fit in to mainstream society but they were interested in understanding that society and reforming it. Many of them were particularly aware of the horrors of the marriage market and the joys of female friendship.

Scott had long been thinking about these things. In 1750, while waiting for George to find himself a job, she had anonymously published her first book, a novel called *The History of Cornelia*. She may have been impelled to write it in the hope of earning a little money so she could expedite the wedding, but Scott had always been bookish. *Cornelia*, the story of a virtuous young woman who undergoes various travails before finding happiness, allowed Scott to explore the ideas that had been nagging her for many years. It deals with questions about how deferential adult children should be towards their parents – something that was often on Scott's mind in those days as she found her father increasingly difficult to get along with. It also raises questions about the power of the patriarchy, and about a woman's right to self-determination. These ideas would appear again and again in Scott's works over the coming decades.

The History of Cornelia did not sell well but the act of writing a full-length book gave Scott confidence. It allowed her to think of herself as a writer; just about the only job a woman of her rank could do. When she feared that George might not keep up his quarterly payments, she was immensely relieved to know that she had a way of securing her own income. Settled in Bath with Lady Bab and their assorted household, Scott began to write again, but now she turned from fiction to translating French literature.

France, the centre of the civilised world in the minds of Scott and plenty of others, was a source of endless fascination. The English upper and middle classes would slavishly copy French fashions, hairstyles and manners. Now Scott saw a chance to profit from this. She wrote to Montagu, who was always well-informed about the latest French literature, to ask if she could recommend a work that was popular in France but as yet unknown in England. If Scott could work quickly enough, she could produce the first translation and earn good money.[18]

The first book Scott translated from French was *La Laideur aimable* by Pierre Antoine de la Place (famous in France as the first translator of Shakespeare, and also of both Henry and Sarah Fielding). She translated it as *Agreeable Ugliness*; it was a meditation on a family dominated by a tyrannical patriarch with more junior members of the family questioning the degree to which filial piety should be stretched. It also highlighted the importance of virtue over physical beauty, something which no doubt appealed to Scott. This work was published anonymously – even the publisher did not know Scott's true identity.

Scott's writing and translating focussed her attention on the unfairness of the society in which she lived. Determined to do more, and aware that her household was beginning to outgrow the rented rooms in the town, she began to look for a larger house. A few miles away from Bath, along a path that followed the banks of the River Avon, Scott and Lady Bab discovered the pretty village of Batheaston. By the summer of 1758, the whole household had decamped there. They rented an old farmhouse that overlooked the river and began to make it their own:

> Lady Bab has put up a sort of a Tent at the bottom of a pretty little Garden, from whence there is a most delightful prospect, We are on a hill from which the decent is very steep, at the bottom of it the River Avon winds thro' the finest enabelld Meadows I ever saw – the town of Bath Easton is in the Valley beyond it rises hills beautifully wooded.[19]

With the extra space afforded by the farmhouse, Scott and Lady Bab were able to expand their household even further. They began to take in children. These were usually orphans or the children of poor families, mostly girls. To these girls, they offered a basic education and training in crafts that might provide a livelihood.

Each morning the household would rise early and pray together. Then there would be lessons in reading, writing and arithmetic for the children, followed by practical lessons on needlework and other handicrafts. From a young age, the girls were skilled enough to earn money for their work. They sewed endless silk flowers, ruffs, pompoms and other adornments that could be sold to the fashionable ladies of Bath. They made bedlinens and clothes to be distributed without charge to the poorer people of the neighbourhood. They also took on larger pieces on commission, things such as stomachers, hoods and decorative aprons. Often these commissions came through Scott's friends and relations. Scott's sister Montagu commissioned many pieces, and Scott would update her on their progress, dropping in details of the girls as she went:

> as for your silk it is not finished but as three pairs of hands are now set to it it will be soon done, but the oldest of the hands are but thirteen, & it contains a prodigious number of flowers so it proceeds slowly.[20]

The girls quickly became adept at working up flowers of all kinds, but sometimes a request would stump them, such as the time Montagu asked for some exotic fruit rendered in silk: 'I am afraid they will make hard work at Grapes,' replied Sarah, 'for we have no picture of any, nor they never saw any.'[21]

None of the work done by the children was sold for profit – the money they earned all went back into their upkeep and education, or was funnelled into other good causes in the neighbourhood. Scott and Lady Bab helped local women find sewing and knitting work that they could do at home, invented an educational card game, set up an impoverished gentlewoman with a shop that was to be at the centre of this cottage industry, established a Sunday school for the children of Batheaston, and even helped women to escape from abusive husbands. One such woman – Betty Pitts – took a job at Montagu's house so that her husband couldn't find her, while Scott and Lady Bab cared for her daughter Nanny.

Though Scott and Lady Bab were willing to help women in distress, they struggled to overlook their 'sins' completely. When a local girl found herself unmarried and pregnant, probably the victim of abuse, Scott and Lady Bab rushed to help, but wouldn't countenance having her in their own household, as Scott explained in a letter to her sister:

> If You or any one You know shall want about five months hence a Kitchen Maid or House Maid, & have no objections to a repentant Sinner, I shall have one at your service; a Young Woman bred up in much ignorance, who has been debauched by her Mother, whom she has now left, & has since [found] she was with Child . . . Where this fact is known she will have no chance for a tolerable place; we woud take her ourselves were it not for the whole affair being known to our Servants, & we dare not let our Girls see we can have so much levity for those offences.[22]

It is not known what happened to this woman or to her child. Presumably the child's father suffered no censure. Scott and Lady Bab were considerably more charitable to this woman than many of their contemporaries would have been, but the story stands as a stark reminder that even someone like Scott – someone who questioned the patriarchy and tried to move away from it – still subscribed to the dominant Christian thinking of the time and believed that the burden of sin always fell on the woman in such cases.

Among all her teaching, organising and other charitable work, Scott still found time to write. She followed up her translation of *La Laideur aimable* with an original novel, *A Journey through Every Stage of Life*. Next, in 1761, Scott published a history of the sixteenth-century Swedish King Gustav I under the pseudonym Henry Augustus Raymond. One reviewer praised the author's style as being 'easy, spirited, and manly'.[23] She followed this with another history – *The History of Mecklenburg* – in 1762. The book was published just a few months after King George III had married Princess Charlotte of Mecklenburg and the public was eager to read anything that might relate to their new queen. When the wedding was first announced, Scott had been sceptical of the furore surrounding the royal event. She grumbled about the cost of the wedding and the attendant folly, but she revelled in hearing all the details from her niece Mary Arnold who had been in London to witness the spectacle. And when she saw a chance to profit from it herself, she jumped at it, and her *History of Mecklenburg* sold well.

The year 1762 was also when Scott began work on the novel that would come to define her: *Millenium Hall*. She wrote this 260-page book in less than a month and published it anonymously in the guise of a travelling gentleman. The novel, purporting to be a letter from this gentleman to a friend, describes how he stumbles across a secluded community of women living in the West Country. These ladies are devoted to the arts and literature, but also to educating children, helping the poor and disabled, running a not-for-profit economy that benefits all, and providing sanctuary for women fleeing violence or abuse. The gentleman narrator, having been beguiled by the perfectly maintained farmland and beautifully manicured gardens, was invited into the house where he found a long drawing room filled with bookcases, orreries and globes. Several women were in the room; two sat by the bow windows with pen, ink and paper; at the further end of the room, one stood painting a Madonna, another drew a landscape, one was carving a wooden picture frame, while the final member of the group was making an engraving. There were several children too. The narrator described seeing a group of girls, from the age of ten years old to fourteen. Of these, one was drawing figures, another a landscape, a third a perspective view, a fourth engraving, a fifth carving, a sixth turning in wood, a seventh writing, an eighth cutting out linen, another making a gown, and by them an empty chair . . . which had been left by a young girl who was gone to practise on the harpsichord.[24]

This was Scott's dream: women working companionably with focussed attention on every kind of craft imaginable. Although her house at Batheaston was not as grand as Millenium Hall, this is an idealised version of the daily life of her own household.

The title was inspired by ideas of millennialism or millenarianism (the single 'N' of Scott's title perhaps indicates that she was thinking more of millenarianism). The first of these two related doctrines refers to a belief that there will be a paradise on Earth prior to the final judgement; the second foretells of a transformation in society which will lead to everything being changed beyond recognition. Scott's utopian women-only community would, in her mind, fit the bill perfectly.

Scott's novel made it clear why such a utopia was needed. Her characters' stories (often inspired by real events that had befallen her friends) are a reminder that eighteenth-century England was very much a man's world. One character is groomed from childhood for later use in her patron's debauched fantasies: 'among his friends he made no secret of his designs in all he had done for her, and boasted frequently of the extraordinary charms which were ripening for his possession.' Upon learning this, the young woman, whose education has been sponsored by this patron, is more concerned with saving appearances than with exposing this man's cruel intentions. 'She was almost as much afraid of appearing ungrateful, as of being imprudent,' wrote Scott, a sentiment familiar to many women down the centuries. Happily, the young lady is saved from his advances when her would-be abuser suffers that most eighteenth-century of maladies – a fit of apoplexy.[25]

Another character is forced into an unhappy marriage with an older man who conspires with his sister to make her life a misery. This may have been based on the first marriage of Mary Delany who, aged seventeen, was pushed by her uncle into marriage with a fifty-seven-year-old whom she found loathsome. Both women – fictional and real – were saved by the early deaths of their husbands. Another character is duped into marrying a bigamist; thankfully, a carriage accident renders her unable to elope to Scotland. Another character, who was born out of wedlock, is 'grieved to the heart' to think of how much trouble her very existence has caused. She was never likely to have had a very high sense of self-esteem, as we learn when her mother tells her how, at her birth, 'I beheld [you] with horror as well as affliction, considering you as the melancholy memorial of and partner in my shame.' Her father calls her 'a constant memorial of the greatest misfortune of [my] life'.[26]

There was very little these women could do to defend themselves from lecherous men, to avoid marriages pressed on them by their parents, or to make their own way in life if their families couldn't or wouldn't support them. 'The woman who is suspected, is disgraced,' wrote Scott, accurately.[27] The merest whiff of a scandal could remove a woman from the marriage market, thus cutting off her best prospect of a livelihood. The now-disgraced woman had to earn her own keep, but had little training to help her do so. Millenium Hall was a sanctuary for such women.

The story tells of the many good works done by the women, and the happiness of all who benefit from contact with their community. Going one step further than Scott in her real-life charitable endeavours, the fictional women do not stop at helping orphans, the poor and the indigent; they even set up a sub-commune for former circus performers so that they can live in peace and dignity.[28]

The women were remedying the problems of tyranny, one by one. Any downtrodden person could come to them for help. Of course, to Scott it seemed that the greatest tyranny faced by most women was marriage. But to say so openly would be far too controversial for what she hoped would be a mass-market book. To show that she was not an out-and-out man-hater, Scott inserted a passage on the general benefits of matrimony, insisting that she considered it 'as absolutely necessary to the good of society', yet not a single one of the main characters in the book has a happy experience of marriage. Just a few pages after Scott's half-hearted defence of marriage, one of the ladies, Miss Trentham (a virtuous and bookish woman whose looks were destroyed by smallpox), compares marriage to standing in front of enemy cannon fire.[29]

While Scott was keenly aware of sex-based tyrannies, she, an upper-middle class woman, seemed utterly unaware of the tyrannies of class. Her characters are happy to help the poor and working class but only, they stress repeatedly, if they are *deserving* of it. Of course, the women made such judgements on their own terms. Though they tended carefully to the education of the orphans they took in, they were mindful to instil in those children a sense of their proper place in society 'lest their being always in our company should make them think their situation above a menial state'.[30] And there was a strict delineation between the gentlewomen who ran the community and their servants. As in Scott's real household, most of the servants in Millenium Hall had some kind of physical or learning disability. The servants were treated much better than could ordinarily be expected, but they were still seen as occupying a different rank in society.

But though there were some holes in Scott's theory of a perfect society, the overall impression left by the book is striking. At its core, the book is a rhapsody of Christian virtue. Christianity was the dominant cultural force in Europe in the eighteenth century. Though some radical and enlightenment thinkers had begun to argue in favour of atheism, it was still a fringe belief in England and few openly confessed to it. In theory, Christianity informed the workings of society at every level. And yet, as Scott and others saw, there was an enormous gulf between the teachings of scripture and the reality of this supposedly Christian world. Scott was interested in weaving practical Christianity into her life and the lives of those around her. The more she thought about it, the more clearly she realised that the patriarchal system that underpinned everything was fundamentally incompatible with true Christianity.

This was a startling revelation. In eighteenth-century England, the patriarchy was so ingrained as to be almost invisible. It centred on land, money and control. Estates and assets were passed from father to son. Women's sexuality had to be fiercely controlled in order to ensure that all heirs and potential heirs were indeed legitimate. There were plenty who pointed out that this obsession with wealth and its transmission to future generations was at odds with Christian teaching, but Scott was one of the first to write such a popular book about how the very notion of the patriarchy – the unquestioned basis of society – was essentially *unchristian*.

The book ends with Lamont, the young travelling companion of the narrator, a carefree and thoughtless young man, coming to see Christianity in a new light. Lamont admitted that 'when he had before considered the lives of Christians, their doctrine seemed to have so little influence on their actions, that he imagined there was no sufficient effect produced by Christianity, to warrant a belief.' In the book's final scene, the narrator finds that Lamont, on their last morning in Millenium Hall, has risen early, found a Bible and lost himself in rapture at the New Testament: 'he now saw what that religion in reality was.'[31] Scott, a devout Christian, saw a women-only commune not just as a way to improve the lives of women, but to improve the world in line with Christian teachings.

It was very much Scott's own work, but it grew out of endless hours of conversation and debate with the other members of her Bath circle and, in particular, was heavily inspired by Sarah Fielding's arguments about the structure of society. It became a kind of manifesto for the group. It was the most successful of Scott's books, going through four editions by the end of the 1770s. It did not earn Scott a huge amount of money (she received a low percentage of the royalties in exchange for her publisher agreeing to back future projects), but because she had written it in a month she reckoned she had earned a guinea a day by it – a very respectable daily rate, when she put it like that. More than that, it won Scott plaudits from two of her harshest critics – her father and her sister. Matthew Robinson considered that Scott had shown wit (high praise indeed from him).[32] Elizabeth Montagu praised both Scott's writing style and her central message, and recommended the book to all her influential friends. Even so, high-minded Montagu privately wondered if her little sister should do 'something of a higher rank in les belles lettres than novel writing'.[33] This support from her family lessened the blow of a few harsh print reviews, with one reviewer questioning the book's concept, its characters, setting and even title: 'His are monsters of excellence; his scene absurdly unnatural; his narrative perfectly cold and tasteless; his precepts trite; and his very title unmeaningly and ridiculously pedantic.'[34] A novel about a women's utopia was never going to be for everyone.

But for Scott, it wasn't just a novel, it was real life. The Batheaston commune was continuing quietly but splendidly. The children grew, they learned; Scott and Lady Bab helped them find positions as maids or other respectable jobs. When they were settled safely, new children came to the community and on the cycle went. Montagu once described her sister's household as a haven of 'virtue, tranquillity and delightful friendship'.[35] Another time she described it as a convent. This was fitting, and Scott would have been pleased with the idea, but of course all English convents had been destroyed in the Reformation. Theological implications aside, the destruction of the convents had left those women who could not or did not wish to marry with one less option. Convents had been a viable career choice that allowed women to exist outside the strictest bounds of the patriarchy. Bookish women especially, could make a good life for themselves there. Men who sought a religious life in the centuries after the dissolution of the monasteries still had options open to them; but what were the women to do? Some talked about creating Anglican convents, but it never came to pass. A community like Scott's was the closest alternative.

Millenium Hall was a triumph, the Batheaston community was flourishing, life seemed at its zenith for Scott and Lady Bab. And then Lady Bab's heart began to fail. They had always known that this would happen. To be closer to the life-giving springs, and to the doctors whom they so dearly hoped could prolong Lady Bab's life, they left Batheaston and returned to Bath. They took a house on Edgar Row, George Street, 'in the best situation in the whole town, being high, airy, & yet convenient'.[36] Scott consoled herself and Lady Bab, who sorely missed their country cottage, that each window in the new house overlooked the countryside, and that the hundred-foot garden would distract them from the loss of Batheaston.

Lady Bab's decline continued. She often had to take opiates to help her cope with the painful spasms that racked her body. She was confined to bed for days at a time, but unable to sleep. By the following year, days in bed had morphed into months in bed, 'for extremely ill she is at best,' lamented Scott, while still holding out hope for a recovery.[37] Lady Bab lingered on for some time but the recovery never came. Scott's hope continued until the end, even through the three final, worst days of Lady Bab's illness. Then, on a cold August morning, as an uncharacteristic fog rolled over Bath, Bab died peacefully, with Scott, as ever, by her side.

Scott found herself almost floored by the shock of this loss. She was comforted by the women around her: Mary Arnold, Sarah Fielding and Elizabeth Cutts (another of the Bath circle). In the last few years of Lady Bab's illness, Scott had had little time to think of anything but the needs of her friend. But now, in the quiet evenings, as she adjusted to a world without her life's partner, she and her circle found that they had time on their hands, and they began to dream again. Together, they began to plot something more ambitious than their modest Batheaston project – they dreamed of a real-life Millenium Hall.

Batheaston had been a good start, but it had not gone far enough. To be truly free of the patriarchy, Scott and her circle needed to be entirely self-sufficient. They needed land of their own that they could farm. Being of modest means, this seemed a stumbling block, but then help arrived in the form of Scott's cousin Grace Freind. A few years older than Scott, Freind had been close to the Robinson girls from childhood and continued so as they all grew and married. Scott had been godmother to Freind's first son Robert – 'little Bobby is a very fine boy,' reported a proud godmother to anyone who asked – and the two women corresponded regularly and visited each other often.[38] In 1766, Freind's husband William, the Dean of Canterbury, died unexpectedly and, like Scott, she found herself alone.

The two women consoled each other about their losses. They spoke of what their futures might hold. And as Scott began to tell of her vision of recreating Millenium Hall in the real world, Freind was entranced. She saw a future for herself there and, more than that, she saw a way to make it happen. Her son Robert, by then in his twenties, had inherited a modest estate in Buckinghamshire upon the death of his father. Not needing it immediately, he was looking for a tenant. The Hitcham estate consisted of 110 acres of lush green land near the banks of the River Thames as well as an ancient manor house whose illustrious visitors over the centuries had included Queen Elizabeth. It was exactly what Scott had envisaged and she at once began negotiations.

Scott agreed that she, along with Grace Freind, Sarah Fielding, Mary Arnold and Elizabeth Cutts would each contribute £50 per year to cover the rent and all expenses. Fielding's portion was to be covered by her patron Elizabeth Montagu, as she could not afford the fee. Sadly, Fielding's health began to fail shortly after Lady Bab's death, and she too began a steady decline. Fielding was not well enough to make the long cross-country journey from Bath to Buckinghamshire, and not well enough to help set up the new house. Unwilling to leave their friend out, the group stayed on in Bath in the hope that Fielding's health would improve. Though her friends nursed her diligently, she died in the spring of 1768.

Heartbroken, again, at the loss of one of their circle, the group threw themselves once more into plans for the future to distract them from their grief. Robert Freind was still holding the Hitcham estate for them, and Scott soon agreed the terms of the lease, with the tenancy to begin, appropriately, on Lady Day 1768.[39]

Shortly after Fielding's death, the move to Hitcham began. There was much to do there. The grounds needed tending, fences repairing, the house decorating. Slowly it began to come together. Montagu sent livestock and farming equipment from Sandleford, about thirty-five miles away. She also plied the women with gifts: whole salmons and sides of bacon, seeds for the farm and plants for the gardens, and newspapers to keep them in touch with the outside world. The women settled in: Scott oversaw the furnishing of the house and the hanging of pictures, while Mary Arnold discovered a love for animals and became quite devoted to a particularly charming black sow. They attended to practical details first, but all the while they were planning for the future: schools and Sunday schools, work schemes for impoverished locals, support for poor women and orphans. After a visit that spring, Elizabeth Montagu thanked her sister for 'the pleasing hours you gave me in your millenium'.[40]

Word of the commune spread. To many it appeared little more than a passing oddity, but to single, educated women, it seemed like a tantalising rumour of a new world order. Elizabeth Carter badgered her old friend Elizabeth Montagu for updates on Scott's progress, and even hoped to visit and see this utopia for herself.

But it was a utopia that could not last. Scott's letters tell of the frequent comings and goings of Freind's children to the house. Robert, of course, as the landlord, had good reason to visit. But Grace, Freind's daughter, inadvertently brought tension to the household. Pretty, impetuous Grace had eloped with a dashing marine but was soon shocked to discover that he (like a villain from *Millenium Hall*) was interested only in her money. When William Freind died, he left £4,000 to his daughter, but she was only to receive the money on the death of her mother. Grace's new husband demanded extravagant payments from Freind for the upkeep of her daughter, pressuring her to hand over increasingly large sums that she could not afford. When Grace became pregnant, he claimed he was unable to provide a suitable house for her.

Freind, naturally, wanted to look after her child and future grandchild and invited Grace to Hitcham for her lying-in. But in the hurry of events, and under the enormous strain of this family drama, Freind forgot to consult Scott and the others. For Scott, this breach of etiquette was a sign of Freind's disrespect for the basic rules of Hitcham where everything was to be decided communally. Freind had put her family before the community.

Unlike the other women in the Bath circle, Freind had been happily married and had known a good family life. It seemed right to her to put her children first. When she needed a safe place for Grace to spend the final months of her pregnancy and to give birth, Hitcham seemed ideal. But the philosophy of Hitcham had somewhat passed her by. For her, the Hitcham project was a pleasant interlude, a nice and economical way to live out her older years with good company, somewhere her children could spend extended periods if necessary. She did not have that same distrust of patriarchal society that the others had. She did not see how the rules of Hitcham were essential to maintaining this world, fundamentally different from the world she had lived in before. But Scott saw it, and saw that her vision was not possible unless every member was fully committed to it. Scott wished dearly to continue at Hitcham, but it could not be done without the reduced rent Robert Freind offered nor without the financial input of Grace Freind. Ever a purist, Scott let it go.

The dream was over. Scott continued making small women-only communities for herself as the years advanced – one with Cutts and Arnold in London, and later just herself and Arnold in Norfolk. She continued to write, but she was racked with headaches for the remainder of her life and could not muster the energy to create another Millenium Hall.

She lived a long and fairly happy life, this unintentional revolutionary. She could look back with pride on her attempt to create a real-world utopia – a place where pioneering women joined together to live lives that seemed unimaginably odd to most. To the women themselves, Scott's Millenium Hall had seemed the only solution to a world ravaged by patriarchy. After she died in 1795, her final wish was granted: she was buried alongside Lady Bab in Bath, just as the two women had always promised each other they would be.[41]

6

MARRIAGE

EVERYONE IN EIGHTEENTH-CENTURY England knew the story of Clarissa Harlowe. Despite pressure from her family, she refused to marry the man they had chosen for her and, as a result, her life was ruined. She was one of the most famous women of the eighteenth century but Clarissa was not a flesh-and-blood woman – she was the heroine of a novel. *Clarissa* (with the unwieldy subtitle *The History of a Young Lady: Comprehending the Most Important Concerns of Private Life, and Particularly Shewing, the Distresses that May Attend the Misconduct Both of Parents and Children, in Relation to Marriage*) first appeared in 1748. It was penned by the famous writer and printer Samuel Richardson. Clarissa was his idea of an almost perfect woman: beautiful, accomplished and, above all, virtuous.

Many readers, then and now, have been struck most by *Clarissa's* dramatic events: kidnappings, imprisonments, sexual assaults, insanity, duels and death. They will remember Mr Lovelace, an evil libertine who claims to love Clarissa even as he brings about her downfall. But for a young woman reading it in the mid-eighteenth century, Mr Lovelace was not the real villain of the piece. Instead, it was Clarissa's parents (together with the avaricious, unkind and unattractive suitor Mr Solmes) who really set her on the road to ruin. To these female readers, it was clear that Clarissa's refusal to marry Mr Solmes was the most significant plot point in the novel. To them, this felt real.

Richardson knew even before publication that his readers would react this way. He made a habit of reading passages of his novels aloud to his friends before publication, and many of those friends were female. Each morning at North End (Richardson's country house at Fulham) guests would gather in the summer-house to hear the latest exploits of his heroines. Richardson's biographer, the Bluestocking Anna Barbauld, described the milieu:

> [Richardson] was always fond of female society. He lived in a kind of flower-garden of ladies: they were his inspirers, his critics, his applauders . . . his chief correspondents. He had generally a number of young ladies at his house, whom he used to engage in conversation.[1]

Richardson, within reason, was supportive of women who wanted to use their brains. He would deliberately engage the women of his coterie in conversation with the aim of highlighting their intellects. He thought that women should be less afraid of showing off their minds, as he wrote to one female correspondent:

> [women] hide their talents in a napkin, and are afraid, lovely dastards, of shewing themselves capable of the perfections they are mistresses of . . . Do they not, by their wilful and studious concealments of the gifts God has blessed them with, confess, at least indirectly, an inferiority to the other [i.e. men]?[2]

He assured his correspondent that even a clever woman could still be attractive to men and encouraged her not to hide her talents for fearing of losing out in the marriage market.

When a female friend said to him that she disliked hearing members of her own sex speak Latin as it sounded too masculine, he defended lady classicists. He thought of Jane Collier, one of the North End circle, when he replied: 'Miss C------ is an example, that women may be trusted with Latin and even Greek, and yet not think themselves above their domestic duties.' It may have been a somewhat qualified statement of support for bookish women, but it was a more liberal position than many of his contemporaries took. At the same time, Richardson could casually produce statements such as – 'women ought to be controuled, if they are like my wife – in pity to themselves, they ought. For when left to their own will, how do they choose! How are they puzzled!'[3] This exasperated comment was sparked by Richardson's wife suggesting an impromptu weekend trip to North End. If he felt that a woman needed to be controlled when it came to her decision about where to spend a weekend, it is not surprising that he thought women were largely incapable of making decisions about whom they should marry.

When Clarissa Harlowe refused to marry Mr Solmes, her disgrace began. To Richardson, it was obvious that a girl disobeying her parents could only end badly. But women were beginning to think that things should be done differently; and they were becoming brave enough to say so aloud.

Hester Mulso was a young lady from a respectable family. Her mother had been celebrated for her beauty, but young Hester had not inherited her looks. Charlotte Burney (sister of Frances) once called Mulso 'dead ugly to be sure . . . and such a clunch figure'.[4] Later in life, compliments about Mulso's great intellect were often framed in terms of her looks – the travel writer Nathaniel Wraxall wrote that '[Hester Mulso], under one of the most repulsive exteriors that any woman ever possessed, concealed very superior attainments, and extensive knowledge.'[5] The elder Mrs Mulso, so vain about her own face and figure, could not reconcile herself to her ungainly little girl. She was cold to her daughter. She was not much of a believer in schooling for girls and so she decided to limit little Mulso's education to a few domestic skills, feminine accomplishments and novel-reading. Mulso hated needlework, she hated dancing and she hated novels. She wanted to read the books her brothers read. Her four brothers adored the sister they nicknamed 'Hecky' and, unable to bear seeing her unhappy, they hatched a plan. Quietly a trail of history books and geography books, primers in Latin and Greek, sometimes even mathematical tomes, would slip from the schoolroom to Mulso's chamber.

Mulso was twenty years old in 1747 when her mother died. For the first time in her life, she felt at liberty to be openly intellectual. She became housekeeper to her widowed father but even with these new domestic duties she felt freer than before. Her father, like her brothers, was happy to see Mulso happy and made no effort to stand in the way of her educational pursuits – provided the house ran smoothly.

Other women of Mulso's rank celebrated their 'coming out' into society by attending balls and races, dinners and pleasure gardens, but Mulso's coming out was a more sedate affair. Now she could order the books she liked, correspond with whomsoever she chose, and begin to show off her learning a little. Slowly she began to build up a network of like-minded friends who would encourage and support her. In 1749 she met the classicist Elizabeth Carter in Canterbury through mutual friends. Mulso was almost overcome with admiration and afterwards she initiated a correspondence that lasted many years. Her first letter to Carter ran:

> I parted from you, dear madam, with more regret than I dared shew; for I could not expect that you should have believed me sincere, had I expressed all the esteem and affection I felt for you, since I could hardly, myself, comprehend how so short an acquaintance should have produced so warm an attachment . . . I have known you long [via your written works] and long honoured and esteemed you; but it is only since I had the pleasure of conversing with you that I have loved you.[6]

The following year, 1750, Mulso made another new friend – Samuel Richardson. Again, she was introduced by a mutual friend and, again, she felt an instant thrill on meeting a famous writer. Where Mulso's relationship with Carter was largely epistolary (at least in the early years), Richardson invited Mulso to North End and welcomed her into his circle. It was a whole new world for her, and she was especially pleased to meet so many women who easily took part in debates on art, literature and philosophy.

Despite Mulso's dislike of novels, she had read and admired *Clarissa*. She liked the skill with which Richardson had fleshed out his heroine. Richardson, for his part, saw Mulso as almost a living version of Clarissa: she was young, supremely virtuous; she knew her own mind; she was still single but was just beginning to contemplate facing the marriage market.

Marriage *was* a market in the eighteenth century, at least for the upper and middle classes. It was common for marriage announcements to include the size of the dowry alongside the names of the bride's father and husband (though, as we have seen in the example of Elizabeth Montagu, the bride herself was rarely named). Hester Mulso viewed parents arranging financially motivated marriages for their daughters as akin to the trading of livestock at Smithfield Market. With clear-eyed fury, she wrote: 'those marriages which are made up by the parents are *generally* (amongst people of quality or great fortune,) mere Smithfield bargains, so much ready money for so much land, and my daughter flung in into the bargain!'[7] The Bluestocking Catherine Talbot echoed this when she wrote how 'we are told to *hold up our heads for there is money bid for us.*'[8]

It was a simple system: parents essentially 'owned' their children. When a boy grew up and attained the age of maturity (generally around twenty-one) he became an independent being. When a girl grew up, her parents began looking around for an eligible man to take ownership of her. 'Daughters are chickens brought up for the tables of other men,' Clarissa's brother once told her.[9]

Chastity was the only real economic asset that a young woman possessed – only by being able to convince potential suitors of her purity might she be able to attract a man good enough for her parents' balance sheet. Debating suitable punishments for women who committed adultery (a crime he considered infinitely graver than male adultery), Samuel Johnson once remarked: 'consider of what importance to society the chastity of women is. Upon that all the property in the world depends. We hang a thief for stealing a sheep; but the unchastity of a woman transfers sheep, and farm, and all, from the right owner.' When Boswell (a well-known philanderer) tried to draw a distinction between a single woman who had pre-marital sex, and an adulterous wife, Johnson replied:

> Yes, sir; there is a great difference between stealing a shilling and
> stealing a thousand pounds; between simply taking a man's purse,
> and murdering him first, and then taking it. But when one begins to
> be vicious, it is easy to go on. Where single women are licentious,
> you rarely find faithful married women.[10]

A family's happiness and wealth depended in part on their daughters' chastity. Hand in hand with a girl's chastity went obedience to her parents. A girl must obey when her parents warned her off the gallant young dandies she might meet at a ball but, more importantly, she must obey when ordered to marry the man chosen for her.

That moment of filial disobedience in *Clarissa* piqued Hester Mulso's interest. When she met Richardson in person, she questioned him on his beliefs. Did Richardson truly believe that a woman should have no veto at all over the match proposed to her by her parents? Liberal though he might be on issues, Richardson held firm that daughters should leave such decisions to their parents. Yet Richardson was intrigued by the real-life Clarissa that had shown up at North End, and he wanted to know more about Mulso's thoughts on the issue. He also wanted to encourage her to practise the art of rational argument so he suggested that she set down her ideas on paper. Mulso was eager for this chance to argue the case for a woman's right to refuse a marriage partner and was ready to spar with Richardson. It was a Friday in October 1750 when she sat down at her writing desk, sharpened a quill, and began to write the letters that would make her name.

Letter-writing in the eighteenth century was an art form. Manuals abounded on how to write the perfect letter. One had to address one's correspondent according to the ranks, sexes and ages of both writer and recipient. There were coded phrases, formulae, unwritten rules that needed to be known. The structure of the perfect letter required careful thought. Mulso knew this. She knew that there was only one acceptable way for her – a young unmarried woman – to write to the older and more worldly Richardson: in the guise of a daughter needing guidance from a father figure.

In the opening of her first letter, Mulso abased herself before Richardson. She wrote of how she would benefit from hearing Richardson's views on filial obedience; she wrote that she was sharing her thoughts with him in order to have them 'rectified'; she wrote that she hoped to come round to his way of seeing things.[11] By framing her letters in this way, Mulso was giving herself more leeway to share controversial views later.

There was another factor that shaped Mulso's thinking as she sat at her desk that day: Richardson was a printer, and was known occasionally to publish parts of his private correspondence. Mulso knew it was likely that her words, addressed to Richardson alone, would end up in print. Even if he did not print them, letters were frequently read aloud or shared in manuscript. Mulso was aware that she was not writing for an audience of one; she was potentially writing for hundreds or thousands to read her words. And though she never sought the role, many readers would see her as representative of all young unmarried women.

With this in mind, Mulso knew that she had to present herself as 'good'. Before she could question the societal norms that governed women's behaviour and the marriage market, Mulso had to prove that she was morally unsullied and quite beyond reproach. To be a good woman was to be a submissive woman. Thus, in the early pages of the first letter Mulso praised the importance of parental authority over their children. This theme recurred throughout the letters. Mulso hoped that this, alongside her deferential attitude to Richardson, would make her more appealing to her readers, thus making her arguments more palatable.

Her central argument, one from which she never wavered, was that a woman's life and happiness could be ruined by a bad husband and that it was cruel to force an unwanted match on a woman. Mulso put the fictional Clarissa to good use in arguing her case. She discussed the wrongs done to Clarissa by her family alongside real-world examples of women who wished to have the right to refuse marriage partners. She used the sympathy readers felt for Clarissa to win sympathy for real women in similar situations. She moved seamlessly between examples from Clarissa's life and her own.

The first letter Mulso wrote to Richardson was short, just eight pages. His reply has not survived, but we can assume he was unconvinced by her arguments. Whatever that reply said, it spurred Mulso on to greater heights, for her next letter ran to fifty-two pages and was much more ambitious in its use of philosophical arguments. Again, she began by abasing herself before Richardson: 'my excellent instructor!' she called him, apologising for making him waste his time on 'so obstinate, so tenacious a girl'. She thanked him for being patient with her in spite of her 'weakness and absurdity'. She reiterated that she submitted to 'a mild and reasonable government' by her father, and that she would willingly make sacrifices to ensure his happiness. These niceties out of the way, Mulso got back to her argument. This time, she began with words from the great philosopher John Locke. His *Treatise on Government* had included passages on parental power which Mulso quoted at length. In one passage, Locke had interchanged the words 'children' and 'sons'. So when Locke wrote that above a certain age and level of reason a son became free, Mulso jumped on this, commenting:

and if his son, I presume his daughter too; since the duty of a child is equally imposed on both . . . it can never be proved that women have not a right to [liberty], unless it can be proved that they are not capable of knowing the law they are under.[12]

For Mulso (and many women) it was an obvious logical step to assume that if only age and reason were needed to confer liberty upon an individual, then an adult woman should be as free as an adult man. Men, of course, saw things differently.

Even if adult women really were free agents (and many themselves denied this), Mulso was careful not to demand too much for them. She was arguing for just one freedom: the right to refuse a proposed match. She did not even go so far as to suggest that women should be able to marry without parental consent. 'Take notice, dear Sir,' she wrote to Richardson, 'that I, as well as Clarissa, only insist on a *negative*; and that it never entered into my mind to suppose a child at liberty to dispose of herself in marriage, without the consent of her parents.'[13]

It seems such a tiny right – the right *not* to marry a particular man – but it could have profound consequences for a woman's life. Mulso tried to convey to Richardson the enormity of this from a woman's point of view, writing that marriage is

an act whereby a woman places in a man a power over her of so great consequence to her ease and quiet, that nothing but death, or a dreadful appeal to the laws of the land in the face of the world, can release her from his tyranny if he should prove a tyrant.[14]

There was no way in advance of knowing what kind of husband a man would make, and almost no way of leaving him if he should prove to be a bad one.

It was a cause of great anxiety to young women. Elizabeth Carter, when explaining to a friend why she had taken the decision not to marry, speculated on all the possible annoyances of having a husband:

what might I have expected to suffer from a husband! Perhaps be needlessly thwarted and contradicted in every innocent enjoyment of life: involved in all his schemes right or wrong, and perhaps not allowed the liberty of even silently seeming to disapprove them![15]

Elizabeth Montagu confessed herself astonished 'when I hear two people voluntarily, and on their own suggestion, entering into a bargain for perhaps fifty years of cohabitation . . . I weep more at a wedding than a funeral.'[16] (Montagu, of course, chose for her husband a man several decades older than herself – fifty years of cohabitation was going to be unlikely in her case.) Mary Wortley Montagu wrote this poem to a friend when she was young and awaiting her parents' decision on whom she should marry. Coming from a wealthy family, she knew she was a prize bride, but that was not necessarily a good thing.

> I know the fate of those by Interest wed,
> Doom'd to the Curse of a vexatious Bed,
> Days without Peace, and Nights without Desire,
> To mourn, and throw away my Youth for hire.
> Of Noble Maids, how wretched is the Fate!
> Ruin'd with Jointures, curs'd by an Estate.[17]

When Sarah Scott's marriage ended in separation, her sister Montagu wrote: 'indeed poor creature her situation is miserable; allied to the faults & infamy of a bad Man . . . In all disagreements in Wedlock blame falls ever on the innocent.'[18]

Everyone knew someone who had been trapped in a disastrous marriage. In the Bluestocking Circle, the story of Mary Delany's first marriage was told and retold in hushed tones. Delany had been a bright girl – fluent in French, well-versed in the classics in translation, a lover of poetry, books and music. She was deft with a needle, showing high artistry in her creations. Her family was well-connected, politically and culturally. When she was ten years old George Frideric Handel visited her home. The only instrument available was her little spinet so he sat down at the diminutive keyboard and coaxed such music from it that the girl was inspired to practise the moment Handel left the house. She declared that one day she would play as well as him.[19]

She was seventeen years old when she was invited to stay with her uncle Lord Lansdown at his country home near Bath. Lansdown was the man who controlled her family's finances. He kept a lively house: every evening his musicians would play and the company would dance. To Delany, these pleasurable weeks were a peek into a grown-up world of sophistication. Behind the scenes though, her father and uncle were squabbling over the family finances. Delany was grieved to see her father upset, but had not yet any idea of the role she would be expected to play in solving the family's troubles.

It was during this visit that Delany was introduced to the fifty-seven-year-old Alexander Pendarves. Pendarves was a member of parliament, a wealthy landowner and a widower. He arrived late one evening as the company sat at dinner, rain lashing at the windows. Pendarves had come on horseback and was thoroughly drenched but Lansdown was delighted to see his old friend and insisted he join them for dinner. The teenage Delany thought this sodden old man joining a gay party a ridiculous sight and could barely contain her laughter: 'I expected to have seen somebody with the appearance of a gentleman,' she recollected years later, 'when the poor, old, dripping almost drowned Pendarves was brought into the room, like Hob out of the well, his wig, his coat, his dirty boots, his large unwieldy person, and his crimson countenance were all subjects of great mirth and observation to me.'[20] Delany thought Pendarves deeply unpleasant, moody and self-absorbed. He was to stay just one night and Delany looked forward to his leaving. But he did not leave. Each day, he decided to stay another. Soon Delany became alarmed, for something told her that *she* was the reason for his lingering. 'You may readily believe I was not pleased with what I suspected,' she wrote, 'I thought him ugly and disagreeable; he was fat, much afflicted with gout . . . and I dreaded his making a proposal of marriage.'

She dreaded this all the more as she knew a proposal was likely to be accepted on her behalf by her uncle. Pre-emptively, she began openly to show her dislike for Pendarves, hoping it would put him off proposing. She went out of her way to be rude. She left a room the moment he entered it. She deployed the greatest weapon at the disposal of a pretty young woman: 'when I dressed, I considered what would become me least.'[21]

For two months, this dreadful game of cat-and-mouse continued. Delany's only defence against Pendarves was wearing the ugliest dress she could muster. It made no difference. Her aunt, usually an ally, told Delany she was ignorant and silly, and that if Delany could not make sensible decisions, others would make them for her. Even decades later, recalling the mounting horror she felt as Pendarves closed in on her could make Delany tremble.[22]

Pendarves approached Uncle Lansdown and asked his permission to marry Delany. Lansdown was delighted: politically, the alliance with Pendarves would greatly strengthen his position. Pendarves, mindful of the advantage he would gain by the alliance, and hopeful for an heir, was much pleased with the arrangement. Delany – a convenient bargaining chip – was not asked her opinion.

One night as the company took itself off to dance, Uncle Lansdown held Delany back. Suspecting what was to come, she paled. He took her by the hand and launched into a speech about her father's lack of money, and her own lack of prospects. He told her of Pendarves's passion for her and his willingness to make her financially comfortable. He praised the many virtues of Pendarves and told the teenager before him how despicable she would appear to the world if she refused a good match just because he was not young and handsome.

Delany was rendered utterly speechless by her uncle's words and simply stared at him for several minutes before bursting into tears. Knowing that her parents' and siblings' future finances were dependent on her decision, Delany agreed to submit to her uncle's demand, but begged not to be made to rejoin the party that evening. She went to her room and cried alone for two hours. After some consideration, she decided to dine with the company after all, hoping that her puffed red eyes and agitation would show Pendarves how very unhappy she was, hoping that he would walk away from the match. Her plan came to nothing. Uncle Lansdown wrote to her parents to inform them of the development and to invite them to their daughter's wedding.

Delany tried to hide her upset from her parents when they came. She knew they could stop the wedding, but it would be greatly to their disadvantage. Good daughter that she was, she resolved to marry without letting them know her true feelings. When the wedding day came, Delany was distressed almost beyond words. Her uncle had arranged a day of great pomp and ceremony, but Delany felt like Iphigenia, compelled to consent to her own sacrifice. 'I lost,' she wrote, 'not life indeed, but I lost all that makes life desirable – joy and peace of mind.'[23]

After the great day, the newly-weds stayed two months with Uncle Lansdown before departing for Pendarves's home. Delany was obliged to travel to what she called 'a remote country' (Cornwall) with a man she saw as 'my tyrant – my jailor'. When she arrived at Pendarves's dwelling near Falmouth, that feeling of being a prisoner intensified. Roscrow Castle was an austere home for a young bride and as Delany imagined living her whole life in this strange and foreboding place, she was overcome by a fit of crying.[24]

To distract her from her woes, Pendarves gave Delany the task of decorating the dilapidated house. She had always had an artistic streak, and she gladly threw herself into the job, finding much comfort in it. The Cornish countryside brought cheer to her too. Looking out from the castle, she could see down the sloping meadows all the way to Falmouth and the boundless sea beyond.

For two years, the couple continued in Cornwall. Pendarves was solicitous of his wife, whom he seemed truly to love. Delany, not wanting to cause any trouble for anyone, meekly settled into her role of subservient wife, trying to keep her distaste for her husband hidden as well as she could. In the third year of their marriage, Pendarves was obliged to live mostly in London on business, and Delany was able to have her parents and sister stay for many months. Delany felt she could breathe freely. But this hiatus from the daily grind of married life could not last and when Pendarves realised that he must extend his London stay, he summoned his wife to his side. Gloomily she packed her bags and obeyed his call.

In Soho's Hog Lane, she found her husband living in a house almost as alarming to her as Roscrow Castle. Even more worrying, Pendarves's older sister was in residence with him. She had disgraced the family by marrying a young fortune-hunter at the age of sixty-one. Now, still desperately in love with her young Scottish husband, she was mourning his absence and optimistically awaiting his return. Delany was wary of her sister-in-law, whom she saw as meddling and controlling. On top of her concerns over the house and the family, Delany experienced a growing realisation that Pendarves's finances were not as healthy as she had once assumed. In Cornwall, it was easy enough to live simply and cheaply; in London, where coaches, gowns and entertainments were called for, Pendarves began to struggle to pay his bills. He began to drink. Occasional drunken evenings became lengthy binges and he was often carried home at six or seven o'clock in the morning. The drink darkened his moods and caused him bouts of ill health.

Delany suffered too: she began to experience nightmares and low spirits. One night, she was tormented by particularly shocking dreams; all the next day a feeling of dread hung over her. She was to dine with a friend that evening but cancelled the engagement on account of her poor spirits. She arrived home to find Pendarves just returned from an evening of carousing. Unusually, he was in a good mood. He spoke kindly to Delany and told her what a good wife she had always been to him. He told her he was going to amend his will to reward her greatly for all she had done for him. He wanted to do it there and then, but Delany was worried for his health and persuaded him to go to bed. Still drunk, he slept fitfully. Delany, fearful of those nightmares, lay awake until four o'clock before drifting off. When she woke the next morning at seven, she drew back the bed curtain and a shaft of light fell on Pendarves's face. It was black. He had died in the night. Delany screamed for her servant who summoned help, but there was nothing to be done for the man.

Once the initial shock had subsided a little, Delany realised that widowhood was not an unwelcome state. She was young – just twenty-three years old – and she was healthy. Pendarves had not altered his will in Delany's favour so all of his property went to his niece, but Delany had a small income and never regretted the loss of Roscrow. 'As to my fortune,' she wrote, 'it was very mediocre, but it was *at my own command.*'[25] It was the happiest possible ending to a story like Delany's, and everyone knew it.

For many years after she was widowed, Delany had grave concerns about her female friends and relations who decided to marry. When her younger sister Ann announced her engagement, the Bulstrode circle watched an anxious Delany grapple with her feelings. Fidget wrote to Don:

> our friend Penny [Delany] is under great anxiety for the change her sister is going to make. I do not wonder at her fears; I believe both experience and observation, have taught her the state she is going into is in the general, less happy than that she has left.[26]

★

Perhaps it was Delany's story that Hester Mulso was thinking of when she wrote to Richardson:

> a marriage with a man I hate would be criminal, it would be of course unhappy . . . so very unhappy, that for my own part I think the sacrifice of my life would seem a trifle in the comparison. I still think that it would be less cruel in my parent to command my death . . . than to exact this instance of my obedience.[27]

She was becoming more forceful. Now Richardson cast her as one of 'a set of Amazonian soldiers, all drest in flame-coloured taffety'.[28] Though she tried to distance herself from anything too militant, Mulso enjoyed imagining these fearless women leaping from windows and scaling walls to escape their dreaded suitors.

Mulso was warming to her theme. Her third and final letter, written in January 1751, was her most robust, and went furthest in arguing that women were (in some respects) equal to men. Richardson had riled her in his previous letter. 'A woman, either as daughter or wife, never can be in a state of independency,' he had written; and, 'God and Nature make women dependent on the parent, as we have seen; and the law of God and their own choice and consent make them dependent on their husbands.'[29] An indignant Mulso took up her quill again.

On the subject of 'God and Nature' making women dependent, Mulso calmly pointed out that this was not true across all social classes. Upper- and middle-class women might not be allowed to work outside the home, but there were plenty of women who did earn their own living. 'Now the laws of God and nature are the same with regard to all conditions and ranks of people,' Mulso wrote to Richardson. She saw this as 'proof that nature makes no such difference between sons and daughters', chiding him for ignoring such a large section of the population when generalising about the nature of women.[30] She pointed out to Richardson that it was societal norms rather than any real differences between men and women that had led to women being seen as submissive and dependent. Women were not uniquely made for subjugation.

She saw clearly the double standard that permeated every aspect of the world she lived in: if a woman transgressed (particularly when it came to marriage), she was far more harshly judged than a man. This was not because her crime was greater, but simply because men had rigged the system. 'The customs of the world make the breach of [rules relating to marriage] more fatal in its consequences to the daughter than to the son,' she wrote; 'the rules of the world being made by *men*, are always more severe on *women* than on themselves.' Though she could see all of these truths, there was little Mulso could do about the broader situation. She only hoped that one day a higher power would reward women for their suffering here on Earth.[31]

Until that day came, Mulso had to content herself with politely arguing for a woman's right to say no to potential husbands. Richardson was vehemently opposed to a woman's right to a veto when it came to marriage; but, as a concession, he had written that he might countenance a woman's 'non-compliance' if she had good enough reasons – what he called 'an *absolute aversion, an utter dissimilitude of mind and manners*'. Mulso pointed out what a ludicrously high bar this was.[32]

It seemed to her that marriage should be undertaken as a voluntary act, not a forced one. With increasing boldness she put this to Richardson:

> I must insist, that *every* woman, whether of equal prudence with Clarissa, or not, whether the man proposed be *quite* as odious as Solmes, or not, whether she have an absolute aversion to him, or only be *indifferent*, or rather averse to him, whether she is in love with some other, or not, and whether that other be a proper match for her, or not, every woman, I say, has a right to a negative.[33]

Mulso wrote these forceful words, and then she must have remembered to whom she was writing, and the wide audience that might read her letter. Though she did not back down, she ended the letter with an apology for expressing her beliefs so clearly. She humbled herself before Richardson, writing, 'spare not to *take me down*, whenever I forget myself so far as to argue with you with unbecoming tenaciousness or decisiveness.' She remembered what it would mean for all the other learned ladies if she was seen to be too forward, or to ask for too much. She apologised for lacking in feminine decorum, and begged Richardson not to let her talk of women's rights cloud his judgement of other bookish ladies. 'However wanting *I* may have been in the characteristic graces of my sex, in *meekness, patience, resignation, submission*,' she wrote with palpable alarm, 'let not, I beseech you, the *reading* and *writing ladies* suffer for this.'[34]

After that, the formal letters on this subject stopped but Mulso and Richardson remained in the same social sphere and perhaps talked of it again at North End. Mulso was right to have suspected that the letters would not remain private. They soon began to circulate and to draw attention. Many of Mulso's young female readers found the letters an inspiration. Elizabeth Carter's very good friend Catherine Talbot wrote to Carter asking, 'Pray who and what is Miss Mulso? She writes very well . . . I honour her and want to know more about her.'[35] Carter replied,

> Did I never tell you any thing about Miss Mulso? O but I will, for she seems to be a person worthy your enquiry . . . she has an uncommon solidity and exactness of understanding, I was greatly charmed with her.[36]

Not all readers were so positive though, and Mulso discovered herself at the receiving end of harsh and personal criticism. She was told that she was 'proud, rebellious, a little spit-fire', she was told that she was not a good woman, that she had low morals, that she was intoxicated by the false notions she had propounded, that she was leading other women astray. A few months after finishing the third letter, Mulso put pen to paper again. She addressed her words to Richardson but all naivety was gone: really, she was writing to those critics who were hounding her. This new piece of writing was later published under the title *A Matrimonial Creed*. As in the previous letters, Mulso began by highlighting her meekness and modesty. She wrote how she looked forward to handing over control of her life to her future husband, that nothing in *A Matrimonial Creed* was

> founded in pride, or in aversion to being governed, or in jealousy of power . . . I have never yet been the mistress of myself, nor ever wished to be so; for I am convinced that it is generally a happiness, and often a relief, to have some person to determine for us, either to point out our duty, or direct our choice.[37]

Then Mulso performed a sleight of hand: though she said she was going to amend the problematic views she had expressed in the earlier letters, in fact she wrote on a different topic altogether. Earlier, she had argued that a woman had a right to some element of choice in her spouse; now, she wrote about the dynamics of a good marriage, after the husband was chosen and the vows made. On this topic, she held somewhat more socially conservative views. She knew that her critics would be appeased by sentiments such as, 'I believe that a husband has a divine right to the absolute obedience of his wife . . . and that, as her appointed ruler and head, he is undoubtedly her superior.'[38] Yet, even as she was toeing the line, she couldn't quite help herself from pointing out that in many marriages she had observed in real life, the woman was intellectually superior to the man.

A Matrimonial Creed painted a picture of Mulso's ideal marriage. She was in her early twenties when she wrote it, perhaps dreaming of her own future husband. She imagined a marriage of dialogue, consideration and willing compromise. She wrote that a wife should acknowledge her husband's superiority, but that a husband in turn had a duty to value his wife's principles and abilities. He should respect her and allow her the same privileges, rights and freedoms he might extend to a male friend.[39]

It was at North End that Mulso met the man she would marry. His name was John Chapone. John's mother Sarah Chapone had written a book titled *The Hardships of the English Laws in Relation to*

Wives; she would come to approve greatly of her daughter-in-law. In 1753, when John Chapone and Hester Mulso met, it was just two years since Mulso's letters on marriage had been circulated – and she retained a reputation as a headstrong girl. But John was used to strong women expressing forthright opinions. Many said that the beliefs Mulso had expressed in her letters made her unmarriageable, but John disagreed.

Now Mulso got a chance to put her beliefs about a woman's right to choose her marriage partner to the test. Mulso's father liked John, but he was worried about the young man's finances. John's father was a vicar, and his mother was a schoolmistress and writer – it was a respectable but not a wealthy background. John was training to become a barrister but it would take some years for him to establish himself professionally. Mulso's father agreed to let John visit his daughter at home, but ordered her not to accept a marriage proposal without his permission. Mulso loved and respected her father, and she abided by his command. She knew that her father liked John, and she hoped that they would not have to wait too long to win his approval. Within a year, Mulso's father gave the couple permission to become engaged – but no more. The wedding was not to take place until Mulso's father was satisfied with John's finances.

To be engaged with no sign of marriage on the horizon was difficult for the couple. Mulso sought solace in her female friendships, in poetry and in writing. To her old correspondent Elizabeth Carter, she sent some odes that touched on the sadness she felt at being unable to marry the man she loved.

Another ode that Mulso wrote during her long engagement would win her much acclaim. It was a poem of thanks to Carter for having introduced her to the Stoic philosopher Epictetus – a philosopher who argued that one must face the vagaries of life with as much fortitude as one could muster. Mulso never meant the ode to be published, but when Carter had finished her magisterial translation of the complete works of Epictetus and asked if she could publish the poem alongside it, Mulso agreed and the ode appeared:

Come, Epictetus! Arm my Breast
With thy impenetrable Steel,
No more the Wounds of Grief to feel,
Nor mourn by others' Woes deprest.

. . .

No longer let my fleeting Joys depend
On social, or domestic Ties!
Superior let my Spirit rise,
Nor in the gentle Counsels of a Friend,
Nor in the Smiles of Love, expect Delight:
But teach me in *myself* to find
Whate'er can please or fill my Mind.[40]

Though the ode was published anonymously, Mulso's identity was well known. Many years later, when Mulso was introduced to the royal family, the princes' tutor murmured to her that 'these gentlemen [the princes] are well acquainted with a certain Ode prefixed to Mrs Carter's Epictetus, if you know any thing of it.'[41] To readers who knew Mulso and the story of her prolonged engagement, the ode's meaning was clear.

For six long years Mulso waited for her father's permission to marry. She often suffered from low moods, overpowered by a sorrow that could only be alleviated by the presence of her sweetheart.[42] Those who had called her a spitfire, a rebellious spirit who disdained male governance must have been surprised to see her wait so patiently. Though a little part of her perhaps dreamed of eloping, she stayed obediently at home, waiting for the menfolk to arrange everything to their liking. This waiting, which Mulso called an 'uncomfortable state of tedious and almost hopeless expectation', finally drew to a close in the winter of 1760.[43] Mulso's father gave her his blessing and simultaneously (to Mulso's great joy) gave her eldest brother Thomas permission to marry Mary Prescott – another young lady from the North End circle.

The wedding took place late in December 1760 at Mulso's parish church. After so many years of quiet and solitude, Mulso Chapone (as she was often known, unusually retaining the vestige of her old name even after marriage) suddenly found herself plunged into a frenzy of activity. There were lodgings to find, domestic arrangements to be made, letters to answer, and visits and engagements to fit into increasingly busy days. 'A time of *flutteration*', she called it.[44]

The couple took a set of rooms just south of Lincoln's Inn Fields – the legal heartland of London. John needed to be there for his work, but it felt a long way from Mulso's friends in west London. The roof leaked, and Mulso Chapone would later recall the place as 'those puddling lodgings'.[45] The couple could not yet afford a house of their own. John worked long hours, and some days the pair would see each other only at mealtimes. But none of these inconveniences weighed heavily on the newly-weds. Mulso Chapone felt alive in her new marriage. She planned not just to be the perfect wife, but to allow her happiness to seep into every aspect of her life. She wanted to fill the world around her with her radiance. 'I flatter myself my heart will be improved in every virtuous affection by an union with a worthy man,' she wrote to Elizabeth Carter.[46] The marriage saw an improvement in Mulso Chapone's physical health and her dark moods disappeared overnight. She wrote to her friends of her joy at 'the beginning of a union which promises to be the best blessing of my life'.[47] She rejoiced in her brother's new-found happiness too and her father looked kindly on his children and their spouses, satisfied that he had made the right decision in permitting the marriages.

Things went well at first. The summer of 1761 saw the couple move to a house a little nearer the river in Arundel Street. It was small but they furnished it neatly and the roof did not leak. John seemed to be prospering at work and Mulso Chapone was settling into married life. The autumn saw Mulso Chapone's health decline a little, but some fresh air and mineral water soon helped. Then, quite suddenly, John succumbed to a fever. For ten days he lay, barely conscious, sweating and shuddering. Mulso Chapone tended to him as best she could. She waited and she prayed. She tried to stay calm. With all her effort, she put into practice the Christian forbearance that was expected of her.[48]

John died late at night on Saturday 19 September. For the last six days of his life, Mulso Chapone had been advised by the physicians and by her friends not to attend upon John herself as 'her presence was judged to be very hurtful to him.'[49] Meekly she agreed to this; she would do anything that might help John. She was not with him when he died. She was only told the news the following morning.

Her brother Thomas and his new wife took Mulso Chapone to live with them. Her grief was quiet and composed. She barely noticed the whirlwind of activity on the streets of London that week as all in the capital prepared for the coronation of a new king. While the nation rejoiced at the crowning of benevolent young George III, Mulso Chapone sat silently in her brother's parlour. She was grateful to her family and friends for their care and attention. She found comfort in having the Psalms read aloud to her: their sentiments resonated with her and their poetry soothed her. Then a fever began to creep upon her. At first it troubled her only at night, but before long it spilled over into the daylight hours. Headaches began, then stomach-aches. She tossed in her bed, unable to find sleep. Despondency descended upon her. Through the autumn she lingered in this illness, but as winter closed in she rallied.

By December she was well enough to take up her pen again. The first to receive a letter was Elizabeth Carter. 'I have been very near death, and at the time he threatened most, it was the most earnest wish of my heart to meet and embrace him,' she confessed. It had been a dismal time but, now that she was recovering, Mulso Chapone wrote that she was grateful to be alive. She could not foresee much future happiness for herself, but she resolved to make the best of things.[50] Above all, she would treasure her friends, and for the next forty years of her life those friendships would sustain her.

Her writing was another source of comfort to her. John had had very little money to leave his widow so it would also become an important source of income. Mulso Chapone gave up the house in Arundel Street and moved into rented lodgings. Her uncle gave her £20 per annum and when her father died two years later he too left her a modest sum. Mulso lived plainly, uncomplainingly.

Her sweet nature drew new friends towards her, and her quick mind, rational conversation, that old reputation as the woman brave enough to take on Samuel Richardson ensured that she received frequent invitations to Bluestocking salons. Elizabeth Montagu was already acquainted with Mulso Chapone, but did not know her well. When John Chapone had died, Montagu had written to Carter:

> I am indeed grieved at the heart for Mrs. Chapone. All calamities are light in comparison of the loss of what one loves, uniquement. After that dear object is lost, the glories of the golden day are forever overcast, and there is no tranquillity under the silent moon; the soft and quiet pleasures are over . . . *the soul's calm sunshine and the heartfelt joy* can never be regained.[51]

Montagu reached out to the younger woman. Mulso Chapone was excited but nervous at the prospect of entering Montagu's inner circle. Before long, the two women became close friends. Mulso Chapone would spend time at Montagu's homes at Sandleford and at Denton Hall in Northumberland and reported happily that

> I am grown as bold as a lion with Mrs Montagu, and fly in her face whenever I have a mind; in short I enjoy her society with the most perfect *gout*, and find my love for her takes off my fear and awe, though my respect for her character continually increases.[52]

In 1770 the two women set off for a tour of the North of England and of Scotland. Mulso Chapone loved the magnificent Scottish landscape. At Loch Tay she marvelled at the sublime views that surrounded her on every side, writing to Carter:

> Such a lake! such variegated hills rising from its banks! such mountains and such cloud-cap'd rocks rising behind them! such a delicious green valley to receive the 'sweet winding Tay!' such woods! such cascades! – in short I am wild that you and all my romantic friends should see it.[53]

This trip was full of intellectual delights too – Edinburgh was a centre of Enlightenment thinking and the two Bluestockings were warmly welcomed to assemblies and dinners with many of the city's greatest thinkers. Seeing Mulso Chapone so inspired, Montagu decided to push her a little.

Montagu knew that Mulso Chapone had been writing letters to her twelve-year-old niece Jenny for some years and she offered to help shape the letters into a book. It was published in 1773 under the title *Letters on the Improvement of the Mind, Addressed to a Young Lady*. It was dedicated to Montagu and having her name so prominently associated with the book was a great help to sales.

The book gave guidance on religious principles, on affairs of the heart, controlling one's temper, running the finances of a household – all the things a girl would need in her daily life. But it also taught the best way of learning history, it encouraged an interest in the classics and in politics, it encouraged a global vision, and even pointed out some of the injustices of colonisation. Mulso Chapone argued that women were just as capable as men when it came to learning, writing that

> it is not from want of capacity that so many women are such trifling insipid companions, so ill qualified for the friendship and conversation of a sensible man, or for the task of governing and instructing a family; it is much oftener from the neglect of exercising the talents which they really have.[54]

She encouraged her niece, and all young women, to strive for more.

The book was popular. Mary Delany said that it was the best educational book for girls she had ever read.[55] Queen Charlotte used it to guide the education of her little princesses.[56] Poems were written to praise '. . . Chapone, who, like a tender guide, / O'er life's smooth surface taught the youth to glide'.[57] Despite this fame and praise, Mulso Chapone made little money from the book – she had sold her rights to the publisher. She never begrudged this loss of income, saying simply that the book had had a wider readership on account of this arrangement and that this made her happy.[58] Her friends would try to think up ways for her to increase her income – they suggested she apply for posts as a governess or companion, but Mulso Chapone preferred to be poor and free rather than subject to the whims of a capricious mistress.[59] Her friends accepted this and slowly the suggestions died out, but they always looked out for her. Montagu especially was a great support – she invited Mulso Chapone for extended visits to her country homes, created space for her to write, or sent gifts of enormous shimmering trout from the streams of Sandleford.[60] Mulso Chapone kept her independence, she wrote, and occasionally she hosted modest Bluestocking gatherings in her rented rooms. It was a good life, though her heart never really healed from the loss of her beloved John. Even years later she struggled to speak of him with composure. She kept a miniature portrait of him but tried not to look at it very often because the grief was too exquisite, the sorrow too much to bear.[61] Still, she had married the man she had chosen, she had lived by her principles, and that brought her much comfort.

Across the Irish Sea, another Bluestocking romance was unfolding on the southern banks of the River Liffey. It was a lively area of Dublin – too lively, some said – with its taverns and ale-houses, and the infamous Maiden Tower brothel. In the mid-eighteenth century, two important stalwarts of Dublin's cultural life nestled into these jumbled lanes: the New Music Hall in Fishamble Street opened in 1741 and enjoyed an early coup by hosting the premiere of Handel's *Messiah* in 1742; around the corner in Smock Alley stood the Theatre Royal. It had had a less illustrious start than the Music Hall: the theatre was built on land reclaimed from the river and in its early decades it collapsed several times as the soft wet earth shifted beneath its foundations. Several theatregoers were maimed or killed, but a new building begun in the 1730s seemed more stable and audiences returned to Smock Alley.

The new theatre could seat three hundred in its horseshoe-shaped auditorium, with stalls below and tiers of galleries and boxes above. The arched stage was lit by hundreds of candles. A twenty-first-century archaeological dig uncovered the original mosaic floor awash with the remnants of oyster shells and clay pipes. Audiences did not watch passively: they ate, they smoked, they heckled or cheered; occasionally a drunk might wander onto the stage; more than once they rioted. Acting in this rough-and-tumble world took more than talent and artistry, it required real physical courage – especially for a woman.

Elizabeth Griffith was twenty-two in 1749 when she first took to the Smock Alley stage in the role of Juliet. She was petite ('a Lilliputian subject', she once called herself) and delicate – perfect for the role, and not at all daunted by the rambunctious crowds.[62] Griffith had grown up in the world of theatre: her father Thomas was the manager of Smock Alley. Thomas had taught his daughter how to read and recite from an early age. He brought her up to be comfortable in front of an audience, he imbued her with easy sociability and a light cheerfulness. His death when she was still a teenager was awful for her, but did nothing to dull her ambition. While her mother moved away from Dublin to stay with family, Elizabeth asked to be allowed to stay in the city. Her aunt who lived across the river in Abbey Street agreed to take the girl in.

In her first season as a professional actress, Griffith played nine different roles – most of them in Shakespearean tragedies. It was an enormous amount of work to prepare for each one. Plays tended to have short runs, perhaps just a few nights each, so performers needed to be agile, to keep on top of several scripts at once, and to perform impressive feats of memorisation. For most actors, the work was neither particularly well paid nor high-status. Griffith last appeared on the Dublin stage in 1751, having had two moderately successful seasons. It was a short career but it was not the low wages, the precariousness, or the insults hurled at actresses that compelled Griffith to make this drastic change. It was love.

In 1746 she had met a man called Richard Griffith (no relation). He was more than a decade older than her and he had a reputation for being a rake. Richard was in a bad way when the pair met: he had been engaged, but the affair had ended badly. That year – between the end of his first engagement and meeting Griffith – was a dark time for Richard. 'You cannot conceive what a wretched vacuum of life I passed during that interval,' he later wrote, 'I led an unsatisfactory, vague dissipated kind of life, during this interregnum.' When he first met Griffith, Richard saw her as an easy conquest, a pleasant distraction from his emotional turmoil. He was a libertine, and she an aspiring actress – what could be more fitting? Griffith was pretty and vivacious, she had what Richard described as 'a lively Eye, double Chin, and saucy Look'. On another occasion he described her as being 'like the French, warm, lively, and restless'.[63] But Griffith did not fit the stereotype that actresses had had to contend with for so long – that they were women of uncertain virtue, often earning a little extra money by selling their bodies.

He made his advances and she instantly rebuffed him. This intrigued him. Other men might have walked away, tried their luck elsewhere, but Richard became fascinated by Griffith. In conversation he found her charming. She had been given an education by her father; probably she was better educated than Richard – his family had accidentally forgotten to teach him very much at all so he had had to educate himself as best he could. Richard enjoyed the company of women. He said that female company brought out the best in him, that it made him more generous, more honourable, more compassionate, more polite, gentler. He liked being able to show off his (somewhat modest, though he would never admit that) learning in front of female admirers. He praised women for their innate sense, which he characterised as 'un-incumbered with logical distinctions, and untainted with the subtleties of the schools'. If Richard's previous lovers had seemed to him unencumbered with logic, Griffith was something new. She was clever and self-possessed and could hold her own in an argument. Richard wanted to know her better, so when he left Dublin and returned to his home a day's ride away in County Kilkenny he began to write to her. Her letters in response were a delight – witty and playful, brimming with literary allusions, philosophical ideas, sense and good cheer. They lifted Richard's spirits. He put real effort into his replies, painting himself as the ideal gentleman farmer-cum-scholar:

> I am, at present, sitting in the midst of a large field of barley, which I reaped the other day; and am taking care of the binders and stackers: There are forty-seven women and fourteen men, at work round me, while I am reading Pliny, and writing to you.[64]

They wrote regularly three times each week for several years. It seems to us now like an innocent pastime but it was a dangerous game, especially for Griffith. A young unmarried woman who corresponded with an older man, especially one known for his gallantry, put her reputation at risk. The letters had to be kept secret. Once, when Richard learned that Griffith had told a friend of their correspondence, he pointed out the danger of this – not to him, but to her: 'my character is libertine, your fortunes are small, your experience of the world but little, your age young, your guardian old.' He advised her to be wary of public opinion. Who was likely to believe that her conversations with this rake were upon innocent subjects?

Ignoring his own advice, Richard also showed the letters to a friend. Griffith wrote to him in a terrified rage, 'Sir, You have behaved with great dishonour . . . Farewel[l] for life.' He rushed to Dublin as fast as he could but she refused to see him. Unable to speak to her, he wrote to her the next morning: 'Madam, I approve of the resentment you have shewn; and am so pleased with the propriety of your behaviour, upon so nice an occasion, that I readily forgive the hastiness of your censure.'[65] It was Richard's standard response to arguments: to turn things around and magnanimously announce that he forgave Griffith no matter that his behaviour was often the cause of their quarrels. After a series of tempestuous notes hastily dispatched between Dublin and Kilkenny, the couple eventually made up. They always did.

Their relationship was stormy but, in between the quarrels (sometimes even in the midst of them), there was fun and real romance in their letters. It was all lightly done, always with humour. With each missive, more and more pet names were introduced: 'dear Sprightly', 'my dear Pauper', 'my dear Stoick', 'my dear Moralist', for a time they even addressed each other as Heloise and Abelard. Richard sent Griffith a lock of his hair. When Griffith asked Richard to write more often he joked that it was because she wanted to sell his letters to keep herself in tea, linen and plays. He tried to stir her jealousy by telling her of a female who was in love with him – it turned out to be his cat Sultana Puss who drank tea with him in the mornings and sat on his desk taking swipes at his quill as he wrote.[66]

Gradually, Richard realised that something in him had changed. Griffith, noticing that his letters were less gallant than they had once been, questioned him on this. He replied that he thought it was time to move on from romantic flights of fancy to a more rational discourse. He was hinting at something but he waited until he was in Dublin to make his first declarations, not quite trusting himself to commit the words to paper. On the banks of the River Liffey at Chapelizod, just west of Dublin, Richard told Griffith that he loved her. She would always remember the tender sentiments and fond endearments that escaped his lips that day. He was leaving his libertine youth behind. 'You see', he wrote to her, 'what a Platonick you have made me; for I speak of intellectual joys now, as warmly, as I used to do of the pleasures of sense.'[67]

For Griffith, the next obvious step was marriage. Her reputation was still at risk and continuing with secret letter-writing was both dangerous and unsatisfying. Richard said that he would quite like to marry her, but that his financial situation at that time would not allow him to support a wife. She was exasperated and proposed putting an end to the whole thing. He wrote back that he still loved her, though he admitted that he had always struggled with the idea of marriage. He invited her to visit him in Kilkenny (with his mother and sister present to act as chaperones); she was unsure if this was wise. He wrote to persuade her, signing his letter,

> I am, my dear, little, cross pet,
>   Your constant, good-humoured, clumsy,
>   Country Farmer[68]

It was hard to resist Richard in this playful mood. That week in Kilkenny, Richard still did not feel he was financially stable enough to propose, but he asked Griffith not to become engaged to anyone else.

For some time, this situation continued: Richard declaring his love for Griffith, but never committing to marrying her. She made her feelings clear, writing long passages to him like this one:

> That you do love me, I verily believe; and the fond hope, that you will ever do so, is all the hold I have of happiness. The charming change, you speak of in your sentiments, has transported me almost beyond my senses. To have you love me with tenderness and delicacy, all gross desires for ever banished from your heart, is joy unspeakable. – Now, and only now, I begin to live, and you to love . . . Oh! Why has not fortune placed me in a sphere to indulge my first, my last, my only wish, of being always and forever your's?

Richard continued to declare his love for her, but largely ignored her allusions to marriage. The tension was too much and they quarrelled again. She wrote to him to end the relationship for good.[69] He ignored the substance of her letter and replied with a long screed about John Locke. It was, apparently, just the thing to win her forgiveness.

The basic problem, however, remained. Griffith's friends looked on her with pity – not just for her unhappiness, but for the damage she might do to her reputation. Many people knew of the relationship by now, and Griffith was in danger of making herself unmarriageable. She wanted children and a family life but Richard seemed unlikely ever to give her this. Every letter she sent him further lowered her in the eyes of society: 'the world, in general, treat me in the severest manner, on your account,' she wrote to him. She was becoming depressed and was plagued by illness and headaches. She decided to try one more ultimatum. She left aside allusions and said plainly that she wanted Richard to make her his wife.[70] Locke could not help him this time. Richard finally saw how serious Griffith was and that he was doing her damage by prolonging their relationship on an unsure footing. He went to Dublin and asked her to marry him.

Still, there were financial details to be ironed out. Richard was waiting for a family lawsuit to be settled that he hoped would ease his situation. The couple waited months for the courts to adjudicate, but the case remained unresolved. Richard accepted his lot: he might not ever be wealthy, but he could do the right thing by the woman he loved.

They wed on 12 May 1751. It was a tiny affair, for Richard made Griffith swear to keep the wedding a secret, even from her aunt with whom she still lived. Griffith however, with her good name to think of, insisted that there be a witness present and that that witness be someone held in high regard by society. The couple agreed to invite Griffith's friend Lady Orrery to fulfil the role. Lady Orrery, born Margaret Hamilton, had a good reputation in Irish and British society – she was known as an upstanding woman with a fondness for music, needlework and literature. She had been a sort of patron to Griffith for many years. Now she would be responsible for vouching for the legality of the marriage and so ensuring Griffith's character.

Two days after the wedding, Griffith took to the stage at Smock Alley playing the Countess of Nottingham in *The Unhappy Favourite*. It was her last ever appearance on a Dublin theatre stage. Perhaps as she left the stage after that final performance, she imagined herself never needing to earn again, imagined Richard looking after the family's financial future. He had a wonderful plan to set up a linen manufactory. He raised over £3,000 on his own credit and was given a grant by parliament. All of this money he poured into his mill. When it was finished he had to get a mortgage before he could afford to set the machines in motion – he mortgaged the buildings, the machinery, the family farm, everything he could. He had been told he could count on further support from government but when he applied he was turned away. The Seven Years War was on the horizon and the Treasury was redirecting funds to the military. Richard lost everything. He had acted, he readily admitted, 'with more spirit than prudence'.[71]

The Griffiths had to think of something else. They had a child now, a son called Richard. He had been born a year after their wedding, his arrival ending any remaining pretence of secrecy around his parents' relationship. Though they were now a family, they rarely lived together. The baby had been born in Abbey Street while Richard dashed about the country trying to set up his linen business. They could not afford a house of their own and moved between lodgings often. Briefly, Griffith moved to London to act on the London stage. Though she appeared at Covent Garden several times, she was given only minor roles and permanent success eluded her. Their son, and a daughter who arrived not long after, were often sent to stay with Griffith's mother. It was a difficult and uncertain time for all of them.

Then an idea struck them. They realised that without really intending to, they had written a book. Their letters made an extraordinary love story: a pretty young actress, a gallant older man, more tiffs than even the most melodramatic novel, philosophical interludes, and a denouement that involved a secret wedding. If they could edit the letters into a coherent whole they would have a publishing sensation on their hands. Though Dublin had presses, they decided that London was a better bet – they would move there, ingratiate themselves with the literary crowd and make their fortune.

It was a good plan, though perhaps not as polished as it might have first appeared. For one thing the letters were a mess; for another, neither had much interest in doing anything about it. Despite this, a London publisher was able to see the potential in the project and agreed to take it on, and an unnamed friend agreed to the mammoth task of editing the letters. They were published in two volumes in 1757 under the title *A Series of Genuine Letters between Henry and Frances* and, apart from changing names and locations, they were a faithful representation of the love, excitement, anger, despair and hope that the two lovers had felt as they had penned them a decade earlier. The books were only moderately popular with the reviewers, but a roaring success with the public.

Most readers found the romance straightforwardly thrilling: a classic 'will they, won't they?' story. The secrecy of the letters added a hint of risqué subterfuge, but the frequent references to morals and religion ensured that parents did not need to worry too much about the book corrupting their daughters. Then there were readers who enjoyed something else about the book – the proof that a woman writer could hold her own. Elizabeth Montagu wrote to a friend that she approved of the way 'Frances' won 'Henry' through the use of wit and reason, while always upholding moral standards: 'you will find sentiment and delicacy triumph at last,' she wrote, '& Mr Henry becomes very platonick. I think her letters extremely pretty.'[72]

A few years later, a teenage Frances Burney read the letters and liked them, she said, prodigiously. She liked the style which she called 'so elegantly natural, so tenderly manly, so unassumingly rational!' She found the letters inspirational, saying that they were 'doubly pleasing, charming to me, for being genuine – they have encreased my relish for *minute, heartfelt* writing.'[73] She wished that she could meet the authors.

That question of whether the letters really were 'genuine' added to their popularity and, in the early days after publication, guessing the identity of the authors was a popular pastime. The excess of what one reviewer called 'that fond kind of fiddle-faddle jargon' – the pet names and in-jokes – was hard to fake convincingly and everyone wanted to know more about 'Henry' and 'Frances'.[74] Though the letters were edited, it was clear to readers that they told a real love story. Following the success of the first two volumes of 1757, several more volumes and editions appeared over the next few years. These were more self-consciously philosophical and grand, and almost certainly written with publication in mind. By the 1760s (when Burney read the letters and wished that she could know the Griffiths), the identities of the authors were common knowledge, which also made for a less natural style in later volumes.

Those early years in London were an exciting time for the Griffiths, especially for Elizabeth who was often alone there. She took lodgings in Bloomsbury – it was on the very edge of the city, not yet fashionable, but it was the best she could afford. Horace Walpole befriended her, telling everyone how she was 'très-précieuse' and inviting her to stay in Strawberry Hill, his newly built Gothic-style mansion. She found herself invited to royal balls, including a masquerade hosted by the King of Sweden, and stayed out dancing until five o'clock in the morning.[75] She delighted in the theatres of the capital, greedily seeing as many plays as she possibly could. She almost certainly attended salons; later she would write a novel in which a character described hearing Elizabeth Montagu and Samuel Johnson conversing:

> When Dr. Johnson speaks, we listen with respect and admiration, and feel our minds impressed with such an attentive kind of veneration as I imagine was paid to the oracles of old. When Mrs. Montagu, in the purest and most elegant language, delivers sentiments equally just and sublime as his, we are surprised and delighted; the gracefulness of her manner seems to add beauty to her thoughts; her words sink into our hearts, like the softest sounds of the most perfect harmony, and produce the same placid effects.[76]

Despite the success of the *Genuine Letters between Henry and Frances*, and despite their popularity in London, the Griffiths still struggled financially. Richard took a job in a customs office, but it was not a particularly high or steady income. Griffith took a job as a companion back in Ireland for a while. When that did not prove to be a long-term option, Griffith decided to pick up her quill as a means of keeping the family afloat. In London again, she was a prolific writer: she turned her hand to plays, translations, novels, criticism, poetry – anything that would sell. She wrote for eight hours a day in her chilly dressing room, her fingers becoming more cramped as the days wore on. In the evenings she would read and converse with her son and daughter. Richard was sometimes present, sometimes not.

Several of Griffith's plays were produced on the London stage during these years. Her brother (also called Richard) even appeared in one called *The Platonic Wife* at Drury Lane. Sadly, a poorly executed set design turned that play into a farce and the audience descended into 'catcalls, hisses, groans and horse-laughs'. A year later, a play called *The Double Mistake* was staged at Covent Garden and fared much better. It fared so well that Griffith felt confident enough to approach the maestro David Garrick and ask him to consider staging one of her works. Garrick was politely encouraging and Griffith felt heartened. She spent some time working on what she called 'undetermined and vague experiments' for him, but nothing seemed quite right.[77] Eventually he suggested that she translate and adapt the French play *Eugénie* by Beaumarchais which was getting rave reviews on the Paris stage. It told the story of a young woman who had married secretly – of course it appealed to Griffith.

Though Beaumarchais had set his play in England, his characters had what Griffith called 'Spanish manners' – they did not speak and behave like English people did, nor were the laws and customs they observed known in England.[78] Griffith had to rewrite the piece substantially for her London audience. Griffith corresponded with Garrick as she worked on the play, but their relationship was never an easy one. She was anxious for success and keen to discuss details of casting and set design and staging; he was not used to having anyone question him so closely and often sent ill-tempered replies. Finally she had a script they were both happy with. She called it *The School for Rakes* and Garrick agreed to stage it at Drury Lane. The play was a success: it ran for several weeks in its first season in 1769 and was replayed every season for several years afterwards.

The year 1769 also saw Griffith publish her first novel, *The Delicate Distress* – a story about a young wife worried that her husband might be about to stray.[79] She published it under the name 'Frances' and it appeared alongside a separate novel written by 'Henry' called *The Gordian Knot*. The couple had encouraged one another to complete their manuscripts; they were living apart at the time and would send pages to each other as they were finished. Noticing that Griffith was falling behind (perhaps busy with her 'vague experiments' for Garrick), Richard pushed her to finish. In a letter he told her, 'I don't care to publish without you. Hand in Hand, and Heart in Heart, let us march together through Life – Amen!' When the novels were complete, there was as always the difficulty of finding a publisher who would pay well. 'The Booksellers will give nothing worth taking for it,' sighed Griffith,

> they say that they do not dispute the Merit of it, but that while the Public continue equally to buy a bad Thing as a good one, they do not think an Author can reasonably expect that they will make a Difference in the Price.[80]

In need of cash, the Griffiths decided to eschew the booksellers and to publish by subscription; subscribers included David Garrick, Samuel Johnson, Edmund Burke and Oliver Goldsmith. *The Delicate Distress* was generally well-received. *The Gordian Knot* inspired one critic to say of Richard, 'novel writing, in short, does not appear to be the gentleman's talent; but he is a good moralist, and a man of sense.'[81] It was not the worst review Richard ever received.

Griffith was a more successful writer than her husband, but she struggled with it. She had never expected to have to work for a living – a part of her would have much preferred to devote herself to her children and to the running of her household. There was also the fact that writing, even anonymously as she tended to do, required putting herself into public view. Though she had some experience of this from her earliest days as an actress, she never really felt comfortable with it. She wrote for money, and she was clear-eyed about it, saying:

> I never was designed for an Author, and feel no Pride in Fame – therefore nought but Profit ever shapes my Quill. I have none of that charming, flattering Enthusiasm about me, that should support one's Spirits when their Works are sent to the Mercy of the Public. On the contrary, I shrink into nothing on such occasions, and the Woman feels at the Mortification the Writer fears.

Griffith dreamed of winning the lottery – 'that I might afford myself to be a *comfortable Fool* for the Rest of my Life'.[82]

Griffith never did win the lottery. She kept writing. She wrote more plays, more novels, produced more translations. In 1775, inspired by Elizabeth Montagu, she wrote a book about the morality of Shakespeare.[83] In 1782, inspired in part by the works of Hannah More and Hester Mulso Chapone, she wrote a conduct book for newly married women.[84] Griffith was not as closely tied to the Bluestocking Circle as these other women, she was not such a frequent attendee at salons as some, but she was well aware of their work, and they of hers. In the public imagination, she was certainly part of the group. Richard Samuel depicted her in an oil painting known as *The Nine Living Muses of Great Britain* which was exhibited in the Royal Academy in 1779. (It was later reproduced as a print for a popular ladies' pocketbook and circulated widely.) This fantastical image showed nine contemporary clever women dressed in classical garb gathered together in the Temple of Apollo. At the centre, the singer Eliza Sheridan performs for the group; to one side, the painter Angelica Kauffmann sits before an easel with Elizabeth Carter and Anna Barbauld standing just behind her; to the other side, Elizabeth Montagu sits in the middle of a knot of women – novelist Charlotte Lennox, historian Catharine Macaulay, playwright and educator Hannah More, and Elizabeth Griffith.

When the painting first appeared, Carter and Montagu joked that they did not know which woman was meant to be which.[85] None of them had sat for a portrait, all the figures appeared to be much the same age. Griffith is usually assumed to be the figure seated furthest to the right. She bends her head over a text she holds in her hands. While everyone else seems to be lost in Sheridan's song, she is lost to the written word.

7

MOTHERHOOD

WHILE AWAITING THE birth of her twelfth child, Hester Thrale began to imagine her own death. Gruesome images had been appearing unbidden in her mind for years, growing increasingly graphic with each pregnancy. Just before this child had been conceived (on 24 August 1777 – a date Thrale could pinpoint with a precision that hinted at a less-than-passionate relationship with her husband) she had dreamed of giving birth to a boy covered in blood. Four months into the pregnancy, not yet having felt any movement within her, she dreamed of a mourning coach about to carry her dead child to the grave. 'Would the mourning Coach might carry *me* off before I see more of my Offspring devoted to Death,' she wrote the next morning, still feeling the horror of the dream pricking at her, 'would it might!'[1]

In addition to Thrale's twelve pregnancies that resulted in live births, she had also suffered two miscarriages earlier in her marriage (and would later experience stillbirth and further miscarriages).* Records for the period show that, on average, Georgian women left a gap of two to three years between babies. Thrale was pregnant almost every year of her first marriage – fifteen pregnancies in sixteen years. It was a larger-than-average number of pregnancies for a woman, but not unheard of. She was worried that this pregnancy might end

---

* Her twelve children born alive were: Hester Maria, nicknamed Queeney (b. 1764); Frances (b. 1765); Harry (b. 1767); Anna Maria (b. 1768); Lucy Elizabeth (b. 1769); Susanna Arabella (b. 1770); Sophia (b. 1771); Penelope (b. 1772); Ralph (b. 1773); Frances Anna (b. 1775); Cecilia Margaretta (b. 1777); Henrietta Sophia (b. 1778). Her miscarriages occurred in 1767 or 1768, in 1770, in 1787 and in 1788; the stillbirth occurred in 1779.

badly, but in April 1778, eight months into the pregnancy, she felt movements that reassured her that the child was alive. It was a relief that the baby seemed all right, but still Thrale was worried. She could not stop thinking about the possibility of an agonising death. She began to write an autobiography, fearing that her *Thraliana* was about to be closed forever.[2]

She recounted tales of her ancestors, she wrote about her parents' unhappy marriage, and of her girlhood. She had been born Hester Lynch Salusbury in 1741, and her birth had helped to heal her parents' relationship: they finally had something in common and her father's violence became less frequent. But though the child brought great joy, Hester's mother (also called Hester) was so traumatised by the birth that she vowed never to endure another pregnancy. Young Hester was a bright and charming child who picked everything up quickly. Her parents taught her French, Spanish and Italian, she learned Latin from the famous philosopher-priest Arthur Collier, and Roman history from her uncle.[3]

The family led a peripatetic life for many years: they began in their native Wales; then when Hester's father took a job in Canada she and her mother went to London and stayed in lodgings or with various friends. Eventually the trio settled with Hester's uncle Thomas Salusbury at his fine house called Offley Place in Hertfordshire. It was here that Hester rounded off her education in her late teens. She learned the elaborate art of being a hostess as she arranged dinners for the neighbourhood and hosted hunting parties. It was also where she began to find herself courted by numerous young men. Their proposals were inspired as much by the £10,000 dowry her uncle Thomas had arranged for her, as by her own personal charms. Her father hated the idea of Hester marrying and leaving him and his wife alone together so he ferociously saw off most of her suitors. Hester was in no rush to marry and let him scare off these young men in a bid to protect her mother.[4]

Hester's father was not at home when Henry Thrale first came to Offley Place in 1758. Without him to scare off this new suitor, the two Hesters began to get to know the charming young Henry. 'My Mother seemed exceedingly struck with Mr Thrale's Person and Behaviour,' wrote seventeen-year-old Hester, 'she had no Notion

She told me that very night, of a Man so handsome, so well educated, and so well bred.'[5]

Henry Thrale's father Ralph had been born at Offley – not in the grand house, but in a cottage in the grounds where his family had once lived as tenants (and that now served as a dog kennel). Ralph worked for his uncle Edmund Halsey who owned the Anchor brewery in Southwark. Like his uncle before him, Ralph rose from the malthouse floor to the counting house. When Uncle Edmund died, the business passed to Ralph who worked hard and prospered. The brewery grew. Ralph married and had a son and three daughters. He began to buy properties – including an estate in Streatham. Ralph sent his son Henry to the best schools, and then to Oxford. He ensured that his son spent time with the nobility so that he would pick up their manners, and encouraged him to go on the Grand Tour to round off his education.

At Offley Place, mother Hester and uncle Thomas doted on Henry Thrale. Very soon after meeting him, they decided he would be the perfect match for young Hester. While mother Hester gushed about his manners and learning and looks, awkward Thomas commended him as a '*real Sportsman*' – one of the highest compliments he ever bestowed. When Hester's father returned to Offley Place, he was not impressed to learn that his wife and brother had conspired to find a husband for his daughter. Nothing could turn him against a plan like knowing that his wife supported it. He raged against the suggested match, telling his daughter (who had little feeling one way or the other) that Henry was a dandy and a poor businessman, and that he had several mistresses. He ordered his daughter to stay away from Henry. Obedient Hester submitted to his authority without question.[6]

Shortly after Hester had thus meekly resigned herself to her father's will, he died very suddenly of an apoplexy. Mother and daughter moved to Soho's Dean Street where Hester's mother gave open encouragement to Henry Thrale to visit them. Mother Hester had never been much provided for by her parents or her husband – she was entranced by the idea of her daughter marrying someone wealthy. She knew that the Thrale brewery reliably produced tens of thousands of barrels of ale each year and yielded a good income.

Henry, son of a self-made man, liked the idea of marrying a woman of high birth who could trace her family back to royalty. It was a marriage of convenience on both sides. Hester never felt particularly attracted to Henry, though she admitted that his 'Person is manly, his Countenance agreeable, his Eyes steady and of the deepest Blue'.[7]

In the summer of 1763, six months after the death of Hester's father, Henry Thrale sent a note to Dean Street asking if he could come and see them to discuss a 'very interesting Subject'. When he arrived that next afternoon, he asked for Hester's hand in marriage. With little thought for romance, he rambled on about dowries and the prospect of her inheriting Offley Place, before remembering his manners and tacking on a hasty assurance that he would marry her even if she inherited nothing. A final declaration that he would marry Hester even if she were in debt concluded his speechifying. 'Such Offers were surely irresistible,' Hester wrote drily in her autobiography many years later.[8] Encouraged by her mother, she said yes. Henry Thrale duly made off for Offley Place to ask consent from Uncle Thomas, who was responsible for the dowry.

Before they wed, Hester and Henry Thrale only spent five minutes alone together and even that was an accident, a slip made by Hester's mother who usually hovered, always anxious that her daughter's reputation remain unsullied. The wedding took place in October 1763, at St Anne's Church in Dean Street. Then the party (which consisted of just five people: Henry and Hester, her mother and her uncle, and the priest who had performed the ceremony) travelled to Streatham to celebrate the event. Years later, Hester Thrale described her first impressions of the house that would come to be the centre of her world: 'a little squeezed miserable Place with a wretched Court before it, & all these noble Elm Trees out upon the Common. Such Furniture too! I can but laugh when it crosses my Recollection.'[9] This was before Henry's mania for building took hold. Soon he would add the wings with their drawing room, dining room and the beloved library. He would lay lawns and shrubberies, dig out a pond, build greenhouses, and design the gravel walk that meandered around the property.

At Streatham, Hester Thrale's mother moved in with the new couple. Mother and daughter spent their days reading aloud to each other, playing backgammon, and working carpets. They barely saw Henry, who passed his days in the brewery's counting house and his evenings at the opera or at the infamous Carlisle House on Soho Square. This was the home of the impresario Mrs Cornelys, an Austrian soprano who had once taken Casanova as a lover. In Soho, Cornelys hosted raucous dances, card parties, concerts and elaborate masquerades. As his wife sat quietly at home with her needlework, Henry Thrale would while away his evenings in the company of male friends and female dancers, singers or courtesans.

Whenever he did spend an evening at Streatham, he wanted peace. He disliked his neighbours: he refused to have them visit, and told his wife to decline any invitations from them. Occasionally he would invite a friend down from London, but these friends were rarely to his wife's taste; the only one she liked was the playwright Arthur Murphy. Thrale's mother thoroughly approved of the situation, telling her daughter that 'Married women should have no *Friends* . . . but their husbands.'[10] Her mother discouraged her from keeping in touch with old friends, and dissuaded her from befriending Henry's sisters. Thrale did not even have the distraction of domesticity. Her husband said that he did not want her to smell like a kitchen; she was barely mistress of her own house, not allowed so much as to plan a menu.[11] Thrale was growing increasingly lonely. Apart from brief visitations from her husband, she saw only her mother, who had always leaned heavily on her for emotional support.

In September 1764, Thrale's first child Queeney was born at Deadman's Place in Southwark 'sorely against my Will – if any Will I had,' wrote Thrale who had disliked that house from the first time she saw it. The labour was long – lasting from Saturday to Monday. When it finally ended and the baby arrived, the (male) doctor in attendance announced to Thrale that 'it is a Lady Madam; destined to bear what you are this Moment freed from.'[12]

During her lying-in, Henry came to visit Thrale formally in her room two or three times a week. Thrale found her husband's coolness difficult to understand, but her mother assured her that it was quite right for a man to be formal at such a time, and so Thrale accepted it.

At the end of Thrale's month of lying-in, her mother moved back to Soho. Thrale and her husband could live together as a couple for the first time. But this chance to improve their relationship was hampered by Thrale's mother insisting that Hester come and visit her in Soho almost daily.

Thrale's mother and husband encouraged her to breastfeed Queeney, according to the latest trend. Thrale herself was never keen on the practice and was almost relieved when her health started to suffer and her family stopped pressuring her to continue. Henry even procured an ass, stabled with the brewery's many horses, so that his wife could drink its milk and build up her strength. Though stopping breastfeeding may have allowed Thrale to regain her former vigour, it also meant that she could fall pregnant again quickly. Within three months of Queeney's birth, Thrale was with child. Her second child, Frances, was born a few days after Queeney's first birthday. The girl appeared strong at first, but died on the tenth day, of the watery gripes – a particularly severe form of diarrhoea that could kill an infant with terrifying speed.[13] Infant mortality was high then: it has been estimated that between a hundred and fifty and four hundred babies out of every thousand born would not survive to their first birthday.[14]

Thrale had been violently ill throughout the pregnancy. Severe sickness would be a hallmark of almost all her pregnancies. Her twenties and thirties consisted of 'holding my Head over a Bason 6 Months in the Year'. The relentless illness was made worse by the fact that her mother and husband cut off her social life in those few precious months each year when she did feel well. They banned her from attending the theatre for six years. Her mother barred her from contact with her uncle Thomas and ordered her to stop writing to her old tutor Arthur Collier because he was encouraging eccentric notions such as choosing her own reading material. Henry insisted that she spend eight months of the year in Deadman's Place where few would visit her and where she was tormented by lying awake 'listening for Mr. Thrale's Carriage at 2, 3, 4 o'clock in the Morning'.[15]

Instead of cultivating friendships or her mind, Thrale was encouraged to devote herself to Queeney's education, just as her mother had done for her. Obligingly, she threw herself into the task and her educational programme for Queeney was impressive. By the time the child turned two, she knew all the letters of the alphabet (lower and upper case), and could count to twenty as well as recognise all the numbers up to a hundred; she could repeat the *Pater Noster*, identify all the signs of the zodiac on a celestial globe, and name all the ancient gods and their attributes.[16] Though Thrale was a diligent teacher, she wondered whether teaching an infant lists of Greek gods and goddesses was the best use of either her or the child's time. She suspected that her mother and husband were trying to fill her days with pointless tasks.[17]

There were two points of light in these earliest years of motherhood that made things a little more bearable for Thrale. The first had been meeting Samuel Johnson when Queeney was four months old. That meeting in January 1765 took place around the same time that Frances was conceived. Thrale's brilliant new friend lifted her spirits through some of her worst months of sickness. More than that, he gave her a new perspective on her life, and especially on her marriage. She was grateful for this, though he was exceedingly blunt in his advice to her. When, one day, she mentioned her husband's coldness towards her (though she said it without any resentment or expectation that things should be different) Johnson launched on a tirade against Thrale's wifely shortcomings:

> Why how for Heaven's Sake Dearest Madam should any Man delight in a Wife that is to him neither Use nor Ornament? He cannot talk to you about his Business, which you do not understand . . . You divide your Time between your Mamma & your Babies, & wonder you do not by that means become agreable to your Husband.[18]

Thrale was intrigued by the idea of trying to take an interest in her husband's business, and his life more generally. Seeing that there was some truth in Johnson's description of her as a dull wife, she asked her mother's advice. Her mother (who had found survival in distancing herself from her husband) instantly quashed the idea and insisted that Thrale remain in the nursery teaching Queeney rather than becoming 'My Lady Mashtub' at the brewery. And so, for several years, loyally taking her mother's advice over Johnson's, Thrale 'went on in the old Way, brought a Baby once a Year, lost some of them & grew so anxious about the rest, that I now fairly cared for nothing else'. Though she knew in her heart that Johnson was right, she could not break free of the chains that held her.[19] Not yet, anyway.

The second point of light for Thrale in those years was her first attempt at a diary. Many years before she began writing her more ambitious *Thraliana*, she wrote the first entries in her *Children's Book*. She began the book on Queeney's second birthday. It was intended as a record of the births, lives and (too often) the deaths of the children she would carry, but it soon became more than that – it was a unique record of the life of a family, charting loves and passions, arguments and infidelities, the mundane next to the sublime.

Thrale's next child Henry (known as Harry) arrived in February 1767, sixteen months after the loss of Frances. 'Strong and lively . . . he appears likely to live,' she wrote with enormous relief.[20] Between the births of her second and third children, Thrale had found herself a hobby to enliven her days, one that doubled as a way to become closer to her husband: she had begun campaigning on behalf of Henry who had embarked on a political career. He had been put forward as the Member of Parliament for Southwark just a few days before the birth and death of Frances. In the months following the loss of her child, Hester Thrale had found a welcome distraction in going out canvassing for him. She soon discovered she had a natural aptitude for it: she won hearts and minds with her pleasant manner, open countenance and honest speeches. Samuel Johnson joined the campaign team too.

Alongside her new interest in politics, Thrale dutifully continued her daughter's education. By the time Queeney was two and a half years old, she knew all the points of the compass and the planets of the solar system, she could recognise individual comets from drawings, as well as pick out all the major constellations in the night sky. She could name every nation on the globe, all of the bigger islands, and all European and Asian capital cities. The toddler could remember basic rules of grammar and some multiplication tables. She was learning to recite stories gracefully – her repertoire included the tales of Adam and Eve, Perseus and Andromeda, and the Judgement of Paris. Her parents' only concern was that the child could not yet read. Even by the time of her third birthday, she remained what her mother called 'a miserable poor Speller'.[21]

Thrale's fourth baby – Anna Maria – arrived in April 1768, a few weeks after Harry's first birthday. She was the first of the Thrale children to be born at Streatham, rather than Southwark – a small victory for Thrale. It had been another unpleasant pregnancy, made more so by the fact that parliament had been dissolved at the beginning of the year and Thrale had had to help her husband campaign for re-election. This time he had had to fend off a new kind of rival. Republican patriot John Wilkes (who was campaigning for such revolutionary initiatives as votes for the working classes) inspired many radical candidates to stand in this election. Wilkes's supporters demonstrated on the streets in large crowds; the number of his followers seemed to increase each day. Wilkes himself was standing in the constituency of Middlesex, while one of his fellow patriots stood against conservative Henry Thrale. The Thrales were as amazed as anyone when Henry managed to hang onto his seat, seeing off his liberal opponent. Wilkes won the seat in Middlesex, but was arrested a few weeks later for having criticised King George III. His supporters gathered outside the King's Bench Prison in Southwark where he was held, protesting at the unfairness of the charges and the abysmal state of politics in the country. The Riot Act was read to the swelling crowd of protesters. When they refused to disperse, government troops opened fire on the unarmed citizens. The shots could be heard from the Thrale brewery just a few streets away. Seven men were killed in the atrocity that became known as the Massacre of Saint George's Fields.

These political upheavals, where men argued for one ideology or another, rarely seemed to impinge much upon the actual day-to-day lives of women. A few months later, like clockwork, Thrale was pregnant again, her head held over a basin for the rest of the year. Baby Lucy Elizabeth was born in June 1769, when Anna Maria was fourteen months old. 'Large strong and handsome likely to live,' her mother recorded. She was called Lucy after a grandmother, and Elizabeth after Samuel Johnson's deceased wife. Johnson had been well established in the Thrale household for several years now (though he always courteously absented himself when Thrale's confinements drew near). He had been campaigning through several of Thrale's pregnancies for the name Elizabeth to be used, oblivious to the fact that the Thrales had never met his late wife. Eventually, they caved. Johnson was delighted at the name, and at being asked to be the child's godfather wrote that 'I think myself very much honoured by the choice that you have been pleased to make of me to become related to the little Maiden. Let me know when she will want me, and I will very punctually wait on her.'[22] That winter, Thrale's mother took Anna Maria (now aged a year and a half) to live with her in Soho. The Thrales were at the brewery for the winter, and the dirty air of Southwark was not considered healthy for a child, especially a delicate one. Anna Maria was small-boned and showed none of the plumpness expected in a toddler. Yet she seemed to have spirit and passion and to understand what was being said to her from a young age. When she learned to walk, she walked 'with an Air' and, thought Thrale, 'seems to intend being Queen of us all if She lives'. Thrale did not expect her to live. She was so very slight.[23]

Each day, Thrale and Queeney would take the carriage from Deadman's Place to Soho and spend five hours with little Anna. The new bridge opened at Blackfriars that November. Though it made the journey shorter, it was a scary experience as the balustrades were not yet built, and any misstep from a horse threatened to hurl beast, carriage and passengers into the dark waters of the Thames below.[24] In Soho, Thrale found her mother happily spoiling her granddaughter. She joked that such treatment would make the child stuck up, but really Thrale was glad to have the infant so well looked after. With Queeney, Harry, baby Lucy at the brewery and another child on the way, Thrale could not have given Anna such attention as she enjoyed in Dean Street.

The attention was not enough. She began violently vomiting in March 1770, a month shy of her second birthday. Her alarmed grandmother sent for the family physician.

> He purged her very roughly, after having first given her a puke . . .
> fits of languor and screaming succeeding each other by turns . . . Fits
> of Rage . . . threw her into a kind of Delirium: on this they blistered
> her . . . they bled her with Leeches till She lay absolutely insensible.

It was the best treatment on offer at the time, but it was too much for Anna's tiny body. When the doctors gave up, her grandmother continued to sit by her, dipping a feather in wine and brushing it on the toddler's lips, taking hope as the child stirred a little. She continued like this for three days. On the fourth day, she was overcome by a fever. On the eighth day she died. 'I never had much hoped to rear her,' Thrale wrote, knowing that such a weak baby had not stood much chance.[25]

In the wake of Anna Maria's death, Thrale's mother went to stay with relatives in Bath to mourn the child. Though Thrale was mourning too, and anxious about her pregnancy, and nursing baby Lucy through a bad cold, she was also suddenly aware of the fact that this was the first time in her life that she had ever been separated from her mother. Almost seven years into marriage, she was getting better at dealing with her husband too. She felt she had a little freedom to do as she pleased for the first time in her life. Her first trip out was to hear an oratorio at Covent Garden, accompanied by one of her sisters-in-law. Overcome by guilt at the thought of being separated from her children entirely, she brought Queeney along with her. The girl was thrilled to glimpse King George III in the Royal Box. Afterwards, she lorded it over her little brother, impressing the three-year-old with the wonders she had seen. She asked him if he even knew what a king was.

Yes replies Harry, a Picture of a Man, a Sign of a Man's head – no, no, cries the Girl impatiently the King that wears the Crown: do you know what a Crown is – Yes I do, says Harry very well, it is 3s. and 6d.[26]

Though she ventured out a little more, still the children took priority for Thrale. Harry was now old enough to have graduated from nursery petticoats to boyish breeches and he followed in Queeney's erudite footsteps. He could recite his catechism and the basic rules of Latin and Greek grammar; he could name the Muses, the Fates, the Furies and the Greek gods; he knew the days of the week, the seasons, the months, and could count to twenty without missing one. More than that, he was a sweet and gentle soul. Where his older sister was obstinate, headstrong, and often sullen and insolent, Harry was sweet and kind. He loved and was loved easily. He was strong too – able to carry a bag containing twenty-seven shillings all in coppers from the brewery's counting house to the breakfast parlour of Deadman's Place.

This painting was displayed at the Royal Academy in 1779 and later printed in a ladies' pocketbook which circulated widely. In it, nine notable women are depicted as the nine Muses of classical mythology. On the left are classicist Elizabeth Carter, writer Anna Barbauld and artist Angelica Kauffmann (sitting at the easel). In the centre is singer Eliza Sheridan. The right-hand group consists of writers Hannah More and Charlotte Lennox standing, with historian Catharine Macaulay, *salonnière* Elizabeth Montagu and writer Elizabeth Griffith sitting.

Elizabeth Robinson (later Montagu) was in her early twenties when this miniature portrait of her dressed as Anne Boleyn was commissioned for a gold and enamel friendship box, *c.*1740.

Elizabeth and Edward Montagu with Elizabeth's younger sister Sarah Robinson (later Scott) at Sandleford, the Montagus' country estate in Berkshire, 1744.

Hester Thrale with her eldest daughter Queeney. This portrait by Joshua Reynolds formed part of the 'Streatham Worthies' series which hung in the library at Streatham Park, 1777–8.

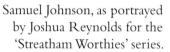

Samuel Johnson, as portrayed by Joshua Reynolds for the 'Streatham Worthies' series.

Samuel Johnson (left) shows off his wit while Hester Thrale pours tea for the assembled guests at one of her literary breakfasts, c.1770.

Frances Burney in her early thirties, sporting a Lunardi bonnet which became fashionable after Vincenzo Lunardi's first balloon flight from London in 1784.

This portrait of Hannah More was commissioned by fellow Bluestocking Frances Boscawen in 1786. More wrote that she had 'a repugnance to having my picture taken', but Boscawen cajoled her into the sitting by promising to read to her throughout.

Mezzotint based on a portrait of Ann Yearsley painted by a supporter named Sarah Shiells in 1787 as part of a campaign to rebuild Yearsley's reputation after her dispute with More.

Hester Mulso (later Mulso Chapone) in her mid-twenties, shortly after writing her famous 'Letters on Filial Obedience' to Samuel Richardson.

Elizabeth Griffith as a young woman in the 1750s.

Samuel Richardson reading aloud from his new book at North End, 1751. From left to right: Richardson in 'his usual morning dress', Mulso's brothers Thomas and Edward, Hester Mulso, Mary Prescott (who would later marry Thomas Mulso), the poet-priest John Duncombe and (in the foreground) his future wife Susanna Highmore.

Elizabeth Carter dressed as Minerva, the Roman goddess of wisdom, c.1735–41. Carter has substituted a volume of Plato for Minerva's spear.

Catharine Macaulay, dressed in Roman-style robes, signals her allegiance to democracy, 1775. Macaulay's own *History of England* rests on a plinth bearing the inscription: 'Government: a power delegated for the happiness of mankind'.

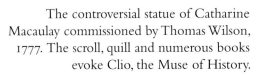

The controversial statue of Catharine Macaulay commissioned by Thomas Wilson, 1777. The scroll, quill and numerous books evoke Clio, the Muse of History.

Catharine Macaulay and Thomas Wilson at Alfred House. This cartoon was published in May 1777, just a few weeks after Macaulay's infamous forty-sixth birthday party.

A satirical print circulated after Hester Thrale's wedding to Gabriel Piozzi in 1784. Thrale (right) declares, 'Your Music has ravished me and your Instrument is large & delightful'; next to her, Piozzi replies, 'And me like de Museek of your Guineas'. Samuel Johnson (far left) observes, 'She has quitted Literature for a Fiddlestick'.

A satirical print showing women brawling at a Bluestocking salon. Circulated in 1815, after the heyday of the Bluestockings, it reflects the early nineteenth-century backlash against learned ladies.

Streatham Park as it appeared in the 1790s when Hester Thrale Piozzi took her second husband to live there. She wrote in the *Thraliana*: 'Streatham looks divinely itself . . . the House has an Appearance of Gayety never attempted in Mr Thrale's time.'

Montagu House, Portman Square, London. Completed in 1781, Elizabeth Montagu lived there until her death in 1800.

Elizabeth Montagu, in her fifties, as portrayed by Joshua Reynolds, 1775.

Thrale spent her days tending to the children, and her evenings (when she could) with Johnson. One May evening in 1770, while sitting up late with Johnson and her husband at Deadman's Place, Thrale was suddenly overcome by violent pains. She was not expecting to give birth for another two months. She hastened to her bed and hoped desperately that the spasms would pass but within two hours she was delivered of a very small and very weak baby girl. They called her Susanna Arabella. She was two months premature – no one expected her to survive. The family physician said he had never seen such a small child make it to her first birthday. Johnson tried to comfort Thrale.

A few months after the birth of tiny Susanna, Thrale was pregnant again when she received an unexpected message to say that her uncle Thomas was dying. Her mother had forced Thrale to cut contact with him soon after he had settled her dowry but now Thrale felt brave enough to stand up to her mother and decided to see him before he died. Her mother tried everything in her power to stop Thrale making the journey to Offley Place but Thrale was determined. At Offley, she was relieved to find Uncle Thomas out of danger. He welcomed her warmly and she stayed the night with her relations. She set off for Streatham the next morning but as the carriage jolted her home over unpaved roads, she began to bleed. 'The agitation of my Mind added to the Journey made me miscarry,' she wrote in a footnote to the *Thraliana* eight years later. 'But as I had now Children enough, nobody much cared about that: my Health indeed never was much the Cause of their Concern.'[27]

She recovered quickly and was pregnant again before the end of the year. Thrale's older children were thriving but Thrale was worried about Lucy, who turned two in the summer of 1771. The bad cold she had had the previous year (around the time of Anna Maria's death) had settled in her head and caused abscesses in her ears. The infected ears ran constantly with pus. Johnson told Thrale of a child he had once known who had died from such a complaint. It shocked Thrale dreadfully and all that night she lay awake fretting about it. It was during this pregnancy too that Thrale's mother, while playing with Harry in the green parlour, was tumbled by the energetic little boy whose head knocked hard into her chest. Within a few days, the bruised area had become a lump.[28]

Worried about her mother and Lucy, Thrale found the final months of this pregnancy especially wearisome. Johnson left Streatham on midsummer's day, clearing out as usual just before Thrale's confinement was expected. Nine days later, still no baby, a visitor described Thrale being 'of pale face and monstrous size'. Johnson used his time away from Streatham to plot the chemistry laboratory he would build in the kitchen garden at Streatham. He bought iron, copper and lead ores so that he could show Queeney and Harry how lead was smelted. He asked if the builders working on the house could leave him a hundred or so loose bricks to make the furnace.

In late July, Thrale gave birth to a daughter and named her Sophia: 'large & likely to live,' she recorded. The baby had come almost a month after she was expected. Her large size had meant that it was a difficult birth. Even Henry Thrale seemed to show some sympathy for his wife.[29]

Johnson's return to Streatham in early August saw a flurry of activity as he started making revisions to his *Dictionary* and, much more excitingly as far as Queeney and Harry were concerned, began work on his laboratory. Thrale was pleased to see the children busy and even joined in the experiments herself once she had recovered from the difficult birth of Sophia. She had five living children now: Queeney and Harry were robust; Lucy, despite her constant ear infections, was large and stout; the premature Susanna, though 'small, ugly & lean', had defied everyone's expectations and made it past her first birthday; and Sophia was a bonny, sturdy baby. Despite seventeen pregnancies, this was the largest number of healthy children Thrale would ever have alive at any one time.* It was one of the happiest summers of her life.

As 1771 slipped into 1772, family life at Streatham continued apace. Harry, now five, was an adept reader. He dutifully turned the pages of *The Pilgrim's Progress*; he enjoyed it, but really he preferred

---

* After the birth of Penelope in 1772, Thrale had six children alive – until Penelope's death ten hours later. Likewise in the summer of 1775, she had a two-month period after the birth of Frances Anna and before the death of Ralph, where she also had six children who lived, but Ralph's ill health did not allow her to enjoy this brief period.

reading gruesome and sensational tales from the newspaper. Always honest, he declared an improving book on Jesus and the apostles to be 'monstrous dull'.[30] Little Susanna reached her second birthday unscathed. Though her mother described her as being the colour 'of an ill painted Wall grown dirty', she was at least alive, against all earlier predictions. She had crooked legs and her sisters and brother called her 'little Crab'. Susanna was prescribed purging, cold baths and a tobacco-smoke enema for a hernia. Little wonder that she cried incessantly. Sophia, not yet one, had to have a boil on her neck lanced. Thrale's mother's illness was troubling her too: the doctors had confirmed the lump in her breast as cancer, but there was little that could be done for her. She was increasingly in pain and suffering from weakness. Thrale herself, pregnant again, had to nurse her children and her mother in between her own bouts of violent vomiting.

It was into this chaotic household that Henry Thrale brought the news that the brewery was about to go bankrupt. Henry had appeared pensive and gloomy for some time, barely able to sleep or eat. Now he admitted to his wife that cartloads of bad hops had spoiled all the beer he had hoped to brew that year. This was indeed bad news, but Thrale suspected that the real reason for his concern was that he had been caught up in the Fordyce scandal – a credit crisis which had hit Britain after the banker Alexander Fordyce had lost hundreds of thousands of pounds by shorting stocks in the East India Company. Twenty banks had gone out of business and thousands of businesses suffered. Thrale, knowing that beer never went out of fashion, was not unduly worried about the bad hops; she suggested trying to save the beer by reformulating it, adding in a few new ingredients to mask any unpleasant taste. Henry turned pale.

When Thrale pressed him further on the state of the beer, he came clean. Together with his friend, the chemist Humphrey Jackson, Henry had deliberately bought the bad hops for a low price.[31] Jackson was a famous chemist and Henry was impressed by him. Jackson was elected that same year as a Fellow of the elite Royal Society – a mark of success that Henry found reassuring. Later, the Royal Society would dismiss Jackson as nothing but a charlatan. Jackson had convinced Henry that he had discovered a way to brew beer without using malt. He had also convinced him that those cheap bad hops could be made good with a little chemical connivance. But Jackson's manipulation of the naively trusting Henry went beyond beer: he had persuaded Henry to spend a vast amount of money on building him a copper still to distil potions to harden the wood used to build ships. The copper alone cost £2,000. The warehouse in East Smithfield where the still was hidden, along with dozens of vats containing thousands of hogsheads of Jackson's experimental liquors, didn't come cheap either.

The brewery clerks all thought Jackson's schemes were mad and had refused to have anything to do with him. When Henry had taken Jackson's side, the clerks turned against him too, threatening to quit en masse. But Hester Thrale had always been beloved by the brewery staff (for she had always taken an interest in them and their wives and their children). She went to talk to the clerks in the hope that she could make them stay. For the first time, she took a stand against her husband and insisted that he distance himself from Jackson. Henry, in a heap, and more than a little awed by his newly confident wife, did as he was told. With Jackson gone, Thrale was able to talk the clerks into staying.

'Money was raised, the Beer was mended,' Thrale wrote lightly in the *Thraliana*. In reality, the brewery was £130,000 in debt – a terrifyingly large amount of money. Thrale, who had never had any experience in business, stepped up to the task of fundraising and restructuring the business. Henry watched in amazed silence as his wife (heavily pregnant again), talked with suppliers and merchants, and arranged loans, even enduring hours in a carriage to Brighton so she could beg a loan from an old family friend. Johnson had been right all those years before when he had advised Thrale to take an interest in her husband's business. 'We soon began to understand each other,' she wrote of the man to whom she had been married for nine years, 'we grew prosperous, and loved each other.'[32]

Things at the brewery were just being brought under control again when Thrale gave birth to baby Penelope in September 1772. The child lived for ten hours. A hurried entry in *The Children's Book* records this brief life: 'Penelope Thrale was born – liv'd but 10 hours, looked black & could not breathe freely – poor little Maid.' Thrale did not have time to grieve for her – the brewery took up much of her time, her mother's illness had progressed and they knew that her death was drawing near too.

Thrale found some comfort in her other children. As soon as her lying-in was over, she was out in the gardens at Streatham enjoying the last warm days of the year. Five-year-old Harry could run as fast as his mother now, his stout legs pounding along the springy lawn; eight-year-old Queeney could run faster but sat out the races so as not to show anyone up. The educational programme at Streatham kept everyone busy. Lucy was three now. She could read some of the Psalms and the Epistles; she knew her two- and three-times tables; she could say how many pennies were in a shilling, and how many shillings in a pound. But Thrale could not fully enjoy her daughter's delight in learning – she was too worried about her ear infections. The pus, which ran constantly, began to smell so bad that none of the nursery maids wanted to share the little girl's bed anymore. The inflammation seemed to be spreading further into the child's head and no remedy could be found. Thrale was heartbroken to see her sweet girl so afflicted. Though she tried not to admit as much, Lucy was her favourite. 'I am indeed accused of a partial Fondness towards her,' was the closest she got. 'She is so lovely one cannot resist her coaxing . . . Lucy is softness & kindness itself.'[33]

That winter, Thrale refused to spend the cold dark months at the brewery. She had done so much for her husband's business that he relented and let her and the children stay in Streatham. She did travel up weekly to Deadman's Place to keep an eye on the books, to visit the clerks and to make sure that there was no sign of any more chemical experimentation in the brewhouse. Thrale's mother moved to Streatham that winter too; her illness meant that she needed more and more care and she was no longer able to live alone in Soho.

Being in Streatham was an improvement on being in Southwark, but between nursing her mother, advancing Harry from being able to recite the rules of Latin grammar to actually reading in the language, and keeping on top of brewery paperwork, Thrale had little time to enjoy it. It didn't help that the press had taken to publishing stories about Henry's sordid dalliances. Thrale had known about Henry's womanising before she married him. She had known where he was on those nights when he stayed out late, and those nights when he never came home at all. It was one thing to put up with this privately, but quite another to have newspapers reminiscing about his former mistresses. The courtesan and sometime actress Grace Hart (often called Polly) specialised in making baronets fall in love with her, but she had briefly stooped to entertaining the self-made brewer – a man 'more famed for his amours than celebrated for his beer', according to one popular magazine.[34] When Henry had first begun courting his future wife, he still brazenly carried a snuff box with a picture of Hart on the outside. That particular affair had fizzled out before too long, but there were plenty of other women. Johnson struggled to see anything wrong in Henry's behaviour, saying that 'between a man and his wife, a husband's infidelity is nothing . . . wise married women don't trouble themselves about infidelity in their husbands.'[35] It was a sentiment very much in keeping with the mores of the time and Thrale accepted it as part of life. Around the same time, another newspaper article appeared, insinuating that Johnson was the real father of little Harry Thrale, a story with no basis in fact, but still more publicity that Thrale could do without.[36]

By now, Thrale was often sleeping in her mother's room to tend to her. The cancer was progressing rapidly, the lump in her breast was swollen and black, and sometimes bled through her clothes.[37] She was often in so much pain she could not sleep, and struggled to breathe unless she was propped up at night. Thrale remembered all that her mother had done for her and vowed to nurse her unceasingly. But she was exhausted, and unable to give everyone the attention they needed. And she was, of course, pregnant again, and ill again. 'Nobody can guess what a Winter this has been to me, & big with Child too again God help me!' Thrale rose one morning after a sleepless night and walked Harry out of Streatham Park and across the common to the village nearby. She deposited him at a small school for boys there run by a respected clergyman well known to the family. Thrale was thankful to have one fewer child to educate; Harry's grandmother was delighted that she lived long enough to see him become a schoolboy; Johnson was pleased that the boy would begin reading Milton; Harry was relieved to find that the school was not overly strict and that he could climb trees between lessons.[38]

He did not board, but ambled home across the common each evening in time for supper.

Susanna – the premature baby nicknamed 'Little Crab' – turned three this year. It was a milestone that meant she was very likely to make it to adulthood. Her health was much improved, the hernia almost healed, though she was still a little off-colour. This green-tinged girl was unusually short and unusually cross-tempered. Even her doting grandmother joked that she must have swallowed a wasp as a baby to make her so peevish. But she was a bright child and had already memorised the catechism and several hymns in Latin. Her big sister Lucy was still having trouble with her ear, so a new lead-based treatment began, alongside a strict diet, severe purging and sarsaparilla tea.[39]

This was the moment that Johnson, who had been at his London house, chose to ask if he could come out to Streatham. He had an infection in his one good eye, and longed for Thrale's maternal ministrations. But looking after her mother, Lucy, and everyone else left no time for Johnson. He came, despite her clearly not wishing to have him there just then. He annoyed her endlessly, with his gloom and constant demands for attention.

He was still at the house when Thrale's mother died in the summer of 1773. After a long illness, Hester Salusbury had a peaceful death, surrounded by her daughter, son-in-law, grandchildren and Johnson, who had become a dear friend. 'The pulse kept beating regularly till 6 in the Afternoon when It fluttered awhile – and then stopt – & stopped forever.' Her mother, though often controlling and manipulative when she had been younger, had mellowed in later years. She was Thrale's closest friend. She had adored her grandchildren and happily pitched in to family life at Streatham, helping to raise and educate the children, and acting as Thrale's confidante through countless family dramas. They had never been apart for more than twelve days. Now she was gone, and to whom, wondered a bereft Thrale,

> shall I tell the little Foibles of my heart, the Tendernesses of my Husband, or the reparties of my Children? to whom shall I now recount the Conversations of the day? & from whom hope Applause for the Labors of Education? to whom shall I carry my Criticism

of a Book, secure of Approbation if the Remark be a good one, &
certain of Secresy if detected in being absurd? with whom shall I
talk over Events long past, Characters known only by ourselves, and
Accidents we have together been sharers in?

She had asked to be buried not with her husband in Wales, but in the
church at Streatham where three of her grandchildren already lay.[40]

The death of Thrale's mother changed the atmosphere at Streatham.
She had always pressured Thrale to keep the family aloof from society
and had discouraged her from making friends. She had even held a
strong dislike of Samuel Johnson for many years, though he had won
her over in the end. Now, without her mother to please, Thrale could
begin to invite guests of her own choosing. Two months after her
mother's death, Thrale invited the painters Frances and Joshua Reynolds for dinner at Streatham. Joshua Reynolds (older than his sister by
six years) was the more famous of the pair, but Frances was a talented
artist in her own right – though her main occupation was keeping
house for Joshua. There seemed always to be a tension between the
siblings, which Thrale put down to jealousy, writing, 'perhaps she
paints too well, or has learned too much Latin, and is a better Scholar
than her Brother.'[41] The Scottish poet and philosopher James Beattie
joined the party that night too, as well as writer Oliver Goldsmith and
the Italian writer and critic Giuseppe Baretti. Despite the absence of
Johnson (in the Hebrides) literary conversation flowed that night in
the library, and Thrale shone as a hostess.

Not long after this dinner party, Lucy began to feel unwell. An
alarmed Thrale tried to guess what the problem might be and to
think up a suitable remedy. The other children laughed at their
mother, always fussing over their health; they assured her that Lucy
was as saucy as ever. Yet a few days later, the foetid smell of her old
ear infection returned. The family physician was not overly concerned and suggested sarsaparilla tea again. The child was fading, but
only Thrale seemed to realise quite how poorly she was. She sought
a second opinion, and Lucy received a blister behind the ear – a
channel through which the infection could drain from the body. It
achieved little. 'The Child was going, & oh what were my Feelings

for my Lucy? my Dear, my favourite Girl!' Another physician said that the infection had got into Lucy's brain, and advised consulting a fourth medic, who recommended rough purging. The maids were enraged at this harsh treatment; they worried that Lucy's illness was exacerbated by years of purgings. Next, a large blister was raised on Lucy's head – this could be done with hot plaster, or with a caustic powder made from the secretions of the blister beetle. The child grew steadily worse. Fever overtook her body and delirium followed. She was bled with leeches, which seemed to have some good effect, even giving her enough energy to sit up and eat something. She was given a camphor julep to drink and her body began to sweat. Her mother hoped that the sweet julep could keep Lucy alive. But it was not enough to sustain her. The little girl died aged four years and five months.[42]

In the midst of all this, Thrale's new baby arrived. Ralph Thrale was born on 8 November 1773, a fortnight before Lucy's death. It was only when writing of Lucy's last days that Thrale hurriedly wrote Ralph's name in *The Children's Book*.

Henry Thrale was proud to have a second son. But Hester Thrale was worried that the stresses during her pregnancy – the deaths of her mother and Lucy, a bout of measles in the household, the additional news that her uncle Thomas had died without leaving her anything in his will – had affected the baby. He was the ninth baby Thrale had borne alive. She knew babies well and, even before he was two months old, Ralph struck her as being less alert than expected. People who saw him only in passing (including his father) thought that he was a fine boy but Thrale was worried. At eight months old, Ralph seemed 'strangely backward somehow in his Understanding'.[43] She tried to gloss over her concerns, telling herself that if he should live and thrive, his understanding would come in time. When he turned one, Thrale recorded, he had a healthy colour in his cheeks but he made no effort to form words as her other children had by that age.

Ralph's big brother Harry was six and a half now – 'the very best Boy in the World', his doting mother thought.[44] A lively cheeky boy, he frequently got into scrapes – earning himself a black eye with over-adventurous climbing, and making himself sick by gorging on cherries. Queeney was ten, a sombre and fiercely intelligent girl who refused to show any affection for anyone. She was old enough now for a live-in tutor. Thrale chose Giuseppe Baretti who had attended that first dinner party. A clever teacher, he did not try to cram Queeney's head with grammatical rules, but instead had her write funny dialogues about the world she knew: the time Harry pulled a cow's tail and the time he got into trouble for throwing a firecracker at Old Nan the maid; stories about Old Nurse who drank too much brandy; imagined chats between the animals of Streatham – a dog and a cat who argued over the unrest in America, a peacock and peahens who debated world affairs, and the grumblings of the coach-horses Poppet and Ramper who had to pull cartloads of heavy children. There were dialogues too about how the serious little girl would forget herself and bounce on the armchairs.[45] Though Baretti may have been an innovative teacher, he was a decidedly undiplomatic house guest. He frequently enraged Thrale by undermining her, or by failing to observe the rules she set for the children. Susanna (Thrale's least favourite child) was sent to a boarding school in Kensington aged three years and ten months. Johnson, who had always championed the 'Little Crab', gave her a Bible and a prayer book as a leaving gift. The toddler Sophia remained at home. She was healthy and stout and promised to be a fine girl.[46]

Thrale wanted peace, and time at Streatham, but news came that parliament was to be dissolved – there was to be an election. Thrale would have to canvass to help Henry keep his seat, which meant the family had to decamp to the brewery. 'I thought to have lived at Streatham in quiet and comfort,' she wrote,

> [to] have kissed my children and cuffed them by turns, and had a place always for them to play in, and here I must be shut up in that odious dungeon, where nobody will come near me, the children are to be sick for want of air, and I am never to see a face but Mr. Johnson's. Oh, what a life that is! and how truly do I abhor it![47]

Thrale's mood was not helped by the fact that she was pregnant again. Still, she threw herself into canvassing and Henry managed to hold onto his seat – just. 'His best Friends say he may thank his Wife for his Seat,' Hester Thrale wrote in *The Children's Book*. But Henry would never do something as unmanly as admit that his wife propped up his political career.

The seat secure, family life began to get back to normal. It was decided to inoculate Ralph against smallpox, as the other children had been. He was just over a year old, and strong enough, they hoped, to fend off infection. Inoculation usually resulted in a few small pustules appearing on the skin. The older Thrale children had never had more than fifty pustules during their inoculations, but now suddenly Ralph's pustules multiplied and enlarged so much that they began to run into each other. The boy was covered with sores. 'Vastly ill – dying I think,' Thrale wrote as the surgeon who had performed the inoculation told her that it was the worst case he had ever seen.[48] She sat up with the little boy, night after night. And then, slowly, his fever came down, and the pustules seemed to recede a little. The boy was through the worst of it. He would live, but he seemed changed by the experience. Never the quickest of the Thrale children, he now struck Thrale as being even further behind in his development than before. He was languid and without any strength. He could barely muster enough energy to cry as new teeth pushed through the soft flesh of his gums.

After so long tending to the sickly Ralph with every cure she could think of, the nursery at Streatham smelt like a hospital. Thrale had the wallpaper taken down and new paper hung, she had all the soft furnishings washed and aired, for fear that the new baby – due in a few months – would catch the smallpox too. 'God give us a quiet Winter!' she implored in December 1774, as she oversaw preparations for the new nursery.[49]

Thrale's wish was granted. Susanna returned from boarding school and seemed a wholly different child. Thrale now found her a joy to be around. No longer a 'crab', the four-year-old could read elegantly and with emphasis and recite the catechism in English and French. She was learning joined-up handwriting, and was good enough at needlework to make little gifts for her siblings. She had grown pretty and graceful in her time at Kensington. Three-year-old Sophia was healthy, handsome and good-humoured. Thrale planned to tutor her at Streatham, with a little help from Queeney. Harry, as always, was the delight of his mother's heart. Each evening he would come to his mother's dressing room to do his school exercises, 'and we always part after that is over pleased with each other,' wrote a contented Thrale, 'he is so rational, so attentive, so good, nobody can help being pleased with him.'[50] This was the winter too that Thrale was first introduced to Elizabeth Montagu. Only Ralph, so lethargic he seemed to be fading away, perturbed Thrale's peace.

That April, Henry Thrale discovered a growth in his nose and called a surgeon to extract it. While the surgeon was at the house, Henry insisted that Ralph be brought downstairs so that the medical man could see him. Hester Thrale resisted, not wanting to wake the sleeping infant. More than that, she knew in her heart what he would say. The surgeon took one look at the child and bluntly cried out, 'What d'ye talk of Sickness & Teething . . . This Boy is in a State of Fatuity.' Thrale had always known that Ralph was not developing like his siblings, but to have a diagnosis, to have a doctor say that his mental powers were unlikely ever to develop further, was devastating – 'Oh how this dreadful Sentence did fill me with Horror!' The surgeon guessed that it might have been caused by an accident, or perhaps had happened during his birth. Thrale fretted that she had brought harm on her son by being so anxious when she was pregnant with him – those awful months nursing Lucy and her mother before their deaths. She fretted that the pride she had always taken in her learning was being punished: 'has the flattery of my Friends made me too proud of my own Brains? & must these poor Children suffer for my crime?' she asked the *Thraliana*.[51]

Now, as well as worrying about Ralph, his health and his future, there was a further pressure on the Thrales. This was a time when disabled children were not accepted by society and Thrale felt that the diagnosis was 'a Thing to hide & be ashamed of whilst we live'.[52] Johnson tried to comfort her, to little avail. Thrale prayed for the fortitude to keep going, and to do her best for the boy. As always, she turned to her armoury of medical cures. She fixed upon cold baths. When she consulted the family physician on this idea, he replied off-handedly, 'any thing Dear Madam that may contribute to quiet your Mind', before adding callously, 'but while you are trying every Means to preserve the Life of little Master I fear your *truest* Friends will scarce be able to wish You Success.'[53] Steadfast in the face of such an attitude, the cold baths began.

Ralph was eighteen months old when his new sister Frances Anna appeared in May 1775 and took her place in the nursery. It was the longest gap that Thrale had ever enjoyed between births. Calling the baby after her two older sisters – Frances who had died aged ten days from the watery gripes, and delicate Anna who had died just before her second birthday – might have seemed to tempt fate, but Thrale was too distracted thinking about Ralph to dwell on the significance of names. 'The Situation of the youngest Boy pierces my very Soul,' she wrote in *The Children's Book*. The birth of Frances and the decline of Ralph were closely intertwined in the pages of the notebook. During her lying-in, Thrale began to plan a trip to the family's holiday cottage in Brighton ('Brighthelmstone' as it still was then) where Ralph could be taken for sea-bathing every day. In the same entry, she first described little Fanny – a 'small delicate Child'. She gave thanks that Frances seemed healthy, despite the stresses Thrale had endured during the pregnancy.[54] She was largely alone with her thoughts during these difficult weeks – Johnson was away from Streatham for the confinement, and Henry (living in the same house) visited her chamber only three times a week.

Johnson thought the trip to Brighton sounded like an excellent idea, though possibly he believed it would do the mother more good than the son. Still, always fond of the Thrale children, he joked about the boy's first tour, writing that 'Ralph like other young Gentlemen will travel for improvement.' Ralph, like other young gentlemen, was to make his tour without his parents. His mother could not be excused from domestic duty, so he was conducted to Brighton by Old Nurse, who wrote often with encouraging words. After a few weeks, Thrale found time to travel down to Brighton. She could not see the cause of Old Nurse's optimism – she found Ralph worse rather than better, 'more heavy more lethargick & insensible than ever I had known him'. A local apothecary confirmed that the boy's 'Brain was oppress'd' – he himself had lost one son with a similar condition, and had another still alive but seriously unwell. The apothecary suggested calling in a physician who practised locally. He recommended blisters and stimulatives for the child. After a few days of this, Ralph seemed to improve a little, even gaining weight. Thrale returned to Streatham leaving Ralph with Old Nurse, the apothecary and the physician. But only five days later, Thrale was summoned urgently to the coast. Ralph had begun having fits. 'When I went down on the 13th I found him dead.'[55] He was buried in Brighton, and Thrale travelled home alone.

The Thrales left Streatham after the death of their son for a trip to France. They travelled to Dover where they boarded a neat little packet boat on a fine sunny day. The packets ran from Dover to Calais, ferrying people and parcels to and fro across the Channel, promising Hester Thrale an escape from her cares. The night before they departed, she prayed fervently, the words tumbling from her pen onto the blank page before her – 'Oh thou most adorable Creator, Redeemer & Comforter of Man – most holy Trinity preserve my Children! . . . Thou who takest account of even the *Sparrow's* Young ones – have mercy upon mine.' Ever since losing Ralph, she had grown more and more concerned about the children. When four-year-old Sophia complained of a headache, Thrale was terrified into agonies, convinced that the child was already as good as dead. A few hours later, Sophia was polishing off a hearty dinner and looking forward to the arrival of her dancing master. 'I believe Ma'amey that Headach of mine was only a Mad Dream,' she lisped complacently to her mother. Such mad and dreadful dreams consumed Thrale now, she saw everywhere signs of her children's imminent deaths.[56]

The trip to France was to be the antidote to Thrale's visions of doom. Clambering awkwardly onto the sloop that bright September morning in 1775, the sea breeze sharp with salt, the cries of the gulls overhead, Thrale looked forward to peace. The tides were favourable and the winds fair. The Thrale party – Hester, Henry and Queeney, as well as Samuel Johnson and Giuseppe Baretti, the manservant Sam, and maid Molly – were the only passengers aboard that day. It was Thrale's first trip overseas and, as the sloop drew away from the shore, she began to anticipate the adventures that lay ahead: the sights she would see, the people she would meet, the new books, the new ideas. Her daydreaming was soon interrupted by Queeney's violent vomiting. It was a memorable eleventh birthday for the girl, who continued ill all the way to Calais. It seemed an omen to Thrale, as her modest attempt at distraction from the cares of motherhood was quickly and messily brought back to earth.

Once landed at Calais, the party began to inch their way towards Paris, stopping frequently to marvel at churches and cathedrals, libraries and colleges, convents and monasteries. Baretti, who was acting as cicerone, insisted that they all rise early to fit in as much sightseeing as possible in each town along the route. They travelled through St Omer and Arras, before heading for Rouen. In the coach – pulled by scraggy-looking post-horses – Thrale was reading *Letters on the English Nation* by Madame du Boccage, the poet and luminary who had graced one of Elizabeth Montagu's earliest literary break-fasts. At Rouen, Thrale was delighted to meet Boccage's sister, who promised an introduction to the great lady herself in Paris.

Leaving Rouen, the party saw their first vineyards – 'not half so pretty to the Eye as a Hop Garden', they declared patriotically (though the fruit was much pleasanter to pluck off the vine and gobble in the late September sunshine than any hop could be).[57] As they rumbled along the fertile Seine valley, there was a sudden commotion. Where the track began to run steeply downwards, the postillion on the lead carriage – bearing Henry, Queeney and Baretti – suddenly lost his seat. The horses were spooked, the traces broken and the carriage picked up alarming speed as it rolled out of control down the hill. Henry jumped from the carriage hoping to be able to take hold of one of the animals and regain control, but he was flung sideways into a chalk pit. It was Sam the manservant who came to the rescue, coax-ing his unwilling mount to catch up with the carriage and bringing the horses to a halt. Queeney and Baretti were shaken but unharmed, but when Henry was pulled out of the chalk pit, he was white as a sheet and barely able to stand.

Henry was helped back into the carriage. Over the bumpy track, they travelled as slowly as they could until they came to the next town. A local surgeon was found and confirmed, to everyone's relief, that Henry had not broken anything. But, said the surgeon, Henry needed to be bled, and Paris was the best place for that. They were just a few hours' ride from the capital but it was late, so Baretti took Henry to Paris alone, while the rest of the party found lodgings for the night. When Hester Thrale and the others arrived in Paris the next day, they found Henry much improved.

They also found that Baretti had been busy. He had secured an elegant house in the rue Jacob, just a few minutes' walk from the Île de la Cité and the heart of Paris. From her window, Thrale could look out onto the narrow street and watch the bustle of Paris life. The high houses on both sides echoed each sound from down below – each coach, each meeting, each quarrel reverberated off the stone, leaving Thrale feeling almost stunned. The road was too narrow for proper footpaths, so the passers-by walked right in front of the door-ways as they made their way along the road. It was a far cry from Streatham but Thrale soon found herself enjoying it, even taking to shouting down to the street in her imperfect French to inquire about the goings-on of the neighbourhood.[58]

A few days after arriving in Paris, the party went to wait on Madame du Boccage. It was a Saturday morning, the weather starting to turn autumnal, when they presented themselves at the great lady's house. Boccage was sixty-five then (a year Johnson's junior, thirty years Thrale's senior) and well used to holding court – she had been hosting a weekly salon in Paris since the 1730s. Boccage welcomed the Thrale party warmly. She lavished them with compliments, and invited them back for dinner the following Thursday.

When they arrived on the appointed day, they were surprised to find the footmen casually playing cards in the entrance hall. They were even more surprised by the meal that was served. Boccage, ever since her visit to England decades earlier, had a fondness for Eng-lish cuisine. She liked its simplicity and she tried to convince her countrymen that it was not as bad as everyone said. That afternoon, she served (her version of) English food to the Thrales: hare that was 'not tainted but putrified', a leg of mutton 'put on the Spit the moment the Sheep was killed & garnish'd with old Beans', a dish containing three lonely-looking sausages, an incongruous bowl of sugar plums, and an English pudding made according to the recipe of the Duchess of Queensbury. Things got even odder after the meal, when the whole group (men and women together) retired to the drawing room. Boccage arranged herself on a red velvet sofa fringed with gold, while above her head hung colossal and ancient cobwebs. Busts of Shakespeare, Milton, Pope and Dryden adorned the room, along with spittoons discoloured and stained from years of use. When coffee was served, the servant plonked sugar cubes into the cups with his fingers. Even Johnson, not renowned for his table manners, found this off-putting. When the teapot refused to pour, Boccage knew just how to sort out the problem: '*soufflez, soufflez*', she shouted. When none obliged, thinking that her guests did not understand the instruction, she lifted the teapot herself, puffed up her cheeks and blew down the spout with all her might until the obstruction was dislodged. She held the pot aloft in triumph. 'France is worse than Scotland in everything but climate,' was Johnson's conclusion at the end of the day.[59]

Johnson did himself no favours by refusing to speak French throughout the whole trip. Even though he could understand spoken French and read it fluently, he was embarrassed by his inability to speak it well so he insisted on using Latin whenever English would not suffice. 'There is no good in letting the French have a superiority over you every word you speak,' he explained later.[60] He regretted not being able to have many conversations in France, and the French in turn found him baffling. Without his elegant wit, his lovely phrasings and his startling tumble of ideas, it was hard to see what all the fuss was about.

Though that first dinner was a disappointment, the Thrales salvaged something from it – a friendship with another of the guests, a young Italian nobleman named Count Manucci. The Count became inseparable from the party. He showed them around Paris, introduced them to his friends and ensured that they became the centre of a small social group that drew in thinkers, artists and people of fashion. They spent their month in Paris visiting and hosting events for these new friends, seeing the wonderful churches, libraries, theatres, museums, palaces and pleasure gardens of the city. They took trips to Versailles, to tapestry factories and to the famous Sèvres porcelain factory. They attended the races, where they caught a glimpse of Marie-Antoinette, just nineteen and married only a year. Johnson (with his bad eyesight) complained that the jockeys were indistinguishable, all wearing green.

Baretti grew tired of Johnson's constant sniping at all things French and assured him that there were many different shades of green. On a two-day trip to Fontainebleau, they saw the King and Queen eat at a public dining. Thrale thought the Queen was beautiful, but the King just looked 'well enough – like another Frenchman'.[61] They visited Paris's largest brewery, and Henry was delighted to learn that they brewed only four thousand barrels a year – a paltry thing next to his eighty thousand barrels. Queeney, much to her displeasure, was sent for dancing lessons. (Dancing would be one of the few things that Queeney never mastered.)

In November, the Thrales dragged themselves away from all this and began heading north. They journeyed slowly through Chantilly towards Lille, carrying letters of introduction and stopping off many times along the way, then on to Dunkirk and Calais. At Calais, they boarded the same sloop they had crossed on in September. Queeney was violently seasick again. At Dover, they fretted about whether the customs officers might tax the Sèvres porcelain, the various knick-knacks, Johnson's new wig or the three silk gowns that Thrale had had made. The white silk gown, trimmed with pale purple and silver in the newest fashion, would become one of Thrale's favourites – it was the one she wore when she sat for Reynolds, immortalised as the Queen of the Streatham Worthies. At Dover, the customs officials waved it through, along with everything else. Back on English soil again, Thrale concluded her account with the patriotic words: 'I see now that [Britain] is better than France.'[62]

On the way home, they picked Harry up from school. He was delighted to see his parents and sister, and not so delighted about his months in boarding school where, he complained, the other boys were childish. The schoolmaster, meanwhile, reported that Harry had polluted the school with bad language. Thrale brushed the criticism aside, focussing instead on how nicely Harry could translate Ovid. When she later found out that Harry had been telling the other boys 'what was done at a Bawdy house', she had to admit that the schoolmaster had probably been correct to administer a flogging. Harry was curious about everything, even topics considered unsavoury for a schoolboy: when he pestered his mother with questions about castrati she was horrified and banned him from ever discussing such a topic with his sisters.[63]

It was late November now, and cold. The Thames froze over that winter, not thick enough for a frost fair – the last one had been held in the year of Thrale's birth – but enough to make still the lighters that plied their trade on the river, bringing the heart of London to a standstill. The cold weather brought ill health. When they arrived at Streatham they found that Fanny, just six months old, was not well. 'Here is little Fanny very ill & of her *head* too,' wrote Thrale, thinking back to Lucy's decline, which had begun with a head cold. The baby's wet nurse was also feeling unwell. Increasingly worried, Thrale consulted the family physician. Influenza was his verdict. It was tearing through the country in those icy months. 'The disease raged exceedingly,' wrote one doctor. It killed thousands. Fanny had it so violently that nothing could be done for her. In December, two weeks after she returned from France, Thrale buried her daughter. Shortly afterwards, the wet nurse was killed by the influenza too. It had passed from one to the other as they had slept huddled side by side.[64]

Thus two more deaths were recorded in *The Children's Book*, and Thrale began to pray again. But her prayers were lacklustre now: 'I hope I may be permitted to keep them,' she intoned weakly. 'I must endeavour not to provoke God's Judgments on my Family,' she chided herself, taking responsibility for all the deaths so far, as she meekly accepted whatever fate God might have in store for her and the little ones: 'be it as it may . . . if I be bereaved of my Children I be bereaved.'[65]

The trip to France had helped to numb Thrale after the loss of Ralph. Now she hoped that a trip to Italy would do the same after the loss of Fanny. Baretti was thrilled to have a chance to show off his native country and began planning a year-long visit. He wrote home to family members to co-opt them as tour guides for the Thrales; he calculated how many carriages, how much luggage, how many servants. He thought of every detail, commanding his brothers to sort out furniture, bedding, plate, a Bible for Thrale and a priest for Johnson to converse with in Latin. He hoped to set out in April 1776 and journey at a leisurely pace through France, across the Alps, down through Turin, Genoa, Milan, Parma, Bologna, Rimini, San Marino and Rome, before wintering in Tuscany, and heading home via Switzerland.[66] Thrale, though excited about the trip, wanted a much shorter route; she wanted to be back in England in October 1776 to see Harry start at Westminster School.

Harry was nine now. At his birthday in February that year, he celebrated with a party in the parlour at Deadman's Place. His mother always said he was old for his age, and his choice of guests reflected that — there was only one other child among a host of his adult friends: Johnson, of course; the playwright Arthur Murphy, who had inspired a love of theatre in the boy; John Perkins, who ran the brewery; his cousin Tom Cotton; his schoolmaster Old Perney; and a surprise appearance from Count Manucci. This odd group filled up the house and brought a festive feeling to the dankness of Deadman's Place. Harry — who always loved the brewery and who spent his free days messing about in the stables or malthouses, running through the coopers' yard or visiting his father in the counting house — asked his parents if a little money could be allowed for the brewery men to make merry. Everyone loved Harry.

A month after the birthday celebrations, with their trip to Italy just a few weeks away, Thrale invited Manucci for breakfast at Deadman's Place on a Friday morning. She wanted to pick his brains about his country, and had offered to show him a little of her own. The children were keen to take him across the river to the Tower of London. On their way, they saw a ship ablaze on the water. At the Tower, Harry delighted in seeing the lions and the arms. He recited passages from his history books for Manucci. He clambered in and out of cannons, blackening himself with old soot. Afterwards, they visited Moore's Carpet Manufactory, before heading for Piccadilly and Brookes's Menagerie. Exotic animal dealers proliferated in London's West End in the late eighteenth century; for those who had the means, almost anything was obtainable. Brookes specialised in birds, but his catalogues also offered porcupines and monkeys, antelopes and lions.[67] It was a tame lion that held Harry's attention that afternoon, while his mother made inquiries about the rather more prosaic peafowl for her own little menagerie at Streatham. After coaxing the children away from the lion, and a particularly beautiful and gentle monkey, the group returned to Southwark. There, a very hungry Harry 'pounced', as he put it, upon a piece of cold mutton and spent the afternoon happily recounting the pleasures of the day. At bedtime, Queeney was feverish and drooping. Thrale checked on her several times in the night, feeling the girl's hot and clammy skin, and beginning to fear the worst, again. In anxiety, Thrale checked on all the children and found them all cool and comfortable as her fingers traced the lines of their peaceful brows.[68]

The next morning, Queeney was still unwell. As her mother tended to her, Harry slipped out to a nearby bakery and watched as a tray of rolls was pulled steaming from the oven. He bought one and carried it back to the brewhouse yard, to the building he called 'Batchelor's Hall' where the young clerks lived. He ate a jolly breakfast with the clerks that morning, then headed for home where he produced two penny cakes, still warm, for Susanna and Sophia who danced minuets in exchange for the treats. He made his little sisters giggle at his antics and the nursery maids joined in too, so that Thrale had to shush them all from Queeney's bedside. With Queeney resting, Thrale went to her dressing room to tutor Sophia until her own breakfast time at ten o'clock. Thrale was just beginning to make her tea when Molly, one of the nursery maids, appeared at her door in a state of alarm. Queeney was feeling better, but Harry was writhing on the floor, curling and uncurling himself from a foetal position and crying as though he had been whipped. Thrale rushed to the nursery.[69]

She sent for a physician immediately and, while she waited, she began to administer her own remedies: a large glass of emetic wine which produced no result, and then a bath as hot as Harry could bear. When the physician arrived, he ordered hot wine, whisky and Daffy's Elixir – a laxative made with senna – for the boy. Mustard poultices were applied to his feet, broth and wine enemas administered, and five grains of the emetic ipecacuanha given. Harry was conscious now, able to talk and even sit up a little; the pain seemed gone but his breath still came in short gasps. Baretti said the boy should be whipped for causing such a fuss. Henry Thrale told his wife to stop crying because it made her look like a hag. The men were unconcerned but Thrale knew that this was serious. A sudden scream from Harry drew them all to his bedside, he vomited again, then turned solemnly to the adults and told them to be calm, 'I *know* I must die.'

Thrale fainted. Manucci and the nursery maids tried to bring her round. When she regained consciousness, she was frantic. Henry, unaccustomed to the sickroom, sat dumbly on an armchair in the corner, his hands thrust deep into his waistcoat pockets, his body stiffly erect, a ghastly look upon his face. The little girls were led away, carried to Kensington by their aunt, to spare them from witnessing the awful scenes. By mid-afternoon, just five hours after he had first begun to contort in spasms of pain, Harry was dead.

Thrale had lost six of her children already and miscarried two pregnancies but this, she said, was the 'most dreadful of all our Misfortunes'. Lovely, bright, cheery, mischievous Harry was gone. The only male heir, dead. He was buried at the church in Streatham with so many of his brothers and sisters.[70]

Two days after the funeral, Thrale fled again. After a sleepless night, she packed Queeney into the carriage, and headed west for Bath. The doctors had advised a change of scene for Queeney who seemed to be sinking into herself, and Thrale needed a distraction too. Baretti offered to come along, and Thrale was grateful to him for cheering the little girl's melancholy away with all the tricks he could think of. Just as the carriage had been about to pull away from Deadman's Place, Johnson had appeared. He had been on his annual tour to Lichfield when news of Harry had reached him. He lamented the loss of the 'poor dear sweet little Boy', and advised Thrale to pray and to keep busy.[71] In the West Country, Thrale took cold baths to stimulate her appetite and her mind.

She returned to London in time for Easter. At a service at St Paul's Cathedral on Easter Sunday, Boswell watched her, observing her tender grief as the liturgy was read. Two days later, she wrote in *The Children's Book* again: 'so ends my Pride, my hopes; my possession of present, & expectation of future Delight.'[72] This was the day the Thrales were to have set off for Italy. They cancelled the trip, much to Baretti's displeasure. Thrale drove out to Streatham that day so that she would not have to hear Baretti and her husband arguing about it. Travel had been her consolation in the past, but not this time. Nothing could distract her from this.

There had been a brief period – just two months – during the previous summer, when Thrale had had six children alive. Now in the summer of 1776, following the deaths of Ralph, Frances and Harry, she had three. Looking at Queeney, Susanna and Sophia, 'the thin remains of my ruined Family', she determined to cling to them. She prayed that God would give her something to live for by keeping the girls alive. 'Let me not,' she begged, 'Oh let me not I most earnestly beseech thee follow any more of my Offspring to the Grave.'[73]

Instead of going to Italy in the spring, the family had gone to Bath again; it was all they could manage. When they arrived back at Streatham, it was a mess. Many of the servants had been redeployed or dismissed in the expectation that the Thrales would be in Italy for most of the year. Now they had to make new arrangements for staff, and get the house up and running again. This was made more difficult by the news that Thrale was pregnant again. She was sick, 'weak as a Cat', she said. Johnson thought it was the best thing for her – a new baby would improve her state of mind, and what was a little sickness to a woman?[74]

Henry jaunted off fishing with a friend, leaving a pale and feeble Thrale to make domestic arrangements. She wrote him a long light-hearted letter in verse, filling him in on the estate, the animals, on local houses bought and sold, and on love affairs played out in public. But though she tried to keep it light, the final lines showed her plunging back into the darkness that had possessed her for months:

> But Oh my sweet Love! – what a sad world is this,
> The sorrow so frequent, so scanty the Bliss;
> That one cannot one's Cares for a Moment beguile,
> And draw from one's Husband an innocent Smile
> But the Gloom of Concern overshadows our Day,
> And shews us that Man was not made to be gay.[75]

Baretti, who had always been such a help with the children, was still peeved that Harry's death had interfered with the planned Italian trip. He showed his annoyance by encouraging Queeney to rebel against her parents, by arguing continually with his hosts, and once even by musing about Thrale (then pregnant) dying in childbirth and which pretty girl Henry should marry after she was gone. One morning during an argument at the breakfast table, Baretti slammed down his half-drunk cup of tea, fetched his hat and stick, and walked out of the house. He walked all the way to London. It would be four years before he would return to Streatham, but never again on such intimate terms.[76]

Sophia, the youngest child, turned five that summer. On her birthday, she read for her mother verses from the Epistles and the Gospels. Thrale listened half-heartedly, unable now to muster much enthusiasm for this kind of learning. 'The Thing is,' she confessed to *The Children's Book*, 'I have really listened to Babies learning till I am half stupefied - & all my pains have answered so poorly.' As she wrote on, her thoughts became increasingly dark:

> I will not make her Life miserable as I suppose it will be short – not for want of Health indeed, for no Girl can have better, but Harry & Lucy are dead, & why Should Sophy live? The Instructions I labor'd to give *them* – what did they end in? The Grave.[77]

Then darker still: 'at Present I can not begin battling with Babies – I have already spent my whole Youth at it & lost my Reward at last.' Thrale had lost not only her children, but her health, her youth, her sense of self.

It was at this low ebb in Hester Thrale's life that Henry showed her his testicles. 'No peace saith my God for the wicked!' exclaimed the beleaguered woman as she examined the grossly swollen appendages. Her immediate guess was that a cancer was causing the swelling – a dire diagnosis. She began suggesting the names of London's most eminent physicians for him to consult – but with a strange expression he dismissed all of the names she mentioned. Instead, he said he would see one Mr Osborne. Hester began to protest that Osborne was a quack, who was known for treating venereal diseases. It was then that the penny dropped. Her father's old prediction rang in her ears: 'If you marry that Scoundrel he will catch the Pox, & for your Amusement set you to make his Pultices.' 'This is now literally made out,' she scribbled in *The Children's Book* as she set about gathering the ingredients for a poultice which she would then have to rub into the affected area. She spent an hour each morning and evening on her knees doing this for her husband, uncomplaining, while he grumbled impatiently.[78] Despite his choice of doctor and treatment, Henry insisted throughout that it was not venereal disease, but an injury arising from his falling off the carriage in France a year earlier.

Thrale did not believe him. It was not the first time he had caught a pox – a few years earlier he had spent the princely sum of fifty guineas curing a similar infection.[79] In any case, the idea of a venereal disease (and the infidelity that caused it) was preferable to the idea that the head of the family had cancer. She could not imagine the family surviving financially without Henry. More than that, she had watched her mother die from that disease just a few years earlier, and could not bear the thought of losing another family member to it. Though she was relieved that Henry did not have cancer, Thrale knew that venereal disease could still have serious ramifications, not least for the unborn child growing now within her. As she showed no symptoms herself, she hoped that the pregnancy would be unaffected.

Despite Henry's churlishness, he did have some appreciation for the care his wife gave him. He knew that in France the year before she had been fascinated by the -ana – miscellany books that combined memoir, observation, witty phrases and striking anecdotes. She had begun collecting them. Now Henry presented her with the notebooks that would become her own *Thraliana*. That gift was not the most expensive he ever gave her, but it was the most thoughtful. Those six calf-skinned notebooks were a sign that Henry knew his wife was capable of something other than bearing children and rescuing him from his own self-inflicted disasters.

Thrale's pregnancy continued. She hoped desperately for a boy. An heir was Thrale's *raison d'être*. Producing several girls was all fine and well, but hardly the point. As Johnson wrote to Boswell around this time:

> Mrs Thrale is big, and fancies that she carries a boy; if it were
> very reasonable to wish much about it, I should wish her not to be

disappointed. The desire of male heirs is not appendant only to feudal tenures. A son is almost necessary to the continuance of Thrale's
fortune; for what can misses do with a brewhouse? Lands are fitter
for daughters than trades.[80]

Even Hester Thrale, who had done so much to save the brewery
from financial ruin when Henry's experiments in chemical beer had
failed, believed in the basic truth of this paradigm, as did many other
women.

As the time for her lying-in drew nearer, Thrale prayed for a son.
If she had to pay for this wish with her own life, 'well no matter!' she
wrote. She began to imagine her own death; then her mind ran on,
picturing Henry's lacklustre grief. Next she pictured the new wife he
would take, and the children he would have with her. She wondered
how her daughters would be treated by their new stepmother. She
decided that Johnson would be the one who would miss her most
of all.

It was February 1777 when the new baby was born, after a labour
that was 'rough and tight'. It was not a boy; Thrale did not die. She
seemed equally surprised by both. The infant was christened Cecilia
Margaretta and her mother described her as, 'large stout, fat, & big
boned . . . a lovely Child sure enough'.[81]

Less than seven months later, Thrale was pregnant again. Once
more, she poured all of her energy into praying for a boy. This
pregnancy was an easier one for Thrale than most of her previous
ones, physically, at least. She did not suffer the violent sickness
that had plagued her before. But then the dreams began – dreams
of children covered in blood, dreams of death and funerals. Four
months into the pregnancy, Thrale was still unable to feel any
movement from within. She bathed in the sea at Brighton in frigid
November waters to improve her constitution, she did everything
she could think of to protect her health and keep the pregnancy.
Still feeling nothing, she began to wonder if the foetus was alive, or
indeed if it ever had been. Expecting a miscarriage or a stillbirth,
she longed for her mother or a female friend to share her worries.
Her husband – as was typical of men of the time – had little interest
in women's affairs. Johnson blithely reported to Boswell that she

was 'in hopes of a young brewer', unaware of or uninterested in her inner turmoil.[82]

A month later, she felt the familiar movements within her belly and suddenly all seemed well again. Henry treated her to a new gown, and she paraded happily off to Court with Elizabeth Montagu, her worst care forgotten for now. To keep herself busy, she stayed in the capital almost two months that year. She reacquainted herself with the joys of society, she attended salons at Montagu's and musical evenings at the Burneys. She gained status as an immensely desirable guest, charming everyone she met, burying her worries about the pregnancy behind her perfectly polished facade. At Court that winter, the King told her that she did not spend enough time in London – a thrilling acknowledgement of her growing celebrity that pleased her immensely. 'Was that not fine?' she sighed happily to Johnson.[83]

It was that winter too that Frances Burney had first caught sight of Hester Thrale at a morning gathering held by her father in St Martin's Street. She wrote to Daddy Crisp afterwards that Thrale was

a pretty woman . . . her nose is very handsome, her complexion very fair; she has the *embonpoint charmant*, and her eyes are blue and lustrous. She is extremely lively and chatty, and showed none of the supercilious or pedantic airs, so freely, or, rather, so scoffingly attributed, by you envious lords of the creation, to women of learning or celebrity; on the contrary, she is full of sport, remarkably gay, and excessively agreeable.

Burney would never forget that first meeting; Thrale, however, paid little attention to the younger woman. Johnson was also present that morning and he too left a deep impression on young Burney – she wrote that she was in a 'twitter, twitter, twitter' to have been in the same room with him. She noted with interest that he wore 'very coarse black worsted stockings', and wondered if he did so to avoid being called a Bluestocking. That morning, the Burney girls played duets on the harpsichord while Johnson examined the family's library. The party drank chocolate while they spoke of the famous Mr Bach (whom Johnson claimed never to have heard of – 'is he a piper?' he enquired), they gossiped about David Garrick and the private performances he was giving for the King, they debated whether

Elizabeth Montagu preferred Thrale or Johnson. It was a delightful visit, cut short only by the fact that Thrale and Johnson had been invited to dine at Montagu's in the early afternoon.[84]

Not long afterwards, Charles Burney gave an evening party. He wished to introduce Thrale and Johnson to his illustrious friends Frances and Fulke Greville. Mrs Greville was a poet, the author of the popular *Prayer for Indifference*, as well as a celebrated socialite and hostess; Mr Greville was a diplomat, sometime author and an early patron of Burney's. Their daughter Frances Crewe – nicknamed 'Baby Crewe' by the Bluestockings – came too. She was famed for her political soirées and sharp wit. It should have been a splendid evening of insightful repartee, but instead it was a complete failure.

The party assembled in St Martin's Street. The Grevilles looked forward to hearing Johnson speak; the Streatham party longed to hear from Mrs Greville. In deference to Johnson's fame, the Greville party waited for him to make the first conversational gambit. They did not know that Johnson, out of modesty, never initiated a conversation. Though he was a master of the spoken word, he never spoke the first word. Thrale had been asked by Charles Burney to let Johnson be the star of the evening, so she politely kept quiet. The two parties sat in silence, each waiting for the other to begin. To cover the awkward silence, the Burneys called upon their friend Gabriel Piozzi, an Italian singer, to provide some background music for the company. He sang beautifully, but only the Burneys cared for music – everyone else was driven into deeper and more awkward silence by his performance, thoroughly uninterested in the music but afraid to interrupt. Eventually Thrale, in a silly mood, tiptoed towards Piozzi who sat at the pianoforte with his back to the room and began to imitate him – squaring her elbows, shrugging her shoulders, and tilting her head back. Charles Burney swiftly and silently pulled her away before Piozzi could see what she was doing and she meekly returned, like everyone else, to solitude for the remainder of the evening. Eventually, recorded young Frances Burney, the party broke up 'and no one from amongst it ever asked, or wished for its repetition'.[85]

Little did Thrale imagine that this was her first meeting with her second husband – the man who would show her true love but who would also, unwittingly, bring about the end of her Bluestocking days. Years later, when Thrale was wrapped in scandal about her Italian lover, people would delight in retelling this odd tale of their first encounter.

Quickly forgetting this unsuccessful evening, Thrale moved on with her social season, fitting in as much as possible before her lying-in. In March, almost seven months pregnant, she recorded that her 'present Companion' was brisk and lively. Thrale had high hopes for this baby, even going to the expense of re-kitting-out her chamber, a thing much out of her ordinary practice. She lavished money on a new bed, sheets, bedgowns for herself and robes for the baby. Henry, who freely spent large quantities of money on his own projects, grumbled about the expense of all these new things. '[I am] conscious that every Man when he begins to wish to *save* Money, always wishes to save it out of his *Wife's* Expenses,' observed Thrale shrewdly, '& when he wishes to *spend* it, wishes to spend it on *his own*.'[86]

Satisfied with her preparations, she turned morbid again: 'and now if I should *dye!*' she wrote in *The Children's Book*, 'Why if I *should* die! what does it signify? Let me but leave a Son, I shall die happy enough.'[87] Again, she began to wonder which of her friends Henry would marry after she was dead.

The baby did not arrive until a month after Thrale expected it – meaning that she had an extra month to torture herself with such thoughts. The baby was large, and the birth was difficult and slow. Thrale was crestfallen that all those long months of pregnancy and the final long day of labour produced another girl – Henrietta Sophia (Harriett). Johnson wrote to Boswell that 'Mrs. Thrale, poor thing, has a daughter.'[88] Disappointment aside, Thrale was delighted to be done with the pregnancy, and revelled in a peaceful lying-in – that same happy lying-in when she discovered *Evelina*.

Elizabeth Montagu, who had seen Thrale often during the pregnancy and knew of her hopes for a son, offered herself as godmother to 'brown, rosy, fat and stout' Harriett, adding that she was glad the baby was a girl. At a time when other friends were offering condolences on the birth of a daughter, Thrale was grateful for this show of solidarity.[89]

She was thirty-seven now, and knew that she had only a few more years to produce an heir. Despite her initial disappointment in having another daughter, Thrale grew immensely fond of charming little Harriett. Contentment was seeping back into Thrale's life. Her other girls – Queeney, Susanna, Sophia and Cecilia – were thriving too. Queeney, now fourteen, was lovely to look at, quick-minded and bookish, though still cold and aloof with almost everyone. (She warmed a little to Frances Burney who wrote after their first meeting: 'indeed, with all her Coldness, distance & gravity, I find she loves a titter as much as any girl.'[90]) Susanna and Sophia were growing taller and cleverer each day; they were healthy and handsome and pleased their mother mighty well.[91] Cecilia was growing her first teeth without any fever or sleeplessness – a great relief to all in the nursery. It was during these months that Thrale began her friendship with Frances Burney and the Streatham salon developed apace. She was publishing (anonymously) too, trying out new metres for her poems and trying her hand at political satire.[92]

On the final day of the year 1778, Thrale wrote her final entry in *The Children's Book*: 'My children are all about me & my house is full of Friends.' She and Susanna were translating a play by Molière while Sophia was working her way through a book in English. Toddler Cecilia was charming everyone, while baby Harriett was peacefully acting the cherubim. Johnson and Murphy and several other literary friends were staying over the Christmas season. The very last paragraph of *The Children's Book* held a secret: 'I *think* I am again Pregnant, I *think* I am,' she confided to its pages. And, as with all such thoughts, she followed with a prayer:

> humble Thanks to Almighty God for all his Mercies thro' Jesus
> Christ our Lord, & most of all for the Health of my dear Children,
> & for the Boon I *hope* I have obtained by my Prayers & Tears – That
> I shall never follow any more of my Offspring to the Grave.[93]

Thrale came heartbreakingly close to seeing her prayer come true. She was indeed pregnant, and the child would have been a boy – had he survived to full term.

★

The year 1779 was a delightful one at Streatham. Thrale skipped her usual winter visit to the capital; instead, she gathered her friends to her. Frances Burney visited more and more often and Thrale encouraged other guests to do the same. Her salon flourished. Johnson took to reciting poetry to the children and Susanna amazed everyone by memorising his words. There was no snow that winter, nor hardly any frost. By February, the creeper that grew outside Thrale's bedchamber window began to blossom, two months earlier than usual. The lilacs poked up from their beds, and the honeysuckle was in leaf already. In a bucolic frame of mind, the Streathamites' in their parlour games turned to comparing themselves and their friends to flowers: Montagu, of course, was a rose; Queeney a pink; Burney a ranunculus; Thrale herself was a sprig of myrtle – 'which the more it is *crushed*, the more it discloses its *Sweetness*'. Henry turned solicitous that winter, running cold baths for his pregnant wife. They were said to be good for pregnant women – for 'bracing up everything that frequent Pregnancy relaxes'.[94]

All proceeded happily until the summer when Henry was suddenly struck by a palsy. He had been dining with his recently widowed sister when he collapsed – they said that the shock of learning that his brother-in-law had died insolvent caused him to fall down paralysed. It would be many years before Thrale learned that it was not concern for his sister, so much as concern for himself that had caused her husband's extreme reaction: his brother-in-law owed Henry £220,000, something that he had kept secret from the family.[95]

For days, Henry lay insensible. A good bleeding helped a little, but the recovery was slow. 'Oh Lord have mercy on us! this is a horrible Business indeed,' Thrale wrote in despair, unsure if her husband would ever be well again, 'five little Girls too, & breeding again, & Fool enough to be proud of it! ah Ideot! what should I want more Children for? God knows only to please my Husband, who now perhaps may be much better without them.'[96] Slowly, Henry recovered his strength and his wits, though the physicians warned that he might never be quite as he was before. By August, he was tolerably well, when another blow struck the family: Thrale seemed about to lose the pregnancy. At eight months' gestation, this was a dire prospect: '[it] will probably kill me,' she predicted, 'or leave me at least so weak as to render Recovery doubtful. Abortions and Profluvia are not easily got through at my Age, & after having had twelve Children.'[97] Philosophically, she turned to poetry for comfort, and found it in some words of Pope's:

> Then what remains but well our Life to use
> And keep Good humour still whate'er we lose.[98]

Thrale, fearing an imminent miscarriage, stayed close to home. As the cramps worsened, she stayed in her chamber, patiently awaiting the worst.[99] That was where she was when word reached Streatham of a minor mismanagement at the brewery. It was an unimportant clerical problem but Henry felt compelled to travel to Southwark at once. Knowing that his wife was always good with the clerks, he insisted that she accompany him. It was six miles on bumpy roads. Thrale could barely stand, but Henry insisted that she make the journey.

Good wife that she was, she allowed herself to be put into the carriage. At the brewery, she mollified the clerks and straightened the paperwork. And then the pains grew worse. She begged Henry to take her home, but he would not be hurried. She began to bleed. She begged Henry to order the coach; he refused to do so until he was ready. Thrale appealed to Henry's valet to hurry him along but it had no effect. Finally, she was lifted into the coach. Unable to sit, she lay on the floor, her blood soaking through her petticoats. She was in so much pain that she lost consciousness five times. After what felt like an age, they reached Streatham but before she could be carried to her bed, she miscarried in agony.[100]

'Tis less a Miscarriage after all than a dead Child,' she would write later, 'a Boy quite formed & perfect.'[101] She barely had time to mourn that perfect little boy, for the stillbirth was not the end of her travails. There followed days of bleeding, vomiting and diarrhoea – all potentially lethal then. Thrale thought she would die, 'that I was as likely to live two Centuries as two Days'.[102] It was five days before she could stand again, still she looked pale as a ghost.[103]

The physical trauma and the grief left a lasting mark on Thrale. She turned to her notebooks for solace. But solace was in short supply, so instead she began to write a series of dialogues imagining her own death. The genre of 'dialogues of the dead' was a popular one at the time, with authors imagining witty or satirical or pious conversations between deceased celebrities, figures from mythology or spikily drawn caricatures. Thrale spun the genre a little differently – imagining what her friends, her husband, her children would think when she had gone. They began morosely, with Johnson so burdened with sorrow that he could hardly bear to hear her name mentioned, with Elizabeth Montagu wishing they could bring her back. In the next dialogue, Thrale's old friends heartlessly toasted the prospect of Henry taking a new wife. By the time she wrote the third dialogue, she was a little cheerier, poking fun at some of the Streathamites, and hardly dwelling on her demise at all.[104]

But thoughts of death still hovered about her. Six weeks after the stillbirth, a creeping feeling of dread stole over her. 'I have got a strange Fit of the horrors,' she wrote in the *Thraliana*, 'something runs in my head that I shall die, or Mr Thrale die . . . I tremble with Terror.'[105] Nothing happened that day, or the next. Gradually, the intensity of the feeling ebbed away. The pregnancy that ended so terribly in August 1779 was the final pregnancy of her marriage to Henry.

For her, as for so many other women in the eighteenth century, producing children had always been presented as her *raison d'être*, and she accepted this without question. Motherhood, society said, was natural and fulfilling, and gave meaning and purpose to women's lives.

Sarah Scott, judging a sister-in-law for spacing out her pregnancies, wrote, 'I look upon it so much as the business of a Married Woman (who was married so entirely on the merit of being a Woman) to breed, that it puts me almost out of humour.'[106] Scott had spent many years thinking about the damage the patriarchy did to women, yet so conditioned was she to think that a married woman's purpose was to reproduce that she could not unthink it. (The fact that she did not like this particular sister-in-law may have clouded her judgement.)

The idea of contraception was utterly unmentionable for women of this class. Men would generally only admit to attempts at contraception where prostitutes were involved. James Boswell famously described using condoms made from animal intestines. Coitus interruptus was another option – a dictionary of slang published in 1785 included a definition for the term 'coffee house': 'to make a coffee house of a woman's *****, to go in and out and spend nothing'.[107] Breastfeeding was often a woman's best bet for delaying the next pregnancy, but it was not always possible, and the fashion for it came and went throughout the century. For a married woman, pregnancy was almost inevitable, and was presented as uncomplicatedly desirable.

Left unmentioned were the downsides of motherhood: the intense sickness brought on by pregnancy; the possibility of death in childbirth; the lifelong health problems that could follow a difficult birth; the extremely high possibility of watching some, if not most, of your children die. It may have been natural, but many women found it far from fulfilling. Traumatised by her own experiences of motherhood, Thrale began quietly to doubt the traditional wisdom. She never said aloud that she deplored the institution of motherhood and throughout her first marriage she continued to try for that elusive boy child. She did everything society said she should, and yet she found herself miserable. She felt that she had wasted her youth – cooped up always in the nursery, bearing and raising children who followed each other to the grave in quick succession.

Instead of relying entirely on her marriage and motherhood for satisfaction, Thrale quietly began to seek out other avenues of fulfilment. There was her friendship with Johnson, her new-found interest in the brewery and political canvassing, her diaries and writing, her travels, and the creation of the Streatham circle – all undertaken to distract herself from the pain, the illness and the loss that motherhood entailed.

The Streatham circle became more than Thrale had ever imagined. What began as a simple gathering of friends grew into a celebrated salon where the brightest lights of the literary world came together. The salon proved to Thrale (and to others) that she and other mothers were capable of more than most people imagined. The public heard tales of the wonderful goings-on at Streatham, they admired Thrale's vivacious personality and quick mind, they envied her friendships with celebrities such as Samuel Johnson. But few knew that behind the lively facade, Thrale's life had long been one of heartbreak. No amount of brilliance could protect her from the fate assigned to women.

Elizabeth Montagu knew that a salon could save your life. Her marriage to quiet, bookish Edward was a world away from Hester Thrale's married life. While Henry disappeared into the bawdy houses of Soho, Edward would settle down in his study with a set of mathematical proofs. Edward gave his wife his blessing to socialise how she saw fit. She would alternate between quiet studious evenings with him, and lively nights of conversation and wit with her friends. While the two women had very different relationships with their husbands, both had a similar experience of motherhood: it left them reeling.

Montagu had become pregnant very soon after her wedding. Her honeymoon was spent at Edward's house in Yorkshire. As was customary, the newly-weds were accompanied by a chaperone. In this case it was Montagu's sister Sarah who travelled with them. The trio travelled for six days to reach Allerthorpe Hall, a few miles east of the city of York. When they reached the house, Montagu was underwhelmed: 'old and not handsome', she declared the seventeenth-century brick dwelling, its stoutness emphasised by two squat turrets. But the flowering meadows, the River Swale that gently wound its way through them, and the lush gardens – overflowing with peaches, nectarines and apricots that warm summer – soon cheered her.

More cheer, and more siblings, came to the house before long. For, as though one adult sister was not sufficient company for a honeymoon, Montagu's three youngest brothers joined the party too. Montagu was particularly glad to be able to surround herself with her vivacious family. She did not think much of her new neighbours: 'merely human', she called them, 'scarce rational'. To escape their dreary and mundane visits, Montagu would go exploring. A three-day expedition to the Dales restored her faith in Yorkshire. The vastness of the mountains, the striking forms of the rocky outcrops, the river rapids and dramatic waterfalls surprised and delighted her. Her enjoyment of that trip was only a little spoilt by feeling ill as her chaise jolted her over the uneven tracks. 'My disorder was owing to fatigue,' she assured her friend the Duchess of Portland.[108]

In another letter written that same week, she thanked her old Bulstrode friend Anne Donnellan for sending her a large mantle (a sort of cape or loose overcoat). Donnellan assumed that the newly married Montagu would soon be pregnant and so had made the mantle extra large but Montagu replied, 'I hope in time I may be worthy of it; but at present the jumps are of a virginal size.'* She continued, 'Do you think I would be guilty of such an indecorum as to be in so unprudish a way already?'[109]

Like any newly married woman in the eighteenth century, the possibility of a pregnancy was never far from Montagu's mind. It was a bittersweet prospect: to be infertile was seen as a fundamental failure; but pregnancy was a life-or-death gamble, especially a first one. And, of course, pregnancy was, at best, a somewhat unpleasant experience for most women. 'Nothing is less divine and angelical than a breeding woman,' wrote Montagu two months into her marriage, 'sick with a piece of toast and butter, or longing for a bit of tripe, liver or black-pudding.' And then there was the fatigue. After that bumpy carriage-ride to Bishopdale, Montagu was so tired that she was unable to hold a pen – she was almost certainly already pregnant. Montagu wrote tentatively to her more experienced friend the Duchess, looking for confirmation that this might be the case. 'How often has the Cardinal miss'd paying you a Visit?' enquired the Duchess, cloaking her meaning in the euphemisms of womanhood. By the end of her honeymoon, Montagu's pregnancy was beyond doubt.

The Yorkshire honeymoon had begun in August. By October, Edward had to return to London as parliament was in session. Travel was considered extremely dangerous in the early stages of pregnancy so Montagu had to stay behind in Allerthorpe. Her little brothers returned to school. Only Montagu and Sarah remained in the dour old farmhouse. The two sisters spent many companionable months sitting by the fireside as autumn passed into winter. They sewed and read, wrote and talked. Having spent much time away from each other when Montagu had become closer to the Duchess, it was a pleasure for both to be together so intimately again. 'Where [my sister] is there will happiness be also,' wrote Montagu in praise of

---

* Jumps are a sort of unboned bodice.

Sarah, 'her temper is continual sunshine; and she smooths the rugged brow of winter, and, without gloom or storm within doors, we sit contented.'[110]

Christmas came and went, with Edward still detained on business in London. Feeling guilty about his prolonged absence, he began his letters with 'My dearest angel', 'My dearest life', and filled them with the tenderest sentiments. Montagu was weak with morning sickness, and suffering from fevers and rashes. She had to be blooded for a headache by a country apothecary who was rumoured to have killed eleven of his patients by the procedure. Finally, in early January, her morning sickness abated somewhat and Montagu's physician said that she was past the dangerous time and could travel down to London, but that she must travel slowly. The normal journey of six days was stretched out to ten. Flooded roads slowed the sisters' journey further, condemning them to unplanned stays in inns along the way, and occasionally forcing them to give up their carriage for a boat.

Eventually Montagu reached London and was elated to be reunited with her friends right in the middle of the social season. She had several months before her confinement, and she threw herself into catching up with the gay life she had missed. However, her joy was short-lived as that March the Duchess of Portland's youngest daughter Frances, just two years old, died from convulsions brought on by whooping cough. The heartbroken Duchess tried to stop Montagu from coming to see her – she was afraid that the grief would be too much for her pregnant friend. But Montagu would not leave Margaret to be alone and she sat with her through the long dark hours as she mourned her infant girl. It was a stark reminder of the fragility of small children, and Montagu must have thought of the precariousness of the life she was growing inside herself.

Just as she arrived back in London, a letter from her mother (who had lost three children herself) gave Montagu a further glimpse into the pain of motherhood. 'For my part I love you too tenderly to rejoice abundantly at your being with child,' wrote Elizabeth Robinson to her daughter, as she recalled her little girl's own childhood illnesses. 'But that is not the worst', she continued, 'children are very precarious Blessings & both Mr Montagu & you are both so passionately fond that any accident that may happen to it pierces very deep, and at the best gives you great anxiety in fears.'[111]

As she thought over her mother's words, and as the Duchess packed away her daughter's clothes, cot and toys, Montagu had to begin preparations for her own child. The last letter written before her confinement tells of a magnificent cradle she had bought. It arrived just in time, as the baby was born at home on 11 May 1743. The Montagus were overcome with joy at the birth of their son, whom they christened John, but always called 'Punch'. A wet nurse named Mrs Kennet was brought up from near Mount Morris in Kent to feed the boy as Montagu recovered. It was a long recovery. Even two months after the birth, Montagu was said to look pale and green, her previously plump face reduced to lankness. But though Montagu was looking wan, her son thrived: he had prodigiously chubby chops, and Montagu proudly informed the Duchess that 'the young Fidget . . . loves laughing and dancing.'[112]

At five months old, Punch was still as jolly, laughing as he played in the sunshine, or staring in wide-eyed amazement as he was driven out daily in his horse-drawn chariot. Montagu had begun to suffer from weakness and fainting fits and was also advised to ride or drive outside daily. Despite her poor health, the early months of mother-hood brought genuine contentment to Montagu. For the first time in her life she was happy to forego the pleasures of society and found all the joy she needed with her baby.[113] Each morning and evening she let him wriggle about unclothed on a blanket spread on the ground. She watched cheerfully as daily he grew more nimble. She wrote that she was becoming like a child herself, so besotted was she by his every move. Gladly, she drifted away from the shining social circles of her youth.

Despite the happiness her son brought her, Montagu was not keen to have more children. Though she liked the idea of Punch having siblings, her unpleasant experience of pregnancy and her long recovery from the birth put her off the idea of bearing another child.[114]

By eleven months, Punch was delighting his parents with rounds of hide-and-seek and bo-peep. For his first birthday, they gave him a pink satin coat, and two fine flowered frocks. When his mother tried the coat on him he loved it so much that he refused to let anyone take it off for the rest of the day. His aunt Sarah, whose letters always asked after 'his little worship', toasted Punch's first birthday with the words, 'I hope he will see more . . . than any of us shall be present to.'¹¹⁵

As a one-year-old, Punch learned to run and prattle, to roll and tumble and bow. He danced like a merry drunken Bacchus. He was weaned that year – much to his mother's distress. It was considered an especially dangerous time for an infant but Punch sailed through the weaning and came to love feasting on milk porridge, bread and rusks.

The next danger faced by the infant Punch was teething. Anxiously watched over by his parents, Punch cut his first tooth in July 1744. The tiny sliver of ivory brought with it much pain and unhappiness, reducing the normally cheery boy to tears and an almost inconsolable anguish. But soon he was well again and the family travelled north to the house in Allerthorpe to enjoy late summer in the fresh Yorkshire air. His next tooth came that August. Again, the pain was excruciating. As the tooth broke through his tender flesh, his temperature began to rise. Montagu and the boy's nurse struggled to keep him cool in the hot summer. As his fever rose and rose, he began to go floppy, then he began to shake. The convulsions shuddered through his tiny body as his mother watched, utterly helpless. Punch died from his second tooth.

'I am well enough as to health of Body,' wrote Montagu, 'but God knows the sickness of the soul is far worse.'¹¹⁶ Montagu tried to submit herself meekly to God's will: she knew that many babies did not survive teething – it was a leading cause of infant mortality at the time. This knowledge offered no comfort. She struggled to come to terms with the loss of her precious boy. She shut herself away for several weeks, depending on her sister to care for her and to write with the sad news to family and friends. Sarah performed her tasks diligently as she mourned her beloved nephew. He never would see all those wonderful things she had wished him in her birthday toast.

Montagu sought distraction. In the early days she found peace with Edward, but then he was called back to London on business, so she turned to books. 'I apply myself to reading as much as I can, and

I find it does me service,' she wrote to the Duchess, with whom she could share the pain of lost children. Montagu was unable to face the outside world just yet, so the sisters stayed on at Allerthorpe into the autumn. They finally decided to return to the capital in November. As they travelled, they must have recalled the last time they made this journey together – when Montagu's belly was just beginning to swell with the promise of new life, and both women were looking forward to the gaiety of London. Now they travelled sombrely along the terrible roads.

The only way Montagu could deal with the loss of Punch was to suppress her feelings as much as possible. Decades later she confessed to Elizabeth Vesey that she had wept uncontrollably night after night until she forced herself to conquer her emotions.[117] Once, when Frances Boscawen's husband was dangerously ill, Montagu advised her to accept God's will – something she had not been able to do herself:

> Be not afraid but commit it all to the great and wise Disposer of all events . . . I remember with sorrow and shame, I trusted much to a continual watching of my son . . . What was the reward of this confidence of my own care and diffidence of His who only could protect him? Why, such as it deserved, I lost my beloved object, and with him my hopes, my joys, and my health, and I lost him too not by those things I had feared for him, but by the pain of a tooth.[118]

She wrote those words thirteen years after Punch's death; at the time, she had not been able to accept what had happened. To dull the pain, she first lost herself in books; but then she found a better cure – she threw herself back into society.

In the summer of 1745 Montagu visited the spa town of Tunbridge Wells in Kent. She went without Edward, who would never be much interested in the place. Tunbridge Wells was less than a day's coach-ride from London and had become a fashionable resort a century earlier. The grassy common on which an iron-rich mineral spring surfaced had, by Montagu's time, been built up into a pretty little town bustling with shops, chapels, coffee-houses, a market and a promenade. People flocked there looking for cures for their various ailments. They would drink a cup of the water each morning before spending the rest of the day promenading, socialising, gambling or dancing.

Montagu fell in love with the place where fashionable English women wore French dresses and copied French manners, while a host of other nationalities – Hungarians, Italians, French, Portuguese, Irish and Scots – added a cosmopolitan feel. The literati were known to haunt Tunbridge Wells in the summer months. On that particular trip, Montagu met the melancholy poet Edward Young, author of the much-admired *Night Thoughts*, who had surprised everyone that week by befriending the notorious actor and playwright Colley Cibber. A trip to Tunbridge Wells became an annual event for Montagu and she spent her season there riding out, attending balls, dining with her new friends and drinking the waters, hoping to restore the good health she had known before her pregnancy.

Meeting literary men at the Wells was pleasing to Montagu, but much more important were the women she met there. It was at Tunbridge Wells that she first met Frances Boscawen in 1749. The two women were staying in neighbouring guest houses and Montagu found Boscawen to be lively yet sensible. They passed many evenings in conversation together, or reading companionably. Montagu wrote to Boscawen as soon as she returned to London, hoping to continue the friendship. She invited Boscawen to dine, hoping for what she called 'a feast of reason'.[119] A friendship blossomed. Later, Boscawen would become a Bluestocking hostess almost as famed as Montagu herself.

Just as Montagu was befriending Boscawen, the new house on Hill Street was nearing completion. The muddy plot that the Montagus had first seen two years earlier had been transformed, and when the house was ready it was magnificent. Montagu had overseen some of the building work herself, watching as the bricklayers coaxed the rooms into existence, the walls progressing steadily upwards until the earth bore the recognisable skeleton of a house. Then she watched as the masons and the carpenters came, and the house seemed to grow flesh. The curve of a balustrade, the perfect coldness of marble, the elegant line of a cornice made the house real for her. Montagu was patient in pursuit of perfection. 'It will be better', she wrote to a friend, 'to stay a year for the finishing than to take what one does not like.'[120] They had already waited two years for the house to be built, and they lived there for another two before the decoration was finished. That too was exquisite. Yards and yards of brocades and damasks softened the rooms, cherubs danced across the ceilings. Dozens of pieces of furniture were made specially for the house, new plate commissioned.

With the passing of time and the distraction of the house, the sickness of Montagu's soul began to recede. In 1748, when she was preparing to move into Hill Street, she gave away most of Punch's old clothes to a cousin who was (unhappily) expecting a fifth child.[121] Before Punch's death, Montagu had said that she did not wish for another pregnancy; now the decision was confirmed. Though they remained tenderly devoted to each other, Elizabeth and Edward slept separately, and there seems to have been little danger of conceiving another child.

It is noticeable that of the women whose stories I tell here, only two (Hester Thrale and Ann Yearsley) had a large number of children. Elizabeth Griffith had two children. Frances Burney, Catharine Macaulay and Elizabeth Montagu had one each. Elizabeth Carter, Hannah More, Hester Mulso Chapone, Catherine Talbot and Sarah Scott did not have any. In a time when marrying and bearing children was the social norm, it is unusual to see such a large group of interconnected women with so few children. The Bluestockings are remarkable in seeming to have rejected en masse the traditional model of womanhood. Their reasons for having small families or remaining child-free were varied and none of them ever talked publicly about it. Like everything else they did, they did this quietly, never trumpeting their decisions as a disavowal of patriarchal structures. Nor do their private letters dwell upon this fact – even saying to a close female friend that one did not desire to be a mother, or to have a large family, was almost taboo. And yet it was only by having few or no children that the many Bluestockings could live the lives that they did.

Instead of trying for more children, Hill Street became Montagu's love. When it was finally ready, Montagu could begin the next phase of her life, now not diverted by the charms of motherhood, but by giving herself over entirely to her new role as hostess. The last room to be decorated at Hill Street was the Chinese Room. And from the beginning of Montagu's literary breakfasts in 1750, that room, that house, became the centre of something new. Where once Montagu had poured all her energy into bo-peep and watching her cherubic boy toddle guilelessly through life, now the salon consumed her. It became a sort of family to her. While she was still fond of Edward, she prioritised spending time with her friends, writing once how 'Mr Montagu passed ye Xmas at Sandleford, I with the Bluestocking Philosophers. I had parties of them to dine with me continually.'[122] And, as she adored her Bluestocking coterie, they adored her. In the salon, Montagu found a joy untinged with pain, and a love far less terrifying than that of a mother for her child.

8

FRIENDSHIP

QUITE EARLY ON in her life Elizabeth Carter decided not to marry. It was not that she lacked suitors; rather, she craved freedom. She wanted freedom for her body – the right not to bear children; she wanted freedom to spend her time as she wished; she wanted freedom to use her mind as she chose. For most women in the eighteenth century, the only way to live a free life was to remain unwed. Of course, one also needed an understanding father and a source of income; Carter was blessed with both.

Carter had been born in Deal, Kent in 1717. Her father Nicolas was a churchman who tended to local parishioners as well as preaching at nearby Canterbury Cathedral. He had studied at Cambridge, where he proved an impressive linguist: he mastered Latin, Greek and Hebrew with incredible speed. Later, when he had been granted his living, had married and fathered his children, he determined to pass on his knowledge to them. Back in Deal, he taught his daughters as well as his sons. His wife died when the children were still young, which perhaps allowed for their unusual and distinctly 'male' education. Elizabeth seemed one of the least promising of the children at first. Nicolas almost gave up on her but, though she seemed to lack aptitude, she was a determined little scholar and devoted hours to deciphering the texts presented to her. Nicolas was impressed by her dedication to study and agreed to continue her lessons.

Carter worked hard at her books through her teenage years. She learned Latin and Greek first, then Hebrew. Like all well-bred young ladies, she learned conversational French. Then she went a step further and taught herself Italian, Spanish and German. She tried to learn Portuguese but struggled to find books in that language. She had the same problem when she began learning Arabic; in the end, she had to make her own Arabic dictionary to aid her studies. As well as her languages, Carter read the Bible daily, she was a devotee of the science of astronomy, an expert on classical geography and was taught all the usual female accomplishments too – sewing and dancing, music and drawing.

All of this activity brought on headaches in Carter. Some thought it was the general nature of study itself that was the problem, others said it was particularly the study of classical languages that caused such symptoms in females. Some thought it was the pinches of snuff and cups of green tea she took to fuel her long study sessions that made her head ache. One (male) friend suggested that marriage was the obvious cure for her problems. Carter ignored this advice, and continued her solitary work. Her headaches would remain with her until old age. Somehow, among all this industry, Carter managed to find time for fun. Her nephew (who would live with her in her old age, and later write her biography) struggled to reconcile the pious scholarly old lady he knew with the girl he heard about in family reminiscences. He was more than a little surprised to hear that she had been 'somewhat, when very young, of a romp'. She loved attending assemblies and dances. Her youthful letters brim over with enthusiasm for Kentish social life:

> I have played the rake most enormously for these two days, and sat up till near three in the morning. I walked three miles yesterday in a wind I thought would have blown me out of this planet, and afterwards danced nine hours, and then walked back again. Did you ever see or hear of any thing half so wonderful?[1]

She would often walk the six miles to Sandwich for the assemblies there. She staged plays with her brothers and sisters (though these were for the amusement of the family only: like many, she was deeply suspicious of actresses who performed on the public stage).

Carter was described as having handsome features, a clear complexion, curled hair and white teeth. She naturally began to attract suitors. She had a flirtatious streak and developed several passing crushes on the men she met at assemblies. She described once to a friend how 'my heart, which I thought so secure and so uninvadable, was yesterday in one half hour intirely given up to a -----; would you believe it? to a *Dutchman* . . . I this morning took a dose of algebra, fasting, which has entirely cured me.' A more serious relationship with an unnamed man looked as though it might be leading some-where, until he published some verses which showed a 'light and licentious' turn of mind.[2] The gentleman was said afterwards to have been most ashamed of himself, but it was too late to win back Carter.

Carter's family naturally assumed that she would marry. Her father – a man comfortably off, but not wealthy – worried about who would provide for his daughters in the event of his death and gently suggested possible suitors to them. Other girls pur-sued romantic relationships, but Carter could not bring herself to consider marriage seriously. As they grew into adulthood, Carter watched happily as her friends and sisters became engaged, but she continued to turn down suitors herself. Her father was concerned but remarkably understanding: he said that she had always been exceptional and that he trusted her to make decisions for herself.[3]

It was a generous position for an eighteenth-century father to take. Perhaps having nurtured this girl into a scholar, he felt that he could not simply abandon her to a marriage that might force her to desert her education completely. With his backing, Carter continued her studies. She spent whole days reading the classics, and began to write works of her own while still a teenager.

Whether Carter already had a notion that this would become a 'career' of sorts for her is unclear. Careers for middle-class women were, of course, practically non-existent. This made writing a god-send for many bright women – it was something that a woman could do at home, alone, and it could be fitted around domestic tasks. Poetry, it was generally agreed, was a suitable medium for women. Novel-writing was considered lowbrow, but not too *déclassé* for a lady, and not overly taxing on her delicate brain. There were genres of lit-erature – including history, classics and literary criticism – that were considered suitable only for male writers.

Being a good girl, Carter stuck obediently to the medium of poetry for her earliest works. Her first piece was a rhyming riddle that appeared anonymously in the *Gentleman's Magazine* in 1734. It began:

Coæval with the world, I lay conceal'd
'Till my existence prying man reveal'd;
Sometimes in caves and mountains make my bed,
And oft beneath the waves in embryo hid
. . .

Like animals I still subsist by breath,
Yet often from its force receive my death.[4]

The answer to the riddle was guessed by several readers, who responded with verses of their own. One was addressed to 'Miss Cart-r'. It praised her as an 'ingenious nymph', skilled both as a poet and as a philosopher.[5] While she might have appreciated its sentiments, Carter was alarmed to see her identity so very nearly revealed and she announced her retirement from poetry.

She was in retirement for less than a year, unable to resist the lure of a literary life. In 1735 Carter took the bold step of departing for London. She stayed with her uncle, a silk merchant in the City, as she tried to establish herself. For the next four years, she would spend much of her time in the capital. Edward Cave, editor of the *Gentleman's Magazine*, was a great supporter and introduced Carter to many other writers, editors and publishers. It was through Cave that she would meet a young Samuel Johnson in 1738. Johnson himself was fairly recently arrived in the city and trying to make a name for himself. He was impressed by Carter, enough to pen her an epigram in Greek which was published by Cave. Carter replied to Johnson in both Greek and Latin verse.[6] Throughout his life Johnson had only praise for Carter; he would later publish her works in his *Rambler* and he subscribed to her books. It was one of the few professional relationships he had that remained on an even keel; it was said that in later years Carter was almost unique in her ability to keep Johnson in line. Carter wrote home to her family in Deal about this schoolmaster-turned-playwright (his lexicography days still far in the future). She wrote in glowing terms, but her father replied coolly: 'You mention Johnson; but that is a name with which I am utterly unacquainted. Neither his scholastic, critical, or poetical character ever reached my ears. I a little suspect his judgment, if he is very fond of Martial.'[7]

Carter published anonymously a small poetry collection in 1738, as well as her first work of prose – a translation from the French of a critique of Alexander Pope. The year 1739 saw Carter translating a popular Italian work on Newton – *Sir Isaac Newton's Philosophy Explain'd for the Use of the Ladies* – a nice opportunity for her to indulge her love of natural philosophy. A male acquaintance wrote admiringly to Carter:

> I hope, Madam, the example you give . . . will allure your own charming part of the creation [i.e. women] to imitate, as well as to admire you, and cure ours [i.e. men] of the prevailing prejudice, that an acquaintance with the sciences inspires [women] with vanity, and an unhappy neglect of the decent offices of the sex.[8]

The book was popular, but the idea that studying science would distract women from more suitable domestic duties would persist for another couple of centuries.

Carter's career was taking flight. As she thought ahead to the next books she would like to write, she was increasingly aware that this career path was only tenable if she remained unmarried. Her previous disinclination for marriage solidified into a firm decision to avoid the institution. Her father, again, was understanding – up to a point. 'If you intend never to marry', he wrote to her, 'then you certainly ought to live retired, and not appear in the world with an expence which is reasonable upon the prospect of getting an husband, but not otherwise.'[9] The expense of keeping a daughter in London was reasonable if there was the possible financial incentive of getting a good marriage out of it; otherwise, Carter might as well work on her books in Deal where there were fewer costs and less risk of impropriety.

Without so much as a murmur, she returned to Deal and settled back into village life. Carter rose early. She employed the sexton to stand below her window each morning between four and five o'clock and pull on a string she had contrived to run up the house, through a crack in her window frame, and across her chamber to a bell placed at the head of her bed. Carter was not a natural morning person but she dragged herself from bed to sit at her desk for a few hours' study before heading out for a long brisk walk – sometimes alone, and sometimes with a sister or a friend from the village. Carter would walk through commons and cornfields, along shady lanes or dew-soaked meadows until the lure of the breakfast table pulled her homewards. Breakfast was a chatty affair in the Carter household, often attended by Carter's siblings or nieces and nephews. Then Carter would water the plants (a lengthy task for someone who kept twenty bowls of pinks and roses in her own chamber alone) before sitting down to practise the spinet. She would spend the rest of the morning 'between reading, working [i.e. sewing], writing, twirling the globes, and running up and down stairs an hundred times to see where every body is, and how they do'. Sometimes she would go visiting in the afternoons, but she always made a point to be home in time for tea. Along with breakfast, this was a favourite time for all the family. 'We have a great variety of topics', she explained to a friend, 'in which every body bears a part, till we get insensibly upon books; and whenever we go beyond Latin and French, my sister and the rest walk off, and leave my father and me to finish the discourse, and the tea-kettle by ourselves.'[10] Carter was happy to be back in Kent. She continued to write poetry and to translate various works. Despite being away from London, her reputation remained high. A portrait of her appeared around this time, showing her sporting a plumed helmet and a breastplate and bearing a shield – viewers would have recognised at once that here was Carter as Minerva, the chaste and wise goddess. In her hand she held a book by Plato, bound in red leather and embossed with gold. A poem praising the portrait (and Carter) was published in the *Gentleman's Magazine* in 1741:

> Have we a nymph, who midst the bloom of youth,
> Can think with *Plato*? – and can relish truth?
> One who can leave her sex's joys behind,
> To taste the nobler pleasures of the mind?[11]

The same year that this poem was published, Carter embarked on one of the most significant friendships of her life. It was January and twenty-three-year-old Carter was paying a visit to friends in London. Through these friends she was introduced to a young woman named Catherine Talbot. Carter and Talbot had heard of each other before this meeting. Carter was reasonably well-known in literary circles; Talbot kept a lower profile but many of her poems had been circulated anonymously and Carter knew of her. A few years before their first meeting, a teenage Talbot had written an unsigned letter of praise to Carter. Intrigued, Carter had tried to find out the letter's author. Carter did eventually discover that Talbot had written the missive, but her efforts to meet the younger woman never came to anything.

Now, following that first brief encounter, Carter determined to get to know Talbot better. She told a friend how ardently she was pursuing Talbot and joked that the whole thing was 'a perfect Romance'. The following Sunday, Carter decided to attend the church where she knew Talbot worshipped. The two women sat in adjacent pews. Carter described the scene: 'She smiled & I smiled, she blush'd and I blush'd, & she looked silly & I looked silly. Well this Intercourse of mutual Confusion lasted all Church Time & when it was over I was in no small difficulty how to act.'[12] After a few moments of this awkwardness, Talbot dropped her fan. It landed in Carter's pew and Carter picked it up and handed it back, grateful to have an excuse for speech at last. Carter reckoned that she had spoken three and a half words, and Talbot two.

Carter wrote to a mutual friend named Thomas Wright afterwards: 'Miss Talbot is my absolute passion; I think of her all day, dream of her all night, and one way or other introduce her into every subject I talk of.' On hearing that Wright was to see Talbot the next day, Carter expressed envy and begged that he present her compliments to the younger lady. Carter longed to converse with Talbot properly. Sounding more like a suitor than a learned lady, she sent dramatic letters to Wright asking 'is she absolutely inaccessible? I cannot long support this . . . Must I never hope for a nearer view till I meet her glittering among the stars in a future state of being?' Unable to see Talbot in person, Carter began to write to her. Carter would agonise over her early letters to Talbot, admitting that it once took her half an hour to compose a single sentence.[13]

In the years that followed, Carter would always mark the anniversary of her first meeting with Talbot. On one such anniversary, Carter sent Talbot some lines from Petrarch: 'Benedetto sia 'l giorno, e 'l mese, e l'anno, / e la stagione, e 'l tempo, e l 'ora, e 'l punto' (Blessed be the day, and the month, and the year / And the season, and the time, and the hour, and the moment). Carter did not continue with Petrarch's lovestruck original, but instead finished in words of her own: '[Blessed be] St. James's church, and Mr. Wright, and the particles yes and no, and every other circumstance, and every other person that contributed to make me happy in the sight and conversation of Miss Talbot.'[14]

Some have speculated that the relationship between Carter and Talbot was a romantic one. There is no evidence that they ever had a sexual relationship; neither is there any evidence against it. Carter's letters were heavily edited by her nephew before publication, meaning that many details of her personal life have vanished. Both women were lauded for their piety and their morals; in an age when homosexuality was more than frowned upon, to defy convention in pursuit of a Sapphic love would seem out of character. And yet, theirs was an intensely close and emotional friendship – one scattered with Italian love poetry. If a physical relationship seems unlikely, perhaps they enjoyed a kind of chaste romance.[15]

Talbot was never far from her thoughts in those early days. Carter, usually so happy in Deal, began to chafe against what felt like a confinement. She began to feel like a misfit in what she called 'these regions of obscurity and uninterrupted dullness'. She was not sure she wanted to live in

> a place where the name of Miss Talbot is a stranger . . . People here are not in the least danger of losing their wits about you, but proceed as quietly and as regularly in their affairs as if there was no such person in being. Nobody had been observed to lose their way, run against a door, or sit silent and staring in a room full of company in thinking upon you, except my solitary self.[16]

Talbot was flattered but perhaps a little embarrassed by Carter's effusiveness.

Over the years, the intensity of Carter's praise, and the bashfulness of Talbot's replies mellowed gracefully into a correspondence between intellectual equals. They ranged over topics from classics to religion, poetry to astronomy, philosophy to physic. Seamlessly, their letters switched from English to French, Italian to Latin. They wrote frequently, they came to know each other's minds, their moods, their tastes in music and literature, their religious values, the mundane details of each other's family lives. But with Carter secluded in Deal and Talbot usually in residence with family friends in Oxfordshire, they had little opportunity to meet. Their letters speak of elaborate plans to see each other again. Carter, sitting at her writing desk one morning at four o'clock, wrote how she would like to appear at Talbot's bedside, speaking quietly and comfortingly in the darkness. The more prosaic Talbot wrote to Carter that she fantasised about them both being in London at the same time – the agreeable afternoons they would spend together, the rational discourse they would enjoy. This letter was accompanied by a single rose.[17]

That year was a dramatic one for the residents of Kent, as the Jacobite Rebellion took off and rumours of a French invasion ran freely through the county. Stories of French fleets massing off the coast caused great alarm; the size of the fleets and the barbarity of the Frenchmen multiplied with each retelling. Carter chose to stay put. Though she put a brave face on it, writing lightly in her letters to Talbot, she was afraid. When one night a messenger arrived to say that a French force had landed a mile from Deal, the townspeople began to panic. An alarm was beaten out to call the men to arms. Alongside just seventy soldiers, they prepared to defend their country to the death. 'Never was such a scene of uproar and confusion,' Carter wrote to her friend,

> women and children squeaking through the streets, drums beating, bells ringing, signals flashing, and the guns from the ships and Deal Castle firing. Various were the accounts that every passenger brought, that the French had taken Walmer Castle, knocked down the village, killed and eat the inhabitants, &c. &c. &c. &c. Well, it was to be our turn next, and every body was in expectation every minute of seeing the cannibals enter the town.[18]

It turned out to be a false report. Two idle young men making a ruckus at Walmer Castle had been mistaken for an invading force; two hundred cows silhouetted on a hillside had been taken for troops. But the fear had been real. Within a few months, the threat from across the Channel abated and the fear lifted. The coastal villages of Kent could return to normal life (much to the relief of the many smugglers who worked the coast – perhaps they had suffered most of all under the watchful eyes of the troops).

The women longed to see each other again. Carter begged Talbot for a self-portrait, even a crude one sketched out in black lead pencil. Talbot, a talented draughtswoman, demurred, claiming that her one attempt at self-portraiture had been an abject failure – worse than seeing oneself in a distorted looking-glass. As each new year rolled in they would write of their hopes for the coming months; among all those hopes, the most keenly felt was that their paths might cross again. Finally, seven years after their first meeting, a reunion seemed possible: both women would be in London at the same time in the spring of 1748. Months in advance, Talbot wrote to Carter in great excitement of how she was looking forward to spending many happy hours with her and to introducing Carter to her mother, and to Thomas Secker who was Bishop of Oxford and protector of the Talbot women since the death of Talbot's father before she was born. 'What castles am I building!' Talbot admonished herself, as she began to imagine the delightful intellectual conversations the four would share. But her visions were accurate – the two women did reunite in London, and their time together brought great happiness to both, as well as to Mrs Talbot and the Bishop.[19]

Their meetings became more frequent after that: perhaps once a year, or every second year. In 1750, Talbot – who had never seen the sea – dreamed up a scheme to visit Carter in Kent so that the two (along with the Bishop of Oxford) could together gaze out upon the waves. It was May, warm and clear, when the pair reunited in Canterbury. The party travelled to Dover to view the magnificent chalk cliffs, then on to Deal to see Carter's home and the pebbly shores of Deal beach. Talbot was charmed by the Carters. 'How much I like, love, and value all your friends, children, and relations!' she wrote afterwards in a letter of thanks. It was on this visit, perhaps sitting on Deal beach, that Carter asked Talbot for a lock of hair. Though Talbot chided her for asking for such a relic she agreed and later sent the lock in a special case she had embroidered with red and blue silk. 'Though not in the form of a heart,' wrote Talbot, 'yet I desire to send with it my sincerest love.'[20]

Though these young women enjoyed sentimentality, at the heart of their relationship was an intellectual connection. They were never happier than when discussing literature. Some of their earliest letters had touched upon translations of classical texts and very early in their friendship Talbot expressed a wish to be able to read the works of the Greek stoic philosopher Epictetus.[21] Epictetus had espoused a system of calmly accepting the events of one's life, whatever they may be. He believed that one had no control over external events, all one could do was manage one's own actions and responses. It was a philosophy that appealed to Talbot.

The year 1748 had seen the death of Catherine Secker, wife of the Bishop of Oxford, and dear friend to Talbot. Talbot felt that she caught glimpses of her departed friend as she walked through the house they had shared. Everything reminded Talbot of her. Though she knew it was unchristian, Talbot wished that Mrs Secker would return. Carter tried to counsel her friend through this period of grief. She attempted to draw her away from excessive introspection and encouraged her to take more of an interest in worldly things.[22] It was around this time that the two women began discussing the works of Epictetus in earnest. Unable to read Greek, Talbot asked Carter if she would translate some chapters for her.

This was the beginning of Carter's most momentous work – a complete translation of all Epictetus' surviving writings. It would take her nine years to complete. It was never meant to be a grand project; Carter embarked on the first translations simply to cheer up her friend. She sent the first tentative sheets to Talbot in summer 1749, along with a note joking that it had taken her so long that Talbot must have assumed she was translating *all* of Epictetus. Little did she realise what she had begun.[23]

Talbot did not know which she loved more – Epictetus' quiet wisdom, or her friend's elegant turn of phrase. With each new bundle of papers that arrived from Kent, Talbot admired the old philosopher more and more. 'There is a nobleness in its simplicity very striking. A superiority of thought, and shortness of expression, that makes both my mother and me wish for more,' she wrote.

Carter, however, had little free time. Though she had chosen not to marry and start a family of her own, Carter was helping to raise and educate her younger half-siblings, born from her father's second marriage. Her brother Henry in particular took up much of her time, for the family hoped that he would be admitted to Cambridge when he was old enough. He was quick, but mischievous. He hated sitting still and, as he declined and conjugated strings of Greek and Latin nouns and verbs, he would walk in constant circles around his tutor sister until she felt dizzy. Keeping the boy inside at his lessons when he would rather be running through the streets with his friends was a chore. Eventually, Carter hit upon the idea of sitting him at a desk and giving him paper and pencil, ruler and compasses and setting geometry puzzles for him. Henry adored this – finally Carter had found a way to keep the boy happy and have a few moments' peace herself. After lessons each day, Carter would take the children with her on her long walks – 'you cannot imagine what odd, good-humoured sociable kind of things these parties of ours are,' she wrote to Talbot one fine July as the family made the most of the Kentish countryside in the blazing sunshine.[24]

Carter's domestic duties did not just extend to teaching grammar and long walks on sunny days. Though she was not much given to complaining, she did once write to Talbot that 'I have been working my eyes out in making shirts for my brother.' In a rare outburst, she wrote how she wanted to reform the world and have men learn needlework so that women might be freed from the drudgery of endless shirt-making. If she ever had sons, she declared defiantly, they would learn how to make their own shirts.[25] This was as far as Carter's rebellion against domestic life ever went. Really she was happy with her lot and loved her siblings dearly. And of course her reputation in the domestic arts was high enough to garner Samuel Johnson's famous remark about Carter's pudding-making skills.

Carter had not always been a natural pudding-maker. Her siblings liked to remind her of her earliest adventures in cooking when, in a bid to save milk, she had substituted brandy and pepper into a recipe. Clearly the pudding had had a striking taste: for the next fifteen years, her brothers and sisters would never let anyone forget 'the day my sister made the brandy pudding'.[26] After the brandy pudding debacle, Carter upped her game in the kitchen until she finally won the highest accolade – the role of christening-cake-maker-in-chief for the whole clan.

Talbot was an only child and spent much of her life in country seclusion with just her mother for company. She longed for tales about Carter's siblings. She longed too for more of Carter's time. Politely but persistently she would write and ask if the next instalment of Epictetus was ready for her. She took to transcribing Carter's work into a special notebook before sending the folios back, creating her own personal volume of Epictetus that she could read again and again. The Talbot–Secker household would read Carter's work aloud and debate and interpret the passages.

Bishop Secker was impressed by Carter's skill as a translator and he encouraged her to continue with the work. As the author of multiple books himself, he was happy to give tips on structure and style. Carter and the Bishop came to enjoy sparring politely over matters of translation. Once, many years later, when he had become Archbishop of Canterbury and she was visiting him at Lambeth Palace, Carter pointed out how women had been disadvantaged by the way certain words in the Bible had been translated. She argued that in Corinthians 7:12 and 7:13, the translators had changed the meaning of words to try to make out that husbands were superior to wives: the same verb (αφιετω) was used for the husband to mean 'let him not put her away', and for the wife to mean 'let her not leave him'. The Archbishop denied that the same verb was used for both in the original Greek and took Carter to his study where he pulled his Greek Bible from the shelf and was astonished to find that she was quite correct.[27]

As the 1750s wore on, Carter worked on her translation whenever she could. By the middle of the decade, she had translated almost all the surviving words of Epictetus, and Talbot and Secker suggested that perhaps she should publish the work. They believed that her translation deserved an audience of more than a half-dozen friends and family members. They thought that engaging with Stoic philosophy could shed new light on Christian beliefs and values. They also knew that as an unmarried woman Carter had little financial security and they hoped that publishing Epictetus would provide an income in the event of her father's death. It took a while for them to convince Carter that publication was a good idea, but eventually she was persuaded. Still, the problem of time remained. By 1756, Henry had been accepted into Cambridge University (his tutors amazed that he had learned classical languages from a woman). This should have freed up some of Carter's time but she found that domestic chores rushed in to fill the void left by Henry's departure. Talbot had insisted that the book needed a preface with a biography of Epictetus, and an explanation of how Epictetus' pagan views could be reconciled with Christian morality. 'Whoever that somebody or other is who is to write the Life of Epictetus, seeing I have a dozen shirts to make, I do opine, dear Miss Talbot, it cannot be I,' Carter wrote tetchily.[28] Talbot and Secker prevailed; Carter gave in and began writing her introduction. She also began to seek subscribers for the publication.

By 1758, the translation of *All the Works of Epictetus* was complete, the introduction was finished and polished, and that ode of resignation by Hester Mulso Chapone was inserted. Over a thousand subscribers had signed up to support the work, paying half a guinea before publication, and another half-guinea on receipt of the book. The printer was Samuel Richardson – known to Carter for over a decade, since she had reprimanded him (or, as she put it, given him a 'twinkation') for including a poem of hers in *Clarissa* without her knowledge or permission and he had abjectly apologised.[29] The text ran to more than five hundred pages across two volumes.

The reviewers greeted the book enthusiastically. They were as delighted by its contents as by the odd fact that it was written by a woman. Unusually, Carter published under her own name and from this time on (despite her unmarried status) she came to be known as 'Mrs. Carter' – a mark of respect in those days. Naturally there were some who refused to believe such a book could have been produced by a woman. Many thought the translation had been done by Archbishop Secker, as an indignant Mulso Chapone reported to Carter:

the story provokes me . . . some how or other they would fain strip the honour from our sex, and deck out one of their own with it.

I question whether there will not be an act of parliament next sessions to banish you this realm, as an invader of the privileges and
honours of the lords of the creation [i.e. men].[30]

The *Monthly Review* stated that many men would be mortified to
learn that women might understand philosophy just as well as their
brothers or husbands. Men were used to assuming intellectual superiority but, as the reviewer pointed out, this was simply because girls
and boys were given such vastly different educations.[31] The *Critical
Review* praised Carter's ability to grapple with difficult questions of
theology. The reviewer was impressed by the moral tone she took
in the Introduction and enthused that Carter seemed to be as good
a Christian as she was a scholar.[32] This was the key to Carter's success – not just with this particular book, but throughout her whole
life. She was beyond reproach. Not a single person who ever met her
had anything but praise for her morals, piety and Christian conduct.
If so much as a hint of scandal, unorthodoxy, or even eccentricity
had ever been associated with Carter, it would have been seen as
proof that learning Greek affected a woman's moral sense. It would
have been proof that intense study made a woman less feminine, less
sane, less healthy, less good. It would have made life harder not just
for Carter, but for any woman who came after her hoping to learn
ancient languages. Carter knew this and she was always careful to
present herself as the perfect woman: meek and modest, diffident and
self-effacing, completely unthreatening to male authority. Her biographer nephew was keen to emphasise that 'her character was truly
feminine, however strong the powers of her mind might be.'[33] Many
of the Bluestockings strived to be more like her.

The *Gentleman's Magazine* celebrated her book by publishing 'An
Ejaculation' written by a reader overcome with religious feeling
while reading Carter's musings on Christianity.[34] Others suggested
(not entirely seriously) that Carter should be made Poet Laureate or
awarded a doctorate by the University of Oxford.[35] The book was as
popular with the public as with the critics, and sales netted Carter
almost a thousand pounds. This was an enormous sum to her and
would allow her that financial independence so rare among women.
Even thirty years after publication, the book remained in the public

consciousness – when Hannah More played a round of twenty questions with the former Prime Minister Lord North in 1786, the clue she made him guess at was the 'earthen lamp of Epictetus'. After his allotted twenty questions, North gave up in defeat and More revealed the answer: 'I am quite provoked at my own stupidity,' declared his Lordship, 'for I quoted that very lamp last night in the House of Commons.'[36] More (a generation younger than Carter) was not the only Bluestocking to have loved the book. Shortly after publication, Epictetus would lead Carter into a whole new world – the world of Elizabeth Montagu's salon.

Elizabeth Montagu considered the Introduction to *Epictetus* to be 'a piece of perfect good writing'.[37] Her friends who could read Greek told her that the translation was a very good one. She wrote to her sister Scott at her new cottage in Batheaston to recommend obtaining a copy if she could.

Montagu and Carter had met briefly the previous year. Montagu had thought Carter modest, amiable and gentle; but Carter had seemed nervous of the great hostess. After Montagu read *Epictetus*, she determined to try again to get to know Carter and so invited her to dine at Hill Street. The dinner was a success and afterwards Montagu wrote a warm letter to her new friend, saying that she looked upon their meeting as one of the luckiest incidents of her life.[38]

Montagu longed to become closer to Carter and, like Talbot before her, she began to dream of visiting Carter at Deal. Montagu imagined Carter reading Livy to her after evening walks along the seashore. Montagu dreamed of learning Greek so that she could read and discuss Xenophon's words with her friend. She resolved never to read Aristotle's *Ethics* after Carter alluded to it being excessively pagan. Montagu's letters in these early days often focussed on classics and religion – she was trying to impress Carter.[39] It was a strange feeling for Montagu who was so used to being an object of veneration, but she rather liked having another woman to look up to.

Within a few months of their first Hill Street dinner, Montagu invited Carter to stay with her in London during the season. Though Carter would have been happy to spend time in London and time with Montagu, she hated the idea of being someone's house guest, bound to their whims and their schedule. Carter wrote truthfully to Montagu that she could not enjoy London unless in a lodging of her own, and that she could not afford a London lodging just then. 'My spirit of liberty is strangely untractable and wild,' Carter explained, 'I must have something like a home; somewhere to rest an aching head without giving any body any trouble.'⁴⁰

Montagu helped Carter to find a set of rooms to rent in nearby Clarges Street, just off Piccadilly. Montagu would invite Carter to dine often, but Carter told her truthfully that she preferred eating alone sometimes. Instead of a hot meal she treated herself to tea and cake which, she told Montagu, was 'mighty consistent with loitering over a book'.⁴¹ She would often winter in Clarges Street, balancing the busy social life of the Bluestockings with her innate need for solitude.

The meeting of Montagu and Carter was a key moment in Bluestocking history. Montagu's fortune and hosting skills, combined with Carter's unquestionable intellectual brilliance, made for a winning combination. It was not just in their semi-public roles as *salonnière* and author that the two women complemented each other: as friends they were also perfect foils, each inspired to better herself by her relationship with the other. When Carter had admonished herself for having a spirit 'strangely untractable and wild', Montagu had recognised that she was the same, but proud Montagu had never considered it a fault. Now, trying to impress the most moral of Bluestockings, she wrote to her:

> I am a little fearful that what you call faults in yourself, I have called virtues, when I have found them in my own mind; particularly when you accuse yourself of a wild and untractable love of liberty, because you want a place where you can enjoy some hours every day uninterrupted. This is my own turn, and I thought it an excellence, a perfection, and almost a virtue.⁴²

As time passed and the two became better acquainted, Montagu's letters took on that more whimsical tone her correspondents knew so well. When Carter went with Talbot to Bristol to take the waters, Montagu joked about the entertainments she imagined the women enjoying there, conjuring an image of 'Miss Betsy Carter gay from a ball, and flippant from the pump-room'. She begged Carter for more details of fashionable Bristol life, imploring, 'I hope you will write to me soon, and pray tell me whether you like pompons or aigrettes [feathers] in the hair; if you put on rouge, dance minuets and cotillions, that I may describe and define you in your Bristol state.'[43] Carter, so often simply seen as serious and pious, was glad to have light-hearted Montagu as a constant source of levity and fun in her life. Montagu in turn admired Carter's seriousness of purpose. 'You would give ballast to an imagination that carries too much sail,' she wrote once, perhaps beginning to contemplate taking on a project that would bring her even deeper intellectual satisfaction than her salons.[44]

In 1760, two years after becoming friends with Carter, Montagu took her first tentative step towards becoming an author: she published three *Dialogues of the Dead* alongside a longer collection of dialogues by her friend George Lyttelton – a statesman, peer, writer and patron of the arts. Like the *Dialogues of the Dead* Hester Thrale would write after the stillbirth of her son, Montagu's dialogues poked fun at the fashionable society in which she moved. The most striking of her characters was Mrs Modish, a *bon ton* lady who is summoned by the god Mercury to the underworld. The lady protests that she does not have time to die just then; it can perhaps be put off until the end of the season. 'I am engaged, absolutely engaged,' she insists to a bemused Mercury:

> look on my Chimney-piece, and you will see I was engaged to
> the Play on Mondays, Balls on Tuesdays, the Opera on Saturdays,
> and Card-assemblies the rest of the week, for two months to
> come; and it would be *the rudest thing in the world* not to keep my
> appointments.

Then her tone changes as she contemplates what the underworld will be like, and imagines herself happily drinking from the River Lethe whose waters brought forgetfulness. Surprised, Mercury asks her why she should wish away the memories of what seemed a happy life. 'Diversion was indeed the business of my Life,' she replies, 'but as to Pleasure I have enjoyed none since the novelty of my amusements was gone off. Can one be pleased with seeing the same thing over and over again?' Her next words summed up the lives of so many eighteenth-century women: 'I was too much engaged to think at all.'[45] It echoed the sentiment Montagu had described to the Duchess of Portland so many years earlier when discussing why men tried to suppress female education: 'they know that fools make the best slaves.'[46]

Many saw the piece as straightforwardly mocking foolish fashionable women (including many fashionable women themselves who, reported Montagu, 'toss'd their heads & said it was abominable satirical'[47]). But if one read between the lines, one could see a deeper criticism of a society that forced women into these narrow and pointless lives. Mrs Modish did the best she could with the hand dealt to her.

Montagu wrote anonymously, and anonymous works always attracted speculation. Several names were proposed, including Elizabeth Carter. In literary London, however, anonymous identities were poorly kept secrets and the true name of the author was guessed soon after publication.

The dialogues were well-received, with one reviewer stating that the author 'is a very great master of the pen'.[48] But the reviewer Montagu cared most about pleasing was Carter. With trepidation she awaited Carter's verdict and was delighted when she received a letter of warm congratulations. She was grateful that Carter had encouraged her to publish, saying, 'at last I may become an author in form. It enlarges the sphere of action, and lengthens the short period of human life.'[49] Montagu's decision to become an author could save her from the dull oblivion that consumed women like Mrs Modish.

So inspired was Montagu by this new direction in her life that she set out to encourage other women to write more. She turned first to Carter who had not produced any more books since the success of *Epictetus* two years earlier. Montagu knew that Carter had a collection of poetry good enough to print and she urged her to send it to press.[50] When Carter wrote her a pretty ode, Montagu encouraged her to lay aside some of her domestic tasks so that she would have more time for poetry. 'Pray write some more odes,' she begged, 'and let your seamstresses do your plain work.'[51] Montagu's pleas worked: in 1762 Carter published her *Poems on Several Occasions*.

Theirs was a productive friendship. They would recommend books to each other and deliberately read the same books at the same time so that they could share their opinions on them. Wealthy Montagu would give Carter books and even have them bound for her. When Carter sent notes of thanks, Montagu would lightly bat her gratitude away: 'you are very good with your thanks,' she wrote once, 'but it seems to me as if my left hand was to thank my right for making a pair of gloves.'[52] Though Montagu might have been the bestower of gifts and hospitality, she was profoundly aware of all the intangible benefits she received from the friendship. There was a sense of sorority between the women that distinguished it from the friendships she enjoyed with the men who attended her salons. There was an innate understanding of just how carefully each woman had had to work to build the life she lived, of the lone-liness one might feel as an intellectual woman, of the experience of being talked down to by men. Carter and Montagu could be equals in friendship in a way that was almost impossible between a woman and a man.

Beyond the simple joys of friendship, Montagu was inspired by Carter. It was like nothing she had ever known before; she found a deep intellectual satisfaction in their correspondence and conversations. Beyond that again, her feelings for Carter (like Carter's feelings for Talbot) seemed tinged almost with a hint of romantic love. Montagu wrote letters to Carter that ran: 'It is but little more than four & twenty hours since I could instantly and immediately breathe every thought into the ear of my Dear Miss Carter,' and,

> you left London only this morning & I am writing to you tonight, does it not seem unreasonable? I hope not, as you must know there are habits which it is hard to break, & alas I was in the habitude of conversing with you every day.

It is easy to see what Carter meant to her.[53] And Carter would write back in kind: 'I longed for you extremely the other night at Reading, to ramble by moonlight amongst the ruins of an old abbey.' Though maybe sensing that she was overdoing it, Carter pulled back into a more humorous vein: 'consider how few people one would chuse for companions in such a scene . . . There are many very good sort of folks whom one may tolerate, and even be mighty well pleased with in broad sunshine, who would be quite insufferable by moonlight.'[54]

Perhaps this intense tone was what led Edward Montagu to a strong dislike of Elizabeth Carter. Edward, the kindest and meekest of husbands, who never refused his wife permission to see any of her friends, or host whatever assemblies she wished, frequently grumbled about Carter. Though Montagu would have loved to have her friend stay in Hill Street, she had to admit that Carter's insistence on taking lodgings did make things easier with Edward. Once he said that she 'would be a good sort of woman *if she was not so pious*'. Another time he complained that the very sight of Carter's face made him melancholy. Montagu retorted briskly – 'I told him it was a jolly round face, and if he found any melancholly it was of his own bringing.' Edward claimed to be able to see the sign of the cross from Carter's baptism still hovering about her visage.[55] (Many years later, when Frances Burney met Carter at Bath for the first time, she would describe how the older lady's 'whole face seems to beam with goodness, piety, and philanthropy'.[56])

Whatever her husband's opinion, Montagu came to see herself and Carter as so close as to be almost inseparable: 'I defy the splitters of a hair, & the dividers of a polype to disunite [us],' she wrote once.[57] (Polyps – those fabulous little creatures that appeared to be half-plant and half-animal – had recently been identified by naturalists.[58]) Their closeness was well-known among their friends, and also more widely, even being written about in newspapers.[59] As Carter was drawn into the Bluestocking world, her friendship with Montagu was much celebrated, symbolising all that was best about this quirky group of women: together they presented a carefully considered picture of rationality, intellect, gentility and fun.

Carter was spending less time at Deal and more time with Montagu. In London she visited Hill Street frequently – attending both gay assemblies and private teas. At Sandleford, Carter spent many happy summer holidays, wandering the beautiful grounds with her friend by day, and conversing, reading or writing by night. The two also travelled to visit mutual friends. Ahead of their visiting the poet Edward Young, he wrote to Montagu:

was I a Saint and could work miracles I would reduce you two ladys to the common level of your sex, being jealous for the credit of my own; which has hitherto presum'd to boast an usurp'd superiority in the realms of genius and the letter'd world.[60]

Though Young was joking, he was right that learned ladies were seen to be encroaching on male territory. And learned ladies, no matter how reputable, no matter how much their male friends insisted they said such things in jest, remained figures of curiosity and suspicion.

In 1763, the two ladies decided to take a trip to the continent together to drink the waters at the famous town of Spa. For both, it was to be their first trip overseas. Carter was nervous about the prospect of travelling abroad but her desire to see the world and to spend more time in Montagu's company emboldened her.[61]

Also along for the trip was Montagu's old friend William Pulteney, the Earl of Bath – a retired politician (and said to be the holder of the record for the shortest term as Prime Minister, a position he occupied for just two days). Montagu had met Pulteney at Tunbridge Wells a few seasons earlier and they had become close – so close that scurrilous rumours circulated about them.[62] Probably the rumours were stoked by Pulteney writing letters to Montagu proclaiming that he was 'at this Instant over head and ears in love' with her. She responded lightly that she would consider him as a suitor if he would wait forty years for her; he bargained her down to twenty. Montagu (then in her forties) saw the letters as a friendly jest and had only platonic feelings for her septuagenarian friend. Though it was a platonic friendship, it was an intense one, with over four hundred letters exchanged in just four years. Montagu introduced Pulteney to Carter and the three got along wonderfully well. They often holidayed together at Pulteney's house. Knowing that she was not wealthy, Pulteney would bestow gifts upon Carter, but he would try to do it in such a way as not to make her feel awkward. Once, he asked Montagu to choose some silk that would be to Carter's taste; he bought it, then told Carter he had found it in his house and no longer needed it.[63] No doubt she saw through these harmless deceptions, and was glad to count this kind, wise old man among her good friends.

With mounting excitement, the three planned their trip to Spa. Edward Montagu grumbled morosely in the background about expense and the difficulties of foreign travel and Elizabeth Carter's pious face. Montagu gently convinced him of the necessity of the trip, and set about arranging everything.

It was a summer crossing. They departed Dover at four o'clock in the morning, the sun just about to rise. Though the weather was fair, Carter was unwell for much of the five-hour passage. At Calais, her mood was lifted by the sight of several burly men wading towards their boat to carry the ladies ashore. These mermen, whom Montagu remembered as being crowned with seaweed, took the women on their backs – saving their petticoats, but undoing their sense of decorum. 'It is better not to be too minute in the description of it,' Montagu joked later in a letter. That same letter poked gentle fun at Carter who found herself transformed by the continent. At first, Carter seemed true to form. When the party stopped at the Jesuit College in St Omer, they requested to see some Greek manuscripts whereupon Carter amazed the librarian by translating them. But by the time they reached Lille, Carter's attention had turned to more frivolous matters, as Montagu reported:

> with the same facility with which [Carter] translated Epictetus from greek into english, she translated her native timidity into french airs, and french modes, bought robes trimmed with blonde and souci denton, Colliers, bouquets, des engageantes and all the most labour'd ornaments of dress.[64]

This was the same Carter who had once written with disgust of how her fellow English men and women

> seem to lose all sense of what is serious and decent in pursuit of French diversions, and are surrounded by French taylors, French valets, French dancing masters, and French cooks . . . Our fine ladies . . . become helpless to themselves, and troublesome to all the world besides, with French hoops, and run into an indecent extravagance of dress, inconsistent with all rules of sober appearance.[65]

Now, in France, Carter read Montagu's letter and found it so amusing (and such an accurate description of the change that had come over her) that she copied it out and sent it to Catherine Talbot. With it, she enclosed a note of her own: 'I am sorry to confirm any part of Mrs. Montagu's scandal but it is an indeniable truth that I am going to dress for the ball.' A few days' stay in Brussels saw Carter buying more clothes and accessories. There was even talk that she might paint her face, but that was a step too far for Carter.[66]

As the party travelled slowly across France and Belgium towards their destination, they stopped off at multiple small towns. In almost every one of these towns, Carter would seek out the local convent. Her letters are filled with the usual anti-Catholic bigotry of the English at this time, with dismissive comments on 'the miserable, trifling fopperies of Popery', and the 'profusion of silly gewgaw finery' in the churches she visited.[67] And yet she was irresistibly drawn towards nuns. Perhaps she felt that if she had been born in a Catholic country she could have found a life for herself among them – though of course, as a good Anglican, she could never admit that.

At Spa the party took the waters, attended the assemblies and tried to identify the many European aristocrats in attendance. They would walk out to the surrounding hills and marvel at the dramatic landscape – craggy summits, green valleys, dense woodlands.[68] For Montagu, the waters seemed to work; she found herself feeling more vigorous than she had for a long time. For Carter, the waters were less successful, and the headaches that had plagued her since girlhood remained. After a few weeks, the party began to make its way home. The route back was different – they travelled through the low countries and Montagu's letters from this leg of the journey reveal the casual prejudices of British travellers against all things foreign: Utrecht was exceedingly dull and its inhabitants inexpressibly stupid; Amsterdam was wealthy but horrible; no one could understand her when she tried to explain that she did not speak Dutch. Home at last, all hailed the general success of the trip.

Though the trip itself had been an amusing excursion, there was only so much that the waters of Spa could do. William Pulteney's health had been failing throughout his seventies. He had suffered a hard blow in 1763 when his only surviving child, a son called William, had died of a fever in Madrid while commanding British forces during the Seven Years War. Though Pulteney had seemed to rally at

Spa, he declined after the group's return to England and died aged eighty in 1764.

Though his death was not a surprise, Montagu took it hard. Carter travelled to Sandleford to grieve with her. Just as when she had grieved for her little son two decades earlier, Montagu desperately sought a distraction. She found it in Shakespeare.

She had loved Shakespeare since the Robinson family used to sit about the fireside at Monk's Horton and listen to his words read aloud. She had loved him since she had first seen his plays on the London stage as she sat in a velvet and gilt box with the Duchess of Portland. She found she loved him more still when 'the saucy Frenchman' Voltaire took a pop at this English hero. Voltaire dismissed Shakespeare's plays as monstrous farces; Montagu dismissed Voltaire as a foolish coxcomb.[69] Voltaire's disparagement had needled the English literati for years, but now Montagu decided to do something about it.

Grief had driven Montagu to look for a distraction; Voltaire had (unwittingly) pointed her towards the perfect subject matter; but it was her friendship with Carter that truly pushed her towards becoming a published writer. Without the friendship of this female scholar who showed, in practical terms, how a woman could be searingly clever but also respectable, Montagu might never have found the courage to write. Inspired and encouraged by her friend, Montagu began a work of criticism of her own.

It really was a project that required courage. It was a much more ambitious project than her earlier *Dialogues of the Dead*, but that was not the main problem. Literary criticism was considered a male pursuit. Furthermore, Montagu's subject was a male writer, and not just any male writer but one considered to be of national importance. Women were seen as ill qualified to make public comments either on men or on matters of national importance.

In trepidation, Montagu began researching her book in 1764 – two hundred years after Shakespeare's birth. She was not the only one thinking about the Bard in that anniversary year. Samuel Johnson was putting the finishing touches to his own edition of Shakespeare's plays. Johnson had had the edition in mind for twenty years. It had coloured much of his work in the previous decades – his *Dictionary* cited Shakespeare more than any other writer. Johnson's new edition contained a preface which analysed Shakespeare's language and explored the backgrounds and deeper meanings of the plays. Upon reading it, Montagu became concerned about her own book and wrote to her sister: 'I don't know whether after Mr Johnson people will desire any more criticisms on Shakespear . . . his Preface is so ingenious it terrifys me.'[70]

Terrified she might have been, but Montagu kept writing. She wrote in London, she wrote in Sandleford, she wrote while visiting Scott's commune in Hitcham. Montagu's friends were supportive: Carter would read through drafts for her; and Benjamin Stillingfleet would later correct the proofs.

The book (titled *An Essay on the Writings and Genius of Shakespear, compared with the Greek and French dramatic Poets; with some remarks upon the Misrepresentations of Mons. De Voltaire*) was published anonymously in May 1769. First came the speculation about the author, with several men proposed as the brains behind this elegant three-hundred-page volume. Next came the reviews praising its author, with male pronouns in abundance.[71] When Elizabeth Carter's brother spoke highly of the book and its author, Carter wrote to Montagu that she listened to him call the author '*he* and *him*' as patiently as she could, 'while I was inwardly wild to oppose such an injury'.[72] Montagu had a similar experience reading the reviews: 'they talk of *him* till they make me feel whether I have not a beard on my chin.' Some reviewers praised the 'classical' tone of the book, which led to speculation that Elizabeth Carter had written it. Edward Montagu was another popular candidate. Joshua Reynolds bet five guineas that it was by one Mr Wharton.[73] 'I cannot help laughing at all the Guessers,' Montagu wrote, '& exult in the guesses when they alight on Ld Lyttelton & Mrs. Carter.' Even the publishers did not know the true author of the manuscript. Montagu communicated with them via anonymous letters, often asking friends to post them from other parts of London.[74]

The author, however, was sniffed out pretty quickly. For modesty's sake, Montagu continued to deny authorship of the *Essay*. Secretly, though, she was happy to have the secret made public. 'Whilst I was young, I should not have liked to have been class'd among authors,' Montagu wrote to her father Matthew, 'but at my age it is less unbecoming.' Matthew was proud of his daughter's success: 'the Gentleman is quite vain that his daughter has written a book,' she reported to her husband.[75]

Voltaire was less impressed by Montagu's performance. David Garrick gleefully informed Montagu that the Frenchman was so cross about her *Essay* that he had banned all English people from his house in perpetuity.[76] It was better than any glowing review. It was more pleasing to her than seeing the first print run sell out; or seeing her book translated into several European languages; or running through multiple editions – all of which came to pass.

Garrick was a great champion of Shakespeare and, perhaps more than anyone else, he was seen as the public face of all things Shakespearean in the eighteenth century. His performances of Shakespeare's leading men were legendary. In 1769 (the same year that Montagu's *Essay* was published) Garrick organised a jubilee event at Stratford-upon-Avon. He built a pavilion (the first theatre in Stratford dedicated to the Bard), and planned a series of plays, concerts and balls, and a grand pageant. Unfortunately the festival was marred by heavy rains, but Garrick's jubilee celebrations put Stratford on the cultural map of Britain and spawned the whole industry of Shakespeare commemoration in the town.

As the public face of the newly emerging Shakespeare industry, Garrick's support was crucial to the success of Montagu's *Essay*. He publicly praised the book and recommended it widely.[77] He even published a poem praising Montagu's performance, and describing the battle between her and Voltaire:

> A Giant He, among the Sons of France
> And at our Shakespeare pois'd his glitt'ring Lance.
> Out rush'd a Female to protect the Bard,
> Snatch'd up her Spear, and for the fight prepar'd.[78]

Many admired Montagu's *Essay* but there was a crucial member of the eighteenth-century literati who did not. Samuel Johnson was never likely to take kindly to a rival author – especially one as significant as Montagu – publishing on a similar topic at around the same time as his own new edition of Shakespeare appeared. The fact that many preferred Montagu's book to Johnson's must have rankled. Johnson dismissed Montagu's book as having no real criticism in it. Those who knew both Johnson and Montagu well attributed his stance to envy and prejudice, rather than any real problem with Montagu's criticism.

Ever philosophical, Montagu knew that her sex coloured the reception of the book. She might have written the most perfect book possible about Shakespeare, but still, 'the Lords of the Creation [i.e. men] wd only say, that I got a good goose quill, had good paper & sat in a Bow window.' It was something she and Carter had discussed numerous times throughout their friendship. Once, chatting about a mutual friend who was known to be an extremely obedient wife, Montagu commented to Carter:

> She would have preferred her husband's discourse to the angels. I am afraid you and I my dear friend should have entered into some metaphysical disquisitions with the angel, we are not so perfectly the rib of man as Woman ought to be. We can think for ourselves, and also act for ourselves.[79]

It was a difficult kind of woman to be: smart enough and independent enough to pursue a life of the mind, but carefully conditioned to put family honour, duty and public opinion above any wishes of their own.

Carter's career was possible because she had remained unmarried; Montagu's because she had married a man who gave her comparative freedom. For these Bluestockings, friendships with other like-minded women were crucial to their success. These friendships operated outside the bounds of patriarchy. Women's relationships with men – be it a father or a husband – demanded a woman's time, a woman's duty, a woman's obedience. Friendships with other women did not make demands; rather they *gave* inspiration, comfort, support and joy.

9

LOVE

I T WAS DURING a parlour game at Streatham that Hester Thrale realised
her husband had fallen in love. The object of his affections was
Sophia Streatfeild, an accomplished young woman who had recently
begun moving in Bluestocking circles. Thrale admired her because she
could read Greek; today, the *Dictionary of National Biography* gives her
occupation simply as 'beauty'. It may have been her looks rather than
her fluency in Greek that first attracted Henry's attention.

At Streatham that afternoon in the winter of 1778, the wits were
toying with Oliver Goldsmith's poem *Retaliation* in which he compared his contemporaries to the dishes at a feast. Goldsmith, whose
portrait hung with the Streatham Worthies in the library, had died
four years earlier. He floated above the gathering as those below
recalled his lines and his descriptions of others among the Streatham
Worthies: he had called Burke 'tongue, with a garnish of brains';
Garrick was a salad – 'for in him we see / oil, vinegar, sugar, and
saltness agree'; Reynolds was lamb. Now the wits added more of
their number to the comparisons: they declared Samuel Johnson
to be a haunch of venison; Elizabeth Montagu was soup *à la reine*;
Charles Burney was a dish of fine green tea; while Frances Burney
was a woodcock. Sophie Streatfeild was a white fricassee.

Thrale neatly listed these comparisons in her *Thraliana* later that
day. A footnote to her entry about Streatfeild reveals, for the first
time, a streak of jealousy: 'I see, I see. My Husband is in Love with
her. Fowl fracassee – broken up will be poor H.L.T. [Hester Lynch
Thrale].'[1] Even in a fit of jealousy, she found time for a pun and a
rhyme.

The Thrales had first met Streatfeild at Brighton in the autumn of
1777 and soon realised that they had something in common: Hester's

girlhood Latin tutor Arthur Collier had also been Greek tutor to
Streatfeild. A friendship grew up quickly. Thrale was struck by the
younger woman and praised her lavishly, admiring her pretty face,
elegant carriage, affectionate nature, lovely manners and her highly
cultivated mind.[2]

A few months later, they had become so close that Thrale permitted Streatfeild to write in the *Thraliana* – the only other hand that
appears in the notebooks. At the start of the third volume (begun in
May 1778) the title stands out in Streatfeild's perfectly formed Gothic-
style script. Later that summer, Thrale asked Streatfeild (along with
Montagu) to be godmother to her new daughter Harriett.[3] Streatfeild was invited to spend more and more time at Streatham. She met
Frances Burney who admired her deeply for her learning, her beauty
and her manners.[4] In the autumn they all holidayed in Brighton,
before the Thrales visited Streatfeild and her mother in Tunbridge
Wells.

After her proficiency in Greek and her looks, the thing people
found most intriguing about Streatfeild was her ability to cry on
command. In a salon full of wits, it was her preferred parlour trick.
At breakfast one morning in Streatham Thrale implored Streatfeild to
show it off. Without a word, reported Burney who was looking on,

> wonder of wonders . . . two Crystal Tears came into the soft Eyes of
> the S.S., - & rolled gently down her Cheeks! – such a sight I never
> saw before, nor could I have believed; - she *offered* not to conceal,
> or dissipate them, - on the contrary, she really *contrived* to have them
> seen by everybody. She looked, indeed, uncommonly handsome.[5]

Everyone agreed that the tears enhanced her beauty. One of the
Streathamites once declared that four days with Streatfeild would
surely make him want to marry her by the fifth. 'You'd be devilish
tired of her . . . in half a year,' pointed out another, 'a *crying* Wife will
never do!'[6] Henry Thrale, watching her at breakfast that morning,
certainly thought her lovely to look at.

In 1778, Streatfeild spent Christmas with the Thrales. It was just a
few weeks since Thrale had first noticed Henry's feelings for her. As
Thrale entertained her guests, she caught herself observing Henry.
She feigned a lightness of manner as she watched him watching

Streatfeild. He was 'so in Love with S:S:', she wrote in *The Children's Book*, 'that it is comical'. The next lines tell of her hopes of a new pregnancy – the pregnancy that would end in agony on the brew-house floor eight months later – before she finished the volume with a prayer asking to lose no more of her children. And then, in a postscript squashed in at the bottom of the page, a more honest admission of her feelings about Streatfeild: if God would answer her prayer, 'I will not fret about this Rival this S.S. no I won't.'[7]

Breezy as Thrale might have tried to appear, she was worried. Henry had had mistresses before, though he had never been very serious about any of the other women he chased. Now, she saw, he was really in love. Thrale knew that the affair was unlikely to become sexual. This was because of Streatfeild's morals and her awareness of the deep double standard that divided a philandering man from an adulterous woman, rather than any concerns Henry may have had about infidelity. Streatfeild enjoyed the attentions of this wealthy older man and was genuinely fond of him but her feelings did not run as deep as his. In any case, she was busy developing a romantic attachment to a chaplain of her acquaintance.

After Christmas, the guests departed Streatham and Thrale watched as her husband pined for Streatfeild. He was counting the days until Parliament sat again and he would have an excuse to go up to town. When he finally escaped back to the capital, Henry took to leaving his carriage at his sister's house in Hanover Square and walking the few minutes to Streatfeild's house. Unlikely as it was that they were having a physical affair, such behaviour lent the whole thing a sordid air and sent the gossip-mongers into ecstasy.

Stories about Streatfeild began to appear in the newspapers. Henry Thrale was not the only man to lust after her: even more newsworthy was the Attorney General's passion for her. Thrale wondered if she was a fool not to intervene in Henry's latest dalliance. The closest she ever came was when the Bishop of Chester fell for Streatfeild. This married man, a quarter-century older than Streatfeild, wrote tender letters to her, filled with all the sentiment a lover might desire. When Streatfeild showed these pages to Thrale, the older woman saw the power of Streatfeild's attractive force and suddenly burst out with these lines from Pope's translation of the *Iliad*:

> Rage uncontrolled through all the hostile crew,
> But touch not Hector; Hector is my due.

If it was meant to warn Streatfeild off Henry, it fell flat. Henry was sitting in the corner listening quietly to the exchange and pointed out that Streatfeild would have been able to quote the original Greek. 'His saying so, piqued me; & piqued me because it was true,' admitted a deflated Thrale. 'I wish I understood Greek!'[8]

The summer of 1779 saw Thrale's belly swell once again with child. It was in August that sudden pangs seemed to augur ill for the pregnancy. As Thrale contemplated her own likely death during a stillbirth, she began to wonder (as she so often did at these times) which of her friends Henry would marry after her demise. Streatfeild was the obvious candidate. But Henry was in poor health too, having been struck down by that palsy after hearing of his former brother-in-law's bankruptcy. This would make him less attractive to Streatfeild. It was one of the few thoughts Thrale found comforting during those dreadful weeks.

By October she had recovered from the stillbirth but Henry's health was declining. Depression and mental fog settled over him. Hoping to lift his spirits, Thrale agreed to a family trip to Tunbridge Wells to see Streatfeild, followed by a stay at Brighton. The first part of the trip was not the success that Thrale had envisioned. The formerly fond couple met with little enthusiasm. Henry was preoccupied by his poor health, and Streatfeild had worries of her own. She had just discovered that the chaplain she had loved, and who was the only man she ever really thought of marrying, already had a wife. Streatfeild's friends were not entirely sympathetic. Thrale thought it was hardly surprising as Streatfeild had loved first, and everyone knew that love should begin on the man's side. Burney agreed and she too chided Streatfeild for having acted unnaturally: 'I am very sorry for her disappointment, but *Ladies* chusing openly for themselves, never appeared to me a *right* thing, - nor does it prove *prosperous*.'[9]

At Brighton, things went better. The sea-bathing seemed to help Henry, and he took once more to riding out, eating with appetite and delighting in the company of his friends. A few pleasant weeks, however, could make little difference to his overall decline. Henry began to suffer from increasingly frequent attacks of palsy and apoplexy in the following years. He could find consolation only in Streatfeild's company. The awkward trip to Tunbridge Wells was forgotten and the pair appeared again almost like young lovers. At a party of tea, cards and supper at Streatham, Henry sat by Streatfeild, 'he pressed her Hand to his Heart . . . & said Sophy we shall not enjoy this long, & tonight I will not be cheated of my *Only Comfort.*' Thrale rolled her eyes and continued her hosting. When his health took a turn for the worse and he was confined to bed, Streatfeild sat by him for hours. 'Who would not suffer even all that I have endured, to be pitied by *you!*' he would sigh at her, quite ignoring his wife, eldest daughter and sisters who had also sat by his bedside through the long hours of many nights.[10] He suggested that they commission a portrait of Streatfeild to hang with the Streatham Worthies, but Thrale drew the line at that.

By the end of 1780, Henry's health was so bad that he required round after round of blisters, bleeding and strong medicines. By the spring of 1781, he was unable to stay awake for more than four hours at a time. April saw Henry looking a little better. Thrale came home from an outing one evening to find him sitting up in the parlour at Deadman's Place with Johnson and Boswell. The next day Johnson came to dine, and Baretti too (who had reappeared in the Thrales's lives as suddenly as he had left four years earlier). Henry ate voraciously – something his physicians had warned him against. His alarmed wife asked him to restrain himself. Johnson was alarmed too and reminded Henry of what the doctors said – to overeat in his condition was tantamount to committing suicide. Henry continued munching his way through the courses.

The following morning, Thrale went out seeking distraction. She found it in an exhibition of drawings from the last voyage of Captain Cook to the South Seas and Pacific Islands. London was caught up in South Seas fever those days as more Europeans ventured further and further from home, and sent back descriptions, pictures and stories of the marvellous lands they saw. A few months earlier, Thrale had attended Court for the Queen's birthday wearing a silk gown inspired by a Hawaiian pattern and trimmed lavishly with feathers and gold to create an even more outlandish effect. 'It was violently admired to be sure,' she recorded afterwards, 'and celebrated in all the Papers of the Day.' Thrale and Burney took to addressing each other as 'tayo' or 'tyo' – they had learned it from Burney's brother James who had sailed with Cook and told them that it was the Tahitian word for a 'bosom friend'. At the exhibition of pictures that morning, Thrale saw many other Bluestockings.[11]

Thrale spent the rest of the day finalising the details of the *conversazione* and musical evening she was to host the next day. Her guests of honour were to be several Asian ambassadors come to London to negotiate a treaty. A high-spirited Henry kept adding to the guest list but, despite the gaiety, Thrale dissolved in floods of tears again and again throughout the day. She was overcome with premonitions about Henry's demise. Henry ate even more at dinner that afternoon and washed down the enormous quantities of food with several pints of strong beer. When Queeney (sixteen years old now) went to see her father in his room later, she found him lying on the ground. The girl began to panic but Henry insisted that he lay like that by choice. Still, the physician was summoned. By the time he arrived, Henry was having apoplectic fits. He was bled, but it was too late. Johnson sat with him through his final day, until he passed away in the early hours of the morning.

Thrale fled first to Streatham, and then to Brighton, desperate for solitude. Henry was buried at Streatham, laid to rest alongside so many of his children. The funeral was a grand one: six men in mourning rode on horseback behind the two mourning coaches, the pews of the church were lined all in black. Thrale saw none of this, for women did not usually attend funerals then. She stayed in Brighton and gathered her thoughts.

Despite his many infidelities and his cruel treatment of her during her final labour, Thrale held no bitterness towards her late husband. Theirs had been a mostly amicable marriage, largely driven by Thrale's awareness that as a woman she had little official power within their relationship. She was a naturally conciliatory person, but below this conciliatory nature lay a deep fear that an argument would show up her low worth as a woman. If she were to fight with her husband and lose, she wrote, 'it would make *me* miserable: to have one's own un Importance presented suddenly to one's Sight, and one's own

Qualities insolently undervalued by those who do not even *pretend* to possess them.'[12] Thrale had made it a rule never to object to anything Henry did, and never to propose anything to which he was likely to say no.

A few weeks after Henry died, Burney asked Thrale if she had ever been in love. She said she had not. To lighten the mood she joked that she had only ever loved herself. She had never been what she called a 'fond wife' and, perhaps consequently, had rarely been a jealous one.[13] It was a marriage without passion which, while it had some disadvantages, did at least mean that there was little marital strife.

Henry Thrale had valued his wife's mind. Ever since she had helped him win his first election, he had respected her intellect and had never tried to interfere with her writing or hosting. When he died, he left a decent will. He trusted Thrale to take over the brewery and gave her more financial freedom than many widows experienced. She was given the use of the houses at both Streatham and Deadman's Place for the rest of her life; the contents of each were hers to do with as she wished; £2,000 a year was left for herself; and an allowance of £150 per year for expenses relating to the younger children and £200 for the older ones. The girls would inherit £20,000 each when they came of age.[14]

The brewery was hers now too. This was Henry's final vote of confidence in her, but she was not entirely sure that his confidence was well placed. Though she had helped in the counting house and had been a guiding force in keeping the brewery solvent, Thrale was not sure that she wanted to become a businesswoman. But just a month after Henry's death, she was back in Southwark. She spent three days a week in the counting house and left each day feeling oppressed by the business and by her surroundings.

When Elizabeth Montagu heard of Thrale's work in the brewery, she declared that a statue should be erected to her for her diligence. Thrale suspected that Montagu was simply happy to have her tied up in Southwark, unable to outshine her at the salon. Samuel Johnson (who was named as a co-guardian to the children in Henry's will) became the greatest champion of the brewery. He rallied around Thrale, exhorting her to run the business to the best of her abilities and even offering practical help. It tickled Thrale to see this great man of letters grappling with the world of commerce, but she never mustered any real enthusiasm for the business and, before the end of the month, she decided to sell it.

By June the brewery was gone – sold to the wealthy Quaker businessman David Barclay for £135,000. For a woman to negotiate such a deal was extraordinary. Thrale considered it the greatest feat of her life. More than the money, she was pleased to have earned peace and stability. Johnson considered it a womanly surrender – to give up the possibility of earning greater sums and to eschew risk seemed weak to him. But Thrale was content. She returned to Streatham directly after the sale, waving a white pocket handkerchief from the carriage window as a signal to Queeney and Frances Burney, waiting impatiently upon the lawn, that all had gone well. The two younger women ran to the coach and, in the midst of endless embraces, Thrale told them of her grand negotiations.

Thrale was delighted to be done with Deadman's Place and spent the summer luxuriating in the gardens of Streatham. As a recently widowed woman it would have been unseemly for her to go out socialising, so she brought her friends to her. Burney, though frantically trying to finish writing her novel *Cecilia*, spent much of the summer at Streatham. The newspapers, obsessing over this intense Bluestocking friendship, wrote about how 'Miss Burney, the sprightly Writer of the elegant Novel Evelina, is now domesticated with Mrs Thrale in the same manner that Miss More is with Mrs Garrick, & Mrs Carter with Mrs Montague.' Burney, who always hated seeing her name in the newspapers, considered this paragraph 'most insufferably impertinent'.[15] But it was true that she became part of the Streatham household that year. Johnson was a near constant presence; as was Jeremiah Crutchley.

The son of an old family friend of Henry's, Crutchley was an executor of Henry's will and another co-guardian of the Thrale children. Henry had once told his wife that Crutchley was in fact his own child, born of an affair long before he married her. It was possible that this was true; Thrale certainly believed it without a second thought and often spotted little resemblances between the two men.[16] It became somewhat awkward for a while as Crutchley appeared to court first Thrale, and later Queeney, but both flirtations petered out

to nothing. The other near constant resident of Streatham that summer was Gabriel Piozzi – the singer that Thrale had mimicked at a
party at the Burneys' a few years before.

In the summer of 1780, two years after that first unfortunate
encounter, Thrale had engaged Piozzi as a singing teacher for
Queeney. Piozzi came highly recommended by the Burney family,
and Thrale hoped that the girl's singing would be better than her
lacklustre dancing. Queeney did turn out to have a sweet voice,
though not a strong one. Piozzi turned out to be an amusing
companion to have about the house. The Thrales took him into
their circle, and he repaid their kindness by singing at their gatherings, adding a suave continental air. Within a month of Piozzi
taking on Queeney as a pupil, Thrale was writing about him in
the warmest terms:

> Piozzi is become a prodigious Favourite with me; he is so intelligent
> a Creature, so discerning, one can't help wishing for his good Opin-
> ion: his Singing surpasses every body's for Taste, Tenderness, and
> true Elegance; his Hand on the Forte Piano too is so soft, so sweet,
> so delicate, every Tone goes to one's heart I think; and fills the Mind
> with Emotions one would not be without, though inconvenient
> enough sometimes.[17]

The day before Henry's death in April 1781, Piozzi had given
Queeney a singing lesson. After the lesson, he found Thrale in tears,
worrying about Henry's health. The 'tenderhearted Italian', as she
called him, tried to soothe her and then, not knowing what else to
do, he began to sing to her in his native language with a great deal
of expression – 'Rasserena il tuo bel Ciglio' (soothe your beautiful
brow).[18] A friend who saw this performance remarked later to Thrale
that she must know that the man was in love with her. She did know,
but she was too anxious about Henry to give any thought to the
matter.

Thrale welcomed Piozzi's presence at Streatham, aware that she
was beginning to feel something for him that she had never felt for
her husband. He sang for the company most evenings, love songs
more often than not. When he began to arrange a trip to Italy to see
his family and entice more singers to join him in London, he took to

singing a Venetian farewell song to Thrale. She translated the lyrics and copied them into the *Thraliana*:

> The fatal Moment is arriv'd
> When of each tender hope depriv'd;
> I come to take my last Adieu,
> Of Love and Happiness and You.[19]

As a wealthy, attractive and relatively young widow, Thrale was already the subject of multiple rumours before Piozzi's interest in her became widely known. In January 1782, nine months into widowhood, she rented a house in central London. She knew that London society would assume that she came husband-hunting and would scrutinise her every move.

She was watched closely. Within a couple of weeks of her arrival in her winter lodgings, she heard that bets were being taken on whom she would marry and when. The newspapers began to report on the visits male friends, including Johnson and even her male physicians, made to the house.

In April 1782 she gave up her residence in town and returned to Streatham. A year had passed since Henry's death and she put her mourning clothes away. Now that she was officially considered to be back on the market, the rumours increased tenfold. Thrale had always had many male friends, and now each became the subject of speculation and wagers. 'Love and friendship are distinct things,' she railed, '& I would go through Fire to serve many a Man, whom nothing less than Fire would force me to go to Bed to.'[20]

The proposals rolled in all through that spring and summer. There was one from Mr Swale, 'a little dapper Macaroni Man', to whom Thrale sent a curt note pointing out that she hardly knew him and ordering him not to write again. Another came from an old family friend, Sir Philip Jennings Clerke: he pursued Thrale openly and intensely, though he was already married. His romantic overtures included details of his wife's terminal illness and his certainty that she would die soon. Thrale was horrified. The wealthy brewer Samuel Whitbread declared his love for Thrale, perhaps thinking how useful it would be to have a wife who already knew something of the trade. 'Oh I would rather', declared Thrale, borrowing a line from Shakespeare, 'be set breast deep in the Earth, & bowled to death with Turneps.' Though she said no to all of them, the newspapers continued to write about Thrale and her supposed lovers.[21]

Thrale wanted none of these men. She had fallen in love with someone else, someone who was not considered husband material. It was Piozzi who had captured her heart. Though she had long known his feelings for her, the realisation that she loved him back dawned on her slowly. Like so many lovers, she thought she did a good job of keeping her true feelings a secret from the world, so she was astonished one day in the autumn of 1782 when Frances Burney – 'that little dear discerning Creature' – said that she knew of Thrale's feelings for Piozzi.[22]

The conversation with Burney threw Thrale into fits of anguish. Although her attraction to Piozzi was clear enough, the idea of marrying for love was not straightforward. It was not acceptable for a woman to seek out a romantic relationship based purely on her feelings. Doing so would subvert the patriarchal idea of a woman as a thing to be bartered away by her menfolk. Furthermore, there were several things that rendered Piozzi an unsuitable husband in the eyes of society: he was a foreigner, a Catholic and of lower social class than his beloved. There were also rumours that he was significantly younger than Thrale, which would have been considered inappropriate at the time (in reality he was six months older).

The entry in the *Thraliana* after her conversation with Burney showed a tumult of conflicting emotions. Thrale praised Piozzi's worthiness, his loveliness, his virtue and his mind, but she stumbled over the problem of his middle-class ancestry. She tried to dismiss it, but she could not stop thinking of what others would say and, indeed, what she herself felt. She tried to convince herself that he was approximately the same social class as Henry Thrale had been; but Henry had been wealthy. But now *she* was wealthy and did not need a husband with money. She worried that she would disgrace her daughters and the Thrale surname that they would still bear. She worried that she was thinking of herself too much. She worried that she had lost the ability to know right from wrong, that she would lose her dignity, that she had never had any dignity to begin with.

More practically, she worried about marrying someone who did not understand English law. As her husband, Piozzi would effectively be her legal guardian and it would be up to him to make financial decisions – if he got it wrong, her children might end up impoverished. She worried that he would insist they move abroad. She worried that if she had children with him they would have to be baptised Catholic. She worried that her looks would fade. She worried that he would die before her and that she would be alone again.

If Thrale had been happy, these concerns might have been enough to dissuade her from considering marrying Piozzi. But she was not happy. Her relationship with Queeney, old enough to be her confidante if either woman had desired it, was strained; she felt that her friends were increasingly disapproving of the turn her widowhood was taking; she was even beginning to suspect that her servants were judging her.

Later that autumn, the household – including Johnson and Burney – decamped to Brighton. Burney was in an excitable mood all that trip: her new novel *Cecilia* had been published in the summer to great acclaim and now the fashionable crowds of Brighton treated her like a celebrity. At balls and dinners, she was sought out by her fans. Though still shy of publicity, she could not help but feel happy to hear her work so praised.

Thrale, who usually found herself renewed by sea-bathing at Brighton, was not herself. She fretted constantly, turning the matter of Piozzi over and over in her mind. She fretted until she began to look pale and ill – so much so that even Queeney became concerned and asked her mother what the matter was. In anguish, Thrale told her the truth – that she had fallen in love with the girl's singing master. It was not just a passing fancy, she told her daughter, but a deep attachment. Thrale felt that she could not live without Piozzi. She felt that her heart was being ripped in two – one half for her daughters and one for him.[23]

Queeney was eighteen years old, prudish, obsessed with notions of respectability, easily embarrassed by her outgoing mother and unsettled by anything that might damage her own marriage prospects. She was aghast at what her mother told her and made her disapproval clear. Thrale invited Burney to join their conversation. Burney was also horrified by the thought of Thrale marrying Piozzi. The two younger women set about trying to talk Thrale out of her relationship with the Italian. She agreed that she would not marry Piozzi without Queeney's blessing.

The party left Brighton late in November. On the last morning, the women of the group went for a final swim in the frigid sea. Hester, Queeney, Susanna and Sophia Thrale, along with Burney, rose at six o'clock and made their way to the shore in the moonlight. They had arranged with the women who operated the bathing machines to be ready for them at this early hour and they plunged into the dark waters. Their cares momentarily forgotten, they splashed around together until they could bear the cold no longer. Wide awake now, they hurried back to the cottage where they dressed by candlelight, woke Johnson, clambered into the coach and chaise, and set off on the road back to London.[24]

Thrale had again taken a house in London that winter. She let Streatham out for three years to save money. She hoped to go abroad where living expenses were lower to save even more money. Really though, when she thought of going to Europe, she was dreaming of Piozzi following her out, the two of them being together without being watched. But she wanted a final season in London first. That season was everything she wished for, and she was the star of it. 'I am all the Mode this Winter,' she wrote in the *Thraliana*, 'no parties are thought highly of, except Mrs Thrale makes one of them; my Wit, & even my Beauty – God help me!! is celebrated; and I have three or four Engagements of a Night among the very first Company this great Town can produce.'[25]

Throughout December and into the new year, Piozzi was always nearby, though the two tried not to be seen alone together. Her passion for him grew, as did his for her. Neither could resist meeting privately. Queeney and Burney were utterly scandalised when they learned about these private meetings, with Burney writing, 'her reputation must be utterly gone . . . no innocence in the World could support her character, after all that has passed, if they have any further interviews. – My wonder will never cease at her blindness to her own destruction.'[26]

Queeney's dislike for Piozzi grew daily. She became bolder in her campaign against him: in January 1783, she demanded that he hand over all the letters her mother had written to him. It was just a few years since Thrale had overseen her daughter's correspondence, intercepting clandestine letters from thirteen-year-old Queeney to a neighbouring girl in Streatham – 'a Wench I do not much like'.[27] Now it was Thrale being treated like an unruly teenager. Piozzi, hoping to alleviate tension in the Thrale household, complied with Queeney's demand. Queeney inveigled the girls' governess and other servants to spy on her behalf; she asked them to report any visits Piozzi made to the house when Queeney was out. She begged her guardians – especially Crutchley – to try to stop her mother from going abroad, or at least to forbid her from taking the girls with her.[28]* Thrale was mortified when Crutchley appeared at her door to confront her with the rumours he had heard.

Queeney implored Burney to intervene. Dutifully, Burney appeared and gave Thrale an ultimatum: marry Piozzi at once or never see him again. 'I actually groaned with Anguish, threw myself on the Bed in an Agony which My fair Daughter beheld with frigid Indifference,' Thrale wrote in the *Thraliana*. Queeney poured hot scorn upon her as she lay on the bed, accusing her of abandoning her children and disgracing Henry's memory. She said she would never speak or write to her mother again. Susanna and Sophia (twelve and eleven respectively) said nothing, but told little Cecilia and Harriett (five and four) that their mother was considering leaving them all. 'Where are you going Mama,' the little girls cried, 'will you leave us, and die as our poor papa did?' Thrale could not bear it. She wrote to Piozzi to come and see her the next day – her forty-second birthday. She spent the rest of the night vomiting, crying and praying.[29]

In the morning, after a sleepless night, she went to Queeney's bedchamber. Her decision was made: she chose her children over her lover. In the *Thraliana*, the page relating to this day has been ripped out. What passed between Thrale and Piozzi is unknown. A few days later, a devasted Thrale wrote: 'Adieu to all that's dear, to all that's lovely. I am parted from my Life, my Soul! My Piozzi: Sposo

---

* Queeney was not yet of age, and so the guardians could ensure that she remained in Britain.

promesso! Amante adorato! Amico senza equale . . . Oh Misery!'[30]
The next two pages were again ripped from the *Thraliana*.

Thrale could bear London no longer. The guardians had forbidden her from taking her daughters abroad, so she fixed on going to Bath instead. Life there would be cheaper than in the capital, and saving money would give her increased independence. She still harboured hope of marrying Piozzi, though she worried it would be years before she could persuade her daughters to support the union. By then, she feared that she would no longer be beautiful and that she would no longer be fertile. She feared too that Piozzi would marry someone else before her daughters came round. Unable to see his beloved, Piozzi decided to return to Italy. They had one last breakfast together in London before they both left for their new homes. Judiciously, they asked a friend of Piozzi's to chaperone them. Before they parted, the couple vowed eternal fidelity to each other.

It was April when Thrale, Queeney, Susanna and Sophia moved to Bath. Cecilia and Harriett stayed behind in a boarding school at Streatham called Russell House. Thrale thought they would receive a better education there than with her, as well as benefitting from the fresh Streatham air. Perhaps she also thought that the atmosphere at the school would be nicer for the little girls. At Bath, the relationship between Thrale and her three older girls was so strained as to be icy. Affection and friendliness were gone from the family, replaced by a cold politeness. Piozzi's name was never mentioned, nor were the events of the preceding months.

Within days of Thrale's removal to Bath, bad news came from Russell House: Harriett was seriously unwell with measles, whooping cough and swollen glands in her neck.[31] Thrale had never had whooping cough herself so was advised against nursing the child. Instead, she sent Old Nurse who had looked after the Thrale children in the Streatham nursery. Old Nurse went to stay in Russell House and, along with the headmistress, matron and two of Thrale's favourite physicians, did everything she could for the child.

It was not enough. Harriett died, aged four years and ten months. It was Good Friday when Thrale received the letter bearing this news. The next day she called for the post chaise to be prepared and set off in the afternoon. After an eight-hour run she made it to Reading where she slept for a few hours before setting off again and arriving at Russell House on Easter Sunday morning. Dazed and grief-stricken, she almost wondered why she had gone – there was nothing she could do now, except watch Harriett be buried alongside so many of her sisters and both brothers. But she was happy to be with Cecilia and see for herself that *she* at least was healthy.

Three days later, Thrale returned to Bath. She had not seen Johnson or Burney or any of her usual friends on the trip. She travelled alone, and when she got back to the house in Bath and stepped inside, none of her older daughters said anything to her. They simply continued their sewing and drawing as though she was not there.[32]

Years later Thrale learned that Piozzi had delayed his start for Italy when he heard of the death of Harriett. He had sat by the front window of an inn on the road to Streatham so that he could see Thrale's carriage as it passed. He was the only one who wanted to comfort her, but he could not be near her.

Life in Bath continued uncomfortably. All through that spring and summer, the broken family made a half-hearted pretence at being normal. They attended the Pump Room and took the waters, but without any real pleasure. There were occasional distractions – such as the time Thrale rescued a badger from a baiting session and Queeney set about taming it. Badgers, however, are not easily tamed. Or, as Thrale put it: 'she does not yet seem disposed to Grateful Acceptance of our Favours.'[33] It was to be the last time that Thrale and Queeney ever collaborated.

Thrale missed Piozzi desperately. She was delighted at the end of the summer to be sent a portrait of him – 'lively, lovely Resemblance of my adored Husband', she called it.[34] If Queeney thought half a year in Bath would dim her mother's passion for Piozzi she was wrong. He had, in Thrale's mind, been promoted from fiancé to 'husband' in those few months.

The fiercer Thrale's devotion to Piozzi became, the more her friends worried. Burney began writing secretly to Queeney, saying how ashamed she was of her friendship with Thrale. She accused Thrale of a mad infatuation, of being overcome by ungovernable passions. Burney did have moments of compassion, wondering whether

Thrale was being so emotional over Piozzi on account of the absolute lack of emotion in her first marriage. Mostly, however, she was concerned with public opinion rather than her friend's happiness. When a mutual friend suggested that the best option for Thrale was suicide, Burney, to her credit, took a firm stand against that.[35]

'I am sometimes ready to think Fanny Burney treacherous,' wrote Thrale in her diary as these secret letters passed between her daughter and her best friend, 'but tis a sinful Thought & must not be indulged.'[36] Just a few years earlier Thrale and Burney had been writing to each other about the depth of their friendship, predicting that it would last another forty years until Thrale died at a ripe old age.[37] They were right that Thrale would live for another forty years (Burney lived for another sixty); they were wrong about the enduring nature of their friendship.

Things came to a head late in 1783. Sophia became seriously ill. She began having fits, she seemed at times to be apoplectic, she had episodes of screaming, a strange lethargy came over her, she fainted, her heart beat so irregularly that she seemed on the verge of death. Just seven months after the death of Harriett, Thrale thought she was going to lose another child. As she had done so many times before, she began bargaining: 'Oh spare my Sophia, my Darling, oh spare her gracious heaven – & take in Exchange the life of her wretched Mother!' When the physicians were unable to do anything, Thrale turned to her own remedies. She found that a dram of fine old whisky could revive the twelve-year-old, and that rubbing the girl could increase her heartbeat and restore warmth and consciousness to the sad little figure. Thrale sat watching over her so long, and rubbed her so vigorously, that she herself fainted from exhaustion.[38]

Queeney was impressed by her mother for once. In the terror of the sickroom, the drama over Piozzi was forgotten. Queeney saw the pure love that Thrale had for her girls. She saw how much her mother's health suffered as she wore herself out nursing Sophia. Queeney knew that Thrale's health had already been in decline before Sophia became ill; she knew that her mother was pining for Piozzi and would never be truly well without him. She relented. Though still deeply opposed to her mother's relationship with the music tutor, Queeney agreed to let him be recalled from Italy.

The *Thraliana* records this as an uncomplicatedly blissful event:

[Queeney] beg'd me Yesterday not to sacrifice my Life to her Con-
venience; She now saw my Love of Piozzi was incurable She said . . .
[She] begged me not to endure any longer such unnecessary Misery
. . . I wrote my Lover word that he might come & fetch me.[39]

The letters between Queeney and Burney have a different tone.
On hearing that Piozzi had been sent for, Burney wrote, 'O what
times are those when *such* news should be thought pretty good . . .
Sweet soul, & *simple* as headstrong, to plunge herself thus into
a Gulph of which no one can see the depth!' Burney was of the
opinion that if Piozzi returned and married Thrale the only sensible thing for them to do would be to move to Devonshire, where
no respectable people would see them. Burney further advised
Queeney to deny all prior knowledge of the union in order to save
her own reputation.[40]

It was January when Piozzi received Thrale's letter. Snow made the
Alps impassable and forced him to delay his journey until the weather
improved. Then a dozen little events conspired to detain him. It was
May, when spring suddenly appeared after a dreary winter, before
Thrale travelled to London to begin making wedding arrangements.
On that trip she saw Burney for the first time in a year. There was a
change in the friendship, clear to both women: 'Dear Burney who
loves me *kindly*, but the World *reverentially*', seemed to be equally
delighted and pained by Thrale's presence. Burney was ashamed of
Thrale, but also eager to speak to one of the few people she had ever
connected with so intensely. Burney's diary entry for this week mir-
rored Thrale's exactly: '[Thrale's] society was truly the most delightful
of cordials to me, however, at times, mixed with bitters the least palatable.'[41]

Thrale saw Samuel Johnson that week too. As with Burney, she
had not seen him for a year. Unlike Burney, Johnson seemed to know
almost nothing about the Piozzi affair: everyone had been too afraid
to tell him. He heard the rumours at the beginning but he thought the
affair at an end once Thrale had gone to Bath – a small folly, all blown
over. Burney had started avoiding him for fear that the topic might
arise. At that May meeting of Thrale and Johnson, the topic of Piozzi

was glossed over once more. But he did suspect something was amiss and in a conversation with Boswell that week, he criticised Thrale harshly, saying, 'Sir, she has done everything wrong, since [Henry's] bridle was off her neck.'[42]

Ever since her husband's death, the old friendship between Thrale and Johnson had been off kilter. Johnson had rallied round and tried to help with the brewery, but when Thrale sold it off he felt slighted. Perhaps there was a more significant slighting too: after Henry's death, many assumed that Thrale and Johnson would marry. The day after Henry's funeral, Boswell penned a tawdry poem entitled 'Ode by Samuel Johnson to Mrs Thrale upon their Supposed Approaching Nuptials'. He circulated it anonymously, well knowing that each of the named parties would see it.

> My dearest lady! View your slave,
> Behold him as your very SCRUB,
> Eager to write as authour grave,
> Or govern well the brewing tub.
> . . .
> Convuls'd in love's tumultuous throws,
> We feel the aphrodisian spasm;
> Tir'd nature must, at last, repose,
> Then Wit and Wisdom fill the chasm.
>
> Nor only are our limbs entwin'd,
> And lip in rapture glued to lip;
> Lock'd in embraces of the mind;
> Imagination's sweets we sip.[43]

Johnson and Thrale pointedly ignored the poem, just as they tried to ignore the newspaper articles, the sideways glances and the whispers. Thrale had no romantic interest in Johnson. He may have had feelings for her, but he never voiced them. If anything, Thrale began to suspect that Johnson did not really like her at all, and that he had spent so much time with the family on Henry's account. In 1782, after her mourning period, when she had considered going abroad, she was surprised that Johnson never hinted that he might miss her:

I fancied Mr Johnson could not have existed without me forsooth, as we have now lived together above 18 Years . . . Not a bit on't! he feels nothing in parting with me, nothing in the least . . . [He] only wish'd to find in me a careful Nurse & humble Friend for his sick and his lounging hours; yet I really thought he could not have existed without *my Conversation* forsooth. He cares more for my roast Beef & plumb Pudden.[44]

After she went to Bath, the two old friends continued to write, but lost their previous intimacy.

In June Thrale finally heard word that Piozzi was on his way back from Italy. Her nerves were frayed as she imagined all the accidents that might befall him on his journey home. Her three older daughters had consented to Piozzi's return but they did not wish to be present to witness it. They left for Brighton, along with a companion. Sophia was just about to turn thirteen, Susanna was fourteen and Queeney was nineteen. By their own choosing, they would never live with their mother again. Seven-year-old Cecilia was still at boarding school.

Thrale wrote a terse letter to the girls' co-guardians, informing them of the situation and confirming that she would marry Piozzi as soon as possible. To Johnson, she included a separate note. She felt that their friendship demanded that she write more than just the businesslike letter which had gone to all the guardians. She apologised for keeping her relationship with Piozzi a secret and explained that she had done so because it would have pained her to reject Johnson's advice (which surely would have been to give up Piozzi). She finished with a heartfelt plea for his blessing.

Two days after she wrote this letter, Piozzi returned. It was, Thrale declared, 'the happiest Day of my whole Life I think – Yes, *quite* the happiest.'[45] Just as she finally relaxed at the end of several very difficult years, Johnson was penning his reply to her. His letter did not bring the blessing that she hoped for. Instead, he accused her of behaving ignominiously and wickedly. He accused her of abandoning her family, her religion, her reputation and her country. He asked God's forgiveness for her. He asked if he could see her before she married – he hoped that he could talk her out of the wedding.

Her reply to him was forthright. She valiantly defended Piozzi. She told Johnson that she did not want a visit from him. She pointed out what a loyal friend she had been to him, reminded him how much she had always esteemed him, and then she finished conclusively: 'but till you have changed your opinion of Mr Piozzi – let us converse no more.'[46]

Seeing that he could not move her, Johnson relented. In one final letter, he gave her his blessing, wished her happiness and acknowledged how good she had always been to him. A few days after he wrote these last words to Thrale, he began to plan a monument and inscription for the grave of his wife Elizabeth (Tetty) who had died more than three decades earlier. In all those long years since her death, he seems never to have visited the grave, nor minded that it was unmarked.[47]

In reply to Johnson's last letter, Thrale sent a final note wishing him health and happiness. The pair never saw each other again.

Thrale and Piozzi were married twice. First there was a Catholic ceremony in London, overseen by the French Ambassador at an embassy chapel on a hot July day. Catholicism was still outlawed in Britain then and only the embassies of certain states (including France, Spain, Florence, Venice, Naples, Portugal, Sardinia, Austria and Bavaria) could safely facilitate Catholic worship and sacraments. Two days later, there was a Protestant ceremony at Bath. 'I am returned from Church', Thrale-Piozzi wrote after that second ceremony, 'the happy Wife of my lovely, my faithful Piozzi: - Subject of my Prayers, Object of my Wishes, my Sighs, my Reverence, my Esteem.'[48]

The newly-weds stayed some weeks in Bath, then returned to London briefly before embarking on a tour of Europe. Before she left, Thrale-Piozzi spent time with Susanna and Sophia who were now boarding at a school in Kensington. Queeney – living with family friends, and now formally called 'Miss Thrale' in her mother's diary – visited the new couple once: 'we parted coldly, not unkindly.'

Thrale-Piozzi did not see Frances Burney during her final weeks in London. Thrale-Piozzi had learned of the letters between her and Queeney and felt betrayed. As with Johnson, Thrale-Piozzi and Burney exchanged a final flurry of letters, which began with recriminations, softened into polite good wishes, and ended with the cessation of their once close friendship.

With so many ties in Britain now cut, Thrale-Piozzi set sail for the continent. She had dreamed of this trip for many years, had longed to see Italy since she first fell in love with Piozzi. From England, the couple sailed to Calais, then travelled to Paris where they stayed a few weeks, then on to Lyons for another short stay before crossing through the Alps into Italy. They travelled through Turin and Genoa before settling in Milan for the winter. Italy enchanted her. She praised its elegance and splendour, she found the women pleasing but the men a little officious. The people of Lombardy reminded her of those in her native Wales. She liked the customs of wearing a veil to church and of gentlemen kissing ladies' hands. She lamented her lack of spoken Italian and struggled with the Milan dialect, but managed to communicate well enough. She loved the merry-making and informality of her new neighbours. She was especially happy to see her husband respected – a great change from their London days. She was flourishing.

Even in Italy though, rumours from England plagued her. Baretti, who had taken against her after he heard that Johnson had broken with her, began a rumour that she and Piozzi had had 'intimacy' before they wed. Baretti sought out Queeney – his former tutee – to tell her this himself. He wrote to Thrale-Piozzi directly to accuse her of 'Murder & Fornication' – a bit rich coming from a man who had once killed a pimp during a street brawl.* Another popular rumour was that Piozzi had taken control of his wife's money, had had her declared insane and had locked her in a convent. Elizabeth Montagu believed it to be true and repeated the story to friends. When she heard this, Thrale-Piozzi wondered how she could ever live happily in England again. One of the Thrale children's co-guardians told Cecilia that Piozzi had locked her mother up and fed her only on bread and water.[49]

---

* This brawl had occurred in October 1769. Baretti was acquitted of murder on the grounds of self-defence; glowing character references were given by Joshua Reynolds, Samuel Johnson, Edmund Burke, David Garrick and Oliver Goldsmith among others.

While most of Thrale-Piozzi's former friends gossiped about her, one tried hard to forget about her. In late November 1784, Frances Burney visited an ailing Samuel Johnson. The conversation turned to Thrale-Piozzi. Burney asked Johnson if he ever heard from his old friend:

> 'No,' cried he, 'nor write to her! I drive her quite from my mind. She has disgraced herself, disgraced her friends and connections, disgraced her sex, and disgraced all the expectations of mankind! If I meet with one of her Letters I burn it instantly. I have burnt all I can find. I never speak of her, and I desire never to hear of her more. I drive her, as I said, wholly from my mind.'[50]

To distract Johnson from this torrent of vitriol, Burney told him a story she had heard about a Bristol milkwoman nicknamed Lactilla who could write extraordinary verse. Soothed, and forgetting Thrale-Piozzi for the moment, he began to debate the nature of genius and the meaning of poetic invention.

In Italy, Thrale-Piozzi was trying desperately to keep her happy memories of home intact. She had a portrait of Johnson with her and had commissioned one of Queeney. 'I do love them dearly still, as ill as they have used me, & always shall,' she wrote in the *Thraliana* the same week that Johnson was telling Burney how he burnt everything that reminded him of Thrale-Piozzi.[51] Within a month, Johnson was dead.

Letters bearing the news took three weeks to reach Thrale-Piozzi in Milan. It was January 1785 when she heard of her old friend's demise: 'Oh poor Dr Johnson!!!' was all she could say at first. It was some weeks before she could gather her thoughts. The one thought that recurred over and over again was that she should write about Johnson; not just to write about him in the *Thraliana* as she so often had, but to write for publication. He had always encouraged her to write, and he had specifically told her that he wished her to write his life. When they had joked about it many years earlier, wondering who his biographers would be and what they would say, he implored her: 'rescue me out of all their hands My dear, & do it *yourself.*' Within a month of Johnson's death at least six others had already decided to attempt a biography, including Boswell. Thrale-Piozzi was nervous about entering such a crowded field, but she had a huge amount of material about Johnson, much of it unique. Also significant was the fact that for the first time in her life she was free from her maternal duties. Though she missed her children, being away from them gave Thrale-Piozzi the time and the space to write something substantial. She loved her *Thraliana* but the idea of writing a whole, coherent book was appealing. Even Piozzi, who (unlike Henry Thrale) had doubts about women becoming professional authors, encouraged his wife to undertake the project.[52]

In Milan that winter, Thrale-Piozzi began to gather together all the fragments she had already jotted down about Johnson. By April, the weather was warm enough to begin on the long-planned tour of Italy. Thrale-Piozzi carried her notebooks throughout their time in Venice and Florence, Padua and Bologna, Rome and Naples. By day she saw the sights, by night she worked on her manuscript. The tour – and the manuscript – concluded in Livorno. There, she had the work neatly transcribed and sent it off to a publisher in London in the autumn of 1785.[53]

The book – *Anecdotes of the Late Samuel Johnson* – was published on Lady Day 1786. The first print run of a thousand copies sold out by nightfall.[54] It was said that the King sent for a copy at ten o'clock that evening and the publisher had to beg one back from a friend to supply His Majesty. Then the King, they said, sat up all night to read it.[55] A second edition was rushed out two weeks later, then a third and a fourth. The book was a sensation.

Thrale-Piozzi presented an intimate portrait of a good friend. Though less exhaustive than the grand book Boswell would publish five years later, Thrale-Piozzi captured the essence of Johnson in her pages. In commemorating her friend, she also secured her own literary reputation. After the *Anecdotes*, Thrale-Piozzi's confidence in her writing grew. There were smatterings of poetry and some writings for children before Thrale-Piozzi returned to her Johnsoniana and published a collection of his and her own correspondence under the title *Letters to and from the Late Samuel Johnson* in 1788. The serious reviews welcomed it as a useful addition to the already burgeoning world of Johnson scholarship; the newspapers that had hounded Thrale-Piozzi over her second marriage called it a vulgar betrayal of trust; the poet Anna Seward – the 'Swan of Lichfield' – considered it proof that

Thrale-Piozzi was a better writer than Johnson. Some years later, an aspiring young novelist called Jane Austen liked Thrale-Piozzi's letters so much that she told her sister she planned to emulate the epistolatory style of 'my dear Mrs Piozzi'.[56]

Ever since she had begun writing her first book about Johnson, Thrale-Piozzi had felt tense, so tense that her shoulders ached just thinking about what the critics and her old friends would say.[57] After publication, letters of congratulation flowed to her; but she was wary of this sudden outpouring of enthusiasm.[58] With each new poem or book she published, the thaw continued a little more. Still she was wary. Despite her fears, Thrale-Piozzi's books were successful – both financially and artistically. Many of them were reprinted well into the nineteenth century.

The main opponent of Thrale-Piozzi's writing career was her beloved husband. Though he happily spent the money she earned for her writing (often several hundred guineas per book), he complained that he thought he was marrying a '*Dama* not a *Virtuosa*'.[59] Thrale-Piozzi, having always gone along with the wishes of her first husband, suddenly found herself standing up to her second. She curtly dismissed his concerns as mere Italian prejudice against 'writing ladies' and continued her work. Piozzi relented and soon reconciled himself to having married a clever woman.

After nearly three years in Europe, the happy couple returned to London in March 1787. Though her writing was winning her admirers, the generally accepted view of Thrale-Piozzi as something of a pariah had changed little in her years away. Her daughters barely saw her and she wrote in the *Thraliana* that 'the old Blue Stocking Society as the folks call them, appear to be shy of me this Spring.'

The Bluestockings were desperate to maintain the respectable facade they had built up over many years and so felt compelled to distance themselves from any hint of scandal that attached to a learned lady. They feared that Thrale-Piozzi would taint their carefully constructed air of moral rectitude. Hester Mulso Chapone explained to a friend:

> Surely there must be really some degree of *Insanity* in that case for such mighty overbearing Passions are not natural in a 'Matron's

bones' . . . It has given great occasion to the Enemy to blaspheme and to triumph over the Bas Bleu Ladies.[60]

If she was not invited to the Bluestocking salons, she would host her own. In a rented house in Hanover Square, Thrale-Piozzi began a series of salons to rival anything else in the capital. She would invite a hundred guests to her soirées. It was said that Queeney – who was always invited but never attended – would sometimes walk by the house just to cast insulting looks through the windows. When the actress Sarah Siddons and the retired dancer Eva Garrick – two of the only people who remained friends with both Thrale-Piozzi and the Bluestockings – praised Thrale-Piozzi's new salons, the Bluestockings tried hard to ignore them. 'Charming Blues!' laughed Thrale-Piozzi, 'blue with Venom I think; I suppose they begin to be ashamed of their paltry behaviour.'[61]

Deserted by her friends and daughters, Thrale-Piozzi distracted herself with new hobbies: an interest in fossils; a dabbling in the craze for animal magnetism; a new pet dog, Florin; looking through William Herschel's famous telescope to see the craters of the moon in detail. Most happily, she convinced her daughter Cecilia to come and live with her again after a brief tussle, in which Queeney tried to send the ten-year-old away to boarding school on the Isle of Wight to be further from her mother. 'I hold her to my Heart all Day long . . . If they steal her away from me now, I shall lose my life: 'tis so very comfortable to have *one* at least saved out of *twelve*,' she wrote.[62]

Thrale-Piozzi was filled with relief to have one of her children back. The return of Cecilia softened the blow of the miscarriage she suffered that month – her first pregnancy of her second marriage. The doctors thought the cause might have been a fall Thrale-Piozzi had had, but she suspected that the real cause was the stress of the custody battle for Cecilia. There was another high price to pay for custody of Cecilia – Thrale-Piozzi's three older daughters would not speak to her for the next six years.[63]

In the summer of 1789 Elizabeth Montagu began making overtures of friendship. An entry in the *Thraliana* shows the pain Thrale-Piozzi still felt at her treatment by London society:

Mrs Montagu wants to make up with me again; I dare say She does; but I will not be taken & left . . . Mrs Montagu wrote creeping Letters when she wanted my help, or foolishly *thought* She did; & then turned her Back upon me & set her Adherents to do the same: I despise such Conduct; & [several other Bluestockings] now sneak about, & look ashamed of themselves. Well they may![64]

Without her old friends, and without all her daughters, London lost its appeal. Even her ever-popular salons could not make up for what Thrale-Piozzi had lost. Instead, Thrale-Piozzi turned her eyes homewards – to Wales. Following their return from their European tour, Thrale-Piozzi had taken her new husband for a holiday there, and he too had fallen in love with the Welsh landscape and the people. She decided to return to Wales for good in the 1790s. On a plot of land that had once belonged to her father, Thrale-Piozzi began to plan what she called 'a cottage', and what most people would call a mid-sized mansion.[65] The house would be called Brynbella – a mixture of Welsh and Italian, meaning 'beautiful hill'. From the hill behind the house there was a magnificent view of Mount Snowdon and the blue sea beyond.

Thrale-Piozzi and her husband immersed themselves in the local community. She felt at home in Wales. She found time to write, she began learning Hebrew, she undertook charitable work for the poor. She re-established communication with her daughters and though there was never any real warmth there, it was more than she had dared to hope for in earlier years.*

Thrale-Piozzi had taken a great risk in her second marriage. Many thought that she had acted foolishly and had paid an appropriate price – a banishment to Wales and the loss of her children and her previous social status. She, however, saw things differently. She felt that she had become a new woman – one who knew true love and the abiding contentment of being a professional writer. By rejecting the norms of society she had found liberation.

---

* In 1808 Queeney (aged forty-four) had married. Thrale could not help writing in the *Thraliana*: 'The Lady four Years older than when I made my second Marriage; & She hooted me (among other Things) for being *superannuated*.'

For their twentieth wedding anniversary, the Thrale-Piozzis distributed beef, pudding and sixpences to all the children of the neighbourhood. And Thrale-Piozzi wrote these lines to her husband:

> Accept my Love this honest Lay
> Upon your Twentieth Wedding Day:
> I little hop'd our Lives would stay
> To hail the Twentieth Wedding Day.
> If you're grown Gouty—I grown Gray
> Upon our Twentieth Wedding Day—
> Tis no great Wonder;—Friends must say
> 'Why tis their Twentieth Wedding Day.'[66]

In this house, with the man she loved, Thrale-Piozzi was happy at last.

IO

INDEPENDENCE

CATHARINE MACAULAY WAS born Catharine Sawbridge in 1731 in Kent. The family lived in a large and ancient house on the banks of the River Stour near the village of Wye. Catharine was one of four children; a fifth pregnancy killed their mother Elizabeth at just twenty-two years old. The children's father was devasted by the loss and locked himself and his family away in the forlorn house. Catharine and her sister Mary were put under the care of a governess, whom they remembered as antiquated, ignorant and ill-qualified.[1]

Within her own lifetime, a mythology of Catharine as a child prodigy grew up. It was said that she had no interest in the things girls usually learned; instead, she was a voracious reader. They said that she began with the fairy tales and romances on the nursery shelves, but soon graduated to reading the weighty bound volumes that adorned her father's library. History was supposed to be her favourite, and for hours on end she would disappear into the realms of Greece and Rome. The reality was probably more mundane – she herself said that she was a 'thoughtless girl' until she reached about the age of twenty.[2] She had no aversion to the domestic arts, and, in fact, when she came to write a book on education many years later, she recommended that needlework be taught to both girls *and* boys: 'I would rather see my [male] pupils engaged in the innocent employment of forming a button, than in spending whole days in hunting down a harmless animal,' she wrote, surprising many with such novel ideas.[3]

In 1757 she visited Canterbury where she met another Kent resident – Elizabeth Carter. At a summer assembly, young Catharine recognised the older woman and addressed her. She spoke of Spartan laws and Roman politics, Epicurean philosophy and French wit; Carter was astounded by her erudition. 'She is a very sensible and agreeable woman, and much more deeply learned than beseems a fine lady,' wrote Carter afterwards. As they spoke, the pair wandered sedately through the assembly rooms. In the custom of the times, other women occasionally joined them as they walked, listening to their conversation and hoping to join in. But the beauties of Kent could make neither head nor tail of Catharine's conversation. Carter, however, was entranced – as much by the young woman's boldness as by her mind:

> to be sure I should have been mighty cautious of holding any such conversation in such a place with a professed philosopher or a scholar, but as it was with a fine fashionable well-dressed lady, whose train was longer than any body's train, I had no manner of scruple.[4]

Catharine Sawbridge met George Macaulay late in the 1750s through a mutual friend. George was a male midwife who worked at a lying-in hospital for poor married women. It was one of the first maternity hospitals in London. He was widely respected for his work there and for the tenderness and humanity he showed his patients.[5]

George met Catharine at the end of a decade of loss. He and his first wife Leonora had seen three of their children buried; Leonora herself had died in 1751; and he lost his two remaining daughters within a few years.[6] George never gave much thought to remarriage, until he met Catharine. She was fifteen years younger than him, attractive, fashionable and well-off. Anyone would have considered her a good catch on those grounds alone, but George saw something else in her – he was drawn to her striking intellect and fierce independence. She, in turn, admired his liberal and progressive views. Catharine had always been scathing about the limited education given to boys by British public schools and the colleges of Oxford and Cambridge.[7] But George, a Scot, had studied in the far more forward-thinking medical centres at Edinburgh and Padua. He had come of age in the Scottish Enlightenment, and been exposed to all sorts of new ideas in Italy. His erudition, open-mindedness and benevolence were what convinced Catharine to become his wife.

The day before their wedding, George wrote to a friend of his high hopes for his second marriage. But George did not just *hope* for marital bliss, he *worked* for it. In a society where many men gave little thought to the dynamics of a marriage George was unusual. Two weeks after the wedding he wrote to his friend again: 'I have been pretty much engaged lately or I would sooner have acknowledged the honour of your last [letter] . . . I have been laying a foundation for domestic happiness, which I hope will last as long as my life.' Perhaps the most important step George took in ensuring a happy marriage was giving his wife financial independence. The couple wed in June 1760 in the parish church in Wye, near Catharine's family home. On that day, George settled £5,000 on his bride. It was a significant sum and the interest on it could provide an independent income for Catharine unimaginable to most women.[8]

With this show of support from her husband, Catharine Macaulay felt invincible. The couple moved to St James's in London where she immediately took to metropolitan life. This part of London was well-located for the capital's coffee-houses, theatres, museums, and the thing that interested Macaulay most of all – parliament. The Macaulays began hosting dinner parties, welcoming anyone who could make good conversation. Before long, it was clear that the guests most likely to hold Macaulay's attention were those with unorthodox political views – the radicals, the dissenters, the republicans. Macaulay herself was by now extremely well-read and not shy of expressing her opinions. She was a brilliant conversationalist. 'Her spirit rouses and flashes like lightning upon the subject of liberty and upon the reflexion of anything noble and generous. She speaks undaunted and freely and disdains a cowardly tongue or pen,' wrote one admirer. The American writer and political pamphleteer Mercy Otis Warren was impressed by the 'commanding genius and brilliance of thought' shown in Macaulay's conversation.[9]

Unlike the other Bluestockings, Macaulay's immediate coterie was mostly male. Warren (who lived across the Atlantic in Massachusetts and met Macaulay only once) was one of the few female writers who publicly shared Macaulay's interest in republicanism. The majority of Bluestockings tended to be politically conservative or were completely apolitical (at least in public). Women could not take any official part in British politics at the time, and they were heavily discouraged from showing any strong interest in this male realm. But though none of the Bluestockings shared Macaulay's passion, they recognised her as a kindred spirit, and she them. The Bluestockings did not tend to frequent Macaulay's dinners but she would visit their salons, and she would often converse with them in resort towns such as Bath. She corresponded with some, such as Hannah More who sent her a copy of her work *A Search After Happiness* along with a pheasant.[10]

Like the rest of the Bluestockings, Macaulay had to deal with an enormous amount of male prejudice. Even an innocuous-seeming comment from a man that her interest in politics was 'not unbecoming' was dripping with insinuations about what women should be interested in and how women should strive to make themselves 'becoming'.[11] Male commentaries on Macaulay's abilities only got worse after the publication of her first book.

The themes of the book had been brewing in her head for many years but it was not until she married and moved to London that Macaulay was able to begin her research properly. She envisaged a history book that would span the years from the accession of James I to the English throne in 1603 to the accession of George I in 1714. *The History of England* would not simply be a recounting of events, it would have a clear ideological slant. Macaulay believed that history books *should* shape current politics, and that highlighting instances of virtue in the past would set a good example for her contemporaries. Women could not participate in politics directly, but Macaulay hoped to have indirect influence through her books.

Macaulay saw herself as a patriot which, to her, meant putting the good of the country ahead of loyalty to a particular leader. Samuel Johnson, in his *Dictionary*, had originally defined a patriot as 'one whose ruling passion is the love of his country'. In the fourth edition he added that the word 'is sometimes used for a factious disturber of the government'.[12] Famously, he was once heard to exclaim that 'patriotism is the last refuge of a scoundrel'.[13] A majority of people would have agreed with Johnson: most saw the patriots as an unsettling force within the country. Macaulay was no admirer of royalty – a stance which many viewed with suspicion. When Johnson commented to her once that there was a monarchy in Heaven, she replied, 'if I thought so, Sir, I should never wish to go there.'[14]

Though the average reader might have been alarmed by Macaulay's political views, they could not deny that *The History of*

England was thoroughly researched and elegantly written. For many years, Macaulay had been buying up seventeenth-century political pamphlets and sermons until her collection totalled more than five thousand works.[15] She also used the reading room at the British Museum Library. There she faced occasional barriers, as when the librarian tried to bar her from accessing certain letters between James I and the man believed to have been his lover. The librarian offered to select the less explicit ones for her perusal, excising those that were 'unfit for the inspection of any one of her sex'. 'Phoo,' she is said to have replied, 'a historian is of no sex,' before reading through the whole pile of letters.[16]

When the first volume of *The History of England* appeared in 1763, readers were impressed. Those who shared Macaulay's republican sympathies were always going to like it. The political philosopher Thomas Hollis, for example, noted in his diary that 'the history is honestly written, and with considerable ability and spirit; and is full of the freest, noblest, sentiments of Liberty.' The Whig Horace Walpole agreed that it was 'the most sensible, unaffected and best history of England that we have had yet'. The future Whig Prime Minister Pitt the Elder was said to have made 'a panegyric of her *History* in the House'. The radical John Wilkes praised Macaulay as 'that noble English historian'. The dissenting chemist Joseph Priestley thought it was a 'very masterly history' – an unusual choice of words for a female author. Macaulay was praised outside Britain too – Benjamin Franklin thought that her book was 'that *rara avis* a true history'.[17]

Even those who could not agree with Macaulay's politics were pleased to see the book doing well. Elizabeth Carter was glad to 'hear Mrs. Macaulay's book so much commended. The few extracts which I have seen of it have given me a high idea of her talents.' Though she was happy to see another woman writer receiving public plaudits, Carter was 'exceedingly vexed' to hear about the work's political leanings.[18] Sarah Scott wrote to her sister Montagu, 'have you seen our old acquaintance Mrs Macaulay's (once Kitty Sawbridge's) book, the first volume of an English History; she seems to have a noble print, & has taken great pains, & as far as I have seen I think she acquits herself well.' Scott and Montagu were a decade older than 'Kitty Sawbridge' but they had known her in their Kent girlhood. Scott, like Carter, was perplexed by Macaulay's politics: 'without knowing how or why, she has taken a great deal of pains to make herself [a republican].'

The *Monthly Review* praised Macaulay's research abilities and writing style but was unable to get past the fact of her being a woman. It was a common response to female scholarship but it was heightened here, for Macaulay was the first woman ever to attempt this kind of history. The review mentioned Macaulay's sex, looks or marital status on almost every page of its ten-page critique of her work – something male writers never had to endure. On the first page the reviewer praised the book, but hinted that he disapproved of women tackling such masculine topics. The next page explained further:

> each sex has its characteristical excellence: and the soft and delicate texture of a female frame, was no more intended for severe study, than . . . Man was formed for [needlework]. Intense thought spoils a lady's features; it banishes *les ris et les graces*, which form all the enchantment of a female face.

This reviewer, like so many others, believed that learned ladies were fundamentally unnatural. By abandoning womanly pursuits and deliberately overtaxing their brains women risked their most valuable possession – their looks. The same reviewer praised Macaulay's writing style by saying, 'we can discover no traces of a female pen.' He then speculated about whether Macaulay might be married and, if so, whether her husband had secretly written this 'manly' prose.[19]

The *Critical Review* managed to write up the book in glowing terms with only one reference to Macaulay's sex. This broad-mindedness was inspired not so much by any kind of belief in the ability of women, as by the fact that the reviewer clearly shared Macaulay's political views.[20]

By the time the second volume of *The History of England* was published in 1765, the novelty of a female historian seemed to have worn off a little and the *Monthly Review* gave the volume a glowing write-up, including only a handful of comments on Macaulay's sex. The reviewer referred back to his earlier piece in which he had speculated on Macaulay's marital status. He had since learned that she was married and confessed himself glad that 'the woman is not lost in the historian.'[21]

There were satires on Macaulay's book too, such as the play *The Devil upon Two Sticks* by Samuel Foote. Sarah Scott saw it at the Haymarket in 1768 and described it as 'a satire on Phisicians the Law & Mrs Macaulay, with a very drole & decent touch at the Methodists'.[22] That night at the Haymarket, Scott caught a glimpse of Macaulay sitting in a box with Horace Walpole and laughing along with everyone else.

Some said that Macaulay exposed herself to these responses by not publishing anonymously as so many of the Bluestockings did. But, as we have seen, leaving one's name off the title page was no real guarantee of anonymity when the literary world was so small and so interconnected. Most of the Bluestockings who wrote books saw their authorship made public within their own lifetime.

Once a woman became a public author, every aspect of her life was up for dissection and debate. In particular, the public fixated on her appearance. They imagined bookish women as hideously deformed and longed for tales of ugly, unlovable women to confirm their prejudices. Of course, bookish women generally looked just like other women. 'I have known many [female authors], both in verse and prose, who were not tolerably decent in their appearance,' began an anonymous letter that appeared in the gossipy *Town and Country Magazine* in the years after Macaulay's fame had spread. The author claimed to be acquainted with Macaulay and gave a flattering description of her, assuring readers that she was thoroughly decent in her appearance. The highest praise he gave was that one could meet Macaulay and *not even realise* that she was a learned lady: 'you may be ten years in her company, without suspecting her to be an author,' he wrote, and, 'though she has come from her study to receive me, I never could discover by her manner or dress that she had been either reading or writing.' Quite how a woman might dress if she had been reading is not made clear in the letter.[23]

Not content just with reading her elegant prose, commentators became obsessed with Macaulay's domestic life. There were many who assumed that home-making skills and intellectual endeavours were mutually exclusive. Everyone felt sorry for those men who were unfortunate enough to have married clever women, but the anonymous *Town and Country Magazine* writer assured his readers that Catharine Macaulay was a surprisingly good wife:

> You have often heard the notables of both sexes say, when speaking of a learned lady, *God pity her husband.* I assure you, from my own experience and knowledge, that Dr. Macaulay was, in a married state, an object of envy; nor do I know any man more happy than he was in a wife.[24]

George Macaulay, a staunch defender of his wife, once wrote to a friend: 'you may think that Catherine from her application to study is not an attentive wife, but there never was a more affectionate wife, or more tender mother.'[25] The couple's daughter, Catherine Sophia, had been born in February 1765 (a few months before the appearance of the second volume of the *History*). The unflappable Macaulay effortlessly combined her maternal duties with her commitment to her work. As was standard for a family of their class, they employed a nurse to see to the more mundane nursery tasks; and it is probable that George, who was used to infants from his work at the lying-in hospital, was a more practical father than most men of the time.

Alongside the assumption that Macaulay lacked domestic skills, sat the sister assumption that she must be ugly. 'Her talents and powers could not be denied; her beauty was therefore called into question, as if it was at all concerned with the subject,' wrote the biographer Mary Hays in 1803, a few years after Macaulay's death. Hays described how Macaulay's adversaries had called her 'deformed', 'unfortunately ugly'.[26] (Hays herself was described as 'a Thing, ugly and petticoated' by Samuel Taylor Coleridge.[27])

Comments about Macaulay's looks were often tied to her political beliefs, as when James Boswell decried her republicanism with the lines:

> Like a Dutch *vrouw*, all shapeless, pale, and fat,
> That hugs and slabbers her ungainly brat,
> Our Cath'rine sits sublime o'er steaming tea,
> And takes her dear Republic on her knee;
> Sings it all songs that ever yet were sung,
> And licks it fondly with her length of tongue.[28]

Boswell's dislike of Macaulay was probably inspired by Samuel Johnson's dislike of Macaulay. Johnson had never cared for her republicanism and enjoyed picking holes in it. He often told the story of how, when he was dining at her house one day, he had teased her by saying that he had been converted to her way of thinking. To prove that all men were equal, he suggested that Macaulay's footman be invited to join them at the dinner table. 'I thus', said Johnson, 'shewed her the absurdity of the levelling doctrine. She has never liked me since.'[29]

It was true that Macaulay's republicanism retained a class system (and it seems never to have occurred to her to extend the franchise to women), but Johnson's dislike of her went beyond a difference of political opinion. When people asked him to give a toast – often expecting a 'loyal' toast to the monarch – he took to mockingly toasting Macaulay instead. Once, while visiting Trinity College Cambridge, it was said that 'he began to be very great; stripped poor Mrs. Macaulay to the very skin, then gave her for his toast, and drank her in two bumpers.'[30] This image of a woman stripped naked in the all-male enclave of a Cambridge college recalls Boswell's grotesque image of her sensuously licking a baby: these men could not deny that Macaulay had brains, so they slandered her body instead.

Macaulay had presented a copy of the first volume of her *History* to Johnson, but he left the pages uncut. A mutual friend noticed this and said it showed Johnson's unfounded contempt for Macaulay. Johnson replied that if the friend told Macaulay this he would deny it, and assured him that Macaulay's vanity meant that she would never believe that anyone would pass up an opportunity to read her work.[31]

Even if Johnson did not care to read the *History*, there were many who did. David Hume requested a copy of the book from the Macaulays (he was a relation of George's) and, though he and Macaulay had little common ground, he said he found her work pleasing.[32] Some of Hume's friends were less polite about the book: the painter Allan Ramsay wrote to Hume to let him know that 'somebody under the name of Mrs Catharine Maccauley [sic] has written a romance, called "James the First", the secret design of which is to abuse you and me, and all the other people of consequence.'[33]

Another of Hume's friends wrote to ask, 'what is this McCaulay [sic] history? I saw in the newspapers an extract of a preface that seemed to me to be the rhapsody of a crazy head. I hear it is in opposition to your History.'[34]

The literati (and their friends) read the book; but so too did ordinary folk. Such was the demand for affordable copies of the *History* that it was serialised: each volume was divided into fifteen parts and one part was published each week at a cost of one shilling. This kind of printing made books much more accessible for those who would struggle to buy expensive full volumes – an unbound volume of the *History* would have cost more than a pound, and a bound one £4 10s. Sales of both the serialised books and the full volumes were strong, and Macaulay earned good money for her work. She was sufficiently famous that portraits of her were sold in print-shops, and a porcelain figure of her was available to buy.[35]

In 1766 George Macaulay died. Catharine was bereft. She lost a loving and supportive husband. George had been a rarity – an eighteenth-century man who saw his wife as his equal. They had had only six years together, and now Macaulay faced an uncertain future as a widow single-handedly raising their one-year-old daughter. There was only one benefit to be derived from George's death: no longer could the critics say that *he* was the true author of *The History of England*, that a woman never could have written such a book. The first two volumes had appeared in 1763 and 1765. When George died in 1766, the eight-volume work was only a quarter complete. The new volumes that were published from 1767 were praised as being every bit as 'masculine' as the earlier ones, but now no one could misattribute them to the man of the Macaulay household.

Those new volumes took a lot out of Macaulay. After finishing the third volume, she developed a fever from working overly long hours for so many months.[36] It was exactly the kind of thing her critics might pounce on as evidence that too much thinking was bad for women. But in spite of bouts of bad health throughout the late 1760s, Macaulay kept working. As well as researching and writing the next volumes of the *History*, Macaulay engaged in wide-ranging correspondences with republicans, radicals and dissenters across Britain; she loaned and borrowed political books and tracts; and, most satisfyingly, she saw her books launched to great acclaim in the American colonies.

Macaulay's American readers adored her republican take on history. One fan wrote to inform her that

> your Name and your History are every day becoming more and more known in this Country . . . to be admired and celebrated here as a patroness of Liberty and a defendant of the rights of Mankind is the highest pitch of honour an ambitious mind can aspire after.

Another praised Macaulay's 'noble zeal'. The great patriot (and future First Lady) Abigail Adams wrote to congratulate Macaulay on her 'superior abilities'. Adams tried to learn more about Macaulay through mutual friends, being eager to know about Macaulay's education and how she had become a historian. Abigail's husband (future President) John Adams wrote to Macaulay, telling her of his esteem for her work: 'I have read, not only with Pleasure and Instruction, but with great admiration, Mrs. Macaulay's History of England . . . [I formed] the highest opinion of the Author, as one of the brightest ornaments, not only of her Sex, but of her age and Country.'[37] After Macaulay's reputation was established, people began to send their books to her for endorsement. James Boswell sent Macaulay a copy of his travelogue of Corsica in 1768, knowing that she was sympathetic to the Corsican general Pasquale Paoli who fought for the island's independence. She described the Corsican volume as 'well timed spirited and elegant' and politely expressed her desire to meet the author.[38] (She did not know of the lines Boswell had written when he had first read her *History* in which he likened her to 'a Dutch *vrouw*'. Though the two met several times, they never much liked one another.)

When she was not writing or reading, Macaulay continued to host the lively social circle she and George had begun. She and her daughter Catherine Sophia moved from St James's to Berners Street, off Oxford Street, a short walk from the British Museum where she undertook much of her research.[39] This new house became famous for its Tuesday evening coteries where all manner of political positions were proposed, analysed and disputed. It was said that her hosting style was both elegant and warm.[40] As well as drawing in the British radicals, Macaulay's Tuesday evenings attracted Americans such as Benjamin Franklin. The coteries were generally serious affairs but, occasionally, Macaulay would break out into frivolity, as when she hosted a Twelfth Night Party which lasted until three o'clock in the morning. 'How unworthy of reasonable beings are modern fashionable amusements!' grumbled one guest who expected more cerebral entertainment at Macaulay's; all the same, he stayed until after midnight.[41]

The fourth volume of the *History* appeared in 1768, and the fifth in 1771. The effort Macaulay expended in finishing that fifth volume made her so ill that she took to her bed for four months. Desperate to be well again, she ate ice-cream to strengthen the stomach (she recommended this practice to friends, who reported that their dinners felt much lighter when accompanied by ice-cream) and she went sea-bathing on the Kentish coast.[42]

Neither ice-cream nor bathing proved successful, so in 1774 Macaulay decided to move to Bath, hoping that its medicinal waters and the city's many practitioners might offer some relief from the symptoms that plagued her. Those symptoms included fevers, chronic stomach pains, trembling and shivering fits, and recurring pains in the ears and throat. She attributed all of these to what she called 'a weak system of nerves'.[43]

In Bath, Macaulay took a house on St James's Parade, not far from the Pump Room. She knew a few people in Bath, but not enough (and few radical enough) to start up a new coterie there. Soon, however, she found herself drawn into the orbit of another Bath resident: Thomas Wilson. Wilson was thirty years older than Macaulay. Like her, he had been widowed a few years earlier, and had moved to Bath for his health. Like her, he was keenly interested in radical politics. Wilson had studied at Oxford, become a doctor of divinity, and been ordained. He held various church positions (including a brief stint as chaplain to George II), but it was politics that really held his attention. He and his wife Mary had been close friends of John Wilkes. Wilson also had in common with Macaulay a passion for books, and his house in Bath contained a fine library.[44]

Some years before either Macaulay or Wilson moved to Bath, a piece appeared in *Town and Country Magazine* which recounted the career and exploits of the (scarcely anonymised) 'Dr. W----n'. The article alleged that Wilson had had several illicit liaisons with various women, but that after he had become embroiled with the Wilkites he had sought out a woman who was 'a female patriot', upon which he had been told that England had but one female patriot – Mrs Macaulay. The article claimed that Macaulay showed no interest in Wilson, and that he then took up with the anonymous 'Mrs. L----n'. Whether or not any of this was true, it was clear that the public was interested in reading scurrilous tales about these unorthodox figures.[45]

What we do know is that in Bath in the mid-1770s, the historian and the churchman began spending time together and became close friends, so close that Macaulay took the unusual step of moving in with Wilson in the winter of 1775. Alfred House in Alfred Street was a five-storey terraced house in honey-coloured Bath stone. Proudly displayed above its porch was a bust of Macaulay's hero King Alfred (he sits there still today, quietly surveying the tourists as he has done for two and a half centuries). No one knows quite why Macaulay and her daughter moved in with Wilson. The relationship was not a romantic one (at least not on Macaulay's side), and Macaulay had enough funds to buy or rent a place of her own. Perhaps she was simply lonely. Perhaps he was. That first spring that the trio lived together, Wilson commissioned a portrait of himself and Catherine Sophia. Wilson had lost his only child, a son, as an infant, and perhaps with the Macaulays he saw a second chance at family life. The artist behind the painting was Joseph Wright of Derby, who had just lately moved to Bath in the hope of building his reputation as a society portraitist. Wright wrote to his brother that he was painting 'Dr Wilson and his adopted daughter' – there had indeed been a ceremonial adoption that spring, and Wilson intended to make her his heir.[46] The completed portrait shows Wilson deep in contemplation and Catherine Sophia gazing respectfully at this new father figure; each has a hand resting on an open volume of Macaulay's *History*.

The domestic set-up was almost certainly innocent but, considering the earlier magazine articles about Wilson's amorous adventures, it is astonishing that there was little public comment on the living arrangement of the pair. They seem to have drawn remarkably little censure from their peers – at first.

For more than a year, the trio lived harmoniously. Macaulay's health was steadily improving thanks to the ministrations of a new medical man she had discovered – one James Graham. In an effusive letter, Macaulay gave a glimpse into some of the methods used by Graham. She said that her symptoms had disappeared thanks to his 'Chemical Essences, [his] Ætherial, Magnetic, and Electric Applications'.[47] Graham also employed balsamic medicines, milk baths, earth baths, dry friction and his famous magnetic throne. Years later, in London, he became known for his 'celestial bed' – a construction nine feet across and twelve long, which rested on forty glass pillars, hooked up to magnets and electrical apparatus. It was said to cure infertility, but mostly it just served to earn Graham an income. Today, the *Dictionary of National Biography* gives his occupation as 'quack'.[48] Macaulay was unbothered by the eccentricities of his methods, so long as they sustained her health and enabled her to write.

Macaulay was feeling positively well again when the spring of 1777 rolled around. To celebrate her recovery, Wilson proposed a party for her forty-sixth birthday which fell on 2 April. Wilson planned an extravaganza unlike anything Bath had seen before. Macaulay's birthday celebrations began with a ringing of bells and, as the day went on, there occurred what Wilson called 'other public demonstrations of the general joy felt for an event so pleasing to the true friends of literature and liberty in these kingdoms'. After the public displays, a large swathe of Bath society was invited to Alfred House. Here an elegantly attired Macaulay was seated upon a stage constructed for the occasion, while six gentlemen read aloud poems and odes, specially composed for her. The odes, recalled Wilson proudly afterwards, were performed 'with great propriety and expression . . . one Ode was delivered with a grace and elocution that would have done honour to *Garrick*; and another, with an energy and action not unworthy of *Demosthenes!*' Next, Wilson advanced towards the stage, presented Macaulay with a gold medal and launched into an exuberant speech. Then it was the turn of James Graham, who presented Macaulay with a copy of his published works and gave a speech likening her to Catherine the Great. At the end of these formalities, wine was served and then the guests dispersed throughout the house, every room lit brightly with candles. There was dancing, cards and conversation until nine o'clock when the doors of the dining room were thrown open and a feast appeared before the guests: 'syllabubs, jellies, creams, ices, wines, cakes, and a variety of dry and fresh fruits, particularly grapes and pine-apples', as one recalled.[49]

Macaulay circulated slowly through the rooms of Alfred House, stopping to converse with each group of guests. At midnight, the festivities came to an end, the guests dispersed, the candles were blown out, and Wilson and Macaulay – overjoyed with the success of the thing – retired to their respective bedchambers.

Others, however, were less pleased. The *Six Odes* were published by Wilson, along with a lengthy description of the day's entertainments. The poems – which likened Macaulay to the Muses and various Roman goddesses – were more than a little over the top. At a private gathering, delivered dramatically, they had been fun; but now, printed in stark black and white, they seemed crassly self-indulgent. One ode in particular attracted attention – this was the final one in the pamphlet, titled 'Britannia's Reward'. In it, the narrator falls asleep on a sweet upland lawn and dreams that Britannia seeks to bestow a laurel wreath on the most worthy British woman. And so begins a comparison of the merits of some of Macaulay's contemporaries:

> . . .
> The figure next presented to my view,
> Resembled learned critic, MONTAGUE;
> Her brow the strength of sentiment exprest,
> And *Shakespeare's* head hung graceful on her breast,
>
> Next Carter came, for wisdom long ador'd,
> Who the vast depth of *Grecian* wit explor'd;
> Made *Epictetus'* moral lessons guide
> The *British* youth by virtue's sacred side.[50]

Excellent though these other women might have been, the ode concluded with Macaulay being crowned with laurels and her triumph sounded in the skies.

The Bluestockings were embarrassed to be linked to any of the ostentatious shenanigans in Bath; not because they lost out in this fictional contest, but because they considered the whole thing vulgar. Elizabeth Carter wrote to Elizabeth Montagu:

> Surely nothing ever equalled that farcical parade of foolery with which [Macaulay] suffered herself to be flattered, and almost worshipped, by that poor old wrong-headed firebrand of party . . . I think one never heard of anybody, above the degree of an idiot, who took pleasure in being so dressed out with the very rags and ribbons of vanity, like a queen in a puppet show.[51]

Even some of Macaulay's good friends thought the party had been excessive, as one wrote:

> the accounts of the extravagant and ridiculous manner, in which, as you observe, my friend Mrs. M-------'s birth-day was celebrated at Bath, gave me extreme disgust; and have contributed to reduce my opinion of her magnanimity and good sense . . . If I live to see her again, I will rally her handsomely.[52]

A review of the *Odes* in the *Monthly Review* openly mocked the whole affair. The reviewer, quite reasonably, pointed out the incongruity of the great republican Macaulay placing herself on what amounted to a throne during the recital of the odes.[53]

The published odes were accompanied by an introduction in which the anonymous author gushed about the 'inexpressible happiness' of sharing a house with Macaulay. He rhapsodised about the honour of being her friend, sharing in her conversation and spending his leisure time with her.[54] These words must have been written by Wilson. Even if they were not, everyone assumed that they were. His reverence for Macaulay seemed to go beyond respect for her intellect or admiration of her books: he was publicly besotted with her. The feeling was not mutual. Macaulay never saw Wilson as anything other than a friend.

Did the odes, the birthday party, Wilson's public joy at sharing a home with her, begin to make her feel uneasy? Perhaps. But it was not until the events of autumn that same year that she saw how truly untenable her position in Alfred House was.

In September 1777 Wilson unveiled a statue that he had commissioned of Macaulay. The white marble sculpture stood more than two metres high and depicted Macaulay in flowing classical robes and sandals. In one hand she held a quill, in the other a scroll. Her arm rested upon a stack of books, her cloak was pinned in place with a brooch bearing an owl – the symbol of Minerva. The elements of the statue – the unfurling scroll, the abundance of books – would have made onlookers think instantly of Clio, the Muse of History, who was always depicted with such paraphernalia. The statue was recessed into a niche, on top of a base inscribed with this curious verse:

> You speak of Mrs. Macaulay:
> She is a Kind of Prodigy!
> I revere her abilities:
> I cannot bear to hear her name sarcastically mentioned:
> I would have her taste the exalted pleasure of universal applause:
> I would have STATUES erected to her memory,
> And once in every age I could wish
> Such a woman to appear,
> As a proof that genius is not confined to sex.
> But, at the same time, you will pardon me,
> We want no more than one Mrs. Macaulay.[55]

Wilson had taken the words from a novel published a few years earlier which purported to be based on the private letters of the recently deceased writer and statesman Lord Lyttelton (though Lyttelton's friends insisted that the novel had nothing to do with him).[56] In the novel, the words had appeared in prose, and the final 'one' was italicised – it was not meant as a straightforward compliment, and the novel went on to suggest that women should stick to less cerebral pursuits.[57] In versifying this passage, Wilson created a strange epitaph to his still-living friend. In the hectic unmetred lines, some saw the unbalancing of Wilson's own faculties.

Another odd thing about the statue was the fact that Wilson had it erected in a church – St Stephen Walbrook in the City of London. Wilson had been rector there since 1737, but it had never been his main focus. The parishioners were deeply unimpressed when he made one of his rare appearances to install this profane statue in a sacred space. It was said that the statue scandalised the devout, astonished the learned and disgusted the royalists.[58] Wilson had consulted no one in the parish about the work or its placement in the chancel. The congregation immediately began to campaign for its removal.

The public, who remembered the ludicrous spectacle of the birthday party earlier in the year, jumped on this new opportunity to satirise Macaulay and Wilson. One magazine piece described the statue before adding: 'we hear that Mrs. Macaulay, in return for the friendly compliment that Dr. Wilson has paid her, in causing a statue to be erected to her memory, is determined to *erect* the Doctor.'[59]

The Bluestockings, again, distanced themselves from Macaulay. A few days after the grand unveiling, Carter wrote to Montagu asking, 'are all the strange representations about Dr. Wilson's statue true?' If they were true, she asserted, polite society would have nothing to do with the statue, nor with Macaulay or Wilson. Carter was particularly shocked by the misattribution of the verse inscribed on the statue's base to Lyttelton. The statesman and literary patron had always been supportive of the Bluestockings and was held in high regard by them. He had been a close friend of Montagu's and he had given her that first chance at publication when he included three of her *Dialogues of the Dead* in one of his collections. Carter called the misattribution 'so very absurd and so very impertinent, that one scarcely knows how to think it could exist, except in a paragraph in a newspaper'.[60]

The furore over the statue, not long after the furore over the birthday party, forced Macaulay to re-evaluate her relationship with Wilson. She had never been one to care much about outward appearances, but now she saw that the relationship was not the straightforward friendship she had always imagined it to be. Wilson seemed to be in love with her; she did not love him; and so she had no choice but to leave. Possibly, she left to spare him. But he did not see it that way.

To gain some distance from Wilson, Macaulay sent her daughter to a boarding school in Chelsea while she herself took a trip to France. She said, truthfully, that her doctors had recommended it but the time away from Alfred House must have come as a relief. She invited

Elizabeth Arnold, the sister of the medical man James Graham, to accompany her. The first leg of the journey – from Bath to London – took six days as Macaulay's poor heath necessitated frequent stops along the way. Then she had to rest in London for two weeks to gather strength before making the crossing to France. There followed two days' rest at Calais as Macaulay battled a fever, then a slow and uncomfortable journey to Paris.[61] In Paris at last, the women took rooms near the Luxembourg Palace and Macaulay contacted a physician recommended to her by Horace Walpole. The physician was shocked by her poor state of health and forbade her from travelling on to her intended destination of Nice. A week in Paris and a bark remedy brought the fever under control. Macaulay's fatigue and frailty began to abate. The women could finally begin to enjoy themselves.

Thanks to numerous letters of introduction from friends, Macaulay soon found herself receiving visits from many notable figures in Paris society. Despite her avowed republican principles, she was as happy to receive aristocratic guests as commoners, though it was once said that she refused to visit Versailles as she considered it to be 'the residence of the tyrants'. Macaulay found her French companions genial and welcoming. They in turn were intrigued by this lady author. Macaulay happily reported that the French complimented her genius and her literary powers, and approved of her republican views.[62]

There were some notable inhabitants of Paris who were off limits to Macaulay – Americans. She wrote apologetically to Benjamin Franklin that she could not entertain him during her visit: the Habeas Corpus Act had been suspended and there was a very real possibility that Macaulay would face imprisonment if she was seen associating with Americans.[63] In the wake of the American Revolution, there was much suspicion surrounding figures like Macaulay who were openly republican. Her transatlantic correspondences with friends such as Mercy Otis Warren were often interrupted in these years, and Warren and many other Americans took to writing in code or leaving their letters unsigned to protect themselves. Macaulay was occasionally accused of being a spy, though no one seriously believed that. She was once linked to a plot to kidnap King George because one of her letters was found in the possession of the man thought to be the chief conspirator – a London-based American called Stephen Sayre. After six days in the Tower, it was decided that Sayre had no case to answer, whereupon he was released and enjoyed a brief period of minor celebrity.

Despite her disappointment at not being able to spend time with Franklin and other Americans in Paris, Macaulay had a pleasant trip. Her only two real complaints were the terrible living conditions of the poor, to whom she distributed alms; and the terrible French food. 'Their meat is car[r]ion,' she railed, 'their poultry and even their game insipid, and their cookery most detestable.'[64] She complained that French food gave her a stomach-ache, and so she cut her trip short, returning to England after just two months.

Having nowhere else to go, on her return in January 1778 she went first to Bath and took up an uneasy residence in Alfred House. A few days afterwards, John Wilkes visited the house and described how ill she looked. 'She was painted up to the eyes, and looks quite ghastly and ghostly,' he told his daughter Polly. Her main topic of conversation was France, the French, and French food – 'she even says their soups are detestable,' he wrote, amused at her vehemence on the subject.[65]

While Macaulay tried to keep the conversation going, a bad-tempered Wilson sat listening in silence. The reason for Wilson's sullenness may have been the rumours that had begun to swirl around Macaulay. It was said that perhaps her relationship with James Graham was not quite what it seemed. Despite obvious tensions, Macaulay and Wilson both remained in residence at Alfred House.

Perhaps to distract herself from her stressful domestic life, Macaulay began to write again. She still had several volumes of *The History of England* to finish, but she put them aside for now and began work on something else – a short, popular, condensed English history, written as a series of letters to Wilson. This book – *The History of England from the Revolution to the Present Time in a Series of Letters to a Friend* – was less scholarly in tone than her multi-volume *History of England* and she deliberately omitted footnotes. The book was dedicated to Wilson, and in the opening pages Macaulay wrote of the happiness she had felt when she first corresponded with him and told of how she aspired to be a better writer thanks to their friendship. She praised

Wilson's character, his conduct, his patriotism, his benevolence, his cheerfulness in the face of ill health. These opening pages read as a reminder to Wilson of the uncomplicated relationship they had once enjoyed and as a plea to return to those days. It was perhaps intended as something of an apology too – an apology for the fact that she did not love him.

No private letters between Wilson and Macaulay have survived; only these formal, stylised missives (which were always intended for publication). She called him 'my friend' throughout, she entered into minute detail of political wranglings and gave sweeping overviews of human society. In the pages of the book, the reader can detect traces of their late-night debates about monarchies and republics, their dissections of theories coming from America or France. More than anything, these debates and discussions had taken place between true equals. Macaulay's sex did not matter when she talked about patriotism, but it came to matter when Wilson publicly courted her. It skewed their relationship. *The History of England from the Revolution to the Present Time in a Series of Letters to a Friend* is deliberately devoid of any emphasis on Macaulay as a *female* historian.

Naturally, the reviews dedicated paragraphs to Macaulay's sex. The *Monthly Review* praised Macaulay's 'manly energy' before launching into a lengthy discussion of the merits (or otherwise) of lady writers. She must have despaired to see so many words given over to her sex rather than her book.

The *Critical Review* prefaced its review of the book with a lengthy discussion of the relationship between Macaulay and Wilson, and a retelling of the story of the statue and the surrounding controversy. Then followed a generally positive review of the book.[66] Again, it was not quite what Macaulay had been hoping for.

It was clear that Macaulay's relationship with Wilson (and the public perception of it) was a distraction that was beginning to affect her career. Later that year, she moved out of Alfred House permanently. She left in October 1778 saying that she wished to care for her friend and former travel companion Elizabeth Arnold who was ill in Leicester. Wilson suspected there was another motivation for Macaulay's departure.[67]

Wilson may have been growing increasingly erratic and paranoid but, here at least, his instinct was correct – Macaulay had fallen in love. The object of her affection was William Graham, the brother of Elizabeth Arnold and James Graham. Like his older brother James, William Graham was medically minded, but he had chosen a more traditional (though less lucrative) career as a surgeon's mate in the navy. The details of how Macaulay and Graham first met and fell in love never became publicly known, but there was one thing that everybody knew: he was twenty-one years old when they married in November 1778 and Macaulay was forty-seven. It was an instant scandal. A middle-aged woman marrying a younger man spoke of unnatural lusts. Widows, in any case, were often viewed with suspicion if they gave any sign that they were husband-hunting. Their role was to fade quietly into the background. Macaulay had never been much of a one for quiet fading.

It had been twelve years since George's death had widowed Catharine. In those years, rumours about her and various of the men in her circle had ebbed and flowed. Wilson, of course, was frequently proposed as a possible husband for her. So too were political philosopher Thomas Hollis (with whom she once drank tea after her first husband's death) and Corsican general Pasquale Paoli (to whom she offered some vague assistance when he visited London). When the British general Charles Lee had joined the American Revolution, Elizabeth Montagu had joked that Macaulay should marry him. John Wilkes (with whom Macaulay shared some political views and not much else) also frequently appeared in rumours about Macaulay's supposed love life. Hester Thrale once published a satirical alphabet which included the line 'W, was a Widow would make Wilkes a Wife'.[68] Wilkes himself joined in the game and accused Macaulay of indiscretions with an unnamed man; specifically, he claimed that she had breakfasted with this man 'in a matrimonial way'.[69] Wilkes heavily hinted that this mysterious breakfaster was James Graham. Several people accused James Graham of trying to seduce Macaulay for her money, or of introducing her to his younger brother as a means to the same end.[70]

When it came to accusations against Macaulay and the Graham brothers, Wilson led the charge. His diary records his disgust at Macaulay's marriage: 'to the great surprise of the world Mrs. Macaulay without giving me the slightest notice at the age of 52 married a YOUNG SCOTCH LOON of 21 whom she had not seen for above a month before the fatal knot was tied.'[71] Since he had organised Macaulay's forty-sixth birthday party the previous year, Wilson would have known that Macaulay was not fifty-two. Did he say it to magnify her offence, or was it a symptom of the senility that his friends said was growing worse? He was correct though that it seemed to be an incredibly quick courtship and a very brief engagement.

Wilson's diary continued with more vitriol against the couple. He called Graham 'a mate to an East India Ship without clothes on his back', and dismissed his family as 'most beggarly'.[72] When Wilkes visited Wilson at Alfred House shortly after the wedding, he found the old man outraged and ranting – Wilson had become convinced (*'from facts'*, he said) that Macaulay had been involved in some kind of intimacy with James Graham. 'He thinks her a monster,' wrote Wilkes.

Anticipating Wilson's likely reaction to her marriage, Macaulay had sat down on her wedding day and written a long letter to him. The letter no longer exists. Maybe it was intended to allay Wilson's fears for her, to ask for his blessing, to explain her feelings for William Graham, or her lack of romantic feelings for Wilson. Perhaps it was a final goodbye, a plea to let her be. Whatever that letter contained sent Wilson into a frenzy of hate. He read it aloud to Wilkes who agreed that this long letter was 'indecent, insolent, mean, fawning, threatening, coaxing, menacing, and declamatory. Such words I believe never escaped a female pen.'[73]

Wilson began to erase all traces of Macaulay from Alfred House. He fired the servants she had hired and promoted the one she had never liked. He banned her from ever visiting the house, though the deeds were actually in her name. He engaged a bookseller to disentangle Macaulay's books from his own library and dispatched four large boxes of them by wagon to her temporary home in Leicester. He had all her clothes taken from their wardrobes and parcelled up to be collected by a maid who arrived bearing a formal written order, rather than the personal letter that Wilson seemed to expect.[74] Much to the relief of the parishioners, he removed the statue of Macaulay from its place at St Stephen Walbrook.[75] He sold the burial chamber he had intended for her future use.[76] His public abuse of Macaulay intensified: he took to calling her 'the modern Messalina' after the wife of Emperor Claudius who was always portrayed as scheming and licentious. He spoke of her only with contempt, and told stories of her 'insolence, capriciousness, and even abandonness'. Most hurtful of all, he began to say that she was not a good historian, that her books were inaccurate.[77] In his diary, he accused her, and women more generally, of insanity: 'the women are all gone stark staring MADD.'[78]

The public lapped up Wilson's dramatic declarations about his former friend. Multiple satirical pamphlets were published soon after the wedding; there were cartoons too and even a play performed at the Haymarket. The play was *A Widow and No Widow*, written by Richard Paul Jodrell. Its main character is a woman called Mrs Sharp who purports to be a widow in order to dupe a man named Dr Alfred into giving her large sums of money. This Mrs Sharp also has a young Scottish lover who has travelled widely.

Jodrell was probably also behind one of the many pamphlets about Macaulay and Graham – *The Female Patriot*. This pamphlet claimed to be based on the letter Macaulay had written on her wedding day. The letter's existence was widely known, though Wilson had not yet followed through on his threat to publish it. In Jodrell's telling of the story, Macaulay's letter bluntly informed Wilson that

> had he not been totally incapacitated for hymeneal rites, she would certainly have preferred him to any other candidates as a husband: but, in consequence of his disability, she was obliged, for the gratification of those natural and irresistible passions which stimulate the sex, to apply to another better qualified to satisfy her warmest wishes.[79]

There is no reason to believe that Jodrell had ever seen the original letter. As a dramatist, he knew what an audience wanted and he was well capable of conjuring salacious details from his imagination. Like many, he had a peculiar fascination with widows. In *A Widow and No Widow* one character had spoken the line: 'we pardon all such false delicacies in an unmarried woman; – but a widow, my dear Mrs. Sharp – a widow is quite another thing.' Later, another character warns a young man: 'A widow! – Oh! beware of widows! They add the experience of mankind to the natural subtilty of their own sex: and the arts they have learned from one husband, they play off upon every other.'[80]

Another pamphlet called *A Remarkable Moving Letter!* also claimed to be based on the one Macaulay had written to Wilson on her wedding day. It too implied that Macaulay had rejected Wilson on account of his inability to satisfy her in bed:

> Hadst thou possess'd (shame checks my falt'ring pen)
> The pow'rs that Heav'n allots to younger men,
> My frailer nature had not dar'd to rove.[81]

There was a general feeling that Macaulay and Wilson had brought such satires on themselves because of their bizarre (and public) conduct.

Her harshest critics were not the satirists, the pamphleteers, the playwrights; they were the other Bluestockings. The gains that the Bluestockings had made were tenuous, too tenuous to allow their project to be derailed by members of the group behaving in any way likely to attract opprobrium. They felt they had little choice but to make a public show of distancing themselves from Macaulay. True, Macaulay had never been central to the circles of Montagu or Thrale, but in the popular imagination all bookish women got lumped together. Being linked to Macaulay was not a risk they could take.

The first to bring news of Macaulay's second marriage was Sarah Scott. Word came to her from mutual acquaintances in Bath and she wrote instantly to her sister Montagu. Scott called Macaulay's actions 'a dishonour to the sex' and took comfort in what she believed was 'the moral certainty that her punishment will equal her offence'. Scott filled Montagu in on all the salacious details of Macaulay's young husband, adding that 'he is a brother to a Dr Graham, who etherized and electrified her, till he has made her electric per se.' Scott mentioned the infamous letter. Wilson had shown it to many of his male friends by now, but the gentlemen said that it was not fit for a woman's eyes and so Scott had not seen it herself. Still, she had heard enough to report that Macaulay was said to have been for some years struggling with nature but found that her life absolutely depends on her complying with her constitution's urgent call . . . and she would have chosen [Wilson], if his age, as he must be sensible, did not disqualify him for answering a call so urgent.

Scott was disgusted by Macaulay's apparently open desire for a satisfying sexual relationship. She denied that such urges were natural in a woman – 'perhaps she calls it nature's [call],' Scott wrote to Montagu, 'but I shall not, for it is not the nature of woman, & woman cannot find her excuse in the nature of a beast.'

Scott showed real venom for Macaulay and her actions – later in the same letter, she wrote: 'If there is any zeal still remaining in the world for virtue's cause the pure Virgins and virtuous Matrons who reside in this place, will unite and drown her in the Avon, and try if she can be purified by water.'[82] Scott had always shown understanding to women who operated outside the normal bounds of society, but she was incapable of extending that understanding to Macaulay. Perhaps it was that Macaulay was too much like herself. It was one thing for Scott to employ servants who had known disgrace, or to give a home to her 'illegitimate' niece. These were acts of charity bestowed on women lower down the social order. It would have been quite another thing to condone scandalous behaviour in someone who was Scott's equal. To support Macaulay would have been to undermine her own social position which was built on a foundation of respectability. Perhaps her venom for Macaulay grew out of fear. For Scott to write a book like *Millenium Hall* and argue that women could form self-contained communes, she had to be beyond reproach, as did those around her.

Montagu was just as fascinated by Macaulay's second marriage as her sister had been and gleefully recounted the details to her friends. To Hester Thrale (still a few years away from taking an Italian lover), she wrote: 'Are you not shock'd that Mrs Macaulay has taken Minerva from her Couch to put Venus couchant & Cupid rampant in the place of ye chaste and prudent Goddess? . . . A surgeon's mate aged 22, ah! it is both passing strange & wondrous pittiful!'[83] To Elizabeth Carter, Montagu wrote:

I should not have thought it strange if Mrs. Macauley had crossed the Atlantick to marry some arch rebel or even the descendent of a Regicide, but to unite herself with a boy and a Scotch boy is quite out of the path of such a comet.[84]

Montagu believed that Macaulay's essential problem was that she was overly manly – as she explained to Thrale:

all this has happened from [Macaulay] adopting Masculine opin- ions, & Masculine manners. I hate a Womans mind in Mans cloaths as well as her Person. I always look'd upon Mrs Macaulay as rather belonging to Jack Cade[*] & other boisterous Rebels than as one of the gentle sex. Indeed she was always a *strange fellow*.[85]

Thrale's replies to these letters have not survived. She was as sur- prised as anyone by Macaulay's conduct, but perhaps she was a little gentler on the woman, recalling that Macaulay had been kind to her following the death of nine-year-old Harry a few years earlier.[86]

Montagu also had moments of compassion for Macaulay. She once compared Macaulay to Medea, the enchantress of classical mythology. 'I believe [Medea] has been much injured by the Poets,' wrote Mon- tagu,

who represented her as a wretch. I imagine she was only a learned lady when learned ladies were not so usual as now a days, and that like Mrs. Macauley she had the misfortune to fall in love with a handsome stripling.[87]

Almost all of the Bluestockings had something to say about Macaulay. Carter despaired of the fact that a woman of such intellec- tual abilities had let the side down.[88] But though she might condemn Macaulay's actions, Carter still acknowledged her genius as a histo- rian. Others were less generous. Hannah More declared herself to be 'extremely scandalized' at Macaulay's conduct. Like Scott, More wanted to distance herself from the notorious female historian. And

* Leader of Jack Cade's Rebellion in 1450.

so she stripped Macaulay of her intellect, writing, 'yet I did not esteem her; I knew her to be absurd, vain, and affected.' But More *had* once esteemed Macaulay. In a poem written in 1773 More had praised modern female learning, and had cited some of her most revered contemporaries:

> . . . in our chaster times 'tis no offence,
> When female virtue joins with female sense;
> When moral Carter breathes the strain divine,
> And Aikin's* life flows faultless as her line;
> When all accomplished Montagu can spread
> Fresh-gather'd laurels round her Shakspeare's head;
> When wit and worth in polished Brookes† unite,
> And fair Macaulay claims a Livy's right.[89]

That esteem had vanished now, replaced by a visceral loathing. Like some of her fellow Bluestockings, More sought to reclassify Macaulay as something other, to banish her from the female realm for fear that Macaulay's scandal would taint all other learned ladies. More noted how the men crowed over Macaulay's alleged disgrace, using it as a weapon with which to castigate clever women. But really, wrote More to another Bluestocking, '[the men] have no real cause for triumph; for this woman is far from being any criterion by which to judge of the whole sex; she was not feminine either in her writings or her manners.' Finally, the harshest dismissal: 'she was only a good, clever man.'[90]

Perhaps the cruellest thing people said about Catharine Macaulay in those years was that she was finished as a writer. New volumes of her scholarly *History of England* had dried up during her Bath years. Now that she was remarrying, everyone assumed that the book would be left unfinished – no woman could be so lucky as to find not one but two husbands who would permit her to write. One of the many satirical pamphlets written about Macaulay in 1779 included the lines:

---

* Aikin was Anna Barbauld's maiden name.
† Brookes may have been the writer Frances Brooke.

Farewell the plumed Pen and Ink!
Which made *Taxation's Champion* shrink;
Here faithful *Hist'ry* ends.
Britain must to her *Centre* shake![91]

But they were wrong. Macaulay had initially found the courage to write during her first marriage; now, during her second, she would not only continue her *History of England* but would branch out into new fields with the support of her husband. She resumed writing and published the sixth and seventh volumes of *The History of England* in 1781, and the final volume appeared in 1783.

She wrote now under the name Catharine Macaulay Graham. It was unusual for a woman to double-barrel her name like this. Most people took no notice and continued to call her Mrs Macaulay. Reviewers would begin by calling her Mrs Macaulay Graham, but often slipped back to Mrs Macaulay by the end of their articles. This may partly have been an unconscious mark of respect to the historian who had made a name for herself; it may partly have been a sign of disrespect to her new husband. When the pair had married, the *Gentleman's Magazine* had announced the union of 'the celebrated historian Mrs Macaulay, to the younger brother of Dr Graham' – a reversal of the usual custom of leaving the bride unnamed, described only as she related to male family members.[92] Even after a decade of marriage, people were still thinking of William Graham as an appendage of his wife. James Boswell dined one snowy evening at the house of the publisher Dilly; afterwards, he jotted down the names of the other guests in his journal, including 'Mr Graham, husband of Mrs Macaulay'.[93]

In the same year that the final volume of her *History* appeared, Macaulay published her first major work of philosophy – *A Treatise on the Immutability of Moral Truth*. Over three hundred pages, Macaulay ranged through many of the most pressing questions in philosophy: from the origins of evil to the nature of liberty; from questions about scepticism to observations on stoicism. She wrote explicitly about the position of women in society, arguing against the common belief that women were naturally formed for subjugation.[94]

The book received mostly good reviews, and Macaulay's success emboldened her to try other genres.[95] Her next major work was *Letters on Education* published in 1790. The book spanned a child's upbringing from infancy to their early twenties. Macaulay gave advice on everything from swaddling and breastfeeding, to which of the Greek authors were most likely to instil moral rectitude. The book touched on other issues too, including prison reform, social justice, vegetarianism and animal welfare. There were occasional nods to Macaulay's beloved Romans, such as her suggestion of state-funded public baths for all. Though the book was diverse, there was a thread that ran through it all: the importance of educating girls.

Macaulay believed that men and women were born equal, but were raised and educated so differently as to seem almost to be two different species. She traced this phenomenon back to what she called 'the barbarous ages of mankind' when physical strength was the principal characteristic that conferred advantage on individuals. Men, having lived a privileged existence for millennia, were unwilling to give up their status. It was in their interests to deny that women were their equals and to refuse education to women who wanted to raise themselves up.[96]

Knowing the opposition she faced and knowing that arguing in favour of female education for its own sake was unlikely to be popular, Macaulay argued that educating women would be an overall benefit to society. According to her theory, education led to wisdom, and people who were wise were more likely to be good. It was an argument that many of her peers had heard before and with which they, broadly speaking, agreed.

Once Macaulay had persuaded her reader of the necessity of female education, she could move on to the particulars of that education. As things stood, if women were educated at all, they were educated to be good wives. 'The admiration of the other sex is held out to women as the highest honour they can attain,' lamented Macaulay. There was rarely any depth to their education. Now Macaulay advocated that girls should receive exactly the same schooling as boys. She outlined a curriculum including English grammar, history, geography, classical languages, French, verse composition, moral readings, the writings of Shakespeare and Milton and Pope, astronomy, natural philosophy, natural history, logic, philosophy, theology and, when the pupils were old enough, politics. The reading of novels was permitted in moderation, though there was always a danger that they could lead to romantic flights of fancy. Macaulay was worried that reading too many love stories could result in what she termed 'trips to Scotland'. She declared that Richardson's *Pamela* was 'totally unfit for the perusal of youth' while Burney's *Cecilia* (which Macaulay admired) 'may fill a young person's mind with too vast an idea of the power of love'.[97]

Alongside this, girls and boys should receive the same moral education. 'There is but one rule of right for the conduct of all rational beings,' wrote Macaulay, 'true virtue in one sex must be equally so in the other . . . *vice versa*, what is vice in one sex, cannot have a different property when found in the other.' This must have had great personal resonance for Macaulay who had, in the matter of her second marriage, acted just as a man might. For this she had been scorned and shunned.

In a chapter titled 'Coquettry', Macaulay wrote: 'the faults of women are treated with a severity and rancour which militates against every principle of religion and common sense.' Particularly when it came to pre- or extra-marital affairs, there were entirely different moral codes for men and women. And yet Macaulay could see why women were drawn to illicit affairs: they had been raised to believe that pleasing men was their highest purpose. Feeling that a lover was in her thrall was the most power a woman could ever experience. Under Macaulay's programme of tutelage, these problems would be swept aside: 'when the sex have been taught wisdom by education, they will be glad to give up indirect influence for rational privileges.'[98] Followed to the letter, Macaulay was sure that her programme of education would lead to a wider move towards equality of the sexes.

The reviewers were not convinced. The *Monthly Review* thought Macaulay's ideas 'rather original than useful'.[99] The public expected history or politics from Macaulay and did not know quite what to make of her books when they veered into new territory. It sold less well than her history books. But there was one reader at least who was heavily influenced by it – Mary Wollstonecraft.[100] Wollstonecraft reviewed *Letters on Education* when it first appeared. She praised it for displaying 'a degree of sound reason and profound thought' and lamented that more women were not raised to think and write so clearly.[101]

Though radicals such as Wollstonecraft admired Macaulay, her star seemed to be fading in the later years of the eighteenth century. Her support for the American and French revolutions proved problematic for her British audience. The Whigs who had loved the earlier volumes of her *History of England* disagreed with much written in the later volumes. Her philosophical works did not achieve the same high sales as her history books. But though she was becoming less popular in her home country, she was still celebrated and revered in America.

After years of longing to visit this new country, she finally travelled there in 1784. She was one of the first British radicals to visit America after Britain formally recognised its independence in 1783, and her departure made headlines. There was much speculation about the nature of her trip. A French-language journal assumed that she was going to seek liberty of a sort unavailable in Britain. Some hoped that she would write the history of the American Revolution. Others joked that she was going to help write up new laws for the country.[102]

The voyage from the old world to the new lasted two months. The sea was rough, the winds unfavourable, the days long and tedious. It had been May when Macaulay and her husband had boarded the *Rosamond* in Kent, and high summer when they finally docked in Boston.[103] There, Macaulay was warmly welcomed by her many admirers. She was famous in America not just for her republican views but for a pamphlet she had published in 1775 called *An Address to the People of England, Scotland, and Ireland, on the Present Important Crisis of Affairs*. In it, she had written about how the British government had imposed unfair taxes and had usurped the rights of the American colonists. She predicted war, she predicted independence. She saw a vision of the British empire falling apart and her compatriots left with nothing but 'the bare possession of your foggy islands'.[104] No wonder she was popular in Boston.

A round of social engagements had been arranged for her, with everyone clamouring for a tea or a dinner or a soirée with the female historian. After more than a decade of exchanging letters, Macaulay was finally able to meet Mercy Otis Warren. Unlike her British contemporaries, Warren defended Macaulay's decision to marry Graham. Pinpointing the double standard on which society was built,

Warren wrote that 'independency of spirit led [Macaulay] to suppose she might associate for the remainder of her life, with an inoffensive, obliging youth, with the same impunity a Gentleman of three score and ten might marry a Damsel of fifteen!' In a private letter to her son, Warren praised Macaulay's 'virtuous worthy character', though she did admit that she blushed 'for the imperfections of human nature' when she thought of that second marriage. Still, it was more support than Macaulay got in Britain. Warren also praised William Graham as a 'Man of understanding & Virtue' – a distinct step up from the person who had called Graham 'a living monument of [Macaulay's] want of common understanding and decency'.[105]

The high point of Macaulay's visit to America was an invitation to visit George Washington at his estate at Mount Vernon, Virginia. They had been introduced by Richard Henry Lee, another of the Founding Fathers. Washington would later thank Lee for introducing him to 'a Lady whose reputation among the literati is high, and whose principles are so justly admired by the friends of liberty and of mankind'.[106] It was July when Macaulay came to Virginia, the air was hot and heavy – unlike anything she had experienced before. Macaulay's letters from Mount Vernon mostly tell of evenings of rational discourse and political debate. She wrote little of the day-to-day life of the place, which is perhaps surprising as this was the first time she had really seen slavery in action. There were hundreds of enslaved people held on the estate, and though she had spoken against slavery in general, Macaulay was remarkably quiet on the topic of her American friends' participation in the trade. Instead, she praised Washington as 'that modern Colossus of human virtue'.[107] She stayed for ten days and enjoyed many long conversations with her host. The two corresponded for several years after her visit.

Macaulay had felt intellectually and politically at home in America. Moreover, she found that Americans were far more likely to overlook her unconventional ways. She must have felt tempted to stay; there was even a rumour in Britain that she did stay and that she later died there. But she missed her daughter too much and so, after a year travelling in America, she sailed home again. She spent some time in France for her health before settling in Berkshire with her husband.

Though she no longer enjoyed the critical success she once had, Macaulay was happy. She was happy with her work. She was happy too that the furore around Thomas Wilson had slowly died down. He had eventually given up on his plan to publish her infamous wedding-day letter (possibly he was helped to this decision by a payment from Macaulay's brother), and the scandal faded from public view.[108] At the time of Macaulay's second marriage there had been rumours that Wilson had cut her out of his will, but when he died in 1784 he left her a small annuity which she passed on to her daughter.[109] She was happy with William Graham. They were a loving and support-ive couple: he encouraged her to write and she encouraged him to attend university. It was a meeting of minds and hearts, but, in a world where appearances mattered so much, few were convinced of its merits.

Of all the Bluestockings, Catharine Macaulay was the one least bothered by traditional notions of respectability. Her political views had always set her apart from the majority – for decades she had been teased or mocked or shunned for holding those beliefs. She had grown a thick skin. When society tried to shame her for her unorthodox friendship with Wilson, or for her supposedly scandalous second marriage, she was largely unperturbed. Macaulay lived out her later life with the same sense of blithe assurance that had always characterised her. She wrote the books that she wanted to write, she travelled where she wanted to go, she lived with the man she loved. Her spirit of independence remained undimmed despite the many criticisms hurled at her. Macaulay's books had always argued in favour of liberty and against tyranny. More powerful than any written word, Macaulay's life showed what liberty truly looked like.

II

THE END OF THE BLUESTOCKINGS

IN 1781, ELIZABETH Montagu left Hill Street for the final time. On her last evening there, she invited Hannah More and Dorothy Gregory to join her in the empty house. The wall hangings, the silk curtains, the chinoiserie furniture were all gone. More later wrote that they 'had about three square feet of carpet, and that we might all put our feet upon it we were obliged to sit in a circle in the middle of the room, just as if we were playing at "hunt the slipper".' The candles were extinguished, and the endless flow of rational conversation was stemmed for the first time in many decades. 'You never saw such an air of ruin and bankruptcy as everything around us wore,' More recalled.[1] But Montagu was not bankrupt, far from it: she was one of the wealthiest women in England, and she was independent.

When her Edward had begun to decline in his later years, she had nursed him tenderly. He died in 1775 aged eighty-three, leaving Montagu (aged fifty-seven) a widow. In death as in life, Edward trusted his wife: he made an extraordinary will, leaving everything to her. She inherited his vast coalfields and estates, and she managed them herself. As a wealthy widow, Montagu occupied the best possible position for a woman in the eighteenth century. She used her money well. Her patronage of the arts increased (including annuities for many friends such as Elizabeth Carter) and she supported much charitable work. She offered healthcare and education to the children of the miners and staff on her estates. For herself, she decided to build a grand new house in London's Portman Square: Montagu House.

Montagu House was intended not just as a home for Montagu and her salons, but as an act of cultural investment in the life of the city. It was seen by many as a moral act to build this temple of wit – a place where the greatest intellects of the day could meet and talk. Their erudite benevolence would seep out into the world around them and gently imbue the institutions of the capital with a spirit of rational enlightenment. Even before it was completed, Montagu House created a stir in the city – the building site became a tourist attraction with tickets sold to visitors.[2] It was far larger and grander than the house on Hill Street. The heart of Montagu House was the Great Room. Enormous pillars of polished green stone rose to a ceiling decorated by the painter Angelica Kauffmann, Italian sculptures were dotted artfully about and even the door panels were painted with chiaroscuro. Montagu delighted the silk merchants of Spitalfields Market by ordering almost five hundred yards of white satin for curtains and wall hangings.[3] 'The whole is an assemblage of art and magnificence which we have never witnessed in a private room,' gushed a popular journal.[4] Hannah More said she had never seen anything so beautiful, while Frances Burney called the house a 'Blue Palace'.[5]

When the house was fully complete, Montagu held a series of parties to mark the beginning of a new era. Everyone came. Every Bluestocking and every person of interest in the capital was invited. Even the hard-to-impress were impressed. Samuel Johnson admitted to visiting Portman Square while the work was still in progress and said that he found the house very handsome. Horace Walpole was invited to one of the house-warmings and declared himself greatly pleased by the elegant interiors: 'Instead of vagaries it is a noble, simple edifice. Magnificent, yet no gilding. It is grand, not tawdry, not larded and embroidered and pomponned with shreds and remnants, and clinquant [tinsel].' This was high praise indeed from Walpole (whom Frances Burney had once described as 'gay, though *caustique*, polite though sneering'[6]).

Guests agreed that the most striking thing in the house was the feather art. For many years Montagu had been collecting feathers: she gathered them from her own birds at Sandleford, procured them from poulterers and asked friends with exotic menageries to send brightly coloured plumes. When finally she had enough, Montagu engaged a craftswoman named Betty Tull to transform the thousands of feathers into a work of art. Tull created six large panels showing exquisitely detailed pastoral scenes.[7] From a distance, they looked like paintings made with the finest brush strokes. 'Macaws she has transformed into Tulips, Kingfishers into bluebells by her so potent art,' marvelled Montagu as she surveyed Tull's work. Everyone else marvelled too. To Montagu's great delight Queen Charlotte and her six princesses came to Portman Square to see the feather work one Monday morning and stayed for breakfast.[8]

With the house now thoroughly warmed, Montagu could return to the more serious business of salons. Occasionally, instead of a salon, she would host a theatre evening. Her dining room would be rearranged to seat an audience of thirty, and she could revel in hearing her favourite speeches by her favourite actors in the comfort of her own home. There were other nights when Montagu would host one of her famous Feasts of the Shells at which guests would drink from an enormous nautilus shell in honour of the mythic Scottish poet Ossian. On summer nights when Montagu was not entertaining she would watch the sun set over the hills of Hampstead Heath, then wander through the grand empty rooms by moonlight with her faithful Newfoundland dog plodding along beside her.[9]

Montagu House felt like the beginning of something new, but really the Bluestocking days were drawing to a close. By the 1790s, Montagu's health was failing. She was in her seventies, and though as bright and witty as ever, her eyesight was going and she was growing weaker. She was the sun around which the Bluestockings had always revolved, but now she was fading. Without her, the group was less clearly defined, more dissipated. As a unit, the Bluestockings had an uncanny ability to break down barriers, to encourage women to think, converse, argue and write in a way previously unseen. Having Montagu at their head had given them a veneer of social respectability that allowed them to act in 'unwomanly' ways with less censure than they might otherwise have expected.

In her later years, Montagu knew that her power was waning. She wrote to a friend: 'I am arrived at an age at which it is no easy matter perhaps to avoid the contempt of the World.'[10] In spite of all that she had achieved, the younger generation saw her simply as an old woman. Each generation looks upon the one that came before as hopelessly old-fashioned and out of touch. Women have always had the additional burden of being seen as essentially useless once they are past childbearing age. Montagu felt the world moving away from her.

She died in August 1800. In her will she asked that her son Punch be reburied alongside her.[11]

Hester Thrale Piozzi was also aware that old age was advancing upon her. In her *Thraliana*, which for so long had contained all the details of her life, and which had buoyed her spirits even in the worst days, she wrote again of death. She drafted the words that she wished inscribed on her grave-stone. She wrote in Latin – a language she was proud to know:

> Pauca fecit, plura scripsit;
> Fæmina tamen magna fuit.
> (She did little, she wrote much;
> However, she was a great woman).[12]

She followed the proposed epitaph with an apology and a question: 'I would I had done more, & written less – but what *could* I do after all?'*

What could any of the Bluestockings have done? Theirs was a revolution that began as a whisper – a handful of women writing, and speaking and having opinions – and rose to a gentle hum. From the 1750s to the 1790s the Bluestockings were tolerated, even celebrated in a few quarters, but more as rare objects of wonder than as role models for the female masses.

The Bluestockings lived in a profoundly patriarchal world. It was a world designed to keep women in their place, and they knew this. They gently pushed back against the limits imposed upon them, they (even more gently) ridiculed the system, but they could not envisage a world without it. Though Elizabeth Montagu might write, 'with all due respect to the superior sex, I do not see how they can be necessary to a woman,' and Hannah More and her friends 'all agreed, that men were by no means so necessary as we had all been foolish enough to fancy,' they never seriously sought to undo the patriarchy.[13]

---

* The plaque that commemorates Hester Thrale Piozzi in Tremeirchion Church, Wales does not bear this inscription but describes her as 'Dr Johnson's Mrs Thrale'.

On a practical level, one of the Bluestockings' greatest achievements was to put their skills to use as a way to earn an income. Many of their books sold well; thus they proved that their work had value in the eyes of the reading public. Esteem translated into money and money conferred (at least a modicum of) power. It could give a woman some control over her own destiny. This was one of the more tangible benefits of life as a Bluestocking.

It went deeper than that, though. The Bluestockings proved that a woman could be as rational as a man. For many, even for other women, this was an utterly new idea. It might seem hardly necessary now to demonstrate what we think of as an obvious truth, but it was an essential foundation for everything that followed. It is the basis for so much we take for granted today – a woman's right to have an education, to vote, to make decisions about her own body, to earn an income, to own property, to run for public office. Moreover, the Bluestockings showed that it was not just one or two isolated individual women who might be able to hold their own in the intellectual realm. They were a numerous and surprisingly diverse group: they could be found in almost every social class; they had vastly different educational backgrounds; they hailed from all parts of the kingdom.

In the ways they lived, the ways they conducted themselves, in their words and in their deeds, the Bluestockings were advocating for the most fundamental woman's right: the right to be acknowledged as an independent individual of inherent worth.

In 1790 the author of *Thoughts on the Education of Daughters* sat at her desk and finally plucked up the courage to write to her hero – Catharine Macaulay. She had read Macaulay's history books and had absorbed her ideas on liberty and republicanism. She read Macaulay's newest book, *Letters on Education*, and agreed wholeheartedly that girls deserved the same kind of education their brothers enjoyed.

She felt a little awkward writing to this great woman, worrying that it would be seen as an intrusion. Still, she picked up her pen and began. She opened with the polite conventions expected of her: 'it is necessary to apologize for thus intruding on you.' Then her awkwardness fell away and, feeling suddenly bold, she continued: 'but instead of an apology shall I tell you the truth? You are the only female writer who I coincide in opinion with respecting the rank our sex ought to attain in the world.' She wrote that she respected Macaulay because she contended for laurels while most other women only wished for flowers. Then she signed her name with a flourish – Mary Wollstonecraft.[14]

Along with her note, Wollstonecraft included a pamphlet she had recently published called *A Vindication of the Rights of Men*. This pamphlet (written in response to a pamphlet by the monarchist Edmund Burke) argued in favour of republicanism. Wollstonecraft wanted to see an end to aristocratic privilege. Catharine Macaulay was fascinated by what she read. In fact she had already heard of the pamphlet but she had not realised that the author behind it was a woman – this pleased her greatly. Macaulay wrote back immediately to congratulate Wollstonecraft on her work. She was delighted to have this new correspondent and hoped that the two could some day meet in person. Sadly, there is no evidence that they ever did. Macaulay died six months later in the summer of 1791. She never saw Wollstonecraft's 1792 book *A Vindication of the Rights of Woman*, a work of which she would surely have approved.

A Vindication of the Rights of Woman was extraordinary. It demanded education for girls and respect for women. Wollstonecraft argued in favour of equality between the sexes and did so without apology. Unlike her Bluestocking forebears, Wollstonecraft did not politely pander to male egos, nor did she spend pages emphasising her own moral rectitude. She simply set out her reasons for believing that women were not all that different from men and let her arguments play out to their logical conclusion.

Wollstonecraft was not the first to argue for such things; indeed, she cited several Bluestockings in the treatise. She praised Hester Mulso Chapone for her *Letters on the Improvement of the Mind, Addressed to a Young Lady* and, though she did not agree with Mulso Chapone on everything, she admired her good sense. Wollstonecraft also cited the works of Catharine Macaulay and advised readers to seek out her books. Wollstonecraft praised Macaulay as 'the woman of the greatest abilities, undoubtedly, that this country has ever produced'.[15] Macaulay was proof that women really were capable of great intellectual achievements. Wollstonecraft built on the views held by many of the Bluestockings; their influences shine through her work. At its heart lay the question of education for girls. Once a girl was educated, she might think for herself, talk for herself and advocate for her own rights.

Wollstonecraft looked back on the career of Catharine Macaulay with mixed feelings. She had found the historian's writings inspirational, but she recognised that Macaulay's fame (at least in England) had dwindled to practically nothing by the end of her life. Wollstonecraft knew that she was almost alone in the reverence she felt for Macaulay and it saddened her greatly. 'Posterity, however, will be more just,' she wrote in the *Vindication*, hoping that Macaulay's genius would be acknowledged again in the future.

Wollstonecraft could not know that she would suffer a similar fate after her own death – her reputation destroyed as details of her unorthodox private life became public knowledge. Wollstonecraft was first ridiculed, and then forgotten. This was just what had happened to the Bluestockings after Elizabeth Montagu had passed away and her salons had fallen silent. Without Elizabeth Montagu, the Bluestockings became a series of individual clever women in a society that did not care for clever women. The turn of the century saw not just the death of Montagu, it also heralded something new – the rise of the Romantics in Britain. The Romantics rebelled against their parents' generation. They rejected the older ideas and everything associated with them. Briefly, Enlightenment culture had allowed a small number of learned ladies to be celebrated. Now that trend was turned on its head.

The incremental steps women had taken towards being seen as equal members of polite society began to be erased. Men began to push back against what they saw as an excess of female liberties. Bluestocking salons lost their sheen. A satire published at the end of the century (in which the author muses on how the Bluestockings got their name) shows how things were changing:

> How they came to *distinguish* themselves by the appellation of *blue stockings*, it would be hard to decide, as the term conveys rather a light and *lascivious* idea; gradually leading the fancy upwards to the garter, and so on, to perhaps an improper and alarming height. Now, it is very well known, that the *fair* members of this *Lyceum*, are in general, chaste

even to a fault; most of them preferring to let their charms be withered by time, than submit them to the *rude mercy* of that *odious monster man*.[16]

The Bluestockings were coming to be seen as figures of fun. For a short while, the salons had provided a space in which women and men had met as equals; without them, the divide between male and female spheres seemed to deepen.

The Romantics were keen to distance themselves from any kind of association with learned ladies. In 1820, Lord Byron mocked what he called the 'benign Ceruleans of the second Sex' in his satirical poem *Don Juan*.[17] A year later, he wrote a farce called *The Blues*, with a character named Lady Bluebottle said to be modelled on Elizabeth Montagu. He sent it to his publisher John Murray with a note asking that it be circulated anonymously because Byron did not want women bothering him with their complaints about it.[18]

In that same note, Byron admitted that he 'sneered' at Bluestockings. This was common amongst this new breed of writer. Samuel Taylor Coleridge signalled his allegiance to manly Romanticism when he wrote to a female friend that he would think less of her if her letters were 'too blue-stocking fine & correct'. He disliked a woman who knew too much of grammar and spelling: 'O curse them,' he wrote to her, 'at least as far as Women are concerned. The longer I live, the more I do loathe in stomach, & deprecate in Judgement, all, *all*, Bluestockingism.'[19] William Hazlitt – critic, essayist, and friend of Coleridge, agreed: 'I have an utter aversion to *blue-stockings*,' he wrote, 'I do not care a fig for any woman that knows even what *an author* means.'[20]

This continued throughout the 1820s and 1830s. When reviewing a new poem by Felicia Hemans, the *British Critic* opened with a five-paragraph rant attacking the Bluestockings. 'We heartily abjure Blue Stockings,' the reviewer railed,

blue stockings are an outrage upon the eternal fitness of things . . .
We would fain make a fire in Charing-Cross, of all the bas blus in
the kingdom . . . Without being positively criminal, a Blue Stocking
is the most odious character in society . . . she sinks, wherever she is
placed, like the yolk of an egg, to the bottom, and carries the filth
and the lees with her.[21]

Only once he had made his feelings about female scholars clear did the reviewer proceed to discuss Hemans's poem and give it a grudgingly positive review.*

Everywhere it was the same. Commentators scrambled to denigrate the Bluestockings. By the time the Victorian period began in 1837, their reputation was largely in tatters. Even those few Victorian readers who were intrigued by the Bluestockings and looked to their original letters, diaries and publications found themselves baffled. The buttoned-up Victorians had no idea how to interpret the playful Bluestockings. Hannah More, easily the most conservative of the group, had to be rewritten to be made palatable for nineteenth-century sensibilities. In one letter included in a posthumous edition of her writings, her editor felt compelled to change More's whimsical 'I am gladerer and gladerer and gladerer' to 'I am very glad'.[22] A Victorian biographer of Hester Thrale wrote that he wished she had died forty years earlier than she did – for then she would have avoided the Piozzi scandal and the biographer would have only good things to write about her.[23] Victorian biographies of Elizabeth Montagu downplayed her intellect, her sense of fun and her intense friendships; instead they praised her for her domestic skills. Though the Bluestockings had actually been deeply religious, politically conservative and socially conventional, they were considered far too frivolous and avant-garde for the austere world of Victorian Britain. Gradually, they ebbed out of the national consciousness.

It was 1845 when the poet Elizabeth Barrett Browning went looking for role models. She pored over the works of previous generations but struggled to find verse written by women. She wrote to a friend, 'England has had many learned women . . . and yet where were the poetesses? . . . I look everywhere for grandmothers and see none.'[24] The evidence of the Bluestockings was being erased. Sometimes it was lost through indifference, sometimes it was deliberately destroyed.

Though their works were fading from memory, the term 'bluestocking' remained in use. It became a word to be hurled as an insult, a word to shame and subdue any girl or woman who thought herself better

---

* The poet Felicia Hemans (1793–1835) is remembered particularly for her poem 'Casabianca' which begins 'The boy stood on the burning deck'.

than she really was. For many decades it remained a term of abuse, but in the latter half of the nineteenth century some women began to reclaim it. This reclamation was part of a campaign for women to be allowed to attend university and to be awarded degrees. The new bluestockings looked back and rediscovered the grandmothers that had been obscured for so long. Then they looked forward and set about doing what needed to be done. They were magnificent, these new bluestockings. Like their forebears, they argued for their rights with spirit and tenacity. Eventually, they won. Women were allowed to pursue higher education alongside men – something that would have seemed a decadent fantasy to Elizabeth Carter or Catharine Macaulay.

In 1928 Virginia Woolf was invited to Cambridge to deliver two lectures to the undergraduates on the topic of 'women and fiction'. The young women of Girton and Newnham colleges listened spellbound as Woolf spoke of the history of female writers. Woolf believed that the rise of the original Bluestockings was one of the most important moments in history. She talked of Montagu and Carter. She admired their intellects but, on a much more practical level, she admired the fact that both women had been able to make money from their writing. 'Money dignifies what is frivolous if unpaid for,' argued Woolf, 'it might still be well to sneer at "blue stockings with an itch for scribbling", but it could not be denied that they could put money in their purses.' Woolf believed that this – the first opportunity for a large group of clever women to earn money by writing – was as important a historical event as the crusades or the Wars of the Roses.

Woolf traced a direct line of descent from the first Bluestockings to Jane Austen, the Brontës and George Eliot. 'Jane Austen should have laid a wreath upon the grave of Fanny Burney,' believed Woolf, 'and George Eliot done homage to the robust shade of Eliza Carter—the valiant old woman who tied a bell to her bedstead in order that she might wake early and learn Greek.'

Woolf spoke clearly and passionately about how books by women, on topics of interest to women, had always been dismissed as inconsequential. A century later, her words still ring true:

> It is the masculine values that prevail . . . And these values are inevitably transferred from life to fiction. This is an important book, the

critic assumes, because it deals with war. This is an insignificant book because it deals with the feelings of women in a drawing-room.

These lectures were later printed under the title *A Room of One's Own*.[25]

It was in these decades, when the century turned and women became bolder in their demand for rights, that the writings of Wollstonecraft were rediscovered. The suffragists saw the power of her arguments and resurrected her as the mother of modern feminism. But what of the women whose writings had so influenced her?

I have told their stories here – some of their stories, at least, for no single book could contain them all. We have learned of the hopes and dreams of these women, of their fears, their sorrows and their tragedies. We have watched as they felt the sting of injustice, or have silently willed them on as they overcame the many obstacles placed in their way.

The Bluestockings enabled change. Against the odds, they laid the foundations for a whole new worldview. Though many have tried to erase them, the Bluestocking legacy lives on. Their ideas have been sewn into the very fabric of our society. Theirs is a call that echoes down the centuries. As Hester Mulso Chapone wrote to Frances Burney when she heard that her young friend was in town – come and see me, 'put on your blue stockings'.[26]

Acknowledgements

I began researching this book before the pandemic and had pencilled in trips to various archives to take place in 2020. Needless to say, I did not make it to any archives that year. For that reason I am extremely grateful to the many scholars who have compiled editions of Bluestocking letters and diaries – without them I could not have continued working on this book at that time. I am also grateful to the team behind the Elizabeth Montagu Correspondence Online project which has digitised so many wonderful letters and made them freely available. Thanks to the Huntington Library and also to the staff of Cambridge University Library for unfailingly supporting research, even in trying circumstances.

I would like to thank Andrew Gordon for patient encouragement and wise counsel. Thanks too to David Evans at David Higham Associates. At John Murray, I have been impressed by the attention to detail of Georgina Laycock and her team – including Katharine Morris, Candida Brazil, Lauren Howard, Sara Marafini, Zoe Ross and Howard Davies. Thanks to Michelle Tessler of Tessler Literary Agency. At W.W. Norton, Amy Cherry has been another much-appreciated source of encouragement and good advice, and thanks too to Huneeya Sidiqui and the rest of the team there.

I am grateful to the many 'bookish slatterns' of my acquaintance who inspire me daily (you know who you are). Finally, and most of all, I am grateful to my family – the Gibsons, the O'Sheas, the Falks, the Campbells, Amos, Oisín and especially Seb.

Picture Credits

Notes

Prologue

1. Reginald Blunt (ed.), *Mrs. Montagu 'Queen of the Blues': Her Letters and Friendships from 1762 to 1800*, London: Constable 1926, vol. II, p. 6.
2. Frances Burney, *Memoirs of Doctor Burney*, London 1832, vol. II, pp. 193–4.
3. Robina Napier (ed.), *Johnsoniana: Anecdotes of the Late Samuel Johnson*, London 1884, p. 122.
4. Hannah More, 'The Bas Bleu: or, Conversation', in *The Works of Hannah More*, London: Henry G. Bohn 1853, vol. V.
5. Blunt (ed.), *Mrs. Montagu*, vol. II, p. 58.

Chapter 1: A Woman's Place

1. Joanna Martin, *Wives and Daughters: Women and Children in the Georgian Country House*, London and New York: Hambledon and London 2004, p. 5.
2. Catharine Macaulay, *Letters on Education* (1790), Cambridge: Cambridge University Press 2014, p. 206.
3. Ann Yearsley, 'On Mrs. MONTAGU', in *Poems on Several Occasions*, 4th edn, London: George and John Robinson 1786, p. 79.
4. Anon., *Man Superior to Woman, or, a Vindication of Man's Natural Right of Sovereign Authority over the Woman*, 4th edn, London 1739, p. 17.
5. Matthew Montagu (ed.), *The Letters of Mrs. Elizabeth Montagu*, London: T. Cadell and W. Davies 1809–13, vol. II, pp. 260–1.
6. Philip Dormer Stanhope, Earl of Chesterfield, *Letters to his Son* (1774), 12th edn, London: Rivington 1806, vol. II, pp. 92–3.
7. Anon., *Man Superior to Woman*, p. 55.

8. James Fordyce, *Sermons to Young Women*, London 1766, Sermon VII.

9. Anon., *The Nunnery for Coquettes*, London 1771, p. 217.

10. Anon., *Female Government! Or, Letters from a Gentleman to his Friend on the Education of the Fair Sex. With Hints for the Conduct of the Men in a Married-State*, London 1779, p. 7.

11. Matthew Montagu (ed.), *The Letters of Mrs. Elizabeth Montagu*, vol. III, Boston: Wells and Lilly 1825, pp. 236–7.

12. Elizabeth Eger, *Bluestockings: Women of Reason from Enlightenment to Romanticism*, Basingstoke: Palgrave Macmillan 2010, p. 97.

13. Lars E. Troide and Stewart J. Cooke (ed.), *The Early Journals and Letters of Fanny Burney. III: The Streatham Years, 1778–1779*, Oxford: Clarendon Press 1994, p. 172.

14. Hannah More, *A Search after Happiness: A Pastoral Drama*, 3rd edn, Bristol 1774, p. 43.

Chapter 2: The Salon

1. Emily J. Climenson (ed.), *Elizabeth Montagu, the Queen of the Bluestockings: Her Correspondence from 1720 to 1761*, Cambridge: Cambridge University Press 2011, vol. I, pp. 262, 271.

2. Ibid., p. 293.

3. Anne-Marie Fiquet du Boccage, *Lettres de Madame du Boccage, contenant ses voyages en France, en Angleterre, en Hollande et en Italie*, Dresden 1771, pp. 7, 28.

4. Climenson (ed.), *Elizabeth Montagu*, vol. I, pp. 30, 68 and vol. II, p. 20.

5. Reginald Blunt (ed.), *Mrs. Montagu 'Queen of the Blues': Her Letters and Friendships from 1762 to 1800*, London: Constable 1926, vol. II, p. 68.

6. Paul Langford, *A Polite and Commercial People: England 1727–1783*, 2nd edn, Oxford: Oxford University Press 1998, p. 100.

7. Anon., *Female Government! Or, Letters from a Gentleman to his Friend on the Education of the Fair Sex. With Hints for the Conduct of the Men in a Married-State*, London 1779, p. 2.

8. Blunt (ed.), *Mrs. Montagu*, vol. II, p. 118.

9. Frances Burney, *Memoirs of Doctor Burney*, London 1832, vol. II, pp. 193–4.

10. Lars E. Troide and Stewart J. Cooke (ed.), *The Early Journals and Letters of Fanny Burney. III: The Streatham Years, 1778–1779*, Oxford: Clarendon Press 1994, p. 144.

11. A. Baker, 'Hamilton [married name Dickenson], Mary (1756–1816), courtier and diarist', *Oxford Dictionary of National Biography*, https://doi. org/10.1093/ref:odnb/48934 [retrieved 18 May 2022]

12. John Gregory, *A Father's Legacy to his Daughters*, Dublin 1774, p. 19. This example is somewhat surprising as John Gregory was a good friend of Elizabeth Montagu's, and his (educated) daughter Dorothy Gregory would later be a companion to Montagu.

13. Quoted in Archibald Edward Harbord Anson, *About Myself and Others, 1745–1920*, London: John Murray 1920, pp. 20–1.

14. Ibid., p. 21.

15. N. William Wraxall, *Historical Memoirs of My Own Time: Part the First, from 1772 to 1780*, Philadelphia: Carey, Lea, & Blanchard 1837, pp. 63–5.

16. Blunt (ed.), *Mrs. Montagu*, vol. II, p. 2; see Climenson (ed.), *Elizabeth Montagu*, vol. II, p. 98 for a use of the phrase in 1756.

17. James Boswell, *Life of Johnson* (1791), Oxford: Clarendon Press 1887, vol. IV, p. 108.

18. Frances Burney, *Diary and Letters of Madame D'Arblay, Vol. I*, London: Bickers & Son 1876, p. 246.

19. Blunt (ed.), *Mrs. Montagu*, vol. II, p. 99.

20. Nicole Pohl (ed.), *The Letters of Sarah Scott*, London: Pickering and Chatto 2014, vol. I, p. 65.

21. Climenson (ed.), *Elizabeth Montagu*, vol. I, p. 11.

22. Ibid., p. 30.

23. Ibid., p. 29.

24. Ibid., pp. 67–8.

25. Ibid., p. 50.

26. Ibid., p. 23.

27. Ibid., pp. 24–5.

28. Ibid., p. 26.

29. Ibid., pp. 45–8.

30. Ibid., p. 58.

31. Ibid., pp. 42, 81.

32. Ibid., p. 87.

33. Ibid., pp. 111, 113.

34. Sarah Scott to Elizabeth Montagu, March 1742, quoted in Pohl (ed.), *Letters of Sarah Scott*, vol. I, p. 25.

35. Climenson (ed.), *Elizabeth Montagu*, vol. I, p. 119.

36. Ibid., pp. 114–15.

37. Ibid., vol. II, p. 203.

Chapter 3: The Streathamites

1. Streatham Park lay just south of Tooting Bec Common. The Thrales' house was demolished in the 1860s. A new residential development on the site is still called Streatham Park, and nearby roads have been named Thrale Road and Dr Johnson Avenue. The brewery covered a large area near Bankside; its southern boundary was at Castle Street (now renamed Thrale Street). Deadman's Place has been renamed Park Street.

2. Katharine C. Balderston (ed.), *Thraliana: The Diary of Mrs Hester Lynch Thrale (Later Mrs Piozzi) 1776–1809*, Oxford: Oxford University Press 2014, vol. I: *1776–84*, pp. 271, 321.

3. Betty Rizzo (ed.), *The Early Journals and Letters of Fanny Burney. Volume IV: The Streatham Years, Part II, 1780–1781*, Montreal and Kingston, Ont.: McGill-Queen's University Press 2003, p. 235.

4. Balderston (ed.), *Thraliana*, vol. I, p. 307.

5. Ibid., p. 455.

6. Lars E. Troide and Stewart J. Cooke (ed.), *The Early Journals and Letters of Fanny Burney. III: The Streatham Years, 1778–1779*, Oxford: Clarendon Press 1994, p. 132.

7. Mary Hyde (ed.), *The Thrales of Streatham Park* (includes *The Children's Book*), Boston, Mass.: Harvard University Press 1972, p. 48.

8. Balderston (ed.), *Thraliana*, vol. I, p. x.

9. Hyde (ed.), *The Thrales of Streatham Park*, p. 167.

10. Balderston (ed.), *Thraliana*, vol. I, pp. 1, 468.

11. Reginald Blunt (ed.), *Mrs. Montagu 'Queen of the Blues': Her Letters and Friendships from 1762 to 1800*, London: Constable 1926, vol. II, p. 276.

12. Balderston (ed.), *Thraliana*, vol. I, p. 158.

13. Ibid., pp. 385, 444 n. 4.

14. Hyde (ed.), *The Thrales of Streatham Park*, pp. 37, 64, 158.

15. Troide and Cooke (ed.), *The Early Journals and Letters of Fanny Burney. III*, p. 100.

16. Balderston (ed.), *Thraliana*, vol. I, pp. 55, 379.

17. P. Rogers, 'Burney [married name D'Arblay], Frances [Fanny] (1752–1840), writer', *Oxford Dictionary of National Biography*, https://doi.org/10.1093/ref:odnb/603 [retrieved 12 July 2022]

18. Annie Raine Ellis, *The Early Diary of Frances Burney, 1768–1778*, vol. I, London 1889, p. 14.

19. Rogers, 'Burney [married name D'Arblay], Frances [Fanny]', *Oxford Dictionary of National Biography*.

20. Troide and Cooke (ed.), *Early Journals and Letters of Fanny Burney. III*, pp. ix, 57, 58, 78–9; Hyde (ed.), *The Thrales of Streatham Park*, p. 203.
21. Troide and Cooke (ed.), *Early Journals and Letters of Fanny Burney. III*, pp. 58, 64.
22. Ibid., pp. 63–4.
23. Ibid., p. 66.
24. Balderston (ed.), *Thraliana*, vol. I, p. 471.
25. Troide and Cooke (ed.), *Early Journals and Letters of Fanny Burney. III*, pp. 61, 73–7.
26. Ibid., pp. 61, 104, 172; Hyde (ed.), *The Thrales of Streatham Park*, p. 208; Balderston (ed.), *Thraliana*, vol. I, p. 368.
27. Troide and Cooke (ed.), *Early Journals and Letters of Fanny Burney. III*, pp. 84–5, 87–8, 90.
28. Ibid., pp. 249, 268, 336, 452 n. 25; Balderston (ed.), *Thraliana*, vol. I, p. 393.
29. Balderston (ed.), *Thraliana*, vol. I, pp. 70, 72, 329–30, 347–8, 366–7, 414.
30. Ibid., pp. 330–1.
31. Blunt (ed.), *Mrs. Montagu*, vol. I, p. 293; M. Postle, 'Reynolds, Sir Joshua (1723–1792), portrait and history painter and art theorist', *Oxford Dictionary of National Biography*, https://doi.org/10.1093/ref:odnb/23429 [retrieved 12 July 2022]
32. Hyde (ed.), *The Thrales of Streatham Park*, p. 114.
33. Blunt (ed.), *Mrs. Montagu*, vol. II, p. 276.
34. Troide and Cooke (ed.), *Early Journals and Letters of Fanny Burney. III*, p. 160.
35. Ibid., p. 151.
36. Blunt (ed.), *Mrs. Montagu*, vol. II, p. 140.
37. Robina Napier (ed.), *Johnsoniana: Anecdotes of the Late Samuel Johnson*, London: George Bell 1884, p. 122.
38. Blunt (ed.), *Mrs. Montagu*, vol. II, pp. 142, 166.
39. Troide and Cooke (ed.), *Early Journals and Letters of Fanny Burney. III*, pp. 151, 152.
40. Ibid., pp. 155–8. A note in the *Thraliana* tells a slightly different story: 'Mrs Montagu cannot bear Evelina - let not that be published'; and a note in Thrale's *Children's Book* reads: '[Burney's] silversmiths are pewterers [Montagu] says': Balderston (ed.), *Thraliana*, vol. I, p. 329; Hyde (ed.), *The Thrales of Streatham Park*, p. 211.
41. Troide and Cooke (ed.), *Early Journals and Letters of Fanny Burney. III*, p. 159.

42. Felicity A. Nussbaum, 'Hester Thrale: "What trace of the wit?"', pp. 187–209 in Elizabeth Eger (ed.), *Bluestockings Displayed: Portraiture, Performance and Patronage 1730–1830*, Cambridge: Cambridge University Press 2013, p. 194.
43. Rizzo (ed.), *Early Journals and Letters of Fanny Burney. Volume IV*, pp. 37–8, 66–7.
44. Nussbaum, 'Hester Thrale' in Eger (ed.), *Bluestockings Displayed*, p. 187.
45. Blunt (ed.), *Mrs. Montagu*, vol. I, p. 289.
46. Anon. [Richard Cumberland], *The Observer*, London 1785, p. 217.
47. Blunt (ed.), *Mrs. Montagu*, vol. I, p. 174. These were the words of John Macpherson, who would later become Governor-General of India.
48. Ibid., vol. II, pp. 4–5.

Chapter 4: The Milking Parlour

1. Jón Steingrímsson (trans. Keneva Kunz), *Fires of the Earth: The Laki Eruption 1783–1784*, Reykjavik: University of Iceland Press 1998.
2. Ann Yearsley, 'Clifton Hill', in *Poems on Several Occasions* (1785), 4th edn, London: George and John Robinson 1786, p. 86.
3. Hannah More, 'A Prefatory Letter' to Ann Yearsley, *Poems on Several Occasions*, p. xiii.
4. S. Skedd, 'More, Hannah (1745–1833), writer and philanthropist', *Oxford Dictionary of National Biography*, https://doi.org/10.1093/ref:odnb/19179 [retrieved 12 July 2022]
5. Anne Stott, *Hannah More: The First Victorian*, Oxford: Oxford University Press 2003, p. 10.
6. Hannah More, 'Prefatory Letter' to Yearsley, *Poems on Several Occasions*, pp. viii–ix.
7. David Little, George M. Kahrl and Phoebe De K. Wilson (ed.), *The Letters of David Garrick*, Cambridge, Mass.: Harvard University Press 1963, vol. III, pp. 1356–7.
8. Skedd, 'More, Hannah (1745–1833), writer and philanthropist', *Oxford Dictionary of National Biography*.
9. When Mozart died, a copy of the German translation of *Percy* was found among his possessions – it is thought that he was considering adapting it into an opera. See Stott, *Hannah More*, p. 47.
10. David Garrick, 'Prologue', in Hannah More, *Percy: A Tragedy*, London 1778.
11. William Roberts, *Memoirs of the Life of Hannah More*, 3rd edn, London: R. B. Seeley and W. Burnside 1836, vol. I, p. 58.

12. Ibid., p. 117.
13. Katharine C. Balderston (ed.), *Thraliana: The Diary of Mrs Hester Lynch Thrale (Later Mrs Piozzi) 1776–1809*, vol. II: *1784–1809*, p. 699.
14. James Boswell, *Life of Johnson* (1791), Oxford: Clarendon Press 1934, vol. III, pp. 293–4 n. 5.
15. Roberts, *Memoirs of the Life of Hannah More*, 3rd edn, vol. I, pp. 33, 39–40, 50, 183.
16. Ibid., pp. 40–1.
17. Ibid., pp. 42, 44, 47–8.
18. Stott, *Hannah More*, p. 64.
19. Roberts, *Memoirs of the Life of Hannah More*, 3rd edn, vol. I, p. 243.
20. Ibid., p. 258.
21. Ibid., pp. 106, 148; Hannah More, 'The Bas Bleu: or, Conversation', in *The Works of Hannah More*, London: Henry G. Bohn 1853, vol. V.
22. Roberts, *Memoirs of the Life of Hannah More*, 3rd edn, vol. I, p. 44.
23. Yearsley, *Poems on Several Occasions*, p. 9.
24. Mary Waldron, *Lactilla, Milkwoman of Clifton: The Life and Writings of Ann Yearsley, 1753–1806*, Athens and London: University of Georgia Press 1996, pp. 53–4.
25. More, 'Prefatory Letter' to Yearsley, *Poems on Several Occasions*, pp. x–xi.
26. Quoted in Waldron, *Lactilla*, p. 57.
27. More, 'Prefatory Letter' to Yearsley, *Poems on Several Occasions*, p. xv.
28. Waldron, *Lactilla*, p. 57.
29. Anon., 'Review of *Poems on Several Occasions*', *Critical Review* 60 (1785), pp. 148–9; Anon. [Samuel Badcock], 'Review of *Poems on Several Occasions*', *Monthly Review* 73 (1785), pp. 216–21.
30. More, 'Prefatory Letter' to Yearsley, *Poems on Several Occasions*, p. x.
31. Yearsley, 'Narrative', in *Poems on Several Occasions*, pp. xix–xx.
32. Ibid., p. xx.
33. Ibid., pp. xxi–xxii.
34. Waldron, *Lactilla*, p. 66.
35. Ibid.
36. Ibid., p. 72.
37. Roberts, *Memoirs of the Life of Hannah More*, 3rd edn, vol. I, pp. 268, 311; Waldron, *Lactilla*, pp. 61, 71.
38. Waldron, *Lactilla*, p. 52.
39. Yearsley, 'Narrative', in *Poems on Several Occasions*, p. xxiv.
40. Kerri Andrews, *Ann Yearsley and Hannah More, Patronage and Poetry*, London: Pickering and Chatto 2013, pp. 43–4.

41. Waldron, *Lactilla*, p. 70.
42. Yearsley, 'Narrative', in *Poems on Several Occasions*, p. xxx.
43. Andrews, *Ann Yearsley and Hannah More*, p. 67.
44. Sir W. Scott (ed.), *Letters of Anna Seward, Written Between the Years 1784 and 1807*, Edinburgh 1811, vol. I, p. 122.
45. Anon., 'Review of *Poems, on Various Subjects*', *Monthly Review* 77 (1787), p. 485; Anon., 'Review of *Poems, on Several Occasions* (fourth edition) and *Poems, on Various Subjects*', *Critical Review* 64 (1787), p. 435.
46. William Roberts, *Memoirs of the Life and Correspondence of Mrs Hannah More*, 2nd edn, London: R. B. Seeley and W. Burnside 1834, vol. II, p. 223.
47. Skedd, 'More, Hannah (1745–1833), writer and philanthropist', *Oxford Dictionary of National Biography*.

Chapter 5: The Commune

1. Emily J. Climenson (ed.), *Elizabeth Montagu, the Queen of the Bluestockings: Her Correspondence from 1720 to 1761*, Cambridge: Cambridge University Press 2011, vol. I, pp. 78–9.
2. Elizabeth Montagu to Sarah Scott, 8 January 1740/1, MO 5592, Elizabeth Montagu Correspondence Online EMCO ID 305.
3. Lady Mary Wortley Montagu was a distant cousin by marriage of Elizabeth Montagu's husband Edward.
4. Celia Fiennes, *Through England on a Side Saddle in the Time of William and Mary, Being the Diary of Celia Fiennes*, London: Field & Tuer 1888, p. 14.
5. Nicole Pohl (ed.), *The Letters of Sarah Scott*, London: Pickering and Chatto 2014, vol. I, pp. 28, 33, 34.
6. Ibid., p. 37.
7. Ibid., p. 5.
8. Ibid., p. xvii.
9. Ibid., p. 45.
10. Elizabeth Montagu to Barbara Montagu, 16 May 1748, MO 1646, Elizabeth Montagu Correspondence Online EMCO ID 712.
11. Pohl (ed.), *Letters of Sarah Scott*, vol. I, p. 314.
12. Ibid., pp. 98–9.
13. Horace Walpole, *Memoirs of the Reign of King George the Second*, London: Colburn 1848, vol. I, p. 80.

14. The church was demolished in 1900. The Barbican Centre sits on the old site.

15. Pohl (ed.), *Letters of Sarah Scott*, vol. I, p. 130.

16. Betty Rizzo, *Companions Without Vows: Relationships Among Eighteenth-Century British Women*, Athens and London: University of Georgia Press 1994, p. 304.

17. Pohl (ed.), *Letters of Sarah Scott*, vol. I, p. 154.

18. Ibid., p. 164.

19. Ibid., p. 226.

20. Ibid., p. 221.

21. Ibid.

22. Ibid., p. 237.

23. Anon., 'Review of *The History of Gustavus Ericson, King of Sweden*', *Monthly Review* 24 (1761), p. 55.

24. Sarah Scott, *Millenium Hall*, London 1762, pp. 7–8.

25. Ibid., pp. 57–63.

26. Ibid., pp. 215–19.

27. Ibid., p. 93.

28. Ibid., pp. 24–5.

29. Ibid., pp. 144–5.

30. Ibid., p. 141.

31. Ibid., p. 261.

32. Pohl (ed.), *Letters of Sarah Scott*, vol. I, p. 313.

33. Elizabeth Montagu to William Pulteney, Earl of Bath, 1762, MO 4554, Elizabeth Montagu Correspondence Online EMCO ID 1268.

34. Anon., *Critical Review* 14 (1763), pp. 463–4.

35. Elizabeth Montagu to Sarah Scott, 12 October 1755, MO 5746, Elizabeth Montagu Correspondence Online EMCO ID 942.

36. Pohl (ed.), *Letters of Sarah Scott*, vol. I, p. 286.

37. Ibid., pp. 297, 326.

38. Ibid., pp. 30–1.

39. Lady Day was another name for the Feast of the Annunciation on 25 March. It was the first day of the year until the Gregorian calendar reform of 1752, and a common start-date for contracts. (The 1752 reforms added eleven days to the calendar so that, thereafter, 6 April became the standard start-date of the financial year.)

40. Sarah Scott, *The History of Sir George Ellison* (ed. Betty Rizzo), Lexington, Ky.: University Press of Kentucky 1996, p. xxviii.

41. Pohl (ed.), *Letters of Sarah Scott*, vol. I, p. xxi. They are buried at St Mary's Church in Charlcombe, just north of the city.

Chapter 6: Marriage

1. Anna Lætitia Barbauld, *The Correspondence of Samuel Richardson . . . to Which are Prefixed, a Biographical Account of that Author*, London: Richard Phillips 1804, vol. I, p. clxi. When Hester Thrale read this biography in 1804 she commented in the *Thraliana* that it was 'edited by Mrs Barbauld of the *Hackney Academy*, whose Notions he [Richardson] & his Friends would have shudder'd at'. Barbauld was a dissenter and known for having liberal, even radical, views. She wrote a treatise on animal rights (*The Mouse's Petition*) as well as numerous educational and political works. Elizabeth Montagu once asked Barbauld to become head of a ladies' college she planned to set up. Barbauld declined on the basis that it would be more likely to turn out '*Femmes sçavants*' rather than 'good wives or agreeable companions'. See Katharine C. Balderston (ed.), *Thraliana: The Diary of Mrs Hester Lynch Thrale (Later Mrs Piozzi) 1776–1809*, vol. II: *1784–1809*, p. 1057; Gary Kelly, 'Bluestocking Work: Learning, Literature, and Lore in the Onset of Modernity', in Deborah Heller (ed.), *Bluestockings Now! The Evolution of a Social Role*, Farnham, Surrey: Ashgate 2015, p. 190.
2. Barbauld, *Correspondence of Samuel Richardson*, vol. I, p. 82.
3. Ibid., pp. 79, 286. Collier was the sister of Arthur Collier who tutored Hester Thrale and Sarah Fielding in classical languages.
4. Barbara Eaton, *Yes Papa! Mrs Chapone and the Bluestocking Circle*, London: Francis Boutle 2012, p. 21.
5. N. William Wraxall, *Historical Memoirs of My Own Time: Part the First, from 1772 to 1780*, Philadelphia, Pa.: Carey, Lea, & Blanchard 1837, p. 70.
6. Hester Mulso Chapone, *The Posthumous Works of Mrs. Chapone*, London: John Murray 1807, vol. I, p. 18.
7. Ibid., pp. 121–2.
8. Sylvia Harcstark Myers, *The Bluestocking Circle: Women, Friendship, and the Life of the Mind in Eighteenth-Century England*, Oxford: Clarendon Press 1990, p. 135.
9. Samuel Richardson, *Clarissa*, London 1747, Letter XIII.
10. James Boswell, *Journal of a Tour to the Hebrides with Samuel Johnson, LLD*, London: H. G. Bohn 1859, p. 164.
11. Hester Mulso Chapone, 'Miss Mulso's First Letter on Filial Obedience', in Chapone, *Posthumous Works*, Cambridge: Cambridge University Press 2011, vol. II, p. 30.

12. Hester Mulso Chapone, 'Miss Mulso's Second Letter on Filial Obedience', in ibid., pp. 37, 38, 46.

13. Ibid., p. 56.

14. Hester Mulso Chapone, 'Miss Mulso's Third Letter on Filial Obedience', in ibid., p. 136.

15. Montagu Pennington (ed.), *A Series of Letters between Mrs Elizabeth Carter and Miss Catherine Talbot from the Year 1741 to 1770*, London: Rivington 1809, vol. II, p. 29.

16. Reginald Blunt (ed.), *Mrs. Montagu 'Queen of the Blues': Her Letters and Friendships from 1762 to 1800*, London: Constable 1926, vol. II, p. 356.

17. Laura E. Thomason, *The Matrimonial Trap: Eighteenth-Century Women Writers Redefine Marriage*, Lewisburg, Pa.: Bucknell University Press 2014, p. 44.

18. Emily J. Climenson (ed.), *Elizabeth Montagu, the Queen of the Blue-stockings: Her Correspondence from 1720 to 1761*, Cambridge: Cambridge University Press 2011, vol. II, p. 6.

19. Sarah Chauncey Woolsey (ed.), *The Autobiography and Correspondence of Mrs Delany*, Boston: Roberts Brothers 1879, vol. I, p. 3.

20. Ibid., p. 18.

21. Ibid., p. 19.

22. Ibid.

23. Ibid., p. 23.

24. Ibid., pp. 24, 27.

25. Ibid., p. 67.

26. Climenson (ed.), *Elizabeth Montagu*, vol. I, p. 56.

27. Chapone, 'Miss Mulso's Second Letter', in Chapone, *Posthumous Works*, vol. II, p. 70.

28. Chapone, 'Miss Mulso's Third Letter', in ibid., p. 104.

29. Ibid., pp. 114, 116.

30. Ibid., p. 117.

31. Ibid., pp. 115–16.

32. Ibid., p. 135.

33. Ibid., p. 137.

34. Ibid., pp. 132, 142.

35. Pennington (ed.), *A Series of Letters*, vol. I, p. 370.

36. Ibid., p. 373.

37. Hester Mulso Chapone, 'A Matrimonial Creed', in Chapone, *Posthumous Works*, vol. II, pp. 147, 155.

38. Ibid., p. 149.

39. Ibid., p. 151.
40. Hester Chapone, 'An Irregular Ode', in Elizabeth Carter, *All the Works of Epictetus Which Are Now Extant*, 3rd edn, London: Rivington 1768, vol. I.
41. Hester Mulso Chapone, *The Works of Mrs Chapone*, Boston: W. Wells and T. B. Wait 1809, vol. II, p. 150.
42. Chapone, *Posthumous Works*, vol. I, p. 101.
43. Ibid., p. 117.
44. Ibid., p. 118.
45. Ibid., p. 123.
46. Ibid., p. 118.
47. Ibid., p. 120.
48. Ibid., pp. 130–1.
49. Ibid., p. 132.
50. Ibid., pp. 141–2.
51. Matthew Montagu (ed.), *The Letters of Mrs. Elizabeth Montagu*, vol. III, Boston: Wells and Lilly 1825, p. 274.
52. Ibid., p. 152.
53. Ibid., p. 155.
54. Mrs Chapone, *Letters on the Improvement of the Mind*, London: E. and C. Dilly 1778, vol. II, pp. 223–4.
55. Eaton, *Yes Papa!*, p. 174.
56. Chapone, *Works of Mrs Chapone*, vol. II, p. 150.
57. Anon., *Six Odes, Presented to that Justly-celebrated Historian, Mrs. Catharine Macaulay, on her Birth-day, and Publicly Read to a Polite and Brilliant Audience, Assembled April the Second, at Alfred-House, Bath*, Bath 1777, pp. 41–2.
58. Chapone, *Posthumous Works*, vol. I, p. 163.
59. Blunt (ed.), *Mrs. Montagu*, vol. II, p. 129; Nicole Pohl (ed.), *The Letters of Sarah Scott*, London: Pickering and Chatto 2014, vol. I, p. 306.
60. Blunt (ed.), *Mrs. Montagu*, vol. II, p. 30.
61. Chapone, *Posthumous Works*, vol. I, p. 129.
62. Anon. [Elizabeth Griffith and Richard Griffith], *A Series of Genuine Letters between Henry and Frances*, vol. I, London 1757, p. 86.
63. Ibid., vol. I, pp. vii, 101; vol. II, p. 285.
64. Ibid., vol. I, pp. 49–50, 249.
65. Ibid., vol. I, pp. 95, 103.
66. Ibid., pp. 12, 41, 42, 53, 65, 81, 227, 230.
67. Ibid., pp. 7, 79, 102.
68. Ibid., p. 122.
69. Ibid., pp. 162, 186.

70. Ibid., p. 197.

71. Ibid., pp. xxxviii–xxxix.

72. Elizabeth Eger, *Bluestockings: Women of Reason from Enlightenment to Romanticism*, Basingstoke: Palgrave Macmillan 2010, p. 90, Elizabeth Montagu to William Pulteney, Earl of Bath, December 1761, MO 4510.

73. Justine Crump (ed.), *A Known Scribbler: Frances Burney on Literary Life*, Peterborough, Ont.: Broadview Literary Texts 2002, pp. 56–7.

74. Anon., 'Review of *Letters between Henry and Frances*', *Monthly Review* 17 (1757), pp. 416–23.

75. Dorothy Hughes Eshleman, *Elizabeth Griffith: A Biographical and Critical Study*, Philadelphia, PA: University of Pennsylvania 1949, pp. 43–4.

76. Elizabeth Griffith, *The Story of Lady Juliana Harley*, London 1776, pp. 14–15.

77. Eshleman, *Elizabeth Griffith*, pp. 61–6.

78. Elizabeth Griffith, 'Advertisement', in *The School for Rakes: A Comedy*, London 1769, p. iii.

79. Elizabeth Griffith, *The Delicate Distress* (ed. Cynthia Booth Ricciardi and Susan Staves), Lexington, Ky.: University Press of Kentucky 2015.

80. Anon. [Griffith and Griffith], *Series of Genuine Letters*, vol. V, London 1770, pp. 15, 39.

81. Eshleman, *Elizabeth Griffith*, p. 79; Anon., *Monthly Review* 41 (1769), p. 232.

82. Anon. [Griffith and Griffith], *Series of Genuine Letters*, vol. V, pp. 124–5, 263.

83. Elizabeth Griffith, *The Morality of Shakespeare's Drama*, London 1775, p. vii.

84. Elizabeth Griffith, *Essays, Addressed to Young Married Women*, London 1782, p. iv.

85. Montagu Pennington (ed.), *Letters from Mrs. Elizabeth Carter, to Mrs. Montagu, between the Years 1755 and 1800*, London 1817, vol. II, pp. 47–8.

Chapter 7: Motherhood

1. Mary Hyde (ed.), *The Thrales of Streatham Park* (includes *The Children's Book*), Boston, Mass.: Harvard University Press 1972, pp. 198, 204.

2. Katharine C. Balderston (ed.), *Thraliana: The Diary of Mrs Hester Lynch Thrale (Later Mrs Piozzi) 1776–1809*, Oxford: Oxford University Press 2014, vol. I: 1776–84, p. 274 n. 1.

3. Ibid., pp. 3, 10, 281, 284, 292, 295, 297 n. 1, 301.

4. Ibid., p. 294.

5. Ibid., p. 299.

6. Ibid., pp. 300, 302, 303.

7. Ibid., pp. 52, 304.

8. Ibid., p. 306 n. 1.

9. Ibid., vol. II: *1784–1809*, p. 782.

10. Ibid., vol. I, p. 305.

11. Michael J. Franklin, 'Thrale's Entire: Hester Lynch Thrale and the Anchor Brewery', in Deborah Heller (ed.), *Bluestockings Now! The Evolution of a Social Role*, Farnham, Surrey: Ashgate 2015, p. 122.

12. Balderston (ed.), *Thraliana*, vol. I, p. 308 n. 2.

13. Hyde (ed.), *The Thrales of Streatham Park*, p. 22.

14. See, for example, Figure 8 in Romola Davenport, Jeremy Boulton and Leonard Schwartz, 'Infant and Young Adult Mortality in London's West End, 1750–1824', https://www.geog.cam.ac.uk/files/people/davenport/davenport2.pdf

15. John Tearle, *Mrs Piozzi's Tall Young Beau: William Augustus Conway*, Teaneck, NJ: Fairleigh Dickinson University Press 1991, p. 39.

16. Hyde (ed.), *The Thrales of Streatham Park*, p. 21.

17. Balderston (ed.), *Thraliana*, vol. I, p. 308.

18. Ibid., p. 309.

19. Ibid., p. 310.

20. Hyde (ed.), *The Thrales of Streatham Park*, p. 24.

21. Ibid., pp. 25, 26.

22. Ibid., pp. 28, 30.

23. Ibid., p. 33.

24. Balderston (ed.), *Thraliana*, vol. I, p. 67.

25. Hyde (ed.), *The Thrales of Streatham Park*, p. 34.

26. Ibid., p. 38. A crown was actually five shillings. A half-crown was two shillings and sixpence which might have been what Harry was thinking of.

27. Balderston (ed.), *Thraliana*, vol. I, p. 311 n. 1.

28. Hyde (ed.), *The Thrales of Streatham Park*, pp. 42–6.

29. Ibid., pp. 47–8.

30. Ibid., p. 49.

31. John H. Appleby, 'Humphrey Jackson FRS, 1717–1801: A Pioneering Chemist', *Notes and Records* 40.2 (1986), pp. 147–68.

32. Balderston (ed.), *Thraliana*, vol. I, pp. 312–13 and p. 313 n. 4.

33. Hyde (ed.), *The Thrales of Streatham Park*, p. 57.

34. Lee Morgan, *Dr. Johnson's 'Own Dear Master': The Life of Henry Thrale*, Lanham, Md.: University Press of America 1998, p. 72; P. Toynbee (ed.), *The Letters of Horace Walpole*, Oxford: Clarendon Press 1903–5, vol. III, Letter 132.

35. James Boswell, *Life of Johnson* (1791), Oxford: Oxford University Press 1934, vol. III, p. 406.

36. Morgan, *Dr. Johnson's 'Own Dear Master'*, p. 73.

37. Hyde (ed.), *The Thrales of Streatham Park*, pp. 65–6.

38. Ibid., pp. 60, 61, 64, 128.

39. Ibid., pp. 62, 63.

40. Ibid., pp. 65, 68–70.

41. Balderston (ed.), *Thraliana*, vol. I, p. 79.

42. Hyde (ed.), *The Thrales of Streatham Park*, pp. 82–4.

43. Ibid., pp. 85, 89.

44. Ibid., p. 107.

45. Ibid., pp. 76–80, 96, 98.

46. Ibid., p. 87.

47. Ibid., p. 105.

48. Ibid., p. 110.

49. Ibid., p. 110.

50. Ibid., pp. 112–13.

51. Ibid., pp. 115, 123.

52. Ibid., p. 115.

53. Ibid., p. 116.

54. Ibid., p. 118.

55. Ibid., pp. 118, 122–3.

56. Ibid., p. 131.

57. Ibid., p. 136.

58. Ibid., pp. 136–7.

59. Ibid., p. 138; Isabelle and Robert Tombs, *That Sweet Enemy: The British and the French from the Sun King to the Present*, London: Pimlico 2007, p. 78; Boswell, *Life of Johnson*, vol. III, p. 288.

60. Boswell, *Life of Johnson*, vol. III, p. 290.

61. Hyde (ed.), *The Thrales of Streatham Park*, pp. 139–40; Boswell, *Life of Johnson*, vol. III, p. 290 n. 1.

62. Hyde (ed.), *The Thrales of Streatham Park*, pp. 142–3.

63. Ibid., pp. 143–4.

64. Ibid., pp. 143, 145; William Grant, *Observations on the Late Influenza, the Febris Catarrhalis Epidemica of Hippocrates, as it Appeared at London in 1775 & 1782*, London 1782, pp. 4, 6.

65. Hyde (ed.), *The Thrales of Streatham Park*, p. 145.

66. Ibid., pp. 144, 146.

67. Christopher Plumb, *The Georgian Menagerie: Exotic Animals in Eighteenth-Century London*, London: I. B. Tauris 2015, p. 23.

68. Hyde (ed.), *The Thrales of Streatham Park*, p. 151.

69. Ibid.

70. Ibid., pp. 152–3.

71. Ibid., p. 155.

72. Ibid., p. 156.

73. Ibid., p. 160.

74. Ibid., pp. 159–60.

75. Balderston (ed.), *Thraliana*, vol. I, p. 267.

76. Ibid., pp. 44, 457–8.

77. Hyde (ed.), *The Thrales of Streatham Park*, p. 163.

78. Ibid., p. 166.

79. Ibid., p. 167.

80. Ibid., p. 173.

81. Ibid., p. 176.

82. Ibid., p. 196.

83. Ibid., p. 199.

84. Frances Burney [Madame D'Arblay], *Memoirs of Doctor Burney*, Philadelphia, PA: Key & Biddle 1833, pp. 102–6.

85. Ibid., pp. 109–16.

86. Hyde (ed.), *The Thrales of Streatham Park*, pp. 198–202.

87. Ibid., p. 201.

88. Ibid., p. 203.

89. Ibid., p. 204.

90. Lars E. Troide and Stewart J. Cooke (ed.), *The Early Journals and Letters of Fanny Burney. III: The Streatham Years, 1778–1779*, Oxford: Clarendon Press 1994, p. 105.

91. Hyde (ed.), *The Thrales of Streatham Park*, pp. 203, 209.

92. Balderston (ed.), *Thraliana*, vol. I, pp. 349–51.

93. Hyde (ed.), *The Thrales of Streatham Park*, pp. 214, 217–18.

94. Balderston (ed.), *Thraliana*, vol. I, pp. 361, 365, 367.

95. Ibid., vol. II, p. 803.

96. Ibid., vol. I, p. 389.

97. Ibid., vol. I, p. 399.

98. Pope, *Rape of the Lock*, Canto 5, line 30. Pope's original 'pow'r' is substituted by Thrale's 'Life'.

99. Balderston (ed.), *Thraliana*, vol. I, p. 401.

100. Ibid.
101. Ibid., p. 400.
102. Ibid., p. 402.
103. Ibid., p. 400.
104. M. Zamich (ed.), 'Three Dialogues on the Death of Hester Lynch Thrale', *Rylands Library Bulletin* 16 (1932), pp. 94–114.
105. Balderston (ed.), *Thraliana*, vol. I, p. 409.
106. Nicole Pohl (ed.), *The Letters of Sarah Scott*, London: Pickering and Chatto 2014, vol. I, p. 288.
107. Anon. [Francis Grose], *A Classical Dictionary of the Vulgar Tongue*, London 1785, p. 38.
108. Matthew Montagu (ed.), *The Letters of Mrs. Elizabeth Montagu*, London: T. Cadell and W. Davies 1809, vol. II, pp. 191–2, 203, 210, 211.
109. Ibid., p. 206.
110. Ibid., pp. 206–7, 229, 231.
111. Sylvia Harcstark Myers, *The Bluestocking Circle: Women, Friendship, and the Life of the Mind in Eighteenth-Century England*, Oxford: Clarendon Press 1990, p. 102.
112. Montagu (ed.), *Letters of Mrs. Elizabeth Montagu*, vol. II, pp. 253, 255.
113. Ibid., p. 292.
114. Ibid, p. 306.
115. Emily J. Climenson (ed.), *Elizabeth Montagu, the Queen of the Bluestockings: Her Correspondence from 1720 to 1761*, Cambridge: Cambridge University Press 2011, vol. I, pp. 182, 186; Pohl (ed.), *Letters of Sarah Scott*, vol. I, p. 57.
116. Climenson (ed.), *Elizabeth Montagu*, vol. I, p. 193.
117. Reginald Blunt (ed.), *Mrs. Montagu 'Queen of the Blues': Her Letters and Friendships from 1762 to 1800*, London: Constable 1926, vol. II, p. 198.
118. Climenson (ed.), *Elizabeth Montagu*, vol. II, p. 119.
119. Ibid., pp. 86, 106.
120. Ibid., vol. I, p. 230.
121. Myers, *The Bluestocking Circle*, p. 104.
122. Elizabeth Eger, *Bluestockings: Women of Reason from Enlightenment to Romanticism*, Basingstoke: Palgrave Macmillan 2010, p. 106.

Chapter 8: Friendship

1. Montagu Pennington, *Memoirs of the Life of Mrs Elizabeth Carter*, London: Rivington 1807, pp. 13, 18.

2. Ibid., pp. 20, 24–5.

3. Ibid., p. 20. See also Montagu Pennington (ed.), *A Series of Letters between Mrs Elizabeth Carter and Miss Catherine Talbot from the Year 1741 to 1770*, London: Rivington 1809, vol. I, p. 155.

4. Anon., 'A Riddle', *Gentleman's Magazine* 4 (November 1734), p. 623. The answer to the riddle is fire.

5. Sylvius [John Duick], 'To Miss Cart-r Author of the Riddle in November', *Gentleman's Magazine* 5 (June 1735), p. 321; Brigitte Roxane Sprenger-Holtkamp, 'Miss Epictetus, or, the Learned Eliza: A Literary Biography of Elizabeth Carter', unpublished PhD thesis, University of London 1996.

6. Anon., 'Epigram', *Gentleman's Magazine* 8 (April 1738), p. 210; Anon., 'Epigram', *Gentleman's Magazine* 8 (May 1738), p. 272.

7. Pennington, *Memoirs of the Life of Mrs Elizabeth Carter*, p. 26.

8. Ibid., pp. 46–7.

9. Ibid., p. 22.

10. Ibid., pp. 92–3.

11. Anon. [Samuel Boyse], 'On Miss Carter's Being Drawn in the Habit of Minerva, with Plato in her Hand', *Gentleman's Magazine* 11 (May 1741), p. 271.

12. Gwen Hampshire (ed.), *Elizabeth Carter, 1717–1806: An Edition of Some Unpublished Letters*, Newark, NJ: University of Delaware Press 2005, pp. 102–3.

13. Pennington (ed.), *A Series of Letters*, vol. I, pp. 2–4.

14. Petrarch (edited and translated by Mark Musa), *Canzoniere*, Bloomington and Indianapolis: Indiana University Press 1999, p. 134.

15. Though Carter had formally eschewed marriage, Talbot had had several romantic entanglements with men before and during her friendship with Carter. In the early 1740s Talbot wrote in a private journal of an infatuation with a man she called 'Comte de S'. He was a neighbour of hers and she felt that perhaps he was attracted to her too. We do not know how serious the relationship ever was, but we know that Talbot felt deeply rejected when she learned that he had married someone else and she had to see the 'Comte' with his new wife around the neighbourhood. A few years later she received a marriage proposal from a man she had never met. She did seriously consider his offer, but her lack of a dowry and the man's parents' reluctance to settle a significant sum on him made the whole thing impossible. In the 1750s George Berkeley (son of the philosopher of the same name) proposed to Talbot and though she loved him she turned him down for fear of 'objections'

from her family and his. See Sylvia Harcstark Myers, *The Bluestocking Circle: Women, Friendship, and the Life of the Mind in Eighteenth-Century England*, Oxford: Clarendon Press 1990, pp. 112–14.

16. Pennington (ed.), *A Series of Letters*, vol. I, pp. 8–9.

17. Ibid., pp. 56, 110.

18. Ibid., p. 83.

19. Ibid., pp. 157–8, 162, 243, 250, 257, 262.

20. Ibid., vol. II, p. 35.

21. Ibid., vol. I, pp. 41–2.

22. Ibid., pp. 254, 263.

23. Ibid., p. 313.

24. Ibid., pp. 308, 350.

25. Ibid., p. 188.

26. Ibid., p. 219.

27. Pennington, *Memoirs of the Life of Mrs Elizabeth Carter*, p. 110.

28. Pennington (ed.), *A Series of Letters*, vol. II, p. 202.

29. Ibid., vol. I, p. 249.

30. Hester Mulso Chapone, *The Posthumous Works of Mrs. Chapone*, London: John Murray 1807, vol. I, pp. 106–7.

31. Anon., 'Review of *All the Works of Epictetus . . . Translated by Elizabeth Carter*', *Monthly Review* 18 (1758), pp. 588–96.

32. Anon., 'Review of *All the Works of Epictetus . . . Translated by Elizabeth Carter*', *Critical Review* 6 (August 1758), pp. 149–58.

33. Pennington, *Memoirs of the Life of Mrs Elizabeth Carter*, p. 104.

34. Anon., 'An Ejaculation Made upon Reading . . . Miss Carter's Translation of Epictetus', *Gentleman's Magazine* 28 (1758), p. 596.

35. Anon. [Jacobina Henriques], 'Humorous Proposal for a Female Administration', *Annual Register* (1766), pp. 209–12; Anon. [L.P.], 'On the Propriety of Bestowing Academical Honours on the Ladies', *Westminster Magazine* (1773), pp. 408–9.

36. William Roberts (ed.), *Memoirs of the Life of Mrs Hannah More*, 3rd edn, London: B. Seeley and W. Burnside 1836, vol. I, p. 334.

37. Matthew Montagu (ed.), *The Letters of Mrs. Elizabeth Montagu*, Boston: Wells and Lilly 1825, vol. III, p. 49.

38. Ibid., p. 90.

39. Ibid., pp. 107–12.

40. Montagu Pennington (ed.), *Letters from Mrs. Elizabeth Carter to Mrs. Montagu between the Years 1755 and 1800*, London: Rivington 1817, vol. I, pp. 19–20.

41. Ibid., p. 24.

42. Montagu (ed.), *Letters of Mrs. Elizabeth Montagu*, vol. III, pp. 173–4.

43. Ibid., pp. 162–3.

44. Ibid., p. 107.

45. Anon. [Elizabeth Montagu], 'Dialogue XXVII', in George Lyttelton, *Dialogues of the Dead*, 2nd edn, London 1760, pp. 300–5.

46. Montagu (ed.), *Letters of Mrs. Elizabeth Montagu*, vol. II, pp. 260–1.

47. Ibid., p. 260.

48. Anon., *Candid and Critical Remarks on the Dialogues of the Dead in a Letter from a Gentleman in London to his Friend in the Country*, London 1760, p. 88.

49. Montagu (ed.), *Letters of Mrs. Elizabeth Montagu*, vol. III, p. 205.

50. Ibid., pp. 259–60.

51. Emily J. Climenson (ed.), *Elizabeth Montagu, the Queen of the Blue-stockings: Her Correspondence from 1720 to 1761*, Cambridge: Cambridge University Press 2011, vol. II, p. 267.

52. Elizabeth Montagu to Elizabeth Carter, 31 December 1762, MO 3091, Elizabeth Montagu Correspondence Online EMCO ID 1397.

53. Elizabeth Eger, *Bluestockings: Women of Reason from Enlightenment to Romanticism*, Basingstoke: Palgrave Macmillan 2010, pp. 98–9.

54. Pennington (ed.), *Letters from Mrs. Elizabeth Carter to Mrs. Montagu*, vol. I, p. 27.

55. Climenson (ed.), *Elizabeth Montagu*, vol. II, p. 246; Reginald Blunt (ed.), *Mrs Montagu 'Queen of the Blues': Her Letters and Friendships from 1762 to 1800*, London: Constable 1926, vol. I, p. 150.

56. Frances Burney, *Diary and Letters of Madame D'Arblay*, London: Henry Colburn 1842, vol. I, p. 366.

57. Elizabeth Montagu to Elizabeth Carter, 31 December 1762, MO 3091, Elizabeth Montagu Correspondence Online EMCO ID 1397.

58. Susannah Gibson, *Animal, Vegetable, Mineral?*, Oxford: Oxford University Press 2015, pp. 43–78.

59. Betty Rizzo (ed.), *The Early Journals and Letters of Fanny Burney. Volume IV: The Streatham Years, Part II, 1780–1781*, Montreal and Kingston, Ont.: McGill-Queen's University Press 2003, p. 354.

60. Climenson (ed.), *Elizabeth Montagu*, vol. II, p. 237.

61. Blunt (ed.), *Mrs Montagu*, vol. I, p. 44.

62. Ibid., p. 93.

63. Climenson (ed.), *Elizabeth Montagu*, vol. II, p. 235.

64. Blunt (ed.), *Mrs Montagu*, vol. I, p. 48.

65. Pennington (ed.), *A Series of Letters*, vol. I, p. 323.

66. Blunt (ed.), *Mrs Montagu*, vol. I, p. 49.

67. Pennington, *Memoirs of the Life of Mrs Elizabeth Carter*, p. 179.

68. Blunt (ed.), *Mrs Montagu*, vol. I, p. 53.

69. Montagu (ed.), *Letters of Mrs. Elizabeth Montagu*, vol. III, p. 48.

70. Elizabeth Montagu to Sarah Scott, 26/27 October 1765, MO 5830, Elizabeth Montagu Correspondence Online EMCO ID 1733.

71. Anon., 'Review of *An Essay on the Writings and Genius of Shakespear*', *Monthly Review* 41 (1769), pp. 130–44; Anon., 'Review of *An Essay on the Writings and Genius of Shakespear*', *Critical Review* 27 (1769), pp. 350–5.

72. Pennington, *Memoirs of the Life of Mrs Elizabeth Carter*, p. 286.

73. Blunt (ed.), *Mrs Montagu,* vol. I, p. 151; vol. II, p. 224.

74. Elizabeth Eger (ed.), *Bluestocking Feminism: Writings of the Bluestocking Circle, 1738–1785, Volume I: Elizabeth Montagu*, London: Pickering and Chatto 1999, pp. 182, 187.

75. Ibid., pp. 186, 189.

76. Blunt (ed.), *Mrs Montagu*, vol. I, p. 227.

77. Ibid., p. 224.

78. Elizabeth Eger, '"Out Rushed a Female to Protect the Bard": The Bluestocking Defense of Shakespeare', *Huntington Library Quarterly* 65 (2002), pp. 127–51.

79. Blunt (ed.), *Mrs Montagu*, vol. II, p. 119.

Chapter 9: Love

1. Katharine C. Balderston (ed.), *Thraliana: The Diary of Mrs Hester Lynch Thrale (Later Mrs Piozzi) 1776–1809*, Oxford: Oxford University Press 2014, vol. I: *1776–84*, p. 348 n. 1.

2. Ibid., p. 323.

3. Mary Hyde (ed.), *The Thrales of Streatham Park* (includes *The Children's Book*), Boston, Mass.: Harvard University Press 1972, p. 204.

4. Lars E. Troide and Stewart J. Cooke (ed.), *The Early Journals and Letters of Fanny Burney. III: The Streatham Years, 1778–1779*, Oxford: Clarendon Press 1994, p. 107.

5. Ibid., p. 316.

6. Ibid., p. 304.

7. Hyde (ed.), *The Thrales of Streatham Park*, pp. 214, 218.

8. Balderston (ed.), *Thraliana*, vol. I, pp. 422, 461. The lines are from Pope, *The Iliad of Homer*, XVI, ll. 112–13.

9. Troide and Cooke (ed.), *Early Journals and Letters of Fanny Burney. III*, p. 374.

10. Balderston (ed.), *Thraliana*, vol. I, pp. 409, 432; Troide and Cooke (ed.), *Early Journals and Letters of Fanny Burney. III*, p. 359.

11. Balderston (ed.), *Thraliana*, vol. I, pp. 480–1, 487 n. 1, 488.

12. Ibid., p. 369.

13. Ibid., pp. 307, 492.

14. Ibid., p. 491 n. 1.

15. Betty Rizzo (ed.), *The Early Journals and Letters of Fanny Burney. Volume IV: The Streatham Years, Part II, 1780–1781*, Montreal and Kingston, Ont.: McGill-Queen's University Press 2003, p. 354.

16. Balderston (ed.), *Thraliana*, vol. I, p. 497.

17. Ibid., p. 452.

18. Ibid., p. 489.

19. Ibid., pp. 497–8.

20. Ibid., p. 531.

21. Ibid., pp. 535, 538, 547. Thrale is citing a line from Anne Page in *The Merry Wives of Windsor*: '. . . do not marry me to yond fool . . . Alas, I had rather be set quick i' the earth and bowl'd to death with turnips', Act III, scene 4.

22. Ibid., p. 544.

23. Ibid., p. 549.

24. Lars E. Troide and Stewart J. Cooke (ed.), *Early Journals and Letters of Fanny Burney: Volume V, 1782–1783*, Montreal and Kingston, Ont.: McGill-Queen's University Press 2012, pp. 175–6.

25. Balderston (ed.), *Thraliana*, vol. I, pp. 553–4.

26. Ibid., p. 558 n. 5 cont.

27. Hyde (ed.), *The Thrales of Streatham Park*, p. 200.

28. Balderston (ed.), *Thraliana*, vol. I, p. 558.

29. Ibid., p. 559.

30. Ibid., p. 557.

31. Ibid., p. 564.

32. Ibid., p. 565.

33. Ibid., p. 566.

34. Ibid., p. 573.

35. Troide and Cooke (ed.), *Early Journals and Letters of Fanny Burney: Volume V*, pp. 393–4, 398.

36. Balderston (ed.), *Thraliana*, vol. I, p. 581.

37. Rizzo (ed.), *Early Journals and Letters of Fanny Burney: Volume IV*, p. 291.

38. Balderston (ed.), *Thraliana*, vol. I, p. 580.

39. Ibid., pp. 581–2.

40. Troide and Cooke (ed.), *Early Journals and Letters of Fanny Burney: Volume V*, pp. 417, 445–6, 448.

41. Balderston (ed.), *Thraliana*, vol. I, p. 593 n. 3.

42. Ibid., p. 599 n. 2.

43. James Boswell, *Ode by Dr. Samuel Johnson to Mrs Thrale, Upon Their Supposed Approaching Nuptials* (1789), London 1784.

44. Balderston (ed.), *Thraliana*, vol. I, pp. 540–1 n. 1.

45. Ibid., p. 599.

46. Ibid., pp. 599–600.

47. Balderston (ed.), *Thraliana*, vol. II: *1784–1809*, p. 615 n. 2.

48. Ibid., p. 611.

49. Ibid., pp. 615, 627 n. 2, 681.

50. Fanny Burney, *Journals and Letters* (ed. Peter Sabor and Lars E. Troide), London and New York: Penguin 2001, 28 November 1784.

51. Balderston (ed.), *Thraliana*, vol. II, p. 617.

52. Ibid., pp. 624–5.

53. Balderston (ed.), *Thraliana*, vol. I, p. xx.

54. James Lowry Clifford, 'The Printing of Mrs. Piozzi's Anecdotes of Dr. Johnson', *Rylands Library Bulletin* xx (1936), pp. 157–72.

55. Michael J. Franklin, '"Thrale's Entire": Hester Lynch Thrale and the Anchor Brewery', in Deborah Heller (ed.), *Bluestockings Now! The Evolution of a Social Role*, Farnham, Surrey: Ashgate 2015, p. 121.

56. Balderston (ed.), *Thraliana*, vol. II, pp. 711–12.

57. Clifford, 'Printing of Mrs. Piozzi's Anecdotes of Dr. Johnson', p. 171.

58. Balderston (ed.), *Thraliana*, vol. II, p. 639.

59. Ibid., p. 813.

60. Sylvia Harcstark Myers, *The Bluestocking Circle: Women, Friendship, and the Life of the Mind in Eighteenth-Century England*, Oxford: Clarendon Press 1990, p. 257.

61. Balderston (ed.), *Thraliana*, vol. II, pp. 681, 729.

62. Ibid., pp. 686, 688.

63. Ibid., pp. 686, 856.

64. Ibid., p. 745.

65. Ibid., p. 846.

66. Ibid., p. 1040.

Chapter 10: Independence

1. Bridget Hill, *The Republican Virago: The Life and Times of Catharine Macaulay, Historian*, Oxford: Clarendon Press 1992, p. 8.

2. Ibid., p. 10.

3. Catharine Macaulay, *Letters on Education* (1787, 1790), Cambridge: Cambridge University Press 2014, p. 65.
4. Montagu Pennington (ed.), *A Series of Letters between Mrs. Elizabeth Carter and Miss Catherine Talbot, from the Year 1741 to 1770*, London: Rivington 1809, vol. II, p. 261.
5. Hill, *Republican Virago*, p. 12.
6. James Wyatt Cook and Barbara Collier Cook, *Man-Midwife, Male Feminist: The Life and Times of George Macaulay, M.D., Ph.D. (1716–1766)*, Ann Arbor, MI: University of Michigan Library 2006, pp. 44, 72, 203. The children were called Charles, Archibald, Caroline, Leonora and Catharine.
7. Catharine Macaulay, *The History of England from the Accession of James I to that of the Brunswick Line*, Cambridge: Cambridge University Press 2014, vol. I, pp. xiii–xiv.
8. Cook and Cook, *Man-Midwife, Male Feminist*, pp. 207–8, 210.
9. Kate Davies, *Catharine Macaulay and Mercy Otis Warren: The Revolutionary Atlantic and the Politics of Gender*, Oxford: Oxford University Press 2005, p. 85.
10. Karen Green (ed.), *The Correspondence of Catharine Macaulay*, Oxford: Oxford University Press 2020, p. 197.
11. Davies, *Catharine Macaulay and Mercy Otis Warren*, p. 85.
12. Samuel Johnson, *Dictionary* (1755), 4th edn, London 1773.
13. James Boswell, *The Life of Johnson*, London: Charles Dilly 1791, vol. I, p. 478.
14. Hill, *Republican Virago*, p. 178.
15. Bridget Hill and Christopher Hill, 'Catharine Macaulay's "History" and her "Catalogue of Tracts"', *Seventeenth Century* 8 (1993), pp. 269–85.
16. Hill, *Republican Virago*, p. 137.
17. Ibid., p. 40.
18. Montagu Pennington (ed.), *Memoirs of the Life of Mrs. Elizabeth Carter, Volume II*, London 1825, p. 172.
19. Anon., 'Review of *The History of England* . . . by Catharine Macaulay', *Monthly Review* 29 (1763), pp. 372, 375. The title 'Mrs' was sometimes used by older unmarried women and so did not necessarily provide any clues about Macaulay's marital status.
20. Anon., 'Review of *The History of England* . . . by Catharine Macaulay', *Critical Review* 16 (1763), p. 329.
21. Anon., 'Review of *The History of England* . . . by Catharine Macaulay', *Monthly Review* 32 (1765), p. 275.

22. Nicole Pohl (ed.), *The Letters of Sarah Scott*, London: Pickering and Chatto 2014, vol. I, p. 82; Samuel Foote, *The Devil upon Two Sticks*, London: T. Cadell 1778.

23. P.M., 'Letter from a Gentleman in Town to his Friend in the Country, Concerning a Celebrated Fair Historian', *Town and Country Magazine* 1 (1769), pp. 91–2.

24. Ibid., p. 92.

25. Basil Cozens-Hardy (ed.), *The Diary of Sylas Neville*, Oxford: Oxford University Press 1950, p. 20.

26. Mary Hays, *Female Biography, or, Memoirs of Illustrious and Celebrated Women, of All Ages and Countries*, London: R. Phillips 1803, vol. V, p. 292.

27. Ernest Hartley Coleridge, *The Letters of Samuel Taylor Coleridge*, London: William Heinemann 1895, vol. I, p. 323.

28. John Wain (ed.), *The Journals of James Boswell 1762–1795*, New Haven, Conn. and London: Yale University Press 1991, p. 87.

29. James Boswell, *The Life of Samuel Johnson*, vol. II, London: Henry G. Bohn 1848, p. 233. For another account of the same incident see Augustus Toplady, *The Works of Augustus M. Toplady*, London 1825, vol. VI, p. 255.

30. Boswell, *Life of Samuel Johnson*, vol. II, p. 284.

31. Ibid., pp. 340–1.

32. Hill, *Republican Virago*, p. 42.

33. John Hill Burton (ed.), *Letters of Eminent Persons Addressed to David Hume*, Edinburgh 1849, pp. 29–30.

34. John Hill Burton (ed.), *Life and Correspondence of David Hume*, Edinburgh: Blackwood 1846, vol. II, p. 186.

35. Hill, *Republican Virago*, pp. 23, 50.

36. Green (ed.), *Correspondence of Catharine Macaulay*, p. 58.

37. Ibid., pp. 69, 93, 192, 115.

38. Ibid., pp. 64–5.

39. Ibid., p. 9.

40. Anon., 'Memoirs of Mrs Macaulay', *London Magazine* (July 1770), p. 332.

41. Hill, *Republican Virago*, pp. 17–18.

42. Green (ed.), *Correspondence of Catharine Macaulay*, pp. 51–2; Hill, *Republican Virago*, p. 17.

43. James Graham, *A Short Inquiry into the Present State of Medical Practice in Consumptions, Asthmas, Nervous Disorders, &c.*, London 1777, p. 18.

44. Bridget Hill, 'Macaulay [née Sawbridge; other married name Graham], Catharine (1731–1791), Historian and Political Polemicist',

Oxford Dictionary of National Biography, https://doi.org/10.1093/ref:odnb/17344 [retrieved 14 July 2022]

45. Anon., 'Histories of the Tête-à-Tête Annexed; or, Memoirs of the Reverend Joiner, and Mrs. L----n', *Town and Country Magazine* (1771), pp. 681–3.

46. Bridget Hill, 'Daughter and Mother: Some New Light on Catharine Macaulay and her Family', *Journal for Eighteenth-Century Studies* 22.1 (1999), pp. 35–50.

47. Graham, *Short Inquiry*, p. 19.

48. Roy Porter, 'Graham, James (1745–1794), Quack', *Oxford Dictionary of National Biography*, https://doi.org/10.1093/ref:odnb/11199 [retrieved 14 July 2022]

49. Anon., *Six Odes, Presented to that Justly-celebrated Historian, Mrs. Catharine Macaulay, on her Birth-day, and Publicly Read to a Polite and Brilliant Audience, Assembled April the Second, at Alfred-House, Bath*, Bath 1777, pp. vii, viii, xiv.

50. Ibid., pp. 42–3.

51. Montagu Pennington (ed.), *Letters from Mrs Elizabeth Carter to Mrs Montagu*, London: Rivington 1817, vol. III, Letter CCXVIII, pp. 98–9.

52. Toplady, *Works of Augustus Toplady*, vol. VI, Letter LXIX, pp. 289–90.

53. Anon., 'Review of *Six Odes Presented to that Justly Celebrated Historian, Mrs. Catharine Macaulay, on her Birth Day*', *Monthly Review* 57 (1777), p. 148.

54. Anon., *Six Odes*, p. iii.

55. Anon., 'On the Statue of Mrs. Macaulay, Erected in the Church of St. Stephen Walbrook, London', *Lady's Magazine; or, Entertaining Companion for the Fair Sex* 8 (1777), pp. 509–10.

56. Anon., *The Correspondents*, London: T. Becket, 1775 p. 114. See, for example, Elizabeth Carter's denial of the work being by Lyttelton in Pennington (ed.), *Letters from Mrs Elizabeth Carter to Mrs Montagu*, vol. III, pp. 40–1.

57. Ibid., p. 114.

58. Hill, *Republican Virago*, p. 101.

59. Claire Brock, *The Feminization of Fame, 1750–1830*, Basingstoke: Palgrave Macmillan 2006, p. 65 n. 23.

60. Pennington (ed.), *Letters from Mrs Elizabeth Carter to Mrs Montagu*, vol. III, pp. 40–1.

61. Green (ed.), *Correspondence of Catharine Macaulay*, p. 79; Hays, *Female Biography*, vol. V, p. 295.

62. Green (ed.), *Correspondence of Catharine Macaulay*, p. 80.

63. Ibid., p. 206.

64. Ibid., pp. 80–1.

65. William Rough (ed.), *Letters from the Year 1774 to the Year 1796 of John Wilkes, Esq, Addressed to his Daughter, the Late Miss Wilkes*, London: Longman 1804, vol. II, pp. 61–2.

66. Anon., 'Review of *The History of England, from the Revolution, to the Present Time . . .* By Catharine Macaulay', *Critical Review* 45 (1778), pp. 130–4.

67. Hill, *Republican Virago*, p. 108.

68. Katharine C. Balderston (ed.), *Thraliana: The Diary of Mrs Hester Lynch Thrale (Later Mrs Piozzi) 1776–1809*, Oxford: Oxford University Press 2014, vol. I: *1776–84*, pp. 121, 123.

69. Rough (ed.), *Letters . . . of John Wilkes*, vol. II, p. 126.

70. Hill, *Republican Virago*, p. 109.

71. Ibid., p. 108.

72. Ibid.

73. Rough (ed.), *Letters . . . of John Wilkes*, vol. II, p. 115.

74. Ibid., pp. 115–16, 142, 145.

75. The statue now stands some two hundred miles away in the entrance of Warrington Public Library, a civic-minded gift from the distant cousin of Wilson's who had inherited it.

76. Hill, *Republican Virago*, p. 110.

77. Rough (ed.), *Letters . . . of John Wilkes*, vol. II, pp. 130, 135, 146, 154.

78. Quoted in Hill, *Republican Virago*, p. 114.

79. Quoted in Devoney Looser, *British Women Writers and the Writing of History, 1670–1820*, Baltimore, Md. and London: Johns Hopkins University Press 2005, p. 129. Richard Paul Jodrell, *The Female Patriot: An Epistle from C-t-e M-c-y to the Reverend Dr. W-l-n on her Late Marriage*, London 1779.

80. Richard Paul Jodrell, *A Widow and No Widow* (performed in 1779), Dublin 1780, pp. 21–2, 28.

81. Anon., *A Remarkable Moving Letter!*, London 1779, p. 6.

82. Nicole Pohl (ed.), *The Letters of Sarah Scott*, London: Pickering and Chatto 2014, vol. II, p. 174.

83. Elizabeth Montagu to Hester Thrale, 19 December 1778, Rylands Library Eng. MS 551/30, Elizabeth Montagu Correspondence Online EMCO ID 1796.

84. Reginald Blunt (ed.), *Mrs. Montagu 'Queen of the Blues': Her Letters and Friendships from 1762 to 1800*, London: Constable 1926, vol. II, p. 64.

85. Elizabeth Montagu to Hester Thrale, 14 December 1778, Rylands Library Eng. MS 551/29, Elizabeth Montagu Correspondence Online EMCO ID 1824.
86. Hyde (ed.), *The Thrales of Streatham Park*, p. 157.
87. Blunt (ed.), *Mrs. Montagu*, vol. II, p. 68.
88. Pennington (ed.), *Letters from Mrs Elizabeth Carter to Mrs Montagu*, vol. III, pp. 98–9.
89. Hannah More, 'Epilogue' to *Search after Happiness* (1773), London: T. Allman 1836, p. 32.
90. William Roberts (ed.), *Memoirs of the Life and Corrrespondence of Mrs. Hannah More*, New York: Harper 1835, vol. I, p. 137.
91. Anon., *A Bridal Ode on the Marriage of Catherine and Petruchio*, London: J. Bew 1779, p. 7.
92. Hill, *Republican Virago*, p. 107.
93. Wain (ed.), *Journals of James Boswell*, p. 372.
94. Catharine Macaulay Graham, *A Treatise on the Immutability of Moral Truth*, London 1783, pp. 156–8.
95. Anon., 'Review of *A Treatise on the Immutability of Moral Truth*', *Monthly Review* 70 (1784), pp. 89–100; Samuel Badcock, 'Review of *A Treatise on the Immutability of Moral Truth*', *Gentleman's Magazine* 59 (1789), p. 777.
96. Catharine Macaulay Graham, *Letters on Education*, London 1790, pp. 203–9.
97. Ibid., pp. 144, 145, 147, 208.
98. Ibid., pp. 210, 215.
99. Quoted in Green (ed.), *Correspondence of Catharine Macaulay*, pp. 288–93.
100. Catherine Gardner, 'Catharine Macaulay's "Letters on Education": Odd but Equal', *Hypatia* 13.1 (1998), pp. 118–37; Florence Boos, 'Catharine Macaulay's *Letters on Education* (1790): An Early Feminist Polemic', *University of Michigan Papers in Women's Studies* 2.2 (1976), pp. 64–78; Elizabeth Frazer, 'Mary Wollstonecraft and Catharine Macaulay on Education', *Oxford Review of Education* 37.5 (2011), pp. 603–17.
101. Janet Todd and Marilyn Butler (ed.), *The Works of Mary Wollstonecraft*, London: William Pickering 1989, vol. VII, pp. 321–2.
102. Hill, *Republican Virago*, p. 126; Green (ed.), *Correspondence of Catharine Macaulay*, p. 226.
103. Green (ed.), *Correspondence of Catharine Macaulay*, p. 227.
104. Catharine Macaulay, *An Address to the People of England, Scotland, and Ireland, on the Present Important Crisis of Affairs*, 2nd edn, London 1775, pp. 7–8, 28–9.

105. Quoted in Hill, *Republican Virago*, pp. 118, 145.

106. Ibid., p. 1.

107. Green (ed.), *Correspondence of Catharine Macaulay*, p. 269.

108. Rough (ed.), *Letters . . . of John Wilkes*, vol. II, p. 179.

109. Green (ed.), *Correspondence of Catharine Macaulay*, p. 231 n. 565.

Chapter 11: The End of the Bluestockings

1. William Roberts, *Memoirs of the Life of Hannah More*, 3rd edn, London: R. B. Seeley and W. Burnside 1836, vol. I, 1836, p. 194.

2. Elizabeth Eger, *Bluestockings: Women of Reason from Enlightenment to Romanticism*, Basingstoke: Palgrave Macmillan 2010, p. 71.

3. Reginald Blunt (ed.), *Mrs. Montagu 'Queen of the Blues': Her Letters and Friendships from 1762 to 1800*, London: Constable 1926, vol. II, pp. 241, 246.

4. From an article in the *St. James's Chronicle*, quoted in Eger, *Bluestockings*, p. 73.

5. Roberts, *Memoirs of the Life of Hannah More*, 3rd edn, vol. I, p. 194; Lars E. Troide and Stewart J. Cooke (ed.), *The Early Journals and Letters of Fanny Burney. Volume V: 1782–1783*, Montreal and Kingston, Ont.: McGill-Queen's University Press 2012, p. 56.

6. Troide and Cooke (ed.), *Early Journals and Letters of Fanny Burney. Volume V: 1782–1783*, p. 366.

7. Beth Fowkes Tobin, 'Bluestockings and the Cultures of Natural History', in Deborah Heller (ed.), *Bluestockings Now!: The Evolution of a Social Role*, Farnham, Surrey: Ashgate 2015, pp. 56–69.

8. Blunt (ed.), *Mrs. Montagu*, vol. II, pp. 228, 257.

9. Ibid., pp. 83, 118, 119.

10. Ibid., p. 112.

11. Nicole Pohl (ed.), *The Letters of Sarah Scott*, London: Pickering and Chatto 2014, vol. II, p. ii.

12. Katharine C. Balderston (ed.), *Thraliana: The Diary of Mrs Hester Lynch Thrale (Later Mrs Piozzi) 1776–1809*, Oxford: Oxford University Press 2014, vol. II: *1784–1809*, p. 938.

13. Roberts, *Memoirs of the Life of Hannah More*, 3rd edn, vol. I, p. 363; Blunt (ed.), *Mrs. Montagu*, vol. II, p. 119.

14. Bridget Hill, 'The Links between Mary Wollstonecraft and Catharine Macaulay: New Evidence', *Women's History Review* 4.2 (1995), pp. 177–92, on p. 177.

15. Mary Wollstonecraft, *A Vindication of the Rights of Woman* (1792), 3rd edn, London: J. Johnson 1796, Section 5.4, p. 241.
16. Charles Pigott, *The Female Jockey Club*, London 1794, p. 199.
17. Lord Byron, *Don Juan*, Canto IV, ll. 857–96.
18. Leslie A. Marchand (ed.), *Byron's Letters and Journals. Volume 8: Born for Opposition*, 1821, London: John Murray 1978, p. 172.
19. A. Taylor (ed.), *Coleridge's Writings*, Basingstoke: Palgrave Macmillan 1994, vol. II, p. 1993.
20. Geoffrey Keynes (ed.), *Selected Essays of William Hazlitt 1778 to 1830*, London: Nonesuch 1930, p. 105.
21. Anon., 'Review of *The Siege of Valencia: A Dramatic Poem*', *British Critic* 20 (1823), pp. 50–61.
22. Anne Stott, *Hannah More: The First Victorian*, Oxford: Oxford University Press 2003, p. viii.
23. William McCarthy, 'The Repression of Hester Lynch Piozzi; or, How we Forget a Revolution in Authorship', *Modern Language Studies* 18.1 (1988), pp. 99–111.
24. Frederic G. Kenyon (ed.), *The Letters of Elizabeth Barrett Browning*, 3rd edn, London: Smith, Elder 1898, vol. I, letter dated 7 January 1845.
25. Virginia Woolf, *A Room of One's Own*, London: Hogarth Press 1929.
26. Sarah Chauncey Woolsey (ed.), *The Diaries and Letters of Frances Burney, Madame D'Arblay*, Boston: Roberts Brothers 1880, vol. II, p. 257.

Index